What They are Saying about
Reb Zalman Gathers Figs

Dana Densmore has done all of us a great service. Reb Zalman is one of the great religious minds and hearts that I've ever witnessed. His style is unique and his message is felt with the heart and soul as much or more than it is understood by the mind. Densmore masterfully gathers the master's words and skillfully supports a deeper understanding of Reb Zalman's wisdom. That she does this difficult task while maintaining the "flavor" of Reb Zalman's powerful voice and heart is a great skill indeed, one that we are all grateful for. *Reb Zalman Gathers Figs* is a must-read for all who yearn for the deeper teachings of the Bible and a connection to G-d/Spirit.

Rabbi David Ingber
Founder and Spiritual Director, Romemu

Dana Densmore's book *Reb Zalman Gathers Figs* is a rare gem. It harkens back to Talmudic dialogue where the voices of sages who lived generations apart from each other seem to talk directly to one another. In this case it is Densmore and Reb Zalman who are having a deep conversation. It would be enough to just to read Reb Zalman's insightful comments on the Bible. But with each teaching by Reb Zalman, Ms. Densmore helps us unpack what the Rebbe is teaching with enlightened commentary. The style is Tamudic, but the insights are contemporary and cutting edge.

Rabbi David Zaslow,
author of *Jesus: First Century Rabbi*

Rabbi Zalman Schachter-Shalomi's Wisdom School was a grand and wild experiment of entering through the primal myths of the Hebrew Bible in order to gather Wisdom for our time. With this important book, Dana Densmore harvests that wisdom for all of us. She invites us to join Reb Zalman and encounter our sacred text as a living, generous Tree of Life that continues to bear fruit when we come to Her as bold, hungry passionate seekers of Wisdom. With *Reb Zalman Gathers Figs*, Ms. Densmore brilliantly conveys and interprets both the method and the substance of Schachter-Shalomi's unique contribution.

Rabbi Shefa Gold, author of *The Magic of Hebrew Chant: Healing the Spirit, Transforming the Mind, Deepening Love,* published by Jewish Lights

Reb Zalman Gathers Figs is a treasure trove of *chiddushim*—new insights—from a master of Jewish thought and practice, a master of renewing the Jewish world, that should grace every lover of Torah's bookshelf. Densmore has given us access to heretofore unreleased material that will inform and illuminate for decades to come. We owe her a significant debt of gratitude for publishing these teachings along with her own remarkable scholarly commentary. Now we can all drink deeply from the well of this neo-Hassidic, deeply ecumenical, psycholigically astute master, held beautifully in the historical and theological container that Densmore so effectively creates, allowing us to study as if we are *talmidim*/students of the rebbe ourselves.

Rabbi Debra Kolodny
Rabbi of P'nai Or of Portland
Executive Director of Nehirim
Former Executive Director of
ALEPH: Alliance for Jewish Renewal

The material for *Reb Zalman Gathers Figs* came through me and Eve during one of our most creative periods. Primal Myth needed to be shaped into a book. Dana Densmore has done a sensitive and remarkable job in presenting this material to the reader in a way that will allow you, in your imagination, to participate in the remarkable process of the Wisdom School.

Rabbi Zalman Schachter-Shalomi,
author of *Davening*

Many jewels of beauty and profound wisdom lie glittering on the surface and hidden beneath it in Jewish text and practice. Scripture, initially given at a moment in time yet relevant for eternity, must always contain both the hidden and the revealed. The particulars of the Hebrew language have given rise to systems of "unpacking the text" that illuminate levels of implied understandings imbedded in the words. For millennia our teachers have inspired us to "turn it, turn it" to discover the intention beneath the intention, offering the practitioner a devotional interactive process with the text so that in every era new light is shown on the workings of the Ancient One. Rabbi Zalman Schachter-Shalomi is one such inspirer of our era.

In this very important work on Reb Zalman's teachings, Dana Densmore shows through careful scholarship and documentation, and with delicious examples of content how Reb Zalman engages the very traditional practice of continual re-visioning that has kept Judaism vibrantly alive, relevant, and evolving. It is a practice that perhaps reflects the Holy Name *ehyeh asher ehyeh*, I am what I am becoming.

Maggid Andrew Gold

Zalman Schachter Shalomi is a genius at bringing the Bible to life, exploring its sometimes hidden mystical and spiritual messages, and showing us a depth of wisdom in the ancient teachings that can enlighten our lives. He is without a doubt the most profound Jewish spiritual teacher alive today.

Rabbi Michael Lerner,
editor, Tikkun Magazine
chair of the interfaith Network of Spiritual Progressives
author of *Jewish Renewal: A Path to Healing and Transformation*

Reb Zalman Schachter-Shalomi is the father of the Jewish Renewal movement of the late twentieth and early twenty-first centuries. Dana Densmore's book, based on unpublished audio tapes, never before transcribed, originates in the seven retreat sessions of the Wisdom School led by Reb Zalman, and his life-partner Eve Ilsen, in 1988-89. Densmore's work makes the breathtaking scope, richness and texture of Reb Zalman's insights available for consideration and reflection by an ever-wider readership. She weaves these teachings into a coherent and sequential whole, contextualizing excerpts from the audio tapes with the experiential elements of the retreat weekends. In this compilation, Reb Zalman's broad secular education and intimate familiarity with the Western intellectual tradition, psychology, theology and comparative religion combine with his bone-deep knowledge of traditional Jewish texts from the biblical, rabbinic, and mystical traditions of Judaism. Through this great teacher, as refracted through Densmore's lens, this critical mass of intellectual, spiritual, and experiential knowledge ignites to create for every seeker a challenging, stimulating, and inspiring path to ever-deeper engagement with our best, most sacred, selves.

Diane M. Sharon, Ph.D.

Reb Zalman
Gathers Figs

Reb Zalman Gathers Figs

A study of Rabbi Zalman Schachter-Shalomi's
Reading of Biblical Text
to Re-Vision Judaism for the Present Day

by Dana Densmore

Kafir Yaroq Books
Santa Fe, New Mexico

Manufactured in the United States of America

Kafir Yaroq Books
an imprint of Green Lion Press
Santa Fe, New Mexico
www.kafiryaroq.com

Cover photograph of Zalman Schachter-Shalomi by Michael Kosacoff.
Cover design by William H. Donahue

Printed and bound by Sheridan Books, Inc.
Chelsea, Michigan

Cataloguing-in-Publication data:
Densmore, Dana
Reb Zalman Gathers Figs / by Dana Densmore
Includes index, bibliography, biographical notes.

ISBN 978-1-888009-39-2
1. Biblical interpretation. 2. Jewish tradition. 3. Zalman Schachter-
Shalomi. 4. Jewish Renewal. 5. Spirituality.
I. Densmore, Dana (1945–), Zalman Schachter-Shalomi (1924–),
III. Title
Library of Congress Control Number: 2013954069

For Uncle Bernie

my godfather, historian Bernard A. Weisberger
in appreciation of a lively and enduring friendship.

Torah is a Tree that Bears Figs for Every Generation

אמר רבי חייא בר אבא אמר רבי יוחנן: מאי דכתיב (משלי
כ"ז) נצר תאנה יאכל פריה, למה נמשלו דברי תורה כתאנה -
מה תאנה זו כל זמן שאדם ממשמש בה מוצא בה תאנים אף
דברי תורה: כל זמן שאדם הוגה בהן - מוצא בהן טעם.

Said R. Hiyya bar Abba said R. Yohanan, "What is the meaning of this verse of Scripture: 'Whoso keeps the fig tree shall eat the fruit thereof' (Prov. 27:18)? How come words of the Torah were compared to a fig? Just as the fig—the more someone examines it, the more one finds in it, so words of the Torah—the more one meditates on them, the more flavor he finds in them."

Babylonian Talmud, Tractate Erubin, 54A-B.
(Translation by Jacob Neusner)

Contents

Schacter-Shalomi's Context in Jewish Tradition

Foreword

Rabbi Zalman Schachter-Shalomi

Rabbi Zalman Schachter-Shalomi is one of the most important, significant, and influential Jewish teachers and thinkers of the 20th and early 21st centuries.

Rabbi Schachter-Shalomi has had a powerful effect on present-day Jewish thinking and practice. A beloved figure in the larger movement for renewal in Jewish practice, "Reb Zalman" is the inspiration behind the Jewish Renewal movement and its organization, ALEPH. He was ordained as an Orthodox rabbi in 1947 within the Chabad Lubavitch Hasidic community. He has a doctorate from Hebrew Union College and is Professor Emeritus at Temple University and at Naropa University. In 1969 he founded the B'nai Or Religious Fellowship out of which the Jewish Renewal movement grew.

A more complete biographical sketch of Schachter-Shalomi's life and contributions is included as an appendix to this book.

Intent of this Study

In this study I investigate the way that Zalman Schachter-Shalomi uses readings of Biblical narratives to provide Biblical warrant for his theological vision and his re-visioning of Judaism. I then place that process in a context of continuous re-visioning in Jewish tradition and in a context of the use of Biblical interpretation to meet a similar need in earlier historical periods.

The first part of this book is based upon case studies of Schachter-Shalomi's Biblical commentary given in a series of weekend retreats.[1] These are an unpublished and hitherto almost

---

1   See the next section, About My Source Material.

unknown set of teachings by Schachter-Shalomi. The material presented here is the only substantial sustained example of his approach to scriptural interpretation, published or unpublished.

The second part develops my claim that this sort of re-visioning is not only the way Judaism has always worked with its Biblical inheritance but also the key to Judaism's survival and continued vitality through the ages. Here I call upon recent scholarly assessments of Jewish use of Biblical interpretation as well as reference to original sources in the Talmudic and Midrashic corpus.

Schachter-Shalomi's Re-visioning of Judaism

What I refer to as Schachter-Shalomi's re-visioning is his approach to keeping a religious tradition alive and relevant while remaining true to its fundamental texts. I show how Schachter-Shalomi finds the means of re-visioning within the tradition itself. Paradoxically, this radical attempt springs from Schachter-Shalomi's grounding in a deeply traditional form of Judaism.

In going to the traditional scriptural texts for these teachings and wisdom, he is expressing a belief that these texts have encoded in them guidance for Jews, and humans, in every age.

Schachter-Shalomi's understanding of the lessons of the texts, and of Hebrew Scriptures as divine teachings, differs in many cases from older interpretations within the Jewish tradition. These evocations of the meanings of the text are part of his re-visioning of Judaism for the present age, with the present day's cosmologies, its world views, and its challenges.

Many of the teachings that Schachter-Shalomi draws from his reading of the Hebrew Bible are very different from the perspectives, rulings, and interpretations passed down as Rabbinic Judaism. The Sages of the Talmud codified what a Judaism without a Temple and a sacrificial cult in Jerusalem would look like, and this was developed and refined through the millennium or two since then.

Some of the results of Schachter-Shalomi's re-visioning, held up against the traditional orthodox system, look so radically different that it may be understandable that he should be accused of abandoning Judaism itself for some sort of new religion. As I will develop more thoroughly in the last chapter of this book, this accusation could be, and has been, made of the Talmudic Sages after 70 CE. Their radical re-visioning was necessary then, and perhaps there is a current imperative, something akin to theirs, that Schachter-Shalomi is feeling. In his view, a Judaism that cannot evolve with the changing world and the spiritual evolution of humanity will be increasingly sclerosed and increasingly irrelevant. But he does not only look forward: he wants to look back to the source text, and draw lessons for our time directly from that.

I offer here Schachter-Shalomi's representation of his re-visioning as he draws from *Tanakh*, from Hebrew Scriptures. I provide extensive direct quotations from him as well as from Scripture, in order to allow the reader to form his or her own judgment as to the rightness of his interpretations, its applicability to present challenges, and whether ultimately it feels Jewish.

Does it look like traditional Rabbinic Judaism? In many ways it does not. But that doesn't make it not Judaism, or make it "post-Judaism" as one scholar suggested might be the way to understand it.[2] There are many ways in which Rabbinic Judaism looks different from the Israelite religion of the Bible. But somehow the Rabbinic vision, particularly its Babylonian version, took

---

2   Shaul Magid, *American Post-Judaism*. Magid's book is a magisterial tracing of threads of American philosophical thinking and American Jewish culture. One might suspect at first that Magid means to be deliberately provocative in including Schachter-Shalomi's vision in the philosophical and cultural movements for which he suggests the term "post-Judaism." But careful reading shows that Magid is using the term with a particular meaning. It is not that Schachter-Shalomi or partisans of Jewish Renewal want to leave Judaism behind, but rather that they have re-visioned some of the foundations (just as the rabbinic sages did in their own era). On page 75 Magid writes: "Post-Judaism is not the erasure of Judaism but a reassessment of some of the founding principles on which Judaism was constructed."

hold and established itself as a continuation of the same Biblical religion that was built around the Temple and its sacrifices.

Even though Schachter-Shalomi goes back to Tanakh for teachings for current times, he does see Judaism as a religion evolving from the earlier form presented Biblically. This evolution follows not only changes in the world and the position of Jews in the world, but also follows our own understanding and moral sense, a larger richer spiritual vision emerging today. Judaism has never been static, and Jews have defined, and will continue to define, what it means.

In the teachings presented in this book, Schachter-Shalomi is looking to *Tanakh* for lessons for the challenges faced by present-day Jews. Because his interest lies in culling the time-capsule gems of teachings which that text offers as a Jewish inheritance, he does not call directly on perspectives and insights of other religions. But his curiosity and openness (not to mention his depth of knowledge and familiarity) reveal themselves in passing remarks and occasional cross-references. So we should perhaps acknowledge that the way Schachter-Shalomi views other religions constitutes a shift from conventional Jewish tradition. This shift looks to the traditional orthodox Jewish eye like a serious departure. Through much of Jewish tradition, starting with the Bible itself, condemnation of idolatry and idolators has been powerful and pervasive. These idolatries are the non-Jewish religions. Schachter-Shalomi's openness to non-Jewish religions leads to the charge of syncretism.

The charge of syncretism, while naming the fear, may be too crude.[3] But his shift may indeed be a radical one. He has rejected

3   The charge of syncretism is arguably too crude on two levels. First, what Schachter-Shalomi is doing is more complicated and nuanced than the term suggests; closer inspection shows that he is not simply turning Judaism into a mishmash of different religions when he finds kindred truths or even lost insights in other traditions. And second, whether it is comfortable to acknowledge this or not, Judaism has historically absorbed identifiable influences from other

the view that one religion, Judaism, is true, and all others are false. Philosophers of religion and others have referred to this view variously as classical or traditional or biblical or "exclusive" monotheism.[4] According to this form of monotheism there is one God and it is "our" God (for Judaism, YHVH). If you have another religion, and your God has a different name, your religion is false and your God is nonexistent, an idol.

But the result of this exclusivist stance is a peculiar kind of monotheism. There is one God, but it is only the diety that *we* worship. This God has dominion over all the earth, but cares almost exclusively about Jews.

Schachter-Shalomi has a different vision of monotheism. For him, there is one God, one reality. This God is the God of all, the one worshipped as every god. All religions are worshipping this one God, envisioning divine being according to their particular perspective and slant, like the blind men describing the elephant.[5] The religions and their theologians do their best to describe a God

---

religions and cultures among which it has lived—from Canaanite to Hellenistic to Zoroastrian to Islamic to Christian. It could be, and no doubt has been, argued that a Judaism purged of all those influences would not look "Jewish" to us now.

4   Schachter-Shalomi's rejection of this exclusive monotheism (which he terms "triumphalist") leads traditionalists to accuse him of opening the gates to idolatry, and leads Shaul Magid to characterize Jewish Renewal's theology as post-monotheistic (*American Post-Judaism*, pp. 69–70). Magid is careful, however, to make his meaning here explicit. He says on page 70 that he describes Schachter-Shalomi's position as post-monotheistic "because it abandons what some view as the negative dimensions or consequences of classial monotheism, replacing it with more universalist and tolerant spiritual alternatives while retaining monotheism's basic structure."

5   A parable that originated in India but has now spread widely and been used for many applications, including, frequently, the nature of God (e.g. 19th Century Indian mystic Ramakrishna) and theological doctrines (e.g. in American poet John Godfrey Saxe's poem "the Blindmen and the Elephant").

who is ultimately beyond human understanding, not graspable or ownable, not available to be placed in a proprietary pigeonhole of dogma or doctrine.

Schachter-Shalomi has written: "God or God's Essence is truly beyond our ken, even beyond our ability to conceive. Nevertheless, as theotropic beings, we long for God and turn our gaze to meet that 'undisclosed' Essence continually. So what does that tell us? Perhaps that our idea of God is less about God than about our capacity to conceive of God. And thus it follows that our idea of God has evolved through the centuries, even as the words delivered to the prophet Malachi have remained true, 'I am Y-H-V-H—I have not changed' (Malachi 3:6)."[6]

All religions, according to his analogies, are like organs of the body, or instruments in a symphony orchestra. Judaism has brought a particular unique and precious perspective, but it is not the only perspective, and although it offers deep truth, the others are not false for that, but may offer other faces of truth.

☙ • ♋

In re-visioning Judaism for our present age, what other shifts does Schachter-Shalomi offer us? Will they be surprising? Unsettling? A great relief? A warm welcoming invitation to come home to a Judaism one didn't know could exist? A catalyst for thinking along rich new paths? Things with which to argue heatedly?

Let's see what Schachter-Shalomi brings out as he reads *Tanakh* with a group of serious students.

And then let's look at how previous readers, and in particular another serious group of students, the Talmudic sages, read *Tanakh* and struggled with what it had to teach *their* present age.

---

6 *Spectrum: A Journal of Renewal Spirituality*, Winter-Spring, 2006, p.14.

About My Source Material

1. The Original Source Material for the Schachter-Shalomi Case Studies

My primary source material is audio tapes made of a series of seven weekend retreats of what Schachter-Shalomi called a Wisdom School, which he led with teacher Eve Ilsen as co-leader. The title of the series was Primal Myths and it undertook to use immersion into specific books of the Hebrew Bible to gain insight into, or wisdom about, present-day personal and societal challenges. These are largely human challenges, but Schachter-Shalomi's main focus is what the particular heritage and strengths of the Jewish tradition can allow Jews to learn and contribute.

The group of participants committed to attending all seven or eight weekends over the winter of 1988–1989. The surviving audio tapes were digitized at Naropa University, filling 114 CDs.

Because the purpose of these retreats was the spiritual growth of the participants, not an academic course on theology or Biblical interpretation, there was much that was not directly applicable to my investigation, although, of course, to know what was and what wasn't illustrative for my exploration required careful and repeated listening all the way through.

From these wide-ranging and loosely organized talks, I have extracted examples which show the scriptural dimensions of Schachter-Shalomi's re-visioning of Judaism. This selection, organization, editing, and annotation is discussed in Section 3 below.

How I Came to this Source Material

I began this project to investigate a modern example of re-visioning against a context of traditional Jewish use of Biblical interpretation to keep Scripture alive and relevant. I wanted to use Schachter-Shalomi as my modern example, and I supposed that I would find plenty of material in published print or audio teachings, by him and perhaps by others about him. What I found was that there were only brief references here and there in published material. But in the course of searching for the material, I learned about about the Primal Myths series of retreats. The material presented in these retreats is previously unpublished and largely unknown.

Because Schachter-Shalomi has not published any significant commentary on the Biblical text, either in written form or audio files of teachings, I rely on this series of teachings, most of which were captured on audiotape and which found their way to the archives of the Reb Zalman Legacy Project,[1] housed at Naropa University in Boulder Colorado.[2] These archives are now housed at the University of Colorado.[3]

2. The P'nai Or Community and the Primal Myths Series of Retreats

In the 1980's in Philadelphia, Schachter-Shalomi was the leading teacher and spiritual guide of a community called P'nai Or. He wished to establish what he called a Wisdom School, in which a community of learners would study the Jewish tradition and texts seriously and with on-going focus, entering into the learning process as participants and finding inspiration and relevance for their own lives and in keeping with their own ideals. In the winter of 1988–1989, Schachter-Shalomi, along with spiritual teacher Eve

---

1   **Reb Zalman Legacy Project.** A collaborative effort of the Yesod Foundation and Naropa University to preserve, develop and disseminate Schachter-Shalomi's teachings. www.rzlp.org.

2   I was given access to these audio files through the kind assistance of the Project's Director, Netanel Miles-Yepez, with the permission of Rabbi Schachter-Shalomi.

3   The Zalman M. Schachter-Shalomi Collection, Archives, University of Colorado at Boulder Libraries, University of Colorado.

Ilsen, proposed a series of weekends to explore Biblical narratives and their teachings. Participants would commit to attend all eight sessions at a rate of one weekend per month.

The Primal Myths series of weekend retreats at which Schachter-Shalomi offers the corpus of Biblical commentary that I use for my case studies here were a project of this Wisdom School. This is one series of intensive learning; Schachter-Shalomi had hoped that there would be more like it, but difficulties of organization and the seriousness of the demands it made on students prevented further incarnations. Instead, there was the ongoing learning through P'nai Or in shorter classes and retreats, and long-term students who continued to learn with him in various ways (in some cases leading to rabbinic ordination).

The focus of the Primal Myths series of retreats was to provide an opportunity to draw from the spiritual depths of the Hebrew scriptures (whose narratives are the "primal myths") for individual spiritual development and nourishment, and also for a vision of Judaism that addresses current individual and global challenges. The presumption, or at least the working hypothesis, was that these Biblical texts had encoded into them the teachings that could meet those needs.

For this Schachter-Shalomi had selected a series of Biblical texts from which specific important insights and guidance could be drawn. The plan changed somewhat over the course of the winter 1988–1989 as Schachter-Shalomi responded to the process the group was undergoing and as his own ideas evolved about how the explorations might unfold, in conjunction with the ideas of his co-leader Eve Ilsen. Originally they announced eight sessions. There are audio files only from seven.[4]

---

4   I have not been able to confirm the existence of an eighth session. It did not follow the last of the seven, and no mention is made in the existing recordings of another retreat having taken place, so the likelihood is that the plan changed. However, Schachter-Shalomi suggested that there might have been a session that wasn't recorded.

3. The Challenges of Working with the Original Source Material

The original audio cassettes recorded at the retreats, or at least those surviving, were digitized by the Reb Zalman Legacy Project and stored at the archives at Naropa University in the form of 114 CDs.

My first step was copying the 114 CDs at the Naropa archives. Then I listened repeatedly, studied, and began transcribing.

Transcription

The transcription was anything but routine. No machine could have done it. It required someone very conversant with Schachter-Shalomi's teachings. It also needed familiarity with Jewish tradition, with spiritual traditions and practices, and with the Western intellectual tradition. All that and a lot of research.

And what was the challenge here? Schachter-Shalomi has a dazzling breadth of erudition both in Jewish tradition and in history of ideas. He knows all the classic texts and thinkers. If he speaks the name of some ancient rabbi or other thinker, or an Egyptian Pharaoh, I can't transcribe it without knowing who it is so that I can find how to spell it. This is, of course, made more challenging by the fact that the original audio files were not always of good quality, and had not improved during digitization and reproduction.

Furthermore, Schachter-Shalomi sprinkles quotations through in many languages, often without identifying the language. Sometimes the concept or phrase would be given without the name of the originator of the concept. To transcribe something I would have to identify the author, then the find the passage, then track it down in its original language. In these selections Schachter-Shalomi has used Yiddish, German, Hebrew, Aramaic, Aramaic of the Zohar, Latin, and French. And for good measure, a few words and phrases in Sanskrit and in Greek.

I sometimes had the sense, as I worked on the transcriptions of these audio files, that my job was like that of a scholar working with an ancient manuscript, damaged and faded with age, that required substantial scholarly effort to identify the words and establish the text, to "transcribe" it into a version that could be published and read.

Selection

Because these audio files represented full weekend retreats, with religious services, experiential exercises, discussions, and other sorts of presentations, I needed to select the segments in which Schachter-Shalomi was giving direct commentary on the Biblical passages that were the focus of the weekend. But since the whole weekend was devoted to particular narratives, Schachter-Shalomi's remarks and insights were also scattered through other material. I carefully extracted everything that contributed to the lines of thought he was bringing out.

But Schachter-Shalomi ranged over many topics, and the scope of this project didn't allow for including everything he talked about. I had to pick a manageable number of what seemed like central threads of his re-visioning of Judaism and then pull together the steps of his development of those ideas and the ramifications and digressions and recursions in which he would challenge his own ideas and introduce new complexities to the considerations.

These might be touched on and returned to throughout the weekend (and occasionally picked up in later weekends). Some material was presented in talks, some as part of the Torah reading in the Saturday morning service, some in connection to discussions or experiential exercises or participant questions. This painstaking gathering was the task of the selection process.

Organizing

Then these diverse and diffused and distributed teachings had to be brought together in a coherent order.

Because the whole weekend was one of deeply experiential immersion, a "wisdom school" directed to inner processes of spiritual development and not a College lecture hall, the teachings wove through the days and nights in different ways, speaking to different levels and styles of learning. The way things were presented early in the retreat differed from what might come in a session after a deep experiential practice, or when participants were awakened in the middle of the night, or during a Torah service.

I brought together presentations and remarks from throughout the weekend to follow particular threads. This was more complicated than it may sound. Because of the breadth of Schachter-Shalomi's understanding of, and engagement with, these topics, and their own inherent complexity, one "thread" typically has many strands that he weaves together, here loosely, there more tightly.

Topics were introduced, then allowed to gestate, then returned to from other angles. The circling around the complexities, the ideas and then the difficulties with the ideas, the engagement with the layers of meaning in the original texts themselves, all created challenges for an organization that would flow in the more linear form of written words.

But it was not my wish to turn these teachings into something resembling a college lecture. It was important to keep, as much as possible, the attunement and the tone and the depth of feeling and connection that Schachter-Shalomi was transmitting to participants. He, like the participants, was committed to this full experience of these weekends with the same group of people. In this community of learning, there was a chance to go very deep, in trust, and explore and share in ways that would not happen in a public venue. As editor, I needed, as much as possible, to preserve that dimension, to allow readers to sense the depth and the personalization out of which these thoughts were coming.

My organization had to allow the material to make sense in a written flow, but also to draw the reader, in some sense, into the retreat consciousness. It also had to honor and preserve

Schachter-Shalomi's complexity of thought, his imaginative breadth, and his skill as a weaver of ideas.

Editing

Then the material had to be edited. This too required some delicacy. Because I wanted to maintain Schachter-Shalomi's voice and the attunement in which various teachings were offered, I didn't want to recast his wording into formal written English.

I have also chosen to quote his words at length so that the reader can get not only the conclusions but the spirit and flavor of his way of working with the text.

For the most part, I left his wording just as he expressed it. In a few places I dropped a false start or a digression that did not apply to the topic I was focusing on, and of course in the selection and organizing I both omitted material and rearranged what was there. But all the words are his as given. Where they are not polished, and where they demand an effort to hear the intonations that helped the transmission in the original, I rely on the reader to understand that these are oral teachings delivered in a particular setting. The reward for that extra effort will be catching the authentic flavor of his personality and characteristic style of presentation.

Annotating

A major contribution of "value added" lies in the annotation. As I identified quotations, thinkers, and other references in the transcription phase, I tracked the quotations to their sources, cited them, and, where helpful, gave additional explanations or quotations.

For example, if Schachter-Shalomi mentions *amor dei intellectualis* (with no other identification) I recognize or track down that this is Spinoza and, knowing Spinoza's work, that the text where he would have developed that idea would probably be his *Ethics*, and find by hunting through that book where he introduces the idea and what he means by it, cross-checking with the Latin text to be sure of the quotation and its orthography.

For another example, if Schachter-Shalomi says "the Rabbis say" I track down where this is said in Talmud, or Midrash, or other ancient commentary, check the reference, cite, and, if relevant, give the context.

I also use the annotations to try to make these teachings accessible to a wide range of readers by translating and explaining (at least the first time they are used) all foreign words and technical terms. Of course I translate all foreign-language quotations that Schachter-Shalomi does not himself translate (and if his translation incorporates some of his commentary, I also provide a literal translation). In Schachter-Shalomi's transcribed passages I transliterate the Hebrew and Yiddish. For Hebrew passages which were transliterated or just translated, I include the Hebrew text in footnotes.

Issues of going from spoken to written form

There is another challenge in presenting the material from the audio files in written form that should be noted here.

Going from the full participation in the original retreats and the extended community of the Wisdom School to an audio recording is, of course, a major reduction in the atmosphere and the experience. This is perhaps easily appreciated.

But going from the audio to the written word involves a reduction in the bandwidth of the experience arguably as significant as not being present in person.

This is true in general. Spoken words carry a wealth of information in tone of voice, volume, rate of speed, and intonation. Tenderness or harshness or any of a whole range of emotional and intellectual attitudes and judgments are carried on the voice.

It is especially true of Schachter-Shalomi. His voice is an instrument of great range and power and expressiveness, and his use of his voice is masterful. He is a musician, a preacher, a story-teller. He conveys more than the usual range of emotions and attitudes both because of the power and subtleties and variety of his voice usage and because of his willingness (particularly in these retreats) to lay himself open, sharing some of the most painful parts of his experience and some of his deepest longings. These moments are not just about sharing facts about himself and his beliefs: he is doing his listeners the honor of placing himself fully in the experience, reporting from the inside.

Knowing the inadequacy of written words to convey intonation and affect, I have done my best. In a few places I have made an effort to describe some of what came across in the audio version that I feared would be diminished or missed in reading over the bare written words. I hope that the reader will try to hear his voice, will enter sympathetically into what the delivery must have been, in those places and, to the extent possible, throughout.

4. Authorization and Permissions

I was authorized to use the material in these audio files by the Reb Zalman Legacy Project, its director Netanel Miles-Yeprez, and I was given permission and blessing by Rabbi Schachter-Shalomi himself. My original intention was to use the material for a PhD dissertation, and it was on that understanding that the original authorizations were given. When I developed the project into a book for publication, I sought and obtained permission from Schachter-Shalomi for that specific use. Schachter-Shalomi has seen a draft of the text of this book and approved my use of his material, my transcription, and my representation of his ideas.

Note on Orthography, Transliteration, Translation

My procedure is to transliterate foreign language words that appear in the main body of the text. My transliterations of foreign words are as close to the source language as possible (although see below for my procedure for Yiddish). With Hebrew and Aramaic, there are limitations on how close that can be, and so I have included the text in Hebrew or Aramaic (generally in footnotes) when I transliterate words or passages. I have also included the original language form for transliterated terms in Yiddish, Sanskrit, Greek, and Arabic.

For Yiddish I uses the standardized orthography of the Yidisher Visnshaftlikher Institut (YIVO) and the YIVO Yiddish dictionary of Uriel Weinreich. For Yiddish transliteration, I use the YIVO Transliteration chart. Yiddish transliteration in practice varies widely and approximates the pronunciations of various dialects, so the standardized conventions, while matching no one's Yiddish mother tongue entirely, serve as a scholarly norm.

Translations where not otherwise indicated are my own. My translations have as their aim maximum transparency into the source language.

Translations and explanations of words used by Schachter-Shalomi (such as Yiddish words and expressions) are generally only given once, in a footnote when they first appear. All such words are included in the index so that the explanation can be found again if the reader comes upon them later.

Shading of Schachter-Shalomi Text

Transcriptions of Schachter-Shalomi's teachings are indented and set off with shading. Extracts and quotations from Eve Ilsen and other scholars (these are quoted more extensively in the final chapter) are indented but not shaded.

Acknowledgments

My gratitude to all who helped me with words, citations, and advice.

When this project was a glint-in-the-eye for a doctoral dissertation, Rabbi Miles Krassen helped me formulate my proposal for a study of Schachter-Shalomi's biblical commentary as foundation for his re-visioning of Judaism. My original Director of Studies, Rabbi Professor Dan Cohn-Sherbok, also helped me focus the project. At this point I still thought I could find enough published material to carry out the project.

I found that that was not the case. The project was saved, and greatly enhanced, by Netanel Miles-Yepez, then director of the Schachter-Shalomi archives at Naropa University. He told me that the archives included tapes from the Primal Myths Wisdom School and graciously opened them to me and allowed me to sit in his apartment copying all the Primal Myths audio files onto 114 CDs.

Rabbi Zalman Schachter-Shalomi was strongly supportive from the beginning of the project and met with me several times to clarify points in the transcription and identify citations of unpublished quotations.

I turned to colleagues, friends, and teachers for specific guidance and leads in tracking down citations for some of the things that Schachter-Shalomi mentioned in the course of his teachings on the audio files.

A number of queries went out on the Aleph Alliance for Jewish Renewal P'nai Or email forum. Some participants remembered things that were mentioned without explanation in the audio files, and many offered enthusiastic support of the project. For specific information I thank Rabbi Marcia Prager, Reb Karen Roekard, Yoram Getzler, Yolie Bloomstein, and Chazzan Jack Kessler. For all who expressed eagerness for the result, I offer this book with appreciation for your encouragement.

Rabbi Jack Shlachter helped me track down quite a few citations in traditional Jewish commentaries, and directed me to many books that allowed me to find many other cited material. His depth and breadth of Jewish learning aided by his magnificent library were valuable support in the early stages.

Rabbi Marvin Schwab gave me early tips in accessing traditional texts. He read a number of chapters of the book and made suggestions of wording and emphasis.

I also called upon, and was helpfully steered to needed citations by Rabbi Mordechai Scher, Daniel Israel, and Naomi Israel. Rabbi Berel Levertov helped me with some of the Yiddish expressions. Professor Shaul Magid directed me to scholarly background articles and Rabbi Samuel Barth gave supportive advice.

Rabbi Shefa Gold, Rabbi David Zaslow, and Rabbi David Ingber all read pre-publication editions of the book and provided enthusiastic support, which was much appreciated. To all who reviewed the book and provided supportive comments that they permitted me to use, my deep appreciation.

Maggid Andrew Gold deserves a special acknowledgment. A long-time student of Schachter-Shalomi, Andy introduced me to Reb Zalman's way of reading Tanakh by doing it himself in Torah study sessions. As teacher, study partner, and friend, Andy planted the seeds that led to this project. He also read through an early draft and offered thoughtful comments.

Hebrew scholar and translator Robert D. Sacks helped open to me the wonders of reading Tanakh in Hebrew. For over ten years we have met weekly to delve into that beautiful and surprising text. Through our study partnership I learned a lot of Biblical Hebrew and had much delight. My appreciation of the Hebrew biblical text was one of the enticements that led me into this project.

Some gave not only comments on the text but needed technical help with the production of the book and the computer technology challenges. The dissertation and early versions of the book were composed in the Hebrew word processor DavkaWriter. However, although DavkaWriter is wonderful at handling the shifting back and forth between Hebrew and English, which I was doing constantly, it has limitations as a program for typesetting a book, and it was not up to the standards of my publisher, Kafir Yaroq Books. So it had to be converted to InDesign, which was a demanding project.

Howard Fisher worked with the text after I had it in InDesign, crafting pages according to book design criteria, as well as doing much work implementing the index. I thank him also for reading through a draft and making suggestions, and for his kind support.

I especially thank William H. Donahue, who was supportive of the project throughout in scholarly, technical, and personal ways. He read drafts and gave me thoughtful and useful corrections and suggestions. I called upon him as a resource for helping me identify and transcribe Schachter-Shalomi's Latin and German quotations. He also was a major help in the conversion from Windows and DavkaWriter to InDesign and Mac. He researched ways of moving the text over (a process which had special difficulties not just because it was both cross-software and cross-platform, but because of nonstandard mapping of DavkaWriter's font) and he implemented the software tapestry that finally did the job.

In the six years over which this project was carried out, there were no doubt colleagues, friends, and teachers who helped in various ways whose names I neglected to note at the time and have slipped away. Forgive the omissions; know that you are part of what is worthy in this book.

Prologue

Every religion that is based on an ancient scripture faces a challenge. The text was written at a certain time and place, for a certain people. The language, the images, the situations, and to a large extent, the morals and laws are not only worded but devised to be appropriate to that context and the cultural understanding of its people.

That this is true for texts written by human beings, the sages and teachers and prophets whose words are handed down, is evident. It is also true, however, if the texts are written by the hand or dictated by the voice of God.

Unless the moral precepts can be put in language and terms that can be understood, and more, in language and terms that can move and inspire people, they will merely seem strange and alien. Laws about ways of life the recipient people aren't living (or perhaps cannot even imagine) cannot give guidance for daily life.

Perhaps even God must recognize that he must speak in language the people can understand. One of the great sages of the Mishnah, Rabbi Ishmael ben Elisha, famous also for the Thirteen Rules of Interpretation of Torah (included in the morning liturgy), taught that "Torah speaks in human language" (*Dibrah Torah k'lashon b'nei adam*).[1]

The God of the Bible clearly understands this: the laws he initially sets up for Adam and Eve are modified for Noah and his descendents and again in the Mosaic laws.

---

1   דברה תורה כלשון בני אדם This principle appears frequently in Talmudic discussions. See, for example, Tractate *Bava Metzia* 31b in Babylonian Talmud.

The survival of these scriptures as living embodiments of divine teachings over millennia is therefore, perhaps, surprising. How do they come to have their ability to continue to move and inspire people spiritually, and to provide day to day guidance, and even to continue to unite people into a religion? How is the universal extracted from the particular?

It is easy enough, perhaps, to identify laws cast in terms of practices that no longer exist. But if the scripture has come to be understood as sacred and perfect, the very Word of God, who could be so foolhardy, and so presumptuous, as to declare them void and superseded? And how could the faith community, the guardians of tradition, allow anyone to presume to make changes? If that were permitted anyone might make up any rules he pleased, or destroy any sacred laws that did not please him, and that would be the end of Judaism.

The faith of the covenant community, and its cohesiveness, is based on the unquestioned sacredness of this text. The tradition has maintained that not just every law, but every letter of the received text, every oddity of phrasing, every quirk of the way it is written, every apparent grammatical error, is a message and teaching from God. How can this be maintained and still make the text give guidance for widely differing circumstances and world views over millennia?

The key has been to interpret and reinterpret the text, and more, to continually re-vision the religion, while still basing it on the same text and insisting on the inviolacy of that text.

There is a tension, indeed a paradox here. If one openly admits to reinterpreting the text, one has abandoned and betrayed tradition, and weakened or destroyed the glue of tradition, and the reliance on this sacred verbal formulation of divine wisdom, that holds the community together. And yet, without reinterpretation the text can no longer give guidance, both because the present situations of life are not addressed and because our world view has changed too radically.

The Biblical text has been reinterpreted and re-visioned within the canonical text itself, beginning with the re-telling (in Genesis Chapter 2) of the creation of humankind first given in Genesis Chapter 1. Reinterpretation and re-visioning continued in the Second Temple period after the canon was closed, and, most radically, after the destruction of the Second Temple, in Rabbinic times and through the centuries of the Gaonic academies.

But times kept changing, and even Rabbinic Judaism, thorough and authoritative as it was, did not suffice. Reinterpretations continued to be needed. In medieval times, new interpreters arose to continue to make the text meaningful (while of course continuing to find ways of denying that this was new). New visions arose with Maimonides' work to place Jewish law and traditions on a rational and scientific basis, with authors of the Zohar finding mystical meanings in the text, with the vision of the Baal Shem Tov and his Eastern European Chasidic followers, with the nineteenth century enlightenment movement centered mostly in Germany. And it continues even into our present day.

This study delves into the work and vision of one influential present day thinker, Rabbi Zalman Schachter-Shalomi. How does he follow the pattern of honoring and holding sacred the ancient text while re-visioning and reinterpreting its teachings? What is his sense of what is needed for our time?

∂•∞

As each generation reads this same scripture, the needs and expectations of their own time color their interpretation of the words. Each generation extracts the teachings that are meaningful and helpful to their situation, ones that make sense in their world view and cosmology and that reflect their own ideals and aspirations.

But what if there is an attempt to put a seal on this process? The teachings as interpreted for an earlier situation then get handed down as an inviolable part of the tradition, and can sclerose the living Torah, the sacred teachings coming through that scripture, into a paradigm that may not be meeting the situation and needs of the later generation.

Schachter-Shalomi is inviting the participants of the Primal Myths Wisdom School to take a fresh look at these texts, to read them with their own questions and (as much as possible) setting aside received traditional interpretations.

It is bold, and some would even rightly say risky, to set the traditions temporarily aside to try a fresh look, to let the scripture speak directly to the soul of a present day reader with his or her own and perhaps differing needs and aspirations. In Schachter-Shalomi's view, we must take that perhaps risky but also perhaps exhilarating path if we are to keep this tradition living.

Otherwise, in his view, Judaism will be imperiled by becoming a relic of former beliefs and practices, honored for the sacred power of tradition, but not speaking to the highest aspirations (or even what comes to feel like simple common sense) of our minds and souls today. It may, as it too often has, come to seem irrelevant to many present-day Jews, or even may seem to some to be representing and advocating a world view that is not only unattractive but morally objectionable.

That seems to him a greater risk, and furthermore a loss of the God-given teachings of this Torah scripture, the teachings hidden in the precious words and letters, waiting for each generation to engage and learn.

How there can be new teachings in the same words that have had a different interpretation in the past is something that Schachter-Shalomi is illustrating over the course of this Primal Myths series of weekends.

๛•๕

The guardians of tradition and orthodoxy must worry that any revision or re-visioning of the received interpretations may destroy Judaism. This is a fear that raises a very high level of anxiety after the Nazi Holocaust of the last century destroyed a third of the world's Jewish population and a horrifying amount of a very rich and deep Eastern European Jewish culture.

But I will argue here, and support in the last chapter, that without this continual re-visioning, Judaism would have died out long ago.[2] The astonishing survival of the religion, the continued cohesiveness of the Jewish people, and the persisting reliance on the Bible as a source of deep wisdom and sacredness and guidance for life, is not in spite of, but because of Judaism's willingness to reinvent itself. This drive to continuous re-visioning, one might say, is in its DNA.

To see that the texts must be reinterpreted to continue to give guidance to members of the covenant community living in different circumstances need not depart from a traditional pious view. Rather it can understand and treat the text as having such divine depth and sacredness that the same words can speak beyond their initial apparent meaning and particularity to convey a universal wisdom, speaking to every generation that has come or will come.

This is indeed the context in which Rabbi Schachter-Shalomi offers his re-visioning, as well as essentially the stance of all the traditional interpreters whose commentary or re-visioning I will cite. It is my claim that Schachter-Shalomi is fully within the tradition, the tradition of extracting the essence over and over in new ways in each era.

Rabbinic Midrash tells us *Shev'im panim laTorah* "There are seventy faces of Torah"[3]—that is, seventy (i.e. a very large number) ways or levels of interpreting the words. And Mishnah

---

2   This has indeed been suggested by a number of scholars and thinkers over the years. The final chapter of this book presents some of these scholarly views.

3   ***Shev'im panim laTorah.*** שבעים פנים לתורה *Bamidbar Rabbah* 13:15.

enjoins, *Hafakh bah, va hafakh bah; d'kolah bah* "Turn it [Torah], turn it, everything is in it."[4]

Although I place Schachter-Shalomi's teachings in a context of a process within the tradition that I argue goes back to the earliest sources, it is not my goal to persuade anyone to agree with Schachter-Shalomi's specific conclusions. What I do want to do is to make the case that what he is doing is very much in the long tradition of living Judaism. The richness of the tradition, as well as its vibrancy and longevity, are based in its passionate and endless arguing with itself, as the many volumes of Talmud document exhaustively, and as study of those volumes has taught many generations.

---

4 ***Hafakh bah v'hafakh bah; d'kolah bah.*** הפך בה והפך בה; דכולא בה. (*Hafakh* could also be overturn or transform.) *Babylonian Talmud, Mishnah,* Pirkei Avot 5:26.

Primal Myths Case Studies

From the First Weekend, "Creation"

1
The Four Worlds of Creation

Although the metaphor or trope of "four worlds of creation" is not one that is featured or developed in the course of the Primal Myths series of retreats, it is an important tool in Schachter-Shalomi's thinking more generally, and so is occasionally referred to in the teachings presented at those retreats and gathered here in this book.

This categorization of levels of reality is based on the kabbalistic tradition. There is an apparent hierarchy of spiritual elevation as one moves from the plane of action and physical manifestation through to the divine unity beyond human grasping.[1] But Schachter-Shalomi teaches that these planes interpenetrate and each is present behind the scenes (as it were) in each other world.

When Schachter-Shalomi was presenting the opening words of the book of Genesis, *b'reshiyt bara elohim et ha shamayim v'et ha aretz*[2] he gave an introduction to these levels of reality.

> One of the things we have to keep in mind is that we are moving, constantly moving, at least on four planes of existence.

The World of Asiyah

The first level as Schachter-Shalomi presents the four worlds is the one that includes our ordinary engagements with palpable, physical reality.

---

1   They are often classically presented as a descent: from *Atziylut*, the divine unity, reality descends to *B'riyah*, creation, then to *Yetziyrah*, the fashioning of that creation, then to *Asiyah*, the world of function, of doing. I follow Schachter-Shalomi's presentation here.

2   Gen. 1:1. בְּרֵאשִׁית בָּרָא אֱלֹהִים אֵת הַשָּׁמַיִם וְאֵת הָאָרֶץ׃

> There's the one plane of existence that's the physical one. The chair tells me where I am and the mike is in front of me and so I'm bounded by space. That's very physical. And I do understand everything about technology on that physical plane. ... You know how to put something together, how to take it apart. To treat the universe in the accusative, in the thingness, in the I-it place. That's one way in which we apprehend things.

The World of Y'tziyrah

The second level in Schachter-Shalomi's presentation, *Y'tziyrah*, is the world of formation, the world of feelings. Schachter-Shalomi here emphasizes the relationship dimension of this level.

> There's another way in which we apprehend things. With feeling. What happens in the hermeneutic of feelings, where feelings matter, facts are not so important. Where feelings matter, something else is important. Relationship is important. So the I-it world is that world in which we deal with facts. The I-thou world is the world in which we deal with relationships and with feeling. Every relationship constitutes for us the feeling.
>
> How would you say "gravity" in the world of I-thou? You call it love. Any two bodies in the universe feel attraction to each other; that's gravity. Any two persons in the universe feel attraction to each other, that's love. So what on one level is called gravity is on another level called love.
>
> So there are at least two levels of interpretation. One is the facticity level and one is the relationship level.

The World of B'riyah

The level of *B'riyah* is the level of thought and nuance, intellect and contemplation. Schachter-Shalomi has called it the place of Plato's forms, the place of myths and ideas and understandings.

> There still is another level in which meaning is being given to something. And what we were talking about before as to why there is a universe, why does God want to create, that's a third level of understanding.

The World of Atziylut

Atziylut is the level out of which emanation proceeds, the level of divine unity.

> Behind this there is still another level which can't even be talked about. "The Tao that can be told is not the eternal Tao." So *b'reshiyt* can also deal with that which is unnameable, which is only accessible to the intuition.

Multiple Levels

Schachter-Shalomi is noting near the outset of the Creation retreat that this first creation must be understood as including multiple levels of being, and not just the physical level explicitly called out in the ensuing verses. Simultaneously, levels or worlds of creativity, understanding, and un-manifest divine reality are all present, and will have their effect as the creation plays itself out over the millennia.

> So these are the four levels of hermeneutic with which we will approach things.

Although, as I say, there is very little if any explicit application of the "four worlds" tool as a hermeneutic during these retreats, it will be helpful to keep them in mind. Schachter-Shalomi has presented us here a context for his own understanding and issued participants an invitation to remember that these levels are always present.

2
Male and Female Images

Metaphors for Creation

Schachter-Shalomi begins his first weekend of the Primal Myths series of his P'nai Or Wisdom School[1] with close reading of the first two verses of the first chapter of Genesis, and then supports some of his observations there with evidence from the immediately succeeding verses. He then adds a further dimension from later in the first chapter.

One of Schachter-Shalomi's central understandings is that Judaism must transcend its historical marginalizing of women and its tendency to shy away from feminine aspects or metaphors for divine being. He notes that Jewish women have always been half of the Jewish community, and an essential part. To fail to fully acknowledge their dimension in the historical narratives robs the inheritors of the tradition of an essential piece of that tradition; indeed it must tend to distort the heritage.

Furthermore, to downplay or be actively embarrassed by feminine dimensions of divine being, or avoid using metaphors that call upon feminine images, limits our understanding of divine being and indeed could be thought of as blaspheming by limiting

---

1 For background on this Wisdom School, offered by Schachter-Shalomi in collaboration with spiritual teacher Eve Ilsen, and for identification of the source of my quotations, see the preliminary section About My Source Material.

God to a reflection of one's own (masculine) self.[2] Naturally, this avoidance, when it occurs, proceeds from, or at least feels like, an impulse of piety. When one's own view of women is of a category inferior, sexualized, and made holy only in her status as property, it becomes uncomfortable and even shameful to associate feminine images or attributes with the God one wishes to praise as powerful and transcendent.

Such an avoidance of feminine metaphors is particularly evident in much of the Talmudic and other traditional commentaries.[3]

Schachter-Shalomi uses the opening verses of Genesis to suggest that the Biblical scripture itself presents a much richer picture of the dimensions of divine being, and of the creation of the world in particular, than that which much of later tradition, particularly Rabbinic, might suggest.

In Schachter-Shalomi's initial discussion in the Creation weekend, he notes the interesting mixture of masculine and feminine elements in the creation account.

"*Bara elohim*"[4] is a complete act, indicated by the qatal or "perfect" or "completed" form of the verb.[5] As such it is one that

---

2   To the extent that women share this discomfort with feminine images of divine being, it is because they too want a God that is powerful, free, and confident. The lack of honor accorded female qualities seems to taint those qualities, at least enough to make one uncomfortable about associating them with the being to whom the natural response should be glorification. One wants to feel lifted up by being associated with this God's magnificence.

3   The mystical traditions are much freer in making use of the feminine and even sexualized images for different aspects and dimensions of divine being.

4   Gen. 1.1. בָּרָא אֱלֹהִים ... God created... .

5   **Qatal.** Biblical Hebrew does not have the modern European sense of past, present, and future. The Biblical Hebrew verb forms of *qatal* and *yiqtol*, are sometimes translated as verbal tenses "perfect" and "imperfect," that is, completed and not completed. However, most grammarians recognize that division into "completed" and "uncompleted" is still an inadequate approximation of these forms

could be done all at once. Our modern image would be the Big Bang. This, in Schachter-Shalomi's view, is a masculine sort of creation.

But then in the next verse we get the image of "the spirit/ breath of God hovering/brooding over the face of the water."[6] *Ruach* (spirit or breath or wind) is a feminine noun. The hovering, *m'rachefet*, is not a single act, but an ongoing state like gestation (expressed by use of the participle, rather than the *qatal*—completed—form as was the initial verb *bara*). The *m'rachefet* image (and it is a feminine form to agree with the feminine noun *ruach*) is one of a mother eagle hovering over the nest (as the word is used later of God's relation to us[7]), brooding over the young.

The waters themselves again suggest the feminine and gestation and a mother sort of birthing process. The gestating offspring starts out apparently "*tohu v'vohu*"[8] and, by processes of gathering waters in one place and separating waters above and below and so on, develops into a more completely formed entity.

Schachter-Shalomi suggests that the text balances the initial masculine ברא image with this extended metaphor of maternal gestation for God's creation of the world.

Here is his teaching on the first evening of the Creation weekend:

---

and many prefer to speak noncommittally of *qatal* and *yiqtol* (using the verb root קטל to illustrate the paradigms) or simply of *suffixed* and *prefixed* (although that has the inconvenience that some of the "prefixed" forms also have suffixes, and not all the "suffixed" forms show a suffix).

6   Gen. 1.2. רוּחַ אֱלֹהִים מְרַחֶפֶת עַל־פְּנֵי הַמָּיִם *Ruach elohim m'rachefet al p'nei ha'mayim.*

7   Deut. 32:11. כְּנֶשֶׁר יָעִיר קִנּוֹ עַל־גּוֹזָלָיו יְרַחֵף יִפְרֹשׂ כְּנָפָיו יִקָּחֵהוּ יִשָּׂאֵהוּ עַל־אֶבְרָתוֹ׃ Like an eagle that would stir up its nest, that would hover over its young, would spread out its wings, would catch them, would bear them on its pinions... .

8   Gen. 1:2. הָיְתָה תֹהוּ וָבֹהוּ the earth was formlessness and emptiness [meaning of בֹהוּ uncertain].

V'ruach elohim m'rachefet al p'nei hamayim.[9] And the spirit of God, it hovered on the face of the water.

And that's all I want to talk about—this one word מְרַחֶפֶת *m'rachefet*, hovering—right now.

There above that which has been made is that liquid which is water. That which is capable of taking any shape yet and hasn't yet taken a shape. Above that there is a template, there is an energy, there is a field, and this field is called *ruach elohim*. It is the spirit of God. Strong wind is how some translations have it.

But *ruach* is a feminine word. It is a word of brooding. And it gives that verb that says "it broods." Just like if there were an egg that has to be called into life, this water has to be called into life. Something has to happen to make this life be lived, to live a life. Now it is not kicking it into life, it is coaxing it, it is inviting it, it is creating that wonderful field that is mother field, so that the matrix, the mat-ter, is mothered into life. So prior to there being any *abracadabra* that says "let there be this" or "let there be that", there is that warm invitation that says "Come!... Come!... Come!"

Schachter-Shalomi stretches out this coaxing mother-field creation image past the initial creation. He paints this as an ongoing invitation coaxing us into life and growth. He even con-nects it to our being "theotropic," always stretching ourselves out toward God.

And if you begin to ask yourself what brings you into life, what makes a morning worth getting up for, what makes a night relaxing, you begin to see that it still is the same *ruach elohim* in the same mother God, that cosmic hen brooding over creation and calling it into life and saying, "Come! I have something nice to coax you into. Give yourself a chance to grow. You'll have to break a shell

---

9   Gen. 1:2. וְרוּחַ אֱלֹהִים מְרַחֶפֶת עַל־פְּנֵי הַמָּיִם׃

and come out after a while. You'll have to see what's on the other side of this thing. But it's good."

And since that time we have been theotropic beings. Just like heliotropic things grow towards the sun, we have been growing towards God.

And so I would like to suggest that that which makes crystals take form, and that which makes us become us, is waiting to be with us, as that Beloved that's been calling us all that time, that's been warming us into life all the time. And that is also that which provides us underneath with the everlasting arms. …

And how Goethe put it, in his language, "*Das Ewig-Weibliche zieht uns hinan.*"[10] The eternally feminine is that which keeps drawing us on and on to this expression.

Jewish Mystical and Philosophical Readings of Creation

The next morning Schachter-Shalomi resumed the exploration by considering the Jewish mystical and philosophical readings.

Rabbi Yitzchak Luria, Isaac Luria, 16th century Safed in the Holy Land, kabbalist who for us would be the Eckhart,[11] the Shankara,[12] the Al-Hallaj[13] if I go to Sufism, that person, that radical monist person, he raised the question. He [Luria] said most philosophers were speaking about how

---

10 German. "The eternal feminine draws us onward." Johann Wolfgang von Goethe, *Faust*, last two lines (12110–111).

11 **Eckhart**. Eckhart von Hochheim, known as "Meister Eckhart," was in influential Christian mystic and neo-Platonist and member of the Dominican Order. Lived c. 1260–c. 1327.

12 **Shankara** (788–820). Adi Shankara, Indian philosopher who promoted the doctrine of *advaita*, nondualism, the unity of all existence.

13 **Al-Hallaj** (c. 858–922). Sufi mystic, executed for proclaiming his union with divine being.

God created the world *ex nihilo*, out of nothing. And he says, "where was there a nothing?"

If אֵין סוֹף *ain sof*, the infinite, the endless one, filled all that there was to fill, then there was no place for nothing. And so the question came, instead of speaking like the philosophers did, that there was this *fiat* that created something out of nothing, it spoke of a condensation, of a contraction. By the way, the three key words in the theology of Luria are: *ibur*, *leda*, *yinikha* (and *tzimtzum*[14] goes with that). *Ibur*, to be pregnant with. To contain that way. *Leda*, birth. *Yinikha*, to give nurturance, to suckle.

And so, this person, kabbalist, speaks like [that]. So today, we're so looking to hear if anyone has a voice that brings in the feminine, and here, he [Luria] spoke about these ways as the ways in which God birthed worlds.

That there was a kind of being-pregnant-with, that the notion "let there be and there was," like papa has babies, one two three and thank you ma'am, is not quite the same situation as you speak of time for gestation. So Luria spoke about *ibur*, being pregnant with, that God was pregnant with the worlds first.

Eli Wiesel likes to put it this way,[15] he said "*Eyder Got hot die velt bashafn, hot er ir oysgezungen.*" Before God created the world, he sang it out. All these are the ways in which you want to talk about that it didn't start when we say it started.

Schachter-Shalomi has been exploring the idea that before the creation recounted in the opening verse of Genesis, the *bara* (he

---

14 **Tzimtzum**. Hebrew צמצום Contraction. Schachter-Shalomi will deal with this shortly.

15 Yiddish, meaning as translated. Remembered from a private conversation between Wiesel and Schachter-Shalomi.

created) said to be *b'reshiyt*,[16] there must have been some sort of gestation, something out of which the creation came.

> A conductor, beginning to conduct something, how does the conductor do it? There is the drawing together of the orchestra, and, with that first downbeat, the whole symphony is contained in that. But the downbeat would not make any sense had it not been for that preparation that is prior to the downbeat.

But if it is so, why did the text start with *b'reshiyt bara elohim*? Perhaps, he speculates, it derives from the limitation of perspective of male scribes.

> So why the Bible chose to tell us, from the downbeat on, and not from the preparation for the downbeat, is quite obvious if you see that there is a male elite that got this to write.

Outering and Contraction

Schachter-Shalomi looks now from a slightly different angle.

> The word ברא, which is the word for creation, which is the one that in Aramaic means outside.[17]
>
> So Samson Rafael Hirsch, in his translation of the Bible, says like this: "*Am Anfang hat sich Gott geäussert.*"[18] In the beginning God outered himself. Get that sense?

---

16 בראשית: "In beginning," or "In a beginning." Some, following the King James version, have translated "In the beginning," but there is no definite article in the Hebrew.

17 בר and ברא: outside, outdoors; outside of, except for. See Frank, 1994, pp. 53 and 55 and Melamed, 2005, pp. 104 and 109.

18 Schachter-Shalomi is remembering something quoted by Hirsch's grandson Isaac Breuer in a talk Schachter-Shalomi [*continued overleaf*]

That outering: how do you manage to outer the infinite into the infinitesimal if not by that which is an utter contraction that takes that and gets to be so heavy that you have that collapse that we call a black hole. So if you begin to see black hole on one side and big bang on the other side, then what disappears as black hole reappears as big bang, so you get this whole sense again of it not being starting at that time, but "once upon a beginning" it had been there and contracted itself.

So Luria speaks of contraction. And if he used the word contraction as we use it today in birthing (and we will have more to deal with this birthing sense), and we feel it

---

heard in Vienna when he was a teenager. This is different from the wording that appears in the published German translation *Der Pentateuch,* vol. 1, 1893. However, in Hirsch's commentary on Gen. 1:1 in that edition, he says something essentially the same: ברא. *Die verwandten Wurzeln:* פרע, פרא, פרח, ברה, ברח, *die sämmtlich ein Hinausstreben und Hinaustreten aus einer Innerlichkeit oder einer Gebundenheit bedeuten, ergeben für* ברא *ebenfalls den Begriff des Hinaussetzens in die Aeusserlichkeit; heisst ja auch Chald.* ברא *ohne Weiteres das draussen Seinde, draussen.* ברא *ist somit das Aeusserlichmachen eines bis dahin nur im Innern, im Geiste vorhanden Gewesenen. Es ist jenes Schaffen, dem nichts Anderes als der Gedanke und der Wille vorangegangen.* ברא *ist somit das Aeusserlichmachen eines bis dahin nur im Innern, im Geiste vorhanden Gewesenen. Es ist jenes Schaffen, dem nichts Anderes als der Gedanke und der Wille vorangegangen.* ("ברא. The related roots ברח, ברה, פרח, פרא, פרע, which together denote an outward striving and a going forth out of an inwardness or out of a bound state, likewise show for ברא the concept of a setting forth into the outwardness. In fact, the Chaldean ברא, without anything further, means the outwardly existing, outside. ברא is accordingly the exteriorization of a being that was hitherto present only internally, in spirit. It is that creation which is preceded by nothing other than thought and will. ברא is accordingly the exteriorization of a being that was hitherto present only internally, in spirit. It is that creation which is preceded by nothing other than thought and will.")

in ourselves too, this rhythmicity that takes over when we can no longer control its coming. It produces something in us and this is where that which was innered first, outed, afterwards. *Tzimtzum*, it goes like this. *Tzimtzum*, contraction.

If God were absent, there would be nothing. if God were totally present, there would be nothing. There's no room. That which is the hiding of the God-light creates space.

Space is made by the contraction, but it is not a space of nothingness but of a deeper hidden presence that lies behind manifest creation.

So if you get the sense that space is being made by the withdrawal of that, and yet it isn't absent, it is only hidden, it is implicate, it isn't explicate.[19] That the presence is implicate, and yet there is space being made. This is part of that mystery.

The Primordial Waters

Schachter-Shalomi then moves into a contemplation and investigation of the metaphor of primordial waters, touching on what some parts of the Jewish tradition have done with that, and also, as he so often does, exploring linguistic and etymological connections.

According to one way of looking at it, when the waters were not separated, they were both male and female, or perhaps they are better understood as neither.

---

19 **Implicate, explicate**. Terms of physicist David Bohm. The *explicate* order is our ordinary and materialist notion of space and time. Bohm said of the deeper *implicate* order "The new form of insight can perhaps best be called Undivided Wholeness in Flowing Movement. This view implies that flow is, in some sense, prior to that of the 'things' that can be seen to form and dissolve in this flow." Bohm, *Wholeness and the Implicate Order,* p. 11.

Another dimension of the metaphor would have the undivided waters evoke the state of nonseparation with divine being; a condition of unity divided by the רָקִיעַ *raqia* in Genesis 1:6. This divider (rather unsatisfactorily and variously translated as expanse and firmament—its root has the meaning of stretching out) now separates the waters above and the waters below.

But Schachter-Shalomi draws attention to the fact that this is not a clean separation: the waters above rain down, the waters below evaporate up. It is as if they long to be re-united.

Dimensions of the rich metaphor of the waters keep calling him. What in one level of the metaphor is male and female becomes God calling the human creature and the human creature calling God. This longing and attraction, this *eros*, suggests to him the action of pheromones in human sexual attraction.

> Let's go back to רָקִיעַ raqia, firmament. And in that firmament there is a separation between waters that are above and waters that are below. Here is where the teaching comes. Once upon a time the water was not separated, but when the firmament was made, some water was above the firmament and some water was below the firmament. And ever since that time, the waters above the firmament have been yearning to reunite with the waters below the firmament and vice versa. This is why the waves are reaching upwards. And why rain is falling downward, because these waters want to unite.
>
> The water above has been likened to the male waters; the water below has been likened to the female waters. This is not what you would hear in Hebrew school when you go at first. But in the Kabbalah it makes it very clear that there are times when there is first a flow that comes from the female, and then there is time when the flow first comes from the male.
>
> And the way in which they're talking about this is as follows. When God initiates action, it is the upper waters

first. When human beings initiate action, when creatures initiate action, it's the lower waters first. So prayer is the attraction that pheromones of the lower water attract the upper waters, and the pheromones of the upper waters attract the lower waters.

There is something being sent into the world that starts saying "Respond!" Respond. Okay? And this sense that there is a rising up, and there is a coming down, so all of the fluidity into which we get in the search for re-establishing the union, and the tension between the upper and the lower, that is the רָקִיעַ raqia, that's the firmament that they speak of. And this tension has to be, because it's in that place between the lower and the upper waters that the rest of the action takes place. If the tension were let go there would be a flooding again, that everything would be absorbed in the fluid.

It's that yearning between the lower waters and the upper waters that influences what happens in the in-between.

Creation of Male and Female in God's Image

Moving on to Genesis 1:26–27[20] and the creation of human-kind on the sixth day, the Biblical text tells us that God creates the earthling (*ha'adam*)[21] in his (God's) image, "male and female he created them." It is often noted that this implies that both male and female are in the image of God. This explicit claim (which the text

---

20 וַיֹּאמֶר אֱלֹהִים נַעֲשֶׂה אָדָם בְּצַלְמֵנוּ כִּדְמוּתֵנוּ God said: Let us make humankind, in our image, according to our likeness! וַיִּבְרָא אֱלֹהִים | אֶת־הָאָדָם בְּצַלְמוֹ בְּצֶלֶם אֱלֹהִים בָּרָא אֹתוֹ זָכָר וּנְקֵבָה בָּרָא אֹתָם: So God created humankind in his image, in the image of God did he create it, male and female he created them. [Everett Fox translation]

21 The name for the human being, the *adam* אָדָם, comes from the word for earth, *adamah* אֲדָמָה. Schachter-Shalomi later offers a fanciful etymology or pun connecting *human* to *humus*.

seems to insist upon through its repetition) has implications for the dignity and status of women. Schachter-Shalomi would fully affirm these implications and this inclusiveness.

It is interesting, however, that what Schachter-Shalomi chooses to bring out in this retreat is not the implication for the dignity of human women, or even for understanding the created male and female earthlings more generally, but for our understanding of *God*. If they, male and female, are in the image of God, then, he observes, there must be something of both male and female in God.

Creation of the human being in God's image is first proposed (in God's planning) in Genesis 1:26: *Vayomer elohim na'aseh adam b'tzalmenu kidmutenu*.[22] "And God said, let us make an earth-creature/human being in our image; according to our likeness." Schachter-Shalomi picks up the story in the next verse:

> *Vayivra elohim et ha'adam b'tzalmo; b'tzelem elohim bara oto; zakhar u'm'qevah bara otam*.[23] "And God created the human in his image; in an image of God he created him; male and female he created them."
>
> Therefore God must look at least an androgyne, because it says male and female he created them in his image.
>
> And [note] how almost all, with very few exceptions, God images of the ancient period had consorts. Tiamat and Apsu. Zeus and Hera. Ba'al and Anat. El and Ashera. The gods are couples. The question is, how did it happen in our Biblical understanding that we no longer had the coupleness of God?

Schachter-Shalomi leaves the human creation story here, with this question raised about an androgyne gender of God. This was suggested by the "image" of God being said to be male and female,

---

22 Gen. 1:26. וַיֹּאמֶר אֱלֹהִים נַעֲשֶׂה אָדָם בְּצַלְמֵנוּ כִּדְמוּתֵנוּ

23 Gen. 1:27. וַיִּבְרָא אֱלֹהִים | אֶת־הָאָדָם בְּצַלְמוֹ בְּצֶלֶם אֱלֹהִים בָּרָא
אֹתוֹ זָכָר וּנְקֵבָה בָּרָא אֹתָם:

and by his reference to God images in contemporaneous cultures personified as both male and female. These questions were raised and left, perhaps to gestate over time.

Conclusion

The opening verses of the Genesis creation account invite us into deeper contemplation of divine action in the creation process, and contemplation of dimensions of unfolding and "outering" that reflect natural processes of gestation and even nurturance. These images for the process of creation have implications for the understanding of the nature of God and his (perhaps we should say his/her) action in the world.

In the course of his exploration of other topics gathered here from the Primal Myths weekends, we will see other expressions showing that Schachter-Shalomi finds value in seeing a less exclusively masculine character to the Biblical story. These emerge in his remarks and insights into women's agency and in other perspectives on God's nature and actions.

I find his most powerful feminist statements seem to be the ones that are implicit. He allows women to function as fully human characters without comment, as if it were natural. The female characters needn't be undermined, nor do they need to be applauded. The next section will provide a striking example of that, to which I will draw attention at the appropriate point.

3
Spiritual Evolution of Humanity

A second key theme in Schachter-Shalomi's re-visioning of Judaism, and one that emerges next in his tracing of the narrative of the first chapters of Genesis, is the theme of what he sees as a spiritual evolution of humanity over time. This includes us all as a species, but it also applies specifically to the carriers of the Jewish tradition.

Schachter-Shalomi sees a progressive development, dimensions of which can be viewed through multiple lenses.

From one perspective we can note that Jewish culture and civilization developed as the Jewish people moved from a shepherding life to monarchy within the borders of the ancestral homeland to exile in the advanced civilization of Babylon to world-wide diaspora.

As this was happening, the world around them changed, as well, in moving from early bronze age through various successive empires to industrial revolution to global integration and the image of earth seen from outer space. As these changes occurred, there was a process of spiritual evolution in ways of experiencing and representing divinity.

From another perspective, we can observe progressive development in a single human being. A human individual evolves from infancy through developing intelligence and judgment in childhood and adolescence and early adulthood, as the brain itself develops, and as experience and education inform and mold character, with the human spiritual understanding becoming deeper, more nuanced, less crude and infantile.

Similarly, Schachter-Shalomi sees the human species evolving over the millennia to a deeper and less crude understanding of divine being and divine action in the world.

Our desire for drawing near to God remains, but its expression moves from animal sacrifice to prayer service and potentially beyond. Our valuing of fairness and ethical behavior remain, but the specific ways that plays out may shift, not just with the demands of the times, but with our inner understanding of kindness. Our treasuring of holiness and purity remain, but the means of ensuring that, and of repairing damage to our sense of it, evolve.

These evolving understandings can be characterized in various ways. One image is that of the continual flow of Torah (teachings) from heaven, from the divine source. That image ascribes to God the teachings that arise in our hearts as we are spiritually ready (individually, but here, importantly, as a species). One could also look at this through the Biblical narrative, in which we see earlier phases of the process unfolding.

An Act of Transformation

In the second day of the Creation weekend Schachter-Shalomi moves on to the story of the state of consciousness before, during and after the eating of the fruit of the tree of good and evil.

He begins by exploring the state of innocence that was the human state before the eating of the fruit. He starts at Genesis 2:25.[1]

> So, the two of them were עֲרוּמִּים *arumim*. The Hebrew word for naked here is skin. They were in their skin. עוֹר *or* is skin, עֶרְוָה *ervah* is shame. *Arumim*, they were in their genitals.
>
> *V'lo yitboshashu*. And they were not—and here comes a Hebrew reflexive; they did not make themselves feel shameful over it. Get that? ... It is the *hitpael*, the reflexive. Both of them were in their skins, and in their genitals, the

---

1 Gen. 2:25. וַיִּהְיוּ שְׁנֵיהֶם עֲרוּמִּים הָאָדָם וְאִשְׁתּוֹ וְלֹא יִתְבֹּשָׁשׁוּ׃ "And the two of them were naked, the earthling and his wife, and they were not embarrassed in themselves/by each other."

man and his wife, and they did not cause themselves to be ashamed.

Now, abruptly, the serpent enters. They were naked, and in the very next verse the serpent is introduced as the craftiest of all the animals using a word with the same spelling as the word for their nakedness but with a different meaning.[2]

> Now, they were *arumim* עֲרוּמִּים, and the serpent it was *arum* עָרוֹם. And all of a sudden here a pun is being played very consciously. They were *arum* and the serpent was *arum*. But the *arum* that they were was naked and the *arum* that the serpent was was subtle. Clever. Deceitful. Okay? "More than all the other animals of the field which Yah Elohim had made."[3]

---

2 Schachter-Shalomi calls it a "pun" because although in the forms they appear here the spelling looks the same, the words come from different roots. One is based on root עוֹר ["be exposed, bare" BDB p. 735] or עָרָה ["be naked, bare" BDB p. 788] and the other is from root עָרֹם ["be shrewd, crafty" BDB p. 790].

3 Schachter-Shalomi here substitutes *Yah* (used in the Song of the Sea celebrating the escape from Egypt and in the later psalms) for the divine name YHVH instead of the more conventional substitute words Lord or Adonai. See page 166 for discussion of name-substitutions following the Jewish tradition that pronouncing God's name is impiety. Schachter-Shalomi often uses *Yah* because it is more poetic and avoids the hierarchical and masculinist character and tone of Lord or Adonai, but it is also the case that it is an actual name of God that it is legitimate to speak, according to Talmud and Rashi. In *Babylonian Talmud*, Tractate Eruvin 18b, Rabbi Yirmiyah ben Elazar says that since the day the Temple was destroyed, it is enough for the world to use the two-letter name of God (יָהּ, Yah). His proof text is Psalm 150:6, which says "All souls praise Yah" (כֹּל הַנְּשָׁמָה תְּהַלֵּל יָהּ). The commentary in the ArtScroll edition say that this implies that *every* soul may use the two-letter name, in contrast to the four-letter name (YHVH) which may only be used by priests in the Temple. The ArtScroll editors cite Rashi as saying that now *Yah* is the only name to be used in the world.

Schachter-Shalomi will lead us to look in detail at the process by which Eve, and humanity through her, moves from that state of innocence to a new state of consciousness and new capabilities, the start of all the psychological and spiritual evolution to come.

The Set-up

But first he interrupts the narrative temporarily to bring out something that to him is a key turning point in the parable that the Biblical narrative is presenting.

This whole scenario has God making a point of forbidding the one tree, and allowing the snake to make the argument it does, so that Eve (representing the human creature and its evolution) will violate the express command, risking (or being willing to accept) death as a price for a wisdom and a fuller and more godlike life. This whole scenario, Schachter-Shalomi will say, is a set-up.

But what is the point of the set-up? He gives two examples to illustrate the central psycho-spiritual truth he wants to assert about this transgressive moment.

> Now I want to stop for a moment with text and raise another thing. When women's liberation first began I gave a talk (I was living in Winnipeg Manitoba at that time) to a sisterhood. Question period came, one of the woman raised her hand and said, "Rabbi, there was the old testament and then there was the new testament, can't we now have a women's testament?" I said "I absolutely forbid it." She got angry and said "Who are you to forbid it?" [Schachter-Shalomi exclaims his reply:] "You got the point!"

He continues, addressing the participants at the Primal Myths retreat, with the insight spelled out.

> You cannot give liberation to someone as a gift. No parent can give a child freedom as a gift. That has to be taken, it has to be owned, it has to be conquered. Women

> cannot get from loving husbands, with their nice ribbon and a rose on top, liberation for their anniversary. It can't come as a gift. It has to be something that is owned, that is taken, it has to go through the separation.

His second example refers to what was at the time a painful break with Lubavitcher Chasidism.[4]

> As I read this I get overwhelmed by a feeling about that. When I last time came to a *farbrengen*[5] with the present Lubavitcher rebbe, and there came to be this kind of thing in which separation happened. In moments when I feel strong and aware, I give him credit for having had the strength to make that attitude that allowed for the break.
>
> Get that sense. It's a set-up! We are dealing with a set-up here.

God can't just give humankind the fruit of knowledge of good and evil, and all that follows from that knowledge. Central to the jump to a new level of psychological and spiritual maturity is the forceful taking of it, the courage to judge for oneself and be willing to take the consequences of asserting one's choice. Something will be lost, perhaps something precious. But the thing to be gained must be taken in an act of transformation.

That act may feel as powerful as this moment in which the human creatures, who seem to have paradise, risk it all to disobey the one command of the presumably all-powerful deity who created them.

---

4   See section on Schachter-Shalomi's life and work in the appendix. The break with Lubavitch occurred in 1968.

5   **Farbrengen** פֿאַרברענגען. Yiddish. Literally, a get-together. Used by Chabad Lubavitch communities as gatherings for inspiration, heart-opening, and self-examination, in which Torah and Chasidic philosophy are discussed, stories told, Chasidic melodies sung, and a certain amount of alcohol consumed as toasts to life.

Eve Thinks it Through

Schachter-Shalomi returns to the narrative, unfolding the process of the argument the snake makes to persuade Eve. Schachter-Shalomi draws us into experiencing, along with her, the invitation being made by the snake, and the new way of being that is imaginatively opening before her.

> And he [the snake] said to the woman: "Also, didn't God say 'don't eat from all the trees of the garden'?" Overstatement.

The snake is showing his cleverness by overstating the commandment so that Eve will deny it, thus beginning the move to leniency.

> "No!" the woman says to him. "From the fruit of the trees of the garden we can eat. And from the tree which is in the midst of the garden, there God said 'eat not of it, touch not in it, lest you die.'"

But now Eve herself has overstated the commandment, which forbade eating the fruit, but said nothing about touching. Had her husband overstated it in conveying it to her?[6] If so, had he gotten it wrong or was he deliberately overstating to frighten her away from the tree? Either way, it functions to blur the commandment's terms.

Conscious Dying

Now Schachter-Shalomi looks at the way the consequence of dying is expressed, and will connect this to what is said about the opening of eyes. The Hebrew repeats the root verb in two different forms, a way of creating emphasis often used in Biblical

---

6   In this Genesis account, she had not yet been created when the commandment was given.

Hebrew. Here Schachter-Shalomi follows the implications of the literal expression.

> And follow now how it says, "The snake says 'you will not die!'" Notice the Hebrew again. *Lo mot t'mutun.*[7] The Hebrew means "you will not die dying." You will not die dying.
>
> I want to say this again so you can hear it. Kübler-Ross when she's talking about the experience of death says "*Ich will mein Sterben erleben.*"[8] I want to experience, I want to live through my dying. I don't want to be dead in my dying.
>
> So the snake is saying "you will not die dying."
>
> "For God knows that on the day of your eating thereof your eyes will become opened."[9]

Schachter-Shalomi explores the implications of this "opening of the eyes."

> Remember what we were talking about perception and apperception? You didn't know how to apperceive before. Because you didn't have a center. The Nowhere Man from Yellow Submarine. He doesn't have a point of view. He doesn't have a position where he stands. His eyes are not smart. Perspective comes when the eyes begin to be smart. And when your eyes become smart, you will be like God, knowers of good and evil.

What Eve is Seeking

The next verse describes what Eve was seeing in this tree, or more accurately, in what was to be gained from eating its fruit.

---

7 Gen. 3:4. לֹא־מוֹת תְּמֻתוּן

8 Remembered from a talk that Schachter-Shalomi attended, given in German by Kübler-Ross.

9 Gen. 3:5. כִּי יֹדֵעַ אֱלֹהִים כִּי בְּיוֹם אֲכָלְכֶם מִמֶּנּוּ וְנִפְקְחוּ עֵינֵיכֶם

Genesis 3:6:[10] "And the woman saw that the tree was good for food, and that it was *ta'avah* (desirable/a delight) for the eyes, and the tree was *nechmad* (pleasurable/desirable) *l'haskiyl* (to make one wise/sensible/prudent/insightful)." The fruit is desirable not just as good for food and delightful to the eye but because it will make her wise and insightful.

> Look at the temptation. It is good to the senses; it is desirable to the eyes, it fills affect; and it promises intellect. On all three levels is the temptation. Most of the time a temptation can come in such a gross way that we say "*Ach*, who's tempted by this kind of stuff?" Or, it'll come only on one level. But when the temptation comes you meet your tempter, and the tempter is pulling and pushing energy with you. And the tempter promises, "*Oy*, are you going to get completed through me!" And the tempter says "You've never been understood as you will feel yourself understood and seen by me." And, "Have you ever experienced boundlessness that you will have with me?" Can you imagine a temptation on all four worlds[11] and all four levels, how that is? Here you get three of these levels.
>
> You are a person who doesn't want to look, but there is something to look. You can keep your eyes from looking but the eyes are going to keep on going in this direction all the time. Notice that again: *V'khi ta'avah hu la'eynayim*.[12] It is a lust for the eyes. The eyes keep on going to nothing else but the tree. Everything that is in the garden, but why

---

10 Gen. 3:6. וַתֵּרֶא הָאִשָּׁה כִּי טוֹב הָעֵץ לְמַאֲכָל וְכִי תַאֲוָה־הוּא לָעֵינַיִם וְנֶחְמָד הָעֵץ לְהַשְׂכִּיל

11 **Four worlds.** The first chapter presented Schachter-Shalomi's description of the four worlds of creation, or levels of reality, drawn from the kabbalist tradition.

12 וְכִי תַאֲוָה־הוּא לָעֵינַיִם (Gen. 3:6.)

is that tree attracting the eye all the time? The set-up is amazing.

Schachter-Shalomi draws attention to the Hebrew word whose root is חָמַד, *chamed*. Depending on context, *chamad* can mean to yearn for, desire, take pleasure in, delight in, or lust after.

> *V'nechmad ha'etz l'haskiyl.*[13] Remember the word "thou shalt not covet"? What's the Hebrew for it? *Lo tachmod.*[14] Get that?[15]
>
> *Nechmad.* It is covetous for understanding. Do you get the sense?

Schachter-Shalomi dwells on this idea of being "covetous for understanding," desiring understanding, and he connects it to the very idea of a Wisdom School—to what it is that has drawn him here to teach and learn with the participants and what has drawn them here to this series of retreats. He wants to paint a vivid picture, to make it something that is alive in their present experience, not merely an intellectual claim about an old legend.

> It keeps saying "*Oy*, will you understand. *Oy*, will you know." In some way, a school is covetous for understanding. I invited you to participate with me in this school, because I wanted to have that coveting of another level of understanding that is dawning, that we might do this together. I coveted with you, and I want you to covet with me, to warm it in our hearts, to get that feeling, "*Oy*, yes, yes, yes."

---

13 וְנֶחְמָד הָעֵץ לְהַשְׂכִּיל (Gen. 3:6.)

14 First appears at Ex. 20:17 in the "ten commandments."

15 As a passive (*nifal*) participle נֶחְמָד in Genesis 3.6 it means something like "desirable" (a being-desired thing). As a negative injunction "you will/must/should not desire/yearn for" it takes the form לֹא תַחְמֹד.

It is an attraction, it is a love, but it is not necessarily a love that's in the flesh. It's a love of the intellect. *Amor dei intellectualis*,[16] in a way. *Amor intellectualis*, a love that says, I will so know, that nagging puzzlement will be gone, I will be sure.

Why does an apple say "I am not green like the rest of the tree. I am red. Every bird in the neighborhood, come and eat, so the seed will fall out." It's like an advertisement for it. And so what is built in is that call, "pluck me, eat me."

Humanity Moves On

Schachter-Shalomi continues reading and in the next line[17] he is struck by the picture stirred in him of Eve, having eaten, giving it to her husband who is said to be "with her." One wonders, of course, about this scene. Has her husband been standing there watching silently as the whole drama of Eve's conversation with the snake transpired, along with her own inner assessments and calculations as narrated? Or does she call him up after she has eaten? Does he have any role in this desire for knowledge? Much room is left there for speculation and *midrash*.[18]

---

16 A phrase used by Baruch Spinoza in his masterwork the *Ethics* (*Ethica ordine geometrico demonstrata*), Part V, Propositions XXXIII–XXXVII. This love is the highest aim for humankind and the devotional bond gives access to the mind of God and the natural causal order. Spinoza, 2000.

17 Gen. 3:6. וַתִּקַּח מִפִּרְיוֹ וַתֹּאכַל וַתִּתֵּן גַּם־לְאִישָׁהּ עִמָּהּ וַיֹּאכַל׃ And she took from its fruit and she ate; and she gave also to her husband with her/beside her, and he ate.

18 **Midrash** מִדְרָשׁ. The word *midrash* has as its root the verb *to seek* דָּרַשׁ (here to seek out meaning in the text). *Midrashim* are re-tellings of the Biblical passages with different emphasis, with explanations of potentially obscure elements of the passages, with expansions of the passage with additional material, and with inserted imaginatively constructed stories.

But Schachter-Shalomi is not thinking about her husband, but about the woman: for Schachter-Shalomi, as for the Biblical narrator, she is still the protagonist. She has eaten, she now is in a new world, already knowing at least one dimension of the consequences.

And she doesn't want to be there alone. This knowing good and evil, this being like a god, this being on the journey to full human-ness, is something that needs partners, comrades. Being human needs the family of humanity. At least, this is what Schachter-Shalomi reads into "with her."

> "With her" [עִמָּהּ], that word is needed. "She gave it to her husband with her": intimacy always says "you aren't with me, I'm not with you, we want to be together." Could you imagine, she is now mortal, and she knows. He is not yet mortal, but he doesn't know. She knows, for the rest of her life she will be lonely. She wants him so much to be with her. So the invitation, eat, join me, it's so strong. So powerful at this point.

And he does join her; he eats. Now humanity is moving on to a new paradigm of being human, of living as human beings, with open eyes, with an awareness of dimensions previously invisible to them, engaging actively with the world.

As Schachter-Shalomi reads from Genesis 3:8,[19] he does so in the cantillation trope[20] indicated in the Masoretic text. He chants וַיִּשְׁמְעוּ *Vayishm'u* ("and they heard") with the drawn out and wavering trope assigned to that word.

---

19 Gen. 3.8. וַיִּשְׁמְעוּ אֶת־קוֹל יְהוָֹה אֱלֹהִים מִתְהַלֵּךְ בַּגָּן לְרוּחַ הַיּוֹם וַיִּתְחַבֵּא הָאָדָם וְאִשְׁתּוֹ מִפְּנֵי יְהוָֹה אֱלֹהִים בְּתוֹךְ עֵץ הַגָּן׃

20 The editors of the Masoretic text of the Hebrew Bible included marks understood to indicate patterns of cantillation, or musical trope. These patterns are used when formal recitation of the text is done from the Torah scroll during services.

> *Vayishm'u et qol Adonai Elohim.* "And they would be hearing the voice and the sound of *Yah* God, as that sound is walking through the garden by the wind of the day, and he hid himself," again the reflexive. You can't hide from yourself, and yet you hide yourself.
>
> "And so he hid, the man and his woman, from before God, in the midst of the trees of the garden." Which trees of the garden? The *other* trees of the garden! I'm not hanging out around *that* tree to be caught *flagrante*, red-handed next to the tree. Among the other trees, the okay, the kosher trees, he was hanging out.
>
> "And the voice of *Yah Elokim*[21] comes to the man and says to him, '*Ayekha*?'" Where are you?

Ayekha? "Where are you?" Where are they now, indeed! Although Adam does attempt briefly to separate himself out by blaming Eve,[22] they are, as Schachter-Shalomi imagines Eve wants, in it together. But what exactly this is, this thing that they are in together, must be discovered, by them and gradually by all of us over all our generations. In the breezy part of the day, this question still seems to come to us.

The first humans are now with the consequences of the transgressive act. There is interrogation from God; excuses are made, the snake is cursed, the human creatures are banished from the garden and told of the difficulties they will face in making their own living and in being what we now know as human.

---

21 **Elokim**. Pious substitution for *Elohim* to avoid pronouncing a Godname. This practice and its motivation and implications is discussed in the section The God of Becoming, The God of Change, on page 166 below.

22 Gen. 3:8. וַיֹּאמֶר הָאָדָם הָאִשָּׁה אֲשֶׁר נָתַתָּה עִמָּדִי הִוא נָתְנָה־לִּי מִן־הָעֵץ וָאֹכֵל׃ "The human said, The woman whom you gave to be beside me, she gave me from the tree, and so I ate." [Everett Fox translation]

The Long Process of Divinization

If being human is being like gods, or like God, it is not a one-step process; it is not magic—no more than leaving Egypt freed the Israelites immediately from the effects of slavery. In both cases the way is opened for a slow, sometimes painful, process of transformation from a more limited state to a more evolved, expanded, state.

Schachter-Shalomi steps back a long step to look at this transition in a big picture of evolution.

He invokes Teilhard de Chardin[23] who described the unfolding of spirit in creation as having the phases of first *geogenesis* in which the physical creation arises, then a *biogenesis* in which life arises, then *anthropogenesis* in which humanity arises, then *noögenesis* in which consciousness emerges, then the final phase, divinization or *christogenesis*.[24]

> According to Teilhard de Chardin, we are moving from into the biosphere, into the noösphere, and now comes the divinization of the planet. We are participants in the divinization of the planet. What did the snake promise us? *Vih'yiytem kelohim.*[25] You will be part of the divinization of the planet. Eat from the apple. Go on that journey. The divinization of the planet begins, you participate in it.

Interestingly, what Teilhard de Chardin sees as a final stage in the process, a stage into which we are just now on the cusp of entering, Schachter-Shalomi sees as at least embryonically present in the first chapters of the first book of the Hebrew Bible.

Built into us from the beginning, he says, is the wish to "be like God." And indeed, it is more than Eve's being moved by

---

23 Pierre Teilhard de Chardin (1881–1955). French philosopher and mystic; Jesuit priest; paleontologist and archaeologist.

24 Teilhard de Chardin, *The Phenomenon of Man.*

25 Gen. 3:5. וִהְיִיתֶם֙ כֵּאלֹהִ֔ים "You will be like gods/like God."

the persuasion of the snake who promises that result (*yih'yiytem kelohim*). Earlier in the creation story we are told about being created in the image of God: *Vayivra elohim et ha'adam b'tzalmo; b'tzelem elohim bara oto*.[26] We feel the call of something present in the very template of our being, and the process of divinization of self and planet proceeds—slowly, perhaps, but by necessity.

Being Human: Challenges and Blessing

The narrative of the Genesis account goes on to specify some of the consequences of our new life as humans (Genesis 3:16–19). Previously the proto-humans enjoyed[27] what was apparently an "edenic" paradise of being effortlessly provided for. Now humans will have to till the land to grow food; children will be brought forth through painful labor of birthing; and there will be new complexity in human relationships—there will be both desire and power struggles between husband and wife.[28]

But these new challenges are not just catalysts for growth; they are sources of deep pleasure. Schachter-Shalomi continues with a line of rhetorical questioning that further undermines the common gloomy and punitive-minded interpretation of this transition as a calamitous disaster, resulting in curses under which we must still suffer many thousands of generations later.

---

26 Gen. 1:27. וַיִּבְרָ֨א אֱלֹהִ֤ים | אֶת־הָֽאָדָם֙ בְּצַלְמ֔וֹ בְּצֶ֥לֶם אֱלֹהִ֖ים בָּרָ֣א אֹת֑וֹ "And God created the earthling in his image; in the image of God he created him."

27 One might, of course, note that we don't hear explicitly that they were enjoying it, and with nothing to compare it to, it was perhaps merely taken for granted. Or perhaps there was a dissatisfaction lurking beneath the surface, at least in Eve: we see, in what she recognizes as attractive, that she may be longing for a more substantive moral, intellectual, and aesthetic experience.

28 God tells Eve in Gen. 3:16: וְאֶל־אִישֵׁךְ֙ תְּשׁ֣וּקָתֵ֔ךְ וְה֖וּא יִמְשָׁל־בָּֽךְ׃ "Your desire/longing/lust will be to your husband and he will rule over you."

> Which person who has had a garden and weeded the
> garden and saw tomatoes grow on the vine and harvested
> them still feels that they are dealing with a curse? Which
> mother who has had conscious childbirth feels that she
> is dealing with a curse? Which person who has loved an
> animal and communicated with the animal feels that they
> are dealing with a curse? Which person who has walked on
> this planet and loved what this planet has produced feels
> that we are working under the curse? There is no more
> curse. The curse was the shadow under which we lived that
> original blessing.[29]

Indeed, the text itself does not call these things curses. The snake is said to be cursed (*arur*)[30] but God simply describes to Eve and to Adam the pains and difficulties they will face now as humans. It is only later commentators who, perhaps wishing to strike into hearers a fear of disobedience of God, term these things curses. God does identify these pains and difficulties as consequences of their choices, as in Genesis 3:17. But he never says that they are curses, or that these are punishments.

Stealth Feminism

The way Schachter-Shalomi treats this lesson about human evolution allows us to return for a moment to something referred to in the previous chapter: what I called Schachter-Shalomi's implicit feminism.

Here Eve is permitted to stand in for the evolution of humanity without any attempt either to undermine her agency, or to find feminine weakness or treachery in her acts, or at the other extreme to celebrate her as a feminist heroine. We would not think twice

---

29 Schachter-Shalomi probably refers here to the theology of **Matthew Fox** and his book entitled ***Original Blessing***. Fox (1940–), formerly a priest of the Dominican Order and proponent of movement called Creation Spirituality, argued against the concept of original sin.

30 Gen. 3:14. אָרוּר

about a male character representing human challenge and progress, the hero who blazes the way for all of us. Schachter-Shalomi sees a female character doing just that and, remarkably, seems to show no discomfort, no consciousness of unseemliness or scandal, nor conversely any self-conscious wish to trumpet it as unusual.

Conclusion

This moment of the choice to enter into full humanity with the consequent price (or liberation) of leaving the garden is, of course, momentous. But this account is, after all, a parable, a thought experiment. Furthermore, even if it were literally or historically a moment in human development, it would still be only one first step in the long process of spiritual evolution that has led through the many millennia of human, and Jewish, development to this present moment.

And within this present moment itself, further stages yet to unfold can be glimpsed, a whiff of their aroma caught, their possibilities speculated upon. There will be more that emerges over the continuing sessions of this Primal Myths series.

From the second weekend,
"Genesis"

4
Introduction to the Genesis Retreat

Territoriality, Sibling Rivalry, Family Systems

The second retreat of the series takes up the rest of the book of Genesis as an opportunity to look closely at how we can get along with the other people with whom we share the planet. Indeed, Schachter-Shalomi sees this as one dimension of the intention of these narratives as spiritual teaching stories.

Of course, when first told and written down, and as they might have been interpreted in earlier ages, they would primarily be seen as opportunities to think about how to get along within families and within the Israelite tribe or tribes. But, Schachter-Shalomi would say, the vision we have in the present time of a planetary or global family necessitates expanding the understanding of the lesson of the scripture to include sharing the planet with all people—or at least to accept the survival necessity of doing so.

There are two elements in connection with this theme that Schachter-Shalomi draws out of the material of this retreat for contemplation and engagement.

Survival and Social Harmony

The first element is the social, ethical, practical—one might even say survival—lesson. This would be how to work things out with another person (in the parables, often a sibling) who is, perhaps, very different in personality, character, and destiny, and who, furthermore, is in competition with oneself for limited resources. These limited resources, as represented in these Bible stories, may be turf, pasture-lands, a birthright, a father's blessing, or a husband's seed. These come out with stories of Abraham and

Lot, Sarah and Hagar, Jacob and Esau, Rachel and Leah, and Josef and his brothers, among others.

Theological implications do enter in here as well, from time to time. I'll mention two examples of theological implications to which Schachter-Shalomi will give attention as he extracts teachings from the Genesis stories.

God gives Cain a teaching about the danger of giving way to the violence (in his feelings and thus potentially acted out) arising from his disappointment and jealousy over what appears to be a favoritism of Abel. "YHVH said to Cain, "Why are you angry, and why has your face fallen?[1] … And if you do not do well, sin is crouching at the door. It has a lust for you, but you must rule over it."[2] This is a much more general teaching about self command than its immediate application to sibling friction. It might be understood to reach even to relationship to God, since it is called a sin (or at least a חטא, a missing of the mark, usually translated as sin in English). The implication would be that when we let that lusting desire for revenge or violence rule over us, that is an offense against God.

We see Jacob, before meeting Esau after twenty years, going through a process[3] which is represented as having a divine or soul dimension. This is his night of wrestling with the strange being only called an *iysh*.[4] Jacob is even described by the *iysh* with whom he has been struggling as a person who has wrestled with God (or perhaps it is divine dimensions of his own soul) and his new name

---

1 Gen. 4:6. וַיֹּאמֶר יְהֹוָה אֶל־קָיִן לָמָּה חָרָה לָךְ וְלָמָּה נָפְלוּ פָנֶיךָ׃

2 Gen. 4:7. הֲלוֹא אִם־תֵּיטִיב שְׂאֵת וְאִם לֹא תֵיטִיב לַפֶּתַח חַטָּאת רֹבֵץ וְאֵלֶיךָ תְּשׁוּקָתוֹ וְאַתָּה תִּמְשָׁל־בּוֹ׃

3 Gen. 32:25–33.

4 אִישׁ In the Hebrew Bible, this word is variously used for a man, a husband, or an unspecified individual person or being ("somebody"). As a messenger from God, it may be a human messenger or some sort of divine being, not always distinguished clearly from God himself. Context usually indicates the usage and consequently the translation, but this is not one of those times.

Israel is a permanent reminder of that. According to the *iysh*, the name means one who exerted himself/persevered/struggled with God.[5] So his struggle within himself may be preparing himself to face Esau, but it is not just about his relationship with Esau but (in some way) about making himself equal to a relationship with divine being or God.

Diversity and Unity

The second element that Schachter-Shalomi draws out in connection with this theme is that of the very large question, which may even at times present itself as a paradox, between diversity and unity. God is *one*, according to the monotheistic perspective, but this God, YHVH, seems to love diversity. This issue has deeply theological implications as well as consequences for whether and how people, including siblings, might get along with one another.

How does one honor and even nurture diversity, but still form a cohesive community? How does one see the astonishing multiplicity of creation and still understand that it is the creation of a single God? How does one know when to lean toward diversity and when to strive more for unity? On what principles might God choose actions that promote one over the other in a particular situation?

Assignment in Preparation for Genesis Weekend

At the end of the first weekend, in preparation for this second weekend, Schachter-Shalomi asked the participants to think about issues of territoriality, sibling rivalry, and family systems, and to read through Genesis with those questions in mind. In particular, he asked participants to start wondering how things might have been different in the Genesis family stories. He further asked participants to consider what their own experience suggested to them.

---

5 Gen. 32:29. וַיֹּאמֶר לֹא יַעֲקֹב יֵאָמֵר עוֹד שִׁמְךָ כִּי אִם־יִשְׂרָאֵל כִּי־שָׂרִיתָ עִם־אֱלֹהִים וְעִם־אֲנָשִׁים וַתּוּכָל׃

He recommended reading Konrad Lorenz, *On Aggression* and Robert Ardrey, *The Territorial Imperative*, along with things that deal with sibling rivalry and family systems. He also invited them to do some self-observation with these questions.

Schachter-Shalomi in the overview at end of the Creation weekend:

> The rest of the book of Genesis deals—from Cain and Abel to Josef and the brothers—with sibling rivalry and family matters. It deals with turf. Territoriality. The reptilian brain and how it makes sure that its territory is protected. The program that sits very deeply in our guts. So that at times when our values of how we wish to share and be nice and good with everybody run into conflict with a very deep seated and reinforced programming that is in us to protect territory and turf.
>
> So we will be dealing with the rest of the book of Genesis and the territoriality in ourselves, and how this affects peoples in the world and in family structures and so on. So you can see it is yoking the intention of what we study in Bible together with where we are looking at the real issues and problems that happen in the world.

Schachter-Shalomi gave some specific suggestions for this time through the participants' reading of Genesis. He invites a "beginner's mind"[6] freshness to the process. The significance of that exercise here is to unlock teachings encoded into the scriptures by God as guidance for each generation.

This fresh reading requires temporarily setting aside received interpretations because those older interpretations (however much wisdom and inspiration were brought to them, and however right

---

6   Schachter-Shalomi is referring to a book by Zen Buddhist teacher Shunryu Suzuki, *Zen Mind, Beginner's Mind*, which begins with the epigraph "In the beginner's mind there are many possibilities, but in the expert's there are few." The text advocates keeping just this freshness and openness to what the Zen practice has to teach.

they may have been for their time) may now constitute a sclerosis of the living Torah, limiting its message of wisdom for our own time and making of it only a holy artifact, an object of veneration but not a living present guide.

> And, the book of Genesis. How to read this time? Edmund Wilson from The New Yorker, when he got to be sixty years old, decided he's going to read the Bible again. And he managed to keep out from his reading everything he ever heard before. And said, "I'm going to read it like for the first time. Beginner's Mind Zen Mind. Let me read this book without any traditional glasses. So I'm going to encounter how Esau is and how Jacob is and how the book itself, without any commentary, tells the story."
>
> And following, then, the brother-brother thing, the sister-sister thing, until the end of Genesis, Josef and the brothers. How they dealt with Judah, how they dealt with Benjamin, how they dealt with each other, how they dealt with Dinah their sister, and check out those family systems that are there. How one dealt with Laban, and Jacob. And as you read this material, really pay attention to the territorial things that are happening there.
>
> Ask yourself the question, at each crisis moment, how could this have gone differently? Here is Esau, for instance... Or here is Cain talking to Abel. Could that have had a different ending? And when we see the possibility for different endings, for these relational crises, options are created for us in our lives to deal differently with territorial issues. So the Bible will be a very good background in which different kinds of scenarios can be checked out. How else could it have happened? How could Josef and the brothers have dealt with it differently? These are the things that I would suggest.

Eve Ilsen: And of course there is the other side of the metaphor. Which is, what does it mean when the whole thing is taking place inside one person?

Schachter-Shalomi's collaborator, Eve Ilsen, is here introducing the inner dimension of the teaching in these stories.
Schachter-Shalomi will develop the implications of dealing with
these conflicting qualities within oneself when he takes on the
Jacob and Esau story.

5
Family Relations

Through the parables of family relations, Genesis can be understood as offering guidance for human relations in a more general and broader application.

1. THE MARRIAGE RELATIONSHIP

Schachter-Shalomi begins the Genesis weekend with consideration of the relationship of husband and wife. Perhaps he chose to begin this way because the Biblical story itself begins this way, with Adam and Eve; perhaps it is that Schachter-Shalomi sees male and female as paradigmatic of sorts of people that have differences (consider the term "the battle of the sexes") and yet must be able to work together in harmony.[1] This is the retreat in which he is concerned with family systems and what it takes to make different sorts of people, with different characters and needs and even destinies, to find ways of getting along.

Schachter-Shalomi slips in some of the teachings about the marriage relationship indirectly using numerology, a traditional means of making pedagogical points. By looking at words of the Biblical text as made up of letters each of which is, in Hebrew, also a number, and adding and comparing and otherwise playing with the numbers, commentators have traditionally made connections and contrasts that they used as grounds for the interpretations or teachings they wanted to give. It offers much leeway but has a scientific and at the same time pious air (pious because it is based on the understanding that every letter was consciously chosen by God).

---

1 Anyone familiar with Schachter-Shalomi will know that one thing this choice is *not* is promotion of a hetero-normative ideology of human mate relationships.

However fanciful it might seem to those unfamiliar with this method, it is a way of drawing attention to certain things and one whose real force is in our recognition of the truth in the conclusions. It is another form of parable.

As he recounted the beginning of earthly married life for Adam and Eve, Schachter-Shalomi made certain points about the creation of male and female by means of a commentary on those Hebrew words, and then on the words man and woman. He is showing that not only are both elements important and necessary, but that in the harmonious balancing of male and female, husband and wife, something divine is present that doesn't come into being when either is standing on its own.

The sum of the numerical value of the letters of the Hebrew word for "male" is 227. The sum of the numerical values of the letters for the Hebrew words for "and female" is 163. Together they make 390. The sum of the numerical values of the letters for the Hebrew word for "heaven" is 390. From this he draws the suggestion that male and female together (presumably in harmony) make heaven, that is, some divine reality is created. He later connects this "heaven" to love-making and to child-making.

> When you take the word for male and the word for female, *zachar u'neqevah*,[2] when you put them together in their numerical value, you get the word שָׁמַיִם *shamayim*, heaven. Heaven is made of *zachar u'neqevah*, of that blend that comes.

Another treatment[3] works with the letters without bringing in numerology. Schachter-Shalomi wants to suggest that to create a harmonious bonding each one has to be connected to a divine

---

2 זָכָר וּנְקֵבָה, as in the phrase "male and female he created them" in Gen. 1:27.

3 Schachter-Shalomi had offered this teaching on *iysh*, *ishah*, and *esh* in a digression in the first weekend; for the sake of coherent organization of my present project I include it here.

quality, represented by the letters *yud* and *heh*, both strongly (and traditionally) associated with names of God, particularly the names יָהּ Yah and יְהוָֹה YHVH. As Schachter-Shalomi will describe, without those letters yud and heh to incorporate divinity (or to include divine participation in their embodiment of their gender), all that would be left of the words for man and woman would be the word for fire. They would tend to burn each other, to to consume each other.[4]

> The word for man is אִישׁ *iysh*, in Hebrew, aleph yud shin. The word for a woman is אִשָּׁה *ishah*, aleph shin heh. The word for fire is אֵשׁ *esh*. The male has a yud, the female has a heh. Yud and heh are the letters of the names of God, like יָהּ *Yah*, as in *hallelu Yah*, "give praise to Yah."
>
> So *iysh* has the letter yud, *ishah* has the letter heh, so in a way these are the two crowns that God gives that when God's presence is there between these two people, then it's Yah. When that presence disappears, all that's left is *esh*, and one fire tries to consume the other fire. And it's not so good anymore.

A similar theme again using numerology is introduced in the present weekend in material discussing the preparation that was necessary for Abram and Sarai to be ready to have the promised child. Here he is suggesting that a certain cooperation existing between the two (in this case with Sarai sharing a richness she had in her name) so that both could have a letter that in its writing stretched open a space that had not been there in their original names, allowed space for them to bring a child into their life.

Schachter-Shalomi is entering tenderly, and with some depth of feeling, into the sacredness of creating a child. Every child, one feels, listening to his account, should have this sort of conscious space made for it.

---

4 Something like this can be found in Rashi's commentary to *Babylonian Talmud*, Sotah 17a.

> Well, here is Avram. There is no room between him and
> Sarai to have a baby. He's being told you must circumcise;[5]
> he is told he must change his name.[6]

The numerological transformation goes this way. The *yud* of
שָׂרַי Sarai, numerical value ten, is divided by her into two *heh*'s,
each numerical value five, and one goes into her name for שָׂרָה
Sarah. The other she gives into Avram's name to make Avraham
(אַבְרָם becomes אַבְרָהָם). Their collective numerological value
remains the same.[7]

> The numerical value of the combination Avram and Sarai
> is not changed although the names get changed. Sarai takes
> five from her name. From Sarai she becomes Sarah. And
> gives that five, ה, to Avram.
>
> The masculine is now also consciously absorbing,
> getting to know the feminine inside, through the ה he gets
> from Sarai. That is what gives space for a child to come in
> between. Look at the י, it's tiny. The ה makes space. The ה
> of Avraham and the ה of Sarah now makes space for a child.
> Every relationship that has been so close, when it has to
> make room for the fruit of that relationship, space has to be
> made. The chemistry changes.

This teaching has, in a way, more to do with the relationship of parents and children than conjugal connection, but the
way he describes the cooperation of the two in making it happen evokes a beautiful sense of the shared project. Note that, in

---

5   Gen. 17:11.

6   Gen. 17:15.

7   One midrash about the division of the yud into two hehs appears in
     Midrash Rabbah Bereshiyt, XLVII.1, commentary on Genesis 17:15
     (Volume 1, p. 399). Unless there is another source, Sarai taking the
     initiative, and the purpose being to make space for a child, and that
     Avram should absorb some of the feminine in order to prepare for
     parenthood, are features of Schachter-Shalomi's midrash.

Schachter-Shalomi's story, it is not God who is performing the transformation. No, this is between husband and wife, and once again it is the woman who is taking the initiative to make a transformational act. "Sarai takes five from her name...."[8]

Along with his charming story of the meaning of the name change, playing with the letters and their numbers, Schachter-Shalomi mentions the circumcision commandment of Abraham also given here as a further suggestion of what is necessary to prepare them to be the parents of a child.

> And the preparation for that! how deep the preparation for that has to go. Circumcision is one way in which we talk about that. People speak of circumcising the heart in this way too. There is something rough and big that has to be taken off and something more sensitive and soft and more vulnerable has to be made available.
>
> It's a way of saying, by bleeding from that place the man experiences something that the woman experiences.

2. SIBLING RIVALRY

Back to Troubled Reality

Of course, this is an idealized picture of what marriage and child-making could or should be with both making space in themselves, with the man consciously absorbing something from the woman, and so on.

---

8   The previous teaching suggests that Sarai's numerological bounty is coming in the form of the divine letter yud. In sharing half of this yud with Avram, it is she (if we combine these teaching parables) who is divinizing Avram as well as herself. Here, of course, Schachter-Shalomi is moving in a different direction: Sarai is converting her divine *yud* bounty into a *heh* bounty of space and sharing that with Avram so that they both can make space for a child.

At this moment, and for his present pedagogical purpose, Schachter-Shalomi is not taking into account the ominous divine alerting to the gender power struggles implied by "your desire will be to your husband and he will rule over you,"[9] or all the troubles that children will bring to parents and to one another before we reach the end of our saga.

Now, with the Genesis story barely begun, we must move from the idealized marriage metaphor to the reality of life among siblings.

> "So she continued to give birth to his brother, to Hevel. And Hevel would become a shepherd and Qayin was the one that worked the soil."[10]

The troubles between Cain and Abel abruptly enter the Biblical narrative.

Domestication of Animals and Plants, Ownership, Territory, and Sacrifice

We are poised to move into consideration of the very prominent stories of sibling rivalry with which the book of Genesis is replete. This is another aspect of family relations and introduces the complexities of territoriality.

In Schachter-Shalomi's tracing of family relations, he first takes a step back and looks to the development of agriculture and animal husbandry as having a connection with territoriality and the sibling rivalry that causes friction between the brothers. There is more than external territory at issue, of course, but Schachter-Shalomi unfolds the complexity this way.

> What they didn't tell us, as the story develops, is that that wasn't the first way people made a living. That there

---

9 Gen. 3:16.

10 Gen. 4:2. Qayin and Hevel are the Hebrew names of Cain and Abel.

was hunting before, and gathering before, isn't part of the story. The story of patriarchy begins with the domestication of flora, plants, and fauna, animals.

This idea was introduced in the previous weekend. There Schachter-Shalomi was seeing in the development of animal husbandry and agriculture the origin of patriarchy, a model in which most of the Biblical stories are set. These forms of production lead to a particular crude and external, but powerful, form of territoriality: the ownership of offspring.

Who was Cain? Cain was agriculture. His brother is animal husbandry. The situation is such that the domestication of both flora and fauna has happened as Bible begins. Prior to the domestication of flora and fauna, the Bible doesn't speak.

We are now aware of the foundations of civilization that came to us during the matriarchal period of matrilineal descent. What does it mean? No mother ever called her child a bastard. To a mother, every child is birth, every child is under the heart. How can you say this child is a bastard? It is only after saying that it was a different sire. When this bitch was in heat, instead of coming to the right sire, another one mounted her first and that is a mixed, this is a bastard child, okay?

This is the way someone who is a breeder would deal with things. And if the breeder happens to be a patriarch, he says "If it doesn't come from me, it's a bastard." It's somebody who snuck in who shouldn't be there. And at earlier time, that's not the way it's being seen. "You got some fruit, you kill the hare, you brought me a deer, I'll be with you. You're a good provider man." So bastardy as we look at this today is a patriarchal thing coming from animal husbandry.

We don't know any more what it was like, we don't have Biblical warrant for what was it like prior to agriculture and animal husbandry. We need to find these in the stories of Diana, Artemis, and so on, and where there are other stories that deal with hunt. We will meet Nimrod later on, also in relation to hunt, and we will meet Esau, in relation to hunt, but other than that we don't have anything but animal husbandry and agriculture.

In the second weekend, Schachter-Shalomi plays the invention of agriculture and animal husbandry out in another direction, that of the conflict that arises between the two forms of domestication.

The commentary following the passage describing Abel and Cain's choices of work starts moving in this new direction. But as Schachter-Shalomi first introduces it, he begins to get carried into delight over the discoveries and their benefits to humankind.

Who is the guy that realizes that the last time I dropped some seed in this place and look what sprouted here? Let me next time do this intentionally, put seed in and let it grow over here so I don't have to go all over the place to look for the rice. I will make it grow in this paddy so I have it close by. So this business of the domestication of things means that I don't have to wait for the pot luck.

Instead of killing that wild goat that I hunted, I keep this wild goat and I breed it here. I put it in the corral and I domesticate that, and before long I don't have to go hunting. I can just go to the corral and take out that sheep from the flock and I don't have to go hunting anymore.

In other words, food supply has been assured. This is my soil, these are my animals. Animals are called in Hebrew *miqneh*,[11] all the things that are my acquisitions. Remember in that amazing movie, Meetings with Remarkable Men, do you remember how they created this thing where goats were carrying things? So when they needed their meat, their meat was walking along with them. When they needed their

---

11 מִקְנֶה n.m. cattle, from root קָנָה vb. get, acquire [BDB p. 888].

milk, their milk was walking along with them. Their food supply is portable, forage place is all that's needed. That's in animal husbandry.

In the midst of his thinking about what is rich and delightful in the human discovery and evolution of agriculture and animal husbandry, Schachter-Shalomi lets in an adumbration of trouble to come.

> But then there's the guy who's planting his plants and all of a sudden the goats come and eat there. The farmer hates the shepherd and says "I need to build fences." Who is the one who breaks down the fences? The one who drives the cattle. So you have enmity already.
>
> But what I want you to notice is who is rooted in the ground. Who said, "Finally! I know how I'm going to get my food next time. I will plant it again, I will grow it again, I'm at home here in this neighborhood. This is my soil."
>
> So it would be that Qayin was the *oved ha adamah*,[12] he worked the earth, and paid attention to planting and sowing. It was no longer serendipity that got someone to find a fruit here and a fruit there and grain here and grain there, but it was the decision that if I plant it here it will grow here, that there is a reciprocity.

And Schachter-Shalomi is drawn back into awe as he shares the human discoveries and learning. Reciprocity! Cause and effect! Heaven-making!

> Remember how they discovered it was their heaven-making that got them a child. If there is a cause to that effect, *ahn-hanh*! So seed brings forth fruit. That recognition that seed and fruit go together is something that starts saying some things to people. So if you plan ahead and if you plant the seed in a particular place, then you will gather it in.

---

12 Servant/worker of the earth. Gen. 4:2. וְקַיִן הָיָה עֹבֵד אֲדָמָה׃

That's how you deal with the season. At the beginning of the spring you will do your planting and in the fall you will do your harvesting, and if you did that right what will happen is that you can manage to live through the winter.

What an invention that was! Finally, we are no longer at the mercy of the elements, having only what we find and what we hunt. Rather than having to make sure that I will find an animal that I might eat of, I corral them, I take them out to pasture, I get those little coyote wolves and tame them too. Before long they help me being shepherds. And so there is a whole way of life being established that this one who is a shepherd establishes.

Schachter-Shalomi brings in yet another thread of this tapestry by touching on the origin of sacrifice.

Ahh. Somehow there's a gnawing feeling in there. Did I perhaps in the domestication of things upset the balance that was there before? Yes, it works well for me but it isn't what it used to be before. I have taken a lot of responsibility here. Is that okay with God? I know what I will do. I will offer a sacrifice. I will build an altar. There I will light a fire. There I will offer something to God. And there, that smoke, that burning, that volatilization of that which I worked for is going to go up and God will smell it, and it will go into his nostrils, and he will be nice to me. He won't be angry that I messed around with his world by domesticating it. He gets his cut, I do what I need to do. Let me offer a sacrifice.

Cain and Abel in Conflict

We now are ready to launch into a careful dissection of the Bible's first exploration of sibling rivalry.

And here as Qayin offers the sacrifice, Hevel too sees, "what a great idea" and brings a sheep. But mark the difference. It is not just any sheep that he took. He went around, he looked, is this a *gezunte*[13] sheep, a fat sheep, and he picks one, as it is said right here, *mib'khorot tzono u'mechelvehen,*[14] "and he takes from the firstborn ones."

Firstborn, watch that. What's so good about firstborn? Ah, he opens the womb. Remember, cause and effect, planting, harvesting, the one that is the first harvest. *Oy!* that first apple that ripens in the season. Before that, almonds! Oh, watch them! They're the ones that blossom early and ripen early. And so you see, the first fruit, the first ones, the *b'khor*, the firstborn, that's something special.

"You know what, God, I so had my eye on this sheep, I figured if I'm going to have a celebration, I'm gonna sit down and eat from that sheep, but you know what, I'm gonna give it to you."

Vayisha' Yah el Hevel v'el minchato.[15] And God turned, he moved, he got excited. It became very clear whose sacrifice was desired and accepted.

"I invented sacrifice! I did it first! Why was mine not accepted in the same way?" The ache! Qayin feels that his sacrifice was not so loved. "I had it so good with my parents before you had to come! Now you got the attention that I first got." And so along with that, something like a worm eating in the heart of Qayin.

---

13 **Gezunt** געזונט. Yiddish: forceful, sturdy, healthy, fat.

14 Gen. 4:4. מִבְּכֹרוֹת צֹאנוֹ וּמֵחֶלְבֵהֶן

15 Gen. 4.4. וַיִּשַׁע יְהֹוָה אֶל־הֶבֶל וְאֶל־מִנְחָתוֹ Literally, God gazed attentively (with favor) at Hevel and at his gift/offering.

Vayichar.[16] It burned in him, it ate in him. It felt like—
The basic semitic word for excrement is חר.[17] It felt shitty.
To have that experience inside of him, what eats in him, his
value, he feels nothing but crap in this situation. His face
falls. His *face* falls. "I could walk into this scene before,
I could look everyone in the face, I could have my face
there, and now, something has happened. I come to where
the people are and they know 'Hah, this is the guy whose
sacrifice God turned away from.' *Oowi*, what this does to
my face. I haven't got my face anymore."

God calls to Qayin and says to Qayin, "What's eating
you? Why did your face fall? If you will do good you could
raise the whole thing up. If you want, change the context
of what's going on. Learn something from it. Give it a
lift. Things get better if you give it a lift. *Im teytiv s'et.*[18]
And if not, there at the gate crouches sin, longing for you,
attracting you, pulling at you. And you, you can *timshal*
תִּמְשָׁל over it.[19] *Timshal*.

The significance of this moment and this teaching seems so
important to Schachter-Shalomi that he spends some time digress-
ing on how far one might do well to go to plumb the depths of its

---

16 Gen. 4.5. וַיִּחַר לְקַיִן מְאֹד וַיִּפְּלוּ פָּנָיו And Qayin was exceedingly
kindled/burning/angry and his face fell.

17 חרא or חרי in later Biblical Hebrew and in cognate languages
means dung [BDB p. 351]. Schachter-Shalomi is bringing out the
fact that the root used here in Gen. 4:5 is חרר for burn or get hot or
be scorched [BDB p. 359]. While not, apparently, etymologically
connected, or intended as a pun by the Biblical author, it
nevertheless strikes a resonance in this situation. Such a
reverberation may have been intentional; at least Schachter-Shalomi
notes the presence of simultaneous descriptive truths.

18 אִם־תֵּיטִיב שְׂאֵת. "If you do well, [there will be] upliftment."

19 Gen. 4.7. וְאִם לֹא תֵיטִיב לַפֶּתַח חַטָּאת רֹבֵץ וְאֵלֶיךָ תְּשׁוּקָתוֹ וְאַתָּה
תִּמְשָׁל־בּוֹ. And if you do not do well, sin is lying at the doorway;
and its lust/longing is for you, and/but you must rule over it.

wisdom. This passage can teach what one can learn about oneself, and about the turning away of sin that is, as it were, crouching at the door and lusting after one (an amazing image, and one that can be felt viscerally). It can teach about the avoidance of the consequences of not so turning away: the scape-goating of another, the social violence and disharmony, and the separation from God.

Schachter-Shalomi at this point reads a long selection from Steinbeck's *East of Eden* in which two characters discuss this passage and investigation into its meaning—an investigation that stretches out involving others to join in puzzling out its meaning: Chinese sages who were practiced in Confucian study took it on, learning Hebrew to help them delve more deeply. And then Schachter-Shalomi makes another aside about Benjamin Lee Whorf at Yale who, Schachter-Shalomi says, studied Hebrew and became a linguist having "started out wanting to understand this book and this story that we're talking about."

Then Schachter-Shalomi's tone changes from one of delight in the recognition that others have thought deeply about the richness of this story, and he sighs a bit and drops into a tone of sadness and regret as he resumes the narrative.

> There was this day. They were out in the field. An argument starts.
>
> The midrash puts it this way.[20] It all started when one of Abel's sheep wandered into the garden that Cain was tending and began to eat some of the plants. Cain tells him "Get off with the sheep." Tells him to get off his land. Abel says, "Then take off the garments that you're wearing made from the wool of my sheep and from the leather of the sheep." The fight gets bigger and bigger.
>
> All the old stash that they had never worked out came up. A stone was handy. It was in his hand. He didn't know

---

20 *Genesis Rabbah* 22:7 describes the quarrel and 22:8 killing with a stone. The first part about Abel's goats helping themselves to Cain's vegetables may be Schachter-Shalomi's contribution to midrash.

how much strength and power he had. He hit him. Abel died. And he didn't even know that there was such a thing that you could kill people. In that way.

And now, there comes a voice, back again, saying to him, "Where is your brother Abel?" And he says "I don't know." And here comes this phrase: "Hanhh? *Shomer achi anokhi?*"[21] Am I my brother's keeper? Am I the one who has to watch over him? And God says to him, "What is it that you have done? The voice of the blood of your brother calls out to me from the soil."[22]

How the Consequences Unfold

The reading of the last statement by God about the voice of the blood calling from the soil brings up many interwoven thoughts and themes for Schachter-Shalomi. These threads work through all his teachings (and all the sessions of this series of Primal Myths retreats) in a complex weaving impossible to fully extract and bundle by subject. One cannot take a rich tapestry and try to pull all the threads of a certain color and collect them into a skein with others of their kind and expect to be able to offer a coherent or useful picture. Each thread is too connected to its scene in the whole to conveniently be extracted. However, what I can do is in these cases is to note some of these as they go by, and identify the significance to Schachter-Shalomi; some connections and coherence will have to emerge gradually.

Schachter-Shalomi is struck by the crying out of the earth as Abel's blood sinks into it—the blood of the first created human to die, murdered by violence.

---

21 Gen. 4:9. הֲשֹׁמֵר אָחִי אָנֹכִי Am I my brother's guardian/watcher/keeper?

22 Gen. 4:10. קוֹל דְּמֵי אָחִיךָ צֹעֲקִים אֵלַי מִן־הָאֲדָמָה The voice of the blood of your brother cries/cries out/calls/clamors to me from the earth.

This act leads to Cain no longer having a productive connection to the earth. He, the inventor of agriculture, the one with the special connection with the earth and with growing things, is cut off from that relationship. The earth rejects him, will not yield for him. His violence in spilling the blood of his brother into the earth, his violation of harmony with creation, has destroyed that precious connection.

Similarly, in Schachter-Shalomi's view, we present-day humans, in our own violence against the earth and our own disharmony with creation, are destroying our own connection with the earth and its ability to yield its nurturing produce for us. We pollute the earth, the soil, the water, the seas, the air. We are in danger of being exiled from it—are already causing ourselves to be separated from its former richness and productiveness.

And we turn to technology, as Cain did, to make up for that. Indeed, technology has helped us accelerate the exploitation and pollution of our natural resources. These themes of violence, disharmony, selfish short-sightedness, which lead to being cut off from the earth, to being exiled, to dependence on technology, all show up in this story of Cain.

But it is not a simple morality tale. There are many aspects of this process that are part of our necessary evolution, of the divine plan for us, just as the disobedience in Eden, and the expulsion from the garden, were necessary for our evolution and part of the divine plan—or so Schachter-Shalomi argues.

As we will see in the ensuing discussion, there are things about technology that are thrilling and valuable. Invention. Crafts. Cities. The whole unfolding of civilization.

In Cain's exile we must also feel a foreshadowing of the diaspora of the Jews, their exile from the homeland of Israel promised to Abraham and his descendents. Even here, in Cain's exile, there is benefit. Through Cain's exile God is creating proliferation and diversity. As Schachter-Shalomi reads this narrative, that must take place before any attempt at unification.

Furthermore, being exiled, being driven out as a pariah, means that Cain is thrown on his own resources. He can't follow in the old way he knows. He must develop his own inner resources. He must grow, diversify, be creative.

And ultimately, too, he must learn to rely on others, to band together with others to do things that could not be done by one person. That teamwork is part of the process of human evolution, a lesson we have to learn, a skill we must develop. These experiences and these skills develop what Schachter-Shalomi will be calling the "amity response," something that will save us when the "territorial response" is not working.

Was there a benefit to Cain killing Abel? Some, albeit mixed, good came in the process set into motion by that act. (If one is to believe that God is sovereign, one must say that it is God's process.) But God doing good with the results is not the same as approving the act. As Josef says to his brothers later,[23] "You intended me harm, but God made good out of it." He doesn't let them off the hook for having tried to kill him—they are still answerable for that, and will be judged by God. But for Josef, knowing that God used the sequence of events that followed to save Jacob's whole family and many others from starvation in the famine allows him to let go of personal resentment.

Cain is answerable for his act, answerable for having, despite God's warning, yielded to the lust of that sin that was crouching at the door. But there is much value in this narrative for us. We can learn from it. Schachter-Shalomi's point is that we can study the dynamics of what happens between the brothers and the dynamics of Cain's psycho-spiritual process. If we don't learn how to manage these processes in ourselves, someone may die, someone may be exiled. (And in the larger picture today, where similar things go on between whole peoples, many may die and many may be exiled. As indeed we see happening, repeatedly.)

---

23 Gen. 50:19–20. "And Josef said to them, 'Do not be afraid, for am I in the place of God? You planned/designed/conceived evil against me. God planned/designed/conceived it for good in order to make many people be kept alive as (they are) this day.'"

Exile

Schachter-Shalomi begins with Cain's alienation from the earth and his condemnation to (or assignment to) restlessness.

> "What is it you have done? The sound of the blood of your brother calls out to me from the earth.[24] And now: Cursed be you from the earth. … For when you will work the ground it will not give her strength to you, but *na'vanad tihyeh va'aretz*."[25] *Na*, moving, *nad*, restless, "moving about restlessly will you be in the land." In other words, whenever you will try to get territory for yourself, the territory will not be yours. It won't hold you.
>
> Can you imagine the fantastic frustration of [what we have] here. The person who has invented, in this story, agriculture, who has domesticated seed and growth there, the curse is that it will no longer work for you. The dust bowl. Whatever you will touch, you won't get any more strength coming back from the earth to you. You will have to be *na vanad*. There is no territory that will hold you, that you be able to call your own.

"Where Can I Go?"
Not Just Cain's Pain but a Human Pain

Schachter-Shalomi now connects this with experience of people (like himself) who were driven from their homes by Nazi persecution.[26] Many faced the sense that there was no land that could be theirs, that they would be *"na vanad"* in the world.

---

24 Gen. 4:10. וַיֹּאמֶר מֶה עָשִׂיתָ קוֹל דְּמֵי אָחִיךָ צֹעֲקִים אֵלַי מִן־הָאֲדָמָה׃

25 Gen. 4:12. כִּי תַעֲבֹד אֶת־הָאֲדָמָה לֹא־תֹסֵף תֵּת־כֹּחָהּ לָךְ נָע וָנָד תִּהְיֶה בָאָרֶץ׃

26 In 1938 Schachter-Shalomi's family fled Vienna, going first to Antwerp, Belgium. They were then in an internment camp in Vichy France before finally escaping to Africa, then the West Indies, and finally to New York in 1941.

I want to bring this to your attention because some of us from time to time experienced that, especially those who survived, went through Holocaust.

Here Schachter-Shalomi sings a fragment of a Yiddish song:

Vu-ahin zol ikh geyn, az farshpart far mir iz a yeder tir; vu-ahin zol ikh geyn? "Where should I go? All the doors are locked to me." I have no space where I might go. There is no place that will take me.

The joke, the cruel joke of those days[27] was about the *yiddele*[28] who in Vienna goes into the travel agent and says "Can you sell me a ticket to some place where I might be able to go?" The guy spins the globe and looks here: "Uruguay" he says, "You have to have a *Taufschein*,[29] you have to be baptized. Paraguay—" he goes from one country to another. "There's no place on this globe where I can sell you a ticket to."

And the *yidele* says "Maybe you got another globe?"

You hear the pain in that joke, "Maybe you got another globe"? Cain is in this situation where he says "I can't find another globe and this globe doesn't hold me anymore." When you begin to look at the second exile, you might say "Oh, this is terrible, this is terrible."

---

27 **Those days.** Schachter-Shalomi refers to the days during which Jews were trying to escape from Nazi-occupied territory. Like the joke's protagonist, he and his family were seeking to escape from Vienna. His own story reflected the truth that underlies the bitter joke.

28 **Yidele** ײדעלע. Yiddish: A sympathetic appellation for an ordinary Jew. A diminutive of affection.

29 **Taufschein**. German: Certificate of baptism.

But Cain's exile proves to be the trigger and catalyst for a significant step in human evolution.[30] Genesis 4:17 tells us that when Cain went forth he became a builder of a city, thus introducing technology into the Bible and into human experience.

> And then you discover that his descendents are the ones, and he too, are the beginnings of technology. That if you no longer have a place, where earth sustains you, you then begin to create situations, extensions of your life.

Technology and Cooperation

Schachter-Shalomi then follows this new thread in the tapestry to discuss the development of technology—another exciting step forward for humankind (although, as Schachter-Shalomi will develop later, not an unalloyed benefit). It is significant that this occurs as a consequence of Cain's exile. It leads not just to the benefits of new tools and crafts, but to a necessity of cooperation between human beings, the "amity response."

Exile and diaspora; growth of creativity and resourcefulness; and human cooperation: these large unfoldings are interleaved through the Biblical narrative and through Schachter-Shalomi's commentary. Their interplay is complex and Schachter-Shalomi doesn't try to force it into more convenient pigeonholes.

> So what is a knife? A claw that you no longer have on your hand. What is a fork? The fork is the canine tooth that you no longer have to tear with. When you begin to see that the weapons and the tools that we have are the extension that keep us from over-adapting. What is said about Cain

---

30 Schachter-Shalomi's juxtaposition of the description of Cain's exile with the joke's indirect reminder of his own exile might make one wonder whether his own uprooting from his European origins was part of what allowed his life to take the rich and surprising turns that it did.

is that he can't, there is no place, no situation where he can adapt himself. And so when there is not adaptation possible he needs to move around. Let's take a look at what it means to move around that way.

Imagine I'm still on all fours. Whether I'm an arboreal creature or running through the pampas. If I'm carnivorous, how do I get to eat something? Imagine the strength that it would take to corner animals to tear them apart and have my food? And so when you get to the place of understanding that situation, you begin to see how animals have banded together in creating a hunting response in which a pack does the hunting.

There is a response that is just the same way as there is a territorial response that says "I need my territory, I need to have the place where I'm going to be sovereign, where I am in control." There is another response. That is the *amity response.* "We won't be able to do it unless we do it together."

Diversity and Cooperation: Forcing Dispersion

In the story of the Tower of Babel, God follows up the exile of Cain and dispersion of the original family with a further dispersion. It seems that God loves diversity.

The peoples of the earth, all speaking one language, moved to a single place to settle and decided to join together cooperatively to build themselves a city and a tower with its head in the sky, "lest we be scattered over the face of all the earth."[31]

One might have thought from Schachter-Shalomi's preceding remarks that such cooperation was a good thing, an advance in our spiritual evolution. That the "amity" being evinced from the people working together to make a city and a fine technologically

---

31 Gen. 11:4.

advanced piece of architecture, with the purpose that they should continue to live together, would be something to celebrate. What's not to love here? Why would God want to sabotage these efforts?

But God responds to this amity by going down and confusing their language so that no one could understand the language of his neighbor, and scatters them from there over the face of all the earth. And they stopped building the city.[32]

Schachter-Shalomi uses this perhaps surprising turn to bring out another dimension of the complexity of the whole matter. Not so fast, he might be saying, don't oversimplify this. We're getting pulled up short for a reason.

> And I want to look at this amity response in another context. Come with me to the next place, which will have us look at the description of the Tower of Babel. We are looking at the beginning of Chapter 11.
>
> "And it came to pass that the whole earth was one language and uniform words. And the people traveled together" (they still were in this pack) "and they found a valley in the land of Sumer and they dwelled there. And they spoke" (and here you have the dialogue) "and they spoke to one another saying 'come! let us brick bricks, let us burn them, and they will be like stone to us. And the clay will be like mortar. Let us build us a city. Let it go up as high to the sky; let us make a reputation for ourselves. And lest we otherwise would spread over the face of the earth.'"
>
> And what troubles us when we look at the next *pasuk*[33] is that not only are the characters of the Bible not fair at times, but it seems that God is depicted as coming into this situation saying "gotta scramble them!" Okay? It was interpreted in the past as they wanted to get into God's

---

32 Gen. 11:5–8.

33 **Pasuk**. Hebrew: verse.

territory, and God said "I'm not gonna let them, I'm going to put a monkey wrench in their social machinery. They rely on communication and language and I will not allow that."

Now go back to the whole issue of *lingua franca*, to have one language that we can all use. Esperanto was the "hoped for" language that would bind us together and connect us together. The hope that we would get a rational language that we would be able to express ourselves so that the endings for verbs is going to be one ending and for adverbs is going to be another ending and for nouns will be another ending and everything would be absolutely linguistically clear. Somehow people didn't accept it. There were other [proposals for universal] languages, people tried so hard.

And God comes at this point as the story is being told here [in which they *have* that hoped-for universal language] and scrambles it.

A Value to Making Things Difficult?

Might there be a value to making things more difficult? Does difficulty bring out a creativity that smooth functioning does not? Could this be another version of what was problematic about the "edenic" life in the Garden of Eden, leading God to set them up to take their freedom, and forge a recognizably-human life, by violating the single commandment?

Let us now ask this kind of question. Let's say you have a computer chess game. And as you boot the chess game it says "At what level of difficulty would you like to play?" So you have an opportunity of playing at the lowest level of difficulty, at Beginner's. And after a while you get bored playing at Beginner's; you can beat the machine. Then you set it at a higher level of difficulty.

So it turns out that the frustration that happens here is in the service of the dispersion that has to happen.

What if these earthlings have formed their amity arrangement without having developed their full diversity? Perhaps they don't even know what the possibilities for their own diversity are. Maybe they need to be on their own to allow the individual propensities and talents to unfold in a way that will later allow a fruitful cross pollination that will enrich the totality.

Or perhaps there are already latent differences that are being squelched in the name of the harmonious interactions which they think are necessary if they are to build this magnificent city.

> If you get too soon to try and force a settlement, a peaceful settlement together, in which the differences have not really been worked out, the differences that have been papered over remain there to create the necessary betrayal of what you want to sort out.

And this can be a paradigm of our own inner community, our inner city. Have we taken the time to know and honor the voices, the aspirations, the talents, the needs within our own psyche? Or have we papered over some voices, some needs, in order to fit in with the expectations of others, or our own ideals, or because we have wishes or even values that are mutually incompatible, and rather than face that we push some underground?

> So if you understand that this is not only something that happens on the outside! Deena Metzger[34] has this marvelous image in which she speaks of how *we* are a people, *we* are a government, and most of us have sections that don't have the freedom of speech.
>
> When I say something is unconscious, by and large I mean to say censored. Sometimes it is my morality, sometimes it is an aspect of my personality [that must be censored], but my integration is something that is somehow

---

34 **Deena Metzger.** (1936–.) American storyteller, writer, teacher, and ritual artist.

forced. I might have a police state sitting on top of all the seething stuff that is in there. There may not be freedom of speech for all the components that are inside of me.

So you have to start figuring, at which point can you proceed with your life and at which point are you still open to all the parliament of talking of all the inner voices?

And it turns out that premature calling of the agenda together wouldn't work. And so this is how I see the Tower of Babel. "Don't run to the amity response until you see all the things in clarity."

Abraham and Lot Deal with Territoriality

Territoriality and something akin to issues of sibling rivalry arise when Abraham and Lot come back from Egypt to Canaan. Their shepherds begin quarreling over the pastureland and Abraham sets an example of one harmonious way of dealing with that conflict.[35]

Lot and his flock go along with Abraham and his flock. Lot is his nephew. And the shepherds can't get along with each other. There's not enough pasture. So it's territory again that we're dealing with. And as this territory gets too small to contain both of them, they come to the first means that people invent for dealing with territorial conflict. Partition. If you go to the left, I'll go to the right. If you go to the right, I'll go to the left. This is the way we'll be able to work it out.

To integrate—it's too early yet in the history of humankind to learn that lesson. The first lesson that one learns at this point is my turf, your turf, and we're going to follow this lesson and see how this comes out. Because it does work for a long time. It does work for a long time.

---

35 Gen. 13:5–12.

There weren't enough human beings around. And if there were too many around there was a war and you'd kill some and then you'd work out the space and the life situation for a while. So Lot goes here, Abram is here.

3. JACOB AND ESAU

The story of Jacob and Esau is a powerful and extended exploration of the themes of sibling rivalry and its problems and resolutions. In the course of it, not only the outer but the inner dimensions are made more explicit than Bible usually offers us.

For new insights, though, the text must be read in a way that goes beyond the well-trodden Sunday School simplifications, and the reading must also go beyond the didactic distortions that depend for their lessons on making the characters two-dimensional (or even one-dimensional) caricatures standing as types for righteousness or evil. Schachter-Shalomi offers such a close reading here, finding clues that he puts together to illuminate his themes.

The account of the unfolding of the extended saga of the sibling struggles of Jacob and Esau emerged in the Saturday Torah Service.[36] Schachter-Shalomi begins at the beginning, at Genesis 25:19,[37] moving through the entire story over many chapters.

---

36 It might be helpful to know that for the whole first part of this tracing of Jacob's story, the part in the weekly Torah portion, Schachter-Shalomi is reading from the Torah scroll. He is reading the Hebrew, adding the vowelization and the cantillation. Then as he goes he translates, generally following the same cantillation for the English, except where he pauses to give commentary on specific words or phrases. That is to say, translations to English of these chapters are happening in real time, as he is reading from the Torah scroll and singing the English that is being made on the spot with the trope the Masoretic text gives to the Hebrew. (This reading with the cantillation is called *leyning*—Yiddish for reading.)

37 The start of the weekly Torah portion entitled Toledot.

Rebecca and the Pre-Natal Struggles

Rebecca has become pregnant. "And the children crushed each other within her (*or* in her womb)."[38] The verb here translated "crushed each other" is a reflexive *hitpolel* of the root רצץ used as mutual action.

Already, Jacob and Esau were feeling the shortage of territory. There was not enough room in their mother's womb for both of them; they crushed each other in the limited space.

> *Vayitrotzatzu habanim b'qirbah.* I want to say that word again, that verb. *Vayitrotzatzu habanim b'qirbah.* What did the two kids in her belly do? *Yitrotzatzu.* [laughs delightedly] Hear the sound? *Rutz* is to run; *ratzon* is will, to want. *Aratz, aratz*, I want, I want. I want this, I want that.[39]

And, according to tradition, they weren't just being passively crushed, they were already actively struggling with each other.

---

38 Gen. 25:22. וַיִּתְרֹצֲצוּ הַבָּנִים בְּקִרְבָּהּ

39 Schachter-Shalomi is experiencing and delighting in the poetry of the text. It is partly the sound of *yitrotzatzu,* which rolls off the tongue in a delectably gratifying way. But it is also the resonances he hears with other words called up in the sounds. The root here is רצץ *ratzatz*, vb. crush, grievously oppress [BDB p. 954]. But in *yitrotzatzu* one can hear with Schachter-Shalomi the root רוץ *rutz*, vb. run [BDB p. 930] and *ratzon,* will, desire, pleasure, from the root רצה *ratzah*, vb. will, be pleased with [BDB p. 953]. Schachter-Shalomi hears these other dimensions overlaying the basic description of crushing or jostling.

The Rabbis[40] tell it that she went by, in Rabbinic language,[41] a *shul*[42]—the kid wanted out. She went by the house of idolatry—the kid wanted out. וַיִּתְרֹצֲצוּ. *Yitrotzatzu* is happening in there.

Rebecca appeals to God about what this means and what purpose it is serving. God replies:

> *Vayomer Yah lah sh'nei goyim b'vitnekh, u'sh'nei l'umim mime'ayikh yiparedu.*[43] There are two nations in your belly. Two nationalities from your innards will be separated out.
>
> *U'l'om mil'om ye'ematz v'rav ya'avod tza'ir.*[44] One will get strength from the other. Get that? *U'l'om,* one nation, *mil'om,* from another nation, *ye'ematz,* is going to get its strength. It's in the wrestling that that strength is going to be.

"It's in the wrestling that the strength is going to be." Schachter-Shalomi doesn't interrupt the Torah reading to expand further on that idea here, although the idea does weave through the teachings in the Primal Myths series.

One might get the impression from some traditional commentaries that it is only to be regretted that Jacob, who for them represents all piety, should have to contend with a thwarting force

---

40 This account is in *Genesis Rabbah* 63,6. The Rabbinic text *Genesis Rabbah* dates from sixth century CE. In the Rabbinic account, of course, it was Jacob who wanted out when they passed a Jewish house of study; Esau, when they passed a house of idolatry.

41 When Schachter-Shalomi says "in Rabbinic language" he is not only giving the source of the commentary but acknowledging that it is frankly anachronistic. This is not history; it is Rabbinic parable.

42 **Shul** שׁוּל. Yiddish: synagogue.

43 Gen. 25:23.   וַיֹּאמֶר יְהֹוָה לָהּ שְׁנֵי גֹיִים [גוֹיִם] בְּבִטְנֵךְ וּשְׁנֵי לְאֻמִּים מִמֵּעַיִךְ יִפָּרֵדוּ

44 Gen. 25:23.   וּלְאֹם מִלְאֹם יֶאֱמָץ וְרַב יַעֲבֹד צָעִיר׃

understood as malevolent. Indeed, some of the stories added later to justify Jacob's actions and demonize Esau seem to have behind their rhetorical force the intention to whip up moral indignation.

Schachter-Shalomi by contrast is seeing in the wrestling a double benefit. There is the benefit for Jacob's growth and for the development in him of a more balanced character. There is also, as Schachter-Shalomi sees in God's prediction, a benefit for the whole nations that proceed from the two brothers, a benefit derived from the struggle between those nations.

Again, as at so many points, Schachter-Shalomi is noting in the Biblical text a teaching about a complex human evolutionary process under divine direction. Slowly, and with many twists and turns, that process is worked out through the course of this long history, through the course of an epic (the Hebrew Bible) tracing a saga over millennia. And it is not finished yet: although the Biblical scripture is closed, Torah continues to unfold.

Esau and Jacob are Born

Vayiml'u yameyha laledet.[45] Her days get filled for birthing. And behold, there are twins in her belly. The first one comes out all red and covered with hair and they called his name "well done," "all finished."[46] After him there comes out his brother, his hand still holding onto the heel of Esau, and they called his name Ya'aqov, "heel-holder."[47] Isaac is sixty years old when that birthing is happening. The two lads grow up. And Esav would become a man knowing to hunt, a man of the field, and Ya'aqov was a simple man, dwelling in the tents.

---

45 Gen. 25:24. וַיִּמְלְאוּ יָמֶיהָ לָלֶדֶת

46 Gen. 25:25. Schachter-Shalomi connects Esau's name עֵשָׂו to the root עָשָׂה, to make or do.

47 Gen. 25:26. עָקֵב is a heel or hinder part; Ya'aqov is described as grasping Esau's *aqev*. A verb derived from עָקַב means to follow at the heel, to over-reach, to supplant. עָקֹב also means deceitful or insidious.

The audio file has a brief drop-out here (perhaps as the tape was turned over in recording). During the unrecorded time Schachter-Shalomi evidently had read and translated and perhaps commented on the first part of verse 28, the lines *Vaye'ehav Yitzchaq et Esav, ki tzayid b'piyv.*[48] "And Isaac loved Esau because [Esau provided] game in his mouth." The audio resumes:

> And Rebecca, she loves Jacob. אֹהֶבֶת *Ohevet.* She's constantly loving, it's in the present, she is putting love into that kid. There is a clue in it.
>
> And then comes the cooking.

The Extortion of the Birthright

We have moved on to the first encounter we see between the grown twins, and really their only interaction that we see between the uterine struggling and the reconciliation after twenty years of separation. This "cooking" encounter appears in Genesis 25:29–34, and tells us, perhaps, all we need to know about Jacob and Esau, at least at this point in the story.

Jacob cooks; he knows his brother and how to manipulate him; he grabs an opportunity for advantage and pursues until he nails it down. Out in the outdoor world, Esau works himself to the end of his endurance and then all he wants is to eat and rest. He is impulsive, careless, straight-forward: with Esau, what you see is what you get.

Schachter-Shalomi continues reading and translating directly from the Torah scroll to complete this passage:

> Jacob is cooking that stew up and Esav is coming from the field, tired, and Esav says to Ya'aqov, "Pour down some of this red stuff in my throat, I am so exhausted."
>
> And Ya'aqov says to him, "Sell, as it is day today, by this day, from this day forward, as clear as it is day, I need you

---

48 Gen. 25:28. וַיֶּאֱהַב יִצְחָק אֶת־עֵשָׂו כִּי־צַיִד בְּפִיו

to make that deed to me of your first-born-ness." And Esau says, "I am about to die anyway. What good will there be in having first-born-ness?" And Ya'aqov says "Okay! Then give it to me like an oath, as it is day" and he swears to him. And he sells his birthright to Jacob. And Jacob then gave to Esau bread and the stew of lentils. He ate. He drank. He got up. He went. "And Esau," comes the commentary, the editor, the editorial note,[49] saying, "And thus Esau shamed the first-born-ness, the primogeniture, being born first."

Knowing When to Fight for Territory

Schachter-Shalomi pauses in the narration of the story at this point to bring attention to the larger questions that concern him in the sibling rivalry stories. His concern, as he alerted participants when he asked them to prepare for this weekend, is what we can learn from them about handling differences between people who must live together in the world. These stories also highlight choices that we make in ourselves, and show the playing out of consequences of different ways any of us might handle a particular situation.

While the Bible remains fairly nuanced and, one might say, realistic about the characters, showing the human complexity even as the characters may overall pull in very different directions, tradition can make the character stand, in a one-dimensional way, for extremes. This certainly happens with Jacob and Esau, for whom stories, *midrashim*, are made up by later commentators to prove that Jacob in every way, even in utero, was righteous and pious and Esau in every way was evil, so that they might stand in for the conflict of good and evil, of Israel and its enemies, and of the right and wrong choices we might make in every moment.

---

49 This "editorial note" follows directly as part of the received Biblical text. The narrator has paused to comment on the story. (Or perhaps a later editor or redactor inserted this pedagogical point: Schachter-Shalomi appears to be feeling how different its moralizing tone is from the style and tone of most of the Biblical narratives.)

While the rabbinical midrashim that make Jacob and Esau one-dimensional types do some violence to the original Biblical story, and might cause a literary mind to object, or might distress someone who relates to the humanity of the characters, they serve a pedagogical purpose for their creators. Schachter-Shalomi has a sensitivity to the literary and human dimensions of the characters, but he similarly sees an invitation to identify characteristics that may stand in opposition, to help us think about our present-day interpersonal life challenges and our own inner life.

At this point Schachter-Shalomi explores the contrast between a tendency to use "brawn" and a choice to use a more prudent calculation of consequences. Brawn, associated with Esau, is simple, straightforward, with physical strength, emotional volatility, and perhaps impulsiveness, certainly not overly concerned with long-range consequences. Jacob in contrast relies on his wits, thinks ahead, is devious and bold in seizing opportunities to get what he wants.

As is characteristic of the sibling rivalry stories, the issue of "territory" in its various forms stands out. It is physical space they must share in the womb, and as we are told that they are crushing each other we see that the uterine space is too limited for what they experience as their needs. The "territory" is also the limited resource of the birthright and the father's blessing of the firstborn.

But the differences in them as different human beings is also striking to us. We are told that Esau is a skilled hunter, who brings his father tasty game and is loved by him. Jacob is a different sort who stays in the tents and is loved by his mother. Then there are the striking differences that the text does not name but illustrates so vividly in the account of their interaction over the lentil stew.

The external question is how two such human beings living in community can create harmonious relations while honoring or at least accommodating the differences of personality, character, and destiny. And there is a parallel internal question of what it means for each of us that, as the unhappy pregnant Rebecca experienced, these tendencies sometimes war inside us.

Time out. Why am I so concerned about this story? About the rivalry? It begins with the search for space. Will I have space to develop? All of us, at birth, find that we run out of room in our mother's womb. The contractions that keep pushing us out are the ones that announce there is no more space left. Can you imagine you had to do this with another brother with whom all the time you have been wrestling? Who wins? Brawn wins. Brawn comes out first. Brawn has the power. Brawn gets the first territory. Brawn is that part where the élan, the vital stuff is most strongly present.

Do justice and brawn go together? Not necessarily so. So, should brawn always get the blessing? If you're too streetwise, you die young. If you're not streetwise enough, you die young. You have to be streetwise enough, but not too much, in order to be able to survive.

How do you put this thing together? Now, we look at where we are on this globe right now. At one point there was plenty of land. But they decided they wanted to be in that valley. But they can't all live in the valley, there's not enough room. So they build a high-rise. You stack the space up so you can have more people.

Babel was too soon. But we are spread over the planet right now. And it is earth that is giving us different kind of models. Remember the rats in the overpopulation situation; they attack each other. The issues that have to do with territory and the need that we have with our territory, and the brawn person who keeps on saying inside of us, "If you don't have me you aren't going to make it."

In the midst of looking at the way brawn and prudence were (on one view) divided between Esau and Jacob, Schachter-Shalomi pauses to remind us that in Abraham we have a character in whom both are present. These reminders assume we remember the Biblical narratives that illustrated the qualities. First he refers to the fact that Abraham, at God's behest, leaves his home, originally

Ur of the Chaldees in Mesopotamia, and goes forth "to the land I will show you"—it turns out to be Canaan. Then, later, when there is a famine, he goes down to Egypt, where he passes off his wife Sarah as his sister on the fear that otherwise they might kill him to get access to her. When his nephew Lot is taken captive by a coalition of five kings, he turns warrior and defeats them all to rescue Lot. And when he thinks God is demanding the sacrifice of his long-awaited, much-promised, much-loved son Isaac, he obeys promptly—or does he obey? In the end Isaac is not killed.

> Remember the new development that had to happen. It was not that Abraham was well-adjusted in Ur of the Chaldees. There was something wild, restless, driving him saying, "Out! You can't stay here!" And then there's the prudent situation that says, "Saraleh,[50] do me a favor, say you're my sister. I don't want always have to deal with the overwhelming odds of power that I have to be involved in." Do you get this kind of mix? You see later on: yes, offer the child; no, not offer the child, the struggle that's going on between the two parts of Abraham. So okay, you got to kill something, kill the ram.

In Jacob and Esau, the polarization is divided, perhaps to stand out more starkly so that we may study the alternative choices, the opposing pulls.

> What happens then is that here we now find, instead of in one person, in two people, the polarization. And this is something that you may at times wonder which one of the two are you.

But then, it folds back again: what you may discover is that you have both. An experiential exercise during the weekend had as its goal to show participants that they carry their twin within.

---

50 **Saraleh**. Yiddish. Affectionate diminutive of the name Sarah.

The Binding of Isaac: Why Didn't he Resist?

Schachter-Shalomi now explores how family relations in Esau and Jacob's family are affected by previous generations.

> The binding of Isaac. It comes out that Isaac was 36, 37 years old.[51] Abraham at this point is 136 years old. This 37 year old *bochur*[52] couldn't give his papa a pop in the nose?
>
> If you start asking yourself what is happening here in that program that says "I want to live!" That program that says "*Je ne veux pas mourir!*" as people would scream before they were taken to the guillotine, "I don't want to die, I don't want to die!" This thing that says "Alive! Alive! I want to be alive!" And when you are that alive, how happy that is. And when that is threatened, the adrenaline, the flow, the whole business and, somehow, *shwooh*![53]
>
> Isaac doesn't have that.
>
> Now you look at Isaac seeing the brawny Esavel.[54] Do you understand why he loves him?

Isaac and Esau Played Out in Schachter-Shalomi's Life

Schachter-Shalomi now gives an example of the struggle of balancing the two—impulsive brawn and prudent self restraint—from his own life, as a young teenager in Vienna under Hitler. In

---

51 This is according to later Rabbinic calculations. Rashi's commentary to Genesis 21:34 figures Abraham's age at this moment (and therefore Isaac's), based on *Bereishit Rabbah* ch. 54 para. 6.

52 **Bokher** בחור. Yiddish: young man, in usage an unmarried one.

53 "**shwooh**": I am approximating the strong vocalized breath sound with which Schachter-Shalomi represented the outflow of powerful impulsive energy .

54 **Esavel**. Yiddish affectionate diminutive of Esav. Schachter-Shalomi is looking at Esau through Isaac's loving eyes.

the audio file his voice and dramatization in this description as it unfolds convey all the depths and contradictory dimensions of the experience for him: the fears, the power welling up wanting to strike out, the inhibitions. One feels how fully and how vividly he is re-living the experience, and his weighing of his choices, and the many levels of pain. One feels that in the moment of his roaring out what the brawn side was demanding, and in the point in the recounting in which his voice cracks a little and the tears are close to the surface—these experiences feel very present in his recollection some fifty years later.

> I'm talking about behavior, having to cut out [that is, suppress the impulse to use physical power to fight for life].
>
> Here I stood under a bridge, the Salztorbrücke, in Vienna, and there were some Nazi kids, Hitler Youth, beating me up. On the other side of the bridge stood a Brown Shirt playing with his Luger. Luger, automatic gun. Felsenberg, Izzy Felsenberg, a friend of mine and I, had been gotten down to that place under the bridge, and these kids were beating us up. Here was the Danube Canal. There was just this much of road and the bridge was over here. Can you imagine?
>
> We had enough *koyekh*[55] to be able to kick them back, to throw them into the water. Why didn't we do it? Not only because there was a gun. The gun was one side of it. There was a point when it hurt so much, you get *zetzed*[56] over here, you hit your head against the granite behind it, but I was worried. What would they do to my family?
>
> It was the larger thing that said "Inhibit those responses that are saying [he roars out the word:] FIGHT!" And I couldn't let that come out. The control I had to set on that in order to survive.

---

55 **Koyekh** כוח. Yiddish: Strength, physical power.
56 **Zetz** זעץ. Yiddish: A strong blow: slam, punch.

> The same program that in brawn would translate itself into kicking back and to let adrenaline come out, this very same program on the other side is creating a moment of quiescence, of saying "It only hurts for a little while, carry it out a little longer."
>
> We did get away; the response that kept me in life, on which I made the blessing *Shehecheyanu v'qiyemanu v'higiy'anu*,[57] was *that* response.
>
> But *oy*! when I see one of my kids not letting himself be beaten, and standing up for his rights, and not letting the *shkotsim*[58] get him, okay? Do you understand how that impresses me? How that is something that I love?

The Alternatives Playing Out in the Complexity of Family Dynamics

As Schachter-Shalomi watches brawn versus prudence play out in the family, it is no longer a simple dichotomy between the twins. There is multi-generational complexity in why Isaac loves Esau and isn't drawn to Jacob, why Rebecca loves Jacob and is leery of Esau. It may be that the one kept at a distance is only too familiar.

> And so Rebecca. She has a father, she has brothers. The people, the Arameans, from Paddan Aram, apparently those guys knew how to fight, when you get to see what

---

57. בָּרוּךְ אַתָּה יְיָ אֱלֹהֵינוּ מֶלֶךְ הָעוֹלָם, שֶׁהֶחֱיָנוּ וְקִיְּמָנוּ וְהִגִּיעָנוּ לַזְּמַן הַזֶּה. Hebrew: a blessing said on a special occasion to express gratitude to have been kept alive to see this day.

58. **Shkotsim** שקצים. Yiddish: Wild, misbehaving, reprehensible young males. If gentile (the primary referent), *shkotsim* are the sort who would assault a Jewish child. Schachter-Shalomi's use of this term here is an indicator of the depth of feeling he has been sharing and the extent to which he is with his memories: it follows the usage of European Jews in the last century struggling under threats and attacks of anti-Semitism—a usage, for them, of bitter contempt.

the Assyrians were like later on, the cruelty that was there, the kind of physical prowess called for! I'm sure that she didn't like that in Esav as much, that she likes Yankele[59] a lot better.

So each one of them had something to fear in the behavior of the other child. Isaac, looking at the one who is quiet, quiescent, the one who sits at home. He sees how his life had become colorless. So you dig another well.[60] But the great adventures, all the stuff that was talked about of what happened to Abraham, nothing like this is happening to him. He doesn't go down to Egypt, he doesn't make great discovery.

But you start looking at what each parent has and how much they are aware of it. Do you think they talked it over? It says they loved each other, they were together in the tent.[61] She understood him pretty well. Did they ever talk about it? I don't have the sense that papa and mama ever sat down and had a family conference, "How we gonna raise those kids? What are we gonna do with them? I see my brother in him; you see yourself, your wasted youth in him; how are we gonna deal with those kids?" There isn't that kind of thing.

---

59 **Yankele**. Yiddish. Affectionate diminutive for Ya'aqov (Jacob).

60 In Gen. 26:15–22 Isaac redigs the wells Abraham had dug which had been filled in by the Philistines. As he digs the first, the herdsmen of Gerar quarreled with him and claimed the water. He moved on and dug another. More quarrels. When he moves on again and digs the third well, they they stop disputing with him.

61 After Sarah's death, Abraham arranges for Rebecca to be brought as a wife for Isaac. Schachter-Shalomi refers to Gen. 24:67. "And Isaac brought her to/into the tent of Sarah his mother and he took Rebecca and she became his wife, and he loved her. And Isaac was comforted after his mother." וַיְבִאֶהָ יִצְחָק הָאֹהֱלָה שָׂרָה אִמּוֹ וַיִּקַּח אֶת־רִבְקָה וַתְּהִי־לוֹ לְאִשָּׁה וַיֶּאֱהָבֶהָ וַיִּנָּחֵם יִצְחָק אַחֲרֵי אִמּוֹ׃

Schachter-Shalomi imagines how the divided preferences of the parents might have played out in their treatment and admonishment of the children, and how that might have intensified the antagonism to which their differences could have already predisposed them.

> And against all that stuff, Jacob experiences an unsaid thing that keeps saying to him, "Why don't you go out and play in the field like your brother does? Why aren't you like Esau? Why aren't you like Esau?" So that every day there is tension in his consciousness of that "Why aren't you like Esau?" Doesn't he want to be like Esau?
>
> On the other hand, doesn't Esau get the same kind of message, "Can't you be a *mentsh*[62] and sit at the table? Look how he *fresses*!"[63] *Vayokhal vayesh't' va yaqam vayelakh.*[64] He doesn't even sit down at the table, he doesn't wash his hands. What you get is this kind of impulsive person, don't you think he got the thing, "Why can't you be like…why can't you be like…" — "GRRRR!"
>
> The model "why can't you be like," how that sits in the craw, and how that creates stash so that when nobody sees I want to give a kick to this guy who, even when he isn't there creates a field around him. The territory which I want to have my own four *ells*[65] to live in is constantly dictated to by who he is and what he models and what I have to be with this thing.

---

62 **Mentsh** מענטש. Yiddish: a decent human being. One that can be relied on to come through with honor, having character and dignity.

63 To **fres** פֿרעסען. Yiddish: to eat, with implication of making a pig of oneself. Eat a lot, without decorum.

64 וַיֹּאכַל וַיֵּשְׁתְּ וַיָּקָם וַיֵּלַךְ The description in Gen. 25:34 of Esau consuming the lentil stew. "He ate. He drank. He got up. He went."

65 **Ell**. Biblical measurement. Approximately a cubit; approximately the length of a man's arm.

The Stealing of the Blessing

We are continuing now at Genesis Chapter 27.

> The opportunity presents itself. Papa says, "I'm getting old. I feel a blessing coming. I need a certain kind of quantum for the blessing. Don't feed me any more of domesticated stuff. I need something wild inside of me before I die. Go and hunt me some venison. Bring me—you know how much I love this kind of food. I don't want the domesticated food. Bring me some of the other."
>
> Rebecca hears this. She is already figuring out how is she going to make not-venison. And she says to Jacob, "I'm going to fix this." And Jacob trembles, he's torn about it, he wants the blessing. Doesn't he want the blessing? … Oy, does he want that blessing.
>
> So he wants it. But Mother is saying also that he should fool papa. Okay, papa can't see, we know that. How is he going to talk to papa? Papa will want to touch him. "My brother Esau is a hairy man and I am a smooth man." How will I be felt by papa? How will he deal with me?
>
> She says, "Don't worry." And she comes up, she sets him up with everything. Every instrumentality to make the deception, and then he says, "But mama! He's gonna curse me!" "I take the curse on me, on me is the curse." Do you hear, the essential Jewish mother talking to her son, "I take the curse on me! *Alai qil'latkha*.[66] "Let me, I'll handle that."
>
> Now he has to go in and he has to impersonate the other brother. And he has such trouble! He says, "May my father please come and partake"—the most polite language! He speaks to him, he says, look, I've brought you the thing.
>
> [Isaac] says "How did you manage it that you brought it so fast?" Esau would have said [boisterous voice:] "You should have seen me *run* when I got that stag!" [Now more

---

[66] עָלַי קִלְלָתְךָ בְּנִי "Let your curse be on me, my son." Gen. 27:13.

politely representing Jacob:] "Oh, the Lord happened to
have it and brings it to me, very quick! The success was a
blessing of the Lord."

[Now Isaac speaking:] "The boy sounds—this is the way
Jacob talks! The hands are the hands like Esau has."

He receives the blessing. Can you imagine the
adrenaline, the hair that stands up on the back of Ya'aqov?
"Please, daddy, make it fast with the blessing, I have to
get the hell out of here before my brother comes!" All this,
while he's very polite and subdued in this situation. He
goes out. Esau comes in. [Schachter-Shalomi, speaking
boisterously as Esau:] "Yep, Dad! I got it for you!"

[Isaac] says, "Who are you?"

Can you imagine the rage? The second time. "He has
caused me to stumble a second time. He has grabbed at my
heel a second time." The murderousness that is in him. Why
doesn't he fulfill that deed right then and there?

"Have you only got one blessing, Dad?" And how he
begs!

When Isaac tells Esau that he ate the game and blessed Jacob
and that that blessing will stand, Esau cries out an "exceedingly
great and bitter cry" and says "Bless me also, Father!" Isaac
demurs that Jacob took away Esau's blessing. Esau persists:
"Have you not reserved a blessing for me?" Isaac replies that he
has already made Jacob master over him, and invested Jacob with
grain and wine. Isaac concludes, "So for you, what then can I do,
my son?"

"Esav said to his father: Have you only a single blessing,
father? Bless me, me also, father! And Esav lifted up his voice
and wept."[67] At this Isaac relents and comes up with a blessing.

And papa gives him a blessing. And papa in the blessing
does this amazing thing. He says, "I will give you this

---

67 Gen. 27:38. Everett Fox translation.

blessing *and* you will live by the sword. *And* it is your brawn that is going to get you out from under the thumb of your brother, in the end." So now he has to live with that consolation blessing, with that second, also-ran blessing that he gets at this point.

Jacob Leaves for Paddan Aram

The story continues. Devastated and bitter over the theft of the blessing from the father with whom he had the special connection, Esau "says in his heart" that he will kill Jacob when his father is dead. Rebecca sends for Jacob and tells him that Esau is "consoling himself with thinking about killing you." She advises Jacob to flee to Paddan Aram and stay with her brother Laban for "some days" until Esau's anger has turned around and he has forgotten what Jacob did to him. (Evidently she knows her other son: Esau's impulsive anger will pass quickly and he will, she thinks, effectively forget even this painful betrayal.)[68]

In fear of his brother's wrath, or again obedient to his mother, Jacob sets out as she advises.

On the way to Paddan Aram Jacob sleeps and dreams of angels going up and down a ladder between earth and heaven. And in the dream God speaks to Jacob and promises that he will have this land, and that his children will be as the dust of the earth, spreading in all directions; and that he, God, will be with him, Jacob, and bring him back here.

This dream is a soul-shaking experience. When he awakes, he says *Ma norah hamaqom hazeh! Ki im beyt elohim vzeh sha'ar hashamayim.*[69] How awesome is this place! It is none other than the house of God and this is the gate of heaven.

---

68 Gen. 27:41–45.

69 Gen. 28:17. וַיִּירָא֙ וַיֹּאמַ֔ר מַה־נּוֹרָ֖א הַמָּק֣וֹם הַזֶּ֑ה אֵ֣ין זֶ֗ה כִּ֚י אִם־בֵּ֣ית אֱלֹהִ֔ים וְזֶ֖ה שַׁ֥עַר הַשָּׁמָֽיִם׃

Morning comes, and he has to do something with all that stuff. So he takes that stone which was under his head and he puts it as a stand-up stone. An erection stone. Very *lingam*[70]-like that these monuments are. And very *lingam*-like, too, he poured oil over its head. (Who has been to an Indian temple and seen people pour milk, cream, over the lingam stone?) Calling that place the God-house.

The Brawning of Jacob

Something, Schachter-Shalomi is saying, has changed in Jacob.

There is something that he got from Esau.

Lifting the stone, brawn has entered into Jacob. The guy who was having his head in the clouds all the time is now the one who is going to have to—. How is he going to get a woman in that wimpy place that he is? So watch the next few sentences.

And Yankev[71] picked up his feet! *Vayisa' Ya'aqov raglav.*[72] …

And behold, he comes to the land of the children of the East. …

Behold, there is a well in the field and there are three flocks there that are sort of crouching around that well, for it is around that well that those flocks are to be getting their water.

---

70 **Lingam** लिंगं. Sanskrit: an upright stone representing Shiva and male creative energy in the Hindu tradition.

71 **Yankev.** Yiddish variant of Ya'aqov, Jacob.

72 Gen. 29:1: וַיִּשָּׂא יַעֲקֹב רַגְלָיו וַיֵּלֶךְ אַרְצָה בְנֵי־קֶדֶם "And Ya'aqov picked up/lifted up his feet, and he went/walked to the land of the children of the East." Charan in Paddan Aram is considerably north (and then east) from Bethel where he has just spent the night and built an altar.

V'ha'even g'dolah al piy hab'er.[73] And this stone, *the* stone, get that, with a definite article, the well-known stone. It is covering the cistern. And it tells that the usual thing was that they would be gathering all flocks around it and all the shepherds would come and they would roll away the stone. …

And so usually they would give to drink to the sheep and then they would roll back the stone on top of the well to its place.

Jacob inquires of them where they are from; they say Charan. He asks if they know Laban; they do. But they add that his daughter Rachel is just approaching with her sheep. Jacob, the just-arrived stranger, starts to argue with them about their practice.

"It still is high day; it's not time to gather the sheep yet, why don't you give the sheep to drink and then take them back to pasture?" And they said, "We cannot, for until the time comes that all the flocks will gather together, then we will roll away the stone from the mouth of the well, and we will give to drink to those sheep." They're still talking to one another, and Rachel comes with the sheep that belonged to her father.

The strength that comes by seeing someone whom you want to impress. "And it was as Jacob saw Rachel the daughter of Lavan who is the brother of his mother and the sheep of Lavan the brother of his mother and Jacob came over and he rolled the stone from away from the top of the well."

The stone that it takes a whole bunch of shepherds to roll away, all of a sudden the wimp has *koyach* like this.

---

73 Gen. 29:2. וְהָאֶבֶן גְּדֹלָה עַל־פִּי הַבְּאֵר "The stone was great upon the mouth of the well."

> And he gives to drink to the sheep of Laban the brother of his mother.
>
> He draws the water for the sheep. "And Jacob kissed Rachel." Didn't even get introduced to her.
>
> And then something happens to him, he starts crying. We haven't heard of Jacob crying the whole time. All of a sudden he starts crying.

How much of Esau is coming through Jacob in this encounter!

He has the impulsiveness—and the brawn—to move the stone off the well, in violation of their custom, and performing a physical feat that normally requires the group of men. He has the impulsiveness, and the lack of decorum, to kiss this strange young woman to whom he has not been introduced. Is he not afraid of the consequences of such an impropriety? Does *any* thought of consequences cross his mind?

Then, an emotional outburst—he bursts into tears, "raising his voice in weeping," in a Hebrew construction exactly quoting the description of what Esau did, shortly before, when his father told him he didn't have another blessing for him.

Jacob Prepares to Face Esau Again

In order to stay focused on the relationship of Jacob and Esau, I now pass over Jacob's twenty years with Laban, and Schachter-Shalomi's commentary on Jacob's relations with Laban as well as the relationships of Jacob with Rachel and with Leah, and the sisters' relationship with each other (although there are applications in all these for family relationships).

> Now he is on his way back. He has just said goodbye to Laban and he is making his way and somebody gives him the good news, Esau and four hundred warriors are on the way to greet you. Think about the fear with which he crossed the Jordan before. The fear with which he left.

Schachter-Shalomi Sees Jacob's Fear in His Own Life

Now I want to take you back to a place that happened to me in my life, and I'm sure you have models in your own. I go very often to Catholic churches and feel okay there. When I would go and visit Thomas Merton at Gethsemene[74] I was really at home there. I knew the Latin mass almost by heart, I could *davven*[75] along with it. [sings some of it:] *"Sursum corda; habemus ad dominum."*[76] It wasn't a problem. I was at home with that.

All of a sudden, on my trip to Europe, the first time I went to Auschwitz, I decided to go and visit Mariazell. Mariazell outside of Vienna. It is a cloister; it is also like a museum, it's an amazing church. It was built in commemoration of driving the Turks back from the gates of Vienna. Our lady of Mariazell is the one who saved the city.

And all of a sudden this guy who is at home in various churches and ashrams and what have you goes to a church at Mariazell and something freezes inside of me. What freezes is not the adult. It is the Jewish kid from Vienna that got beaten up under the bridge.

All of a sudden I'm right back at that place of fear that grips me, and I couldn't stand staying there any more. I had to terminate, I had to get out of there quick. I couldn't breathe, you know, it just grabbed me. Can you then imagine the kind of situation that you sometimes feel,

---

74 **Thomas Merton** (1915–1968). Trappist monk of the Abbey of Gethsemene in Kentucky. A prolific writer, poet, social activist, mystic, and student of comparative religion.

75 **Davven** דאַוונען. Yiddish: to pray.

76 Latin: "Let us lift up our hearts; we have [lifted them] to the Lord." Dialogue between priest and people in which the people give assent to the priest continuing with the Eucharistic prayer.

you, adult, grown-up person who has a whole life and a feeling for yourself, coming back into a scene that is still a childhood scene that caused you pain at that point, and here comes your enemy, the *sheygets*[77] who beat you up on the street corner. It's him who you have to face.

And that child inside that was still frightened is what comes alive at that point. Its fears is what fills you. No matter how you want to talk to your head, at this point, that one that hasn't yet worked the thing through is still aching inside.

And here is Jacob and he hears the good news that his brother is coming with four hundred *shkotsim*[78] to beat him up.

"Meet" is what the objective situation is.[79] But the kid inside doesn't hear "meet." He hears "Confront!"

What Jacob fears that Esau has come to say to him is:

"Finally! Give me back my birthright! Now I'm gonna make you pay for all these things!"

And he knows that there is no place to run to. And it's harder to run because he's got *kinderlekh*,[80] he's got sheep, he's got wives, how is he going to deal with him?

---

77 **Sheygets** שייגעץ. Yiddish: In this context and connotation, a male person dangerous to Jews.

78 **Shkotsim** שקצים. Yiddish: Dangerous or threatening ruffians. See earlier footnote on Schachter-Shalomi's usage there.

79 Gen. 32:7. וַיָּשֻׁבוּ הַמַּלְאָכִים אֶל־יַעֲקֹב לֵאמֹר בָּאנוּ אֶל־אָחִיךָ אֶל־עֵשָׂו וְגַם הֹלֵךְ לִקְרָאתְךָ וְאַרְבַּע־מֵאוֹת אִישׁ עִמּוֹ: And the messengers returned to Jacob saying "We came to your brother, to Esau, and he is also walking to meet you, and four hundred men with him."

80 **Kinderlekh** קנדערלך. Yiddish: Affectionate diminutive for children.

Jacob's Strategy

How does he deal with Esau? He deals with him like Jacob. He is frightened, but he doesn't react to him by trying to out-brawn Esau. His plan is to placate him, to buy him off. And there's something more. Schachter-Shalomi notices that he is sending Esau the hunter not just *many* animals, but breeding stock: four females for each male.

> He is preparing a situation that is amazing. To Esau the hunter he is saying "I'm gonna send you a flock. I'll send you cows and bulls, the proportion one to four. I'll send you sheep and goats, the proportion of males to females one to ten. I'm going to send you donkeys, two she-asses to one jack." In other words, he is sending him the breeding stock. Basic breeding stock is what you would expect from somebody who is into animal husbandry.
>
> And he is trying to *domesticate his brother* with the domestication of his own stuff.

This is one prong of his strategy. But he has readied many.

> And it still is eating inside of him that he has to make this confrontation. He is doing everything that he knows, sitting down with his understanding of how one has to deal with a rowdy, and he is saying (instructing the messengers) "You tell him, 'My lord Esau, this is a gift from your servant your brother.'"
>
> Okay? You get it? "You want *koved*,[81] you get *koved*. You want recompense, you get recompense. You want honor, I give you honor. I give you the status that you want. And now, could you bug off?"
>
> Do you understand that he is not giving Esau these gifts? He is giving *internalized* Esau these gifts. The one who has

---

81 **Koved** כבוד. Yiddish: honor, respect, face.

been eating at his guts all the time, who has always drawn him to out-Esau Esau, who has bent him out of shape, just as he has been bent out of shape from birth on.

So, he has a plan. He's going to have Rachel and her kid, Leah and her kids, make two camps, and he is going to present himself and send those presents, and each group that he sends is going to give this message and he figures these are the buffers, one buffer after another he is going to send. Finally, by the time he is going to meet him it is going to be okay. Everything is set, and now comes the night before.

Wrestling: Who Am I?

That night, Jacob chooses to stay alone on the other side of the river. He needs to prepare himself for what feels like a fateful encounter. This is not about brawn against brawn. He has some inner work to do, perhaps some wrestling with conscience, perhaps some sorting out of who he is in relation to his twin brother.

Boundaries haven't been clear, at least not in the time they were together. He was born grabbing Esau's heel, trying to hold him back, or supplant him, or to get something from him before they left the place in which they have lived together almost as one. Even after they grew up, he seemed to continue to be needing things from Esau: the "firstborn" status, the father's blessing.

He has been on his own for twenty years now, and has become wealthy. Is he yet a whole person?

The night before the battle. The night before the encounter. That's the night when Krishna and Arjuna have their great conversation that becomes the *Bhagavad Gita*.[82]

---

82 ***Bhagavad Gita***. भगवद्गीता Sanskrit: Divine song. Scripture beloved of the Hindu tradition. Part of the *Mahabharata,* epic of ancient India. Just before a great battle, Arjuna the prince is wondering what he should do and whether he should even fight in the battle. The god Krishna gives him teachings about the meaning of the battles of life.

It is the night before. He has to meet this one, this brother of his. On the eve of that encounter he has to look at his life. *Vayivater Ya'aqov l'vado.*[83] "And Ya'aqov remained alone."

This is what I feel in this situation. It's a whole other take on alone when I have to start looking at what is "me," and what are the layers that are on top of me, what are the things that people have put on me that have bent me out of shape. Is it possible that I could just be alone, not just as I stand in relation to others, not as others have imposed on me. Can I be alone and look at myself and see who am I when I'm alone.

Wrestling: Dusting, Embracing, Blessing

Vaye'aveq iysh imo,[84] "And there is a guy dusting with him." *Avaq* means dust, from which you get the sense, rolling in the dust, meaning wrestling. Kicking up the dust. At the same time you also get [reminded of] another root. *Daveq,* to cleave, to stick to. Therefore shall man leave his mother and his father and *daveq* to his wife and they shall be one flesh. *Daveq.* And Jacob met Rachel *vayichabeq otah vayishaq lah.*[85] Get that word *chabeq*? *Chabeq* is to hug, to embrace. So *vayiaveq, vayichabeq, vayidabeq,* get this? The *baq* is there but the one letter in front of it is the one that gives the *baq* that's happening its character.

---

83 Gen. 32:25. וַיִּוָּתֵר יַעֲקֹב לְבַדּוֹ

84 Gen. 32:24. וַיֵּאָבֵק אִישׁ עִמּוֹ "And a man dusted/wrestled with him." The verb is in a *nifal* passive form: he was dusted/dusty with him.

85 "And he embraced her and he kissed her." This is not a Biblical quotation; Schachter-Shalomi made it up as illustration. However, very shortly (as we are proceeding in this narrative) Esau, having run up to Jacob, will embrace and kiss him and the narrative will use these Hebrew words.

> Is this a loving hug? Is it a wrestling? Because in every
> hug there's a *shtikele*[86] wrestle there, okay? There is a little
> bit of that.

This word-play with the roots אָבַק *avaq*, wrestle, דָּבֵק *daveq*,
cleave or stick to, and חָבַק *chavaq*, embrace, draws our attention
to the parallels, the intertwinings, and the resonances between
Jacob's wrestling with the *iysh* and his embrace with Esau the
next day. Both have ambiguities. Are they the same ambiguities?
The first seems in some way a preparation for the second, but in
what way is it so?

> *Vayiaveq, vayichabeq, vayidabeq,* which one of the
> *beq*s is happening over here, all right? And so here this guy
> is doing it with him that night. You don't have any street
> lights on the other side of the river. On a dark night, you're
> wrestling with somebody whose features you don't know,
> but whose strength you feel. And you know that there's a
> whole night's wrestling that is going on.
>
> Wrestling on the outside, wrestling on the inside. He is
> alone. Has he shed all the other things? Will the real Jacob
> please stand up? Which one is the real Jacob? Is the real
> Jacob the one who was wrestling? Is the real Jacob the one
> who was stealing? Who's the real Jacob?
>
> Where, finally, is the person, that self? And if you have
> tried to find that real self…. What is it that I want? What is
> it that *I* want? I know what I'm asked to do, I know what I
> agreed to do, I know what's demanded of me to do. But who
> is the *me*? What do *I* want. And if you have wrestled with
> that and you have had a vigil, an all-nighter wrestling with
> that, you get a sense of what that's like.
>
> And it's morning. And the other guy says "Let me go.
> Dawn is coming, I have to leave."

---

86 **Shtikele** שטיקעלע. Yiddish: A very small piece of something.

CHAPTER 5. FAMILY RELATIONS ❧ 103

> And he says "I'm not going to let you go. You have to
> bless me first. You have to bless the *me* first. I have to hear
> that the guy who wrestled me all night is accepting me and
> is giving me a blessing that says 'As you are, with all your
> flaws, with everything that you are, I accept you, I take you,
> you are *okay* in this situation.'"
>
> And he says "What's your name?" And he says
> "Ya'aqov." And he says "Your name isn't going to be
> Ya'aqov any more. Your name is now wrestler. You wrestled
> all night; you deserve that name."
>
> And Ya'aqov limps into the camp. He comes walking
> in with that victory that is his, that he no longer ever has
> to out-Esau Esau. That he no longer has to be bent out of
> shape. That he can be who he is himself.

As one might gather from the way Schachter-Shalomi has been
ruminating on that wrestling, he has experienced something like
this. The experience, the imagery, the inner journey of it, has a
"great familiarity" for him, and he believes it to be a common
human experience. We all must struggle in that wrestling to discover who we really are and to reach the inner integrity to be that
person.

> I wanted to share this view of the struggle. I have a deep
> deep sense that what touched me about it and what touched
> you about it is the great familiarity with such struggles that
> we go through.

The Meeting

Schachter-Shalomi now moves on to the actual meeting with
Esau.

> So there was Jacob the next morning, he goes to greet
> his brother. Everything was set up in the defensive way.
> There is that moment: which way will it go? Will it go the
> hard way, will it go the soft way? And here it turns out
> that having encountered Esau the night before in him and

found himself not in the place of having to do anything to out-Esau Esau any more, there he stands in front of him.

And the first impulse that this impulsive brother gets is to give him a hug. He gets up, runs over to him, and gives him a hug. It's an amazing hug. Can you imagine, at one moment he is still wondering "Will, along with the hug, come a knife in my back?"

Do you remember that moment when Sadat steps out of the airplane?[87] Can you imagine what this was like for both sides? It's possible that an Egyptian commando would come out and shoot all the people of the Israeli government. It is possible that someone would pick off Sadat as he comes out of the plane.

That was a moment in our history, it was a Shabbes[88] morning, it was noon on the Eastern seaboard when that happened. And I was with Larry Kushner's congregation that Shabbat and instead of the Torah reading we wheeled in a TV set because—do you understand?

It was like Jacob *vayigash,*[89] it was happening right then and there in that moment. The vulnerability of those two meeting each other!

87　Schachter-Shalomi refers to November 19, 1977, when Anwar Sadat made his historic visit to Jerusalem. The next day he declared before Israel's parliament: "We really and truly welcome you to live among us in peace and security." (The text is in *New York Times*, November 21, 1977.) The visit led within a year and a half to the first peace treaty between Israel and an Arab country.

88　**Shabes** שבת. Yiddish: sabbath.

89　וַיִּגַּשׁ "and he drew near." This word is very familiar because the root is used in this form when Judah approached Josef to give the speech that finally melts Josef's heart and allows reconciliation of the brothers. In Gen 33:3, this same verb, נָגַשׁ, is used for Jacob drawing near to Esau. "And he (Jacob) himself passed on before them (his wives and children) and he bowed to the ground seven times, until he came near to his brother (עַד־גִּשְׁתּוֹ עַד־אָחִיו)."

How Do Jacob and Esau Deal with Territoriality, Diversity and Unity?

Are they ready now to live together in harmony? To work cooperatively so that the strengths of each extends and supports what is less developed in his brother? In some situations, this might be an ideal. But it's not the only way, and in this case another path is illustrated.

> And then comes the evening and they're talking, "So, are we going to hang out together?" The first impulse is "yes, buddy, we are now going to stay together forever."
>
> Esau is saying "Come on, let's do it together." Jacob is saying, "You know, I've got my responsibilities, I've got my people, this is a lot of life that has happened for me, that has happened for you. You've got your turf, I've got my turf. I will respect yours. We'll get together from time to time and it's going to be fine. We don't have to now, just because we've had our encounter and our meeting, we don't have to merge. The point is not to merge, the point is to be freely meeting when we need to."
>
> The question that we got to was, when is it premature? And remember the tower of Babel was too early to merge.
>
> So the night before they part ways, the four hundred mighty men of Esau and the people in Jacob's camp are doing that sort of *sulcha*[90] feast. They're going their own ways now.
>
> Jacob is about to settle down, *Vayiqen et chelqat hasadeh,*[91] he buys himself a field, he acquires that. That's going to be his base of operations. Well, what happens

---

90 **Sulcha**, סלחה. Hebrew: reconciliation, ceremony of reconciliation.
91 Gen. 33:19. וַיִּקֶן אֶת־חֶלְקַת הַשָּׂדֶה

afterwards is [voice expresses ominous anticipation] *bom-be-bom-bom*![92] But in the meantime, there is that moment that says the boundaries have been set, but they're permeable.

4. LESSONS FROM THESE STORIES

Encountering and Integrating the Twin Self

The following month, at the beginning of the next session of the Primal Myths series,[93] Schachter-Shalomi reminds participants where they were left in the story. He says:

> We came as far as Jacob's encounter with his brother Esau and we came away with that wonderful and amazing recognition that "we have seen Esau and it was us."[94]

Schachter-Shalomi reminds the participants of their review (and partial re-enactment) of Jacob's engagement with his twin self.

> And in this encounter of being our own twin and walking away from that place, with that limp that this gives us....

He refers to an experiential exercise incorporated into the Genesis weekend in which each participant was led to discover

---

92 Referring to the next chapter (Gen. 34) in which Jacob's daughter Dinah is raped (or at least seduced) and two of Jacob's sons, citing a need to avenge their dishonor, deceive and horrifyingly massacre all the men of the town from which Jacob has bought his land, causing the family to have to flee.

93 The next weekend retreat, the third of the series, focused on the story of Josef and the phenomenon of dreams.

94 Schachter-Shalomi refers to the famous punch line from a Pogo comic strip by cartoonist Walt Kelly in which the character Pogo announces "We have met the enemy and he is us." Kelly parodied a message sent by U.S. Navy Commodore Oliver Hazard Perry after the Battle of Lake Erie that announced "We have met the enemy and they are ours."

in himself or herself a twin self who was selected as particularly alien or opposite in character or personality.

> In other words, if you want to be clean, clear, without any flaws, you must project your shadow [95] on someone else. If you want to own it and integrate it in yourself, then how are you to deal with it except to accept who you are. And this is where we left off.

In recounting the Jacob and Esau saga during the second retreat of the series, most of the account was unfolding during the Torah service, and that limited some of the expatiation Schachter-Shalomi might have made on the implications for human relations in general. But in their preparation for that weekend, participants had been asked to read through the book of Genesis thinking about the implications of the family relations and their difficulties. What, Schachter-Shalomi asked them to ask themselves, could have been done differently? What strategies were used and how did they work out?

What would we want for ourselves in the way of harmonious relations with others in the human family? What might this take when—even in one's own nuclear family of origin—there can arise such striking differences in outlook and values and personality?

One of the points that Schachter-Shalomi did bring out, and one he returned to at the beginning of the following retreat, is the struggle with the inner twin, the shadow side. As long as we are rejecting parts of ourselves, and projecting that on some "other," we are very likely to create intolerance, oppression, or even warfare with those we have named the other. Schachter-Shalomi sees the Biblical text as recognizing that pitfall and offering *torah*, teaching, about avoiding it. This joins some of the other lessons Schachter-Shalomi has flagged.

---

95 **Shadow, shadow aspect**. In Jungian psychology, an aspect of the personality that the conscious self does not recognize or acknowledge.

Other Lessons

There was the lesson illustrated by Cain, whose "face fell" when his sacrifice was not favored, leading to "sin crouching at the door." When Cain didn't overcome that, his sense of outraged entitlement led to violence and the Bible's first death—at the hands of a brother.

There was the lesson in the way Abraham proposed to Lot to divide the territory when their shepherds were quarreling over sharing the pastureland. Abraham allowed Lot to choose what territory he would like for himself, and then went the other way. This was a harmonious solution where there was enough territory to do so. It illustrated how one could exercise the self command not to get caught up in the quarrels but respond generously with an offer that maintained peace and maximized the well-being of the family as a whole.

Jacob had done something similar in the arrangement he had made with Laban over his wages after he had worked off his debt for his wives. Spotted and striped offspring would be his; the more common plain sheep would be Laban's. But in that case the strategy was not successful, because Laban was too deceitful and greedy and just made off with the spotted and striped sheep. So Jacob left Paddan Aram clandestinely with his wives and flocks, with the hope of avoiding or minimizing the strife.

Isaac's choice in continuing to dig wells until the Philistines gave up disputing with him can also be seen in the same spirit.

It may be an example of the same solution when Hagar and Ishmael are sent out from the home of Abraham and Sarah. A great nation is to come from each, God promises, but not the same nation. They have different destinies and need their own space to develop and play out those destinies.

But we also see the situations in which dividing territory cannot work, where there is a limited resource that can't be simply divided. Cain saw God's favor over the sacrifices as a limited resource. Isaac had only one first-born blessing to give out, and Jacob wanted it for himself.

Territorial Imperative and the Amity Response

Having looked at these stories, we must ask how we can work out something better. Schachter-Shalomi emphasizes that we have to know what we're dealing with in such situations of conflict. It's not enough to have ideals and say what "should" happen. If there are more powerful and more primitive forces within us, and even competing values, it would do violence to the psyche to force the supposed ideal on oneself, and violence to the human community to try to force others into an ideal mold.

Later in the third session of the series, Schachter-Shalomi says a little more about why we need caution here, and why we need to not be carried away, by our first glimpses of new ideals, into imagining that anything is possible.

What has been termed our "reptilian brain" can trump all our ideals and the constraints of our social institutions and the conditioning those institutions have worked on us. An ancient force of survival programming takes over.

> Now if you recall that at the beginning of our work together in this series, we talked about how difficult it was for people at this time on the planet to be able to manage to become good instruments for its healing. And one of the things that we are dealing with is that we inhabit an instrument, a body, that took—people talk about long long periods of time just to become what it is. And that we went through at least three levels of formation.
>
> The oldest and strongest one is what has to do with that part of the brain that people speak of as the reptilian part. That part that has to do with survival. It is so strongly set to issues of survival that at times when we move into the survival mode all the values that we have accumulated [are unavailable. These are values we accumulated] not instinctually, but by dint of the civilization that we are a part of, by the structure of our culture, by the reason of our institutions, by who we are as part of the institutions in which we live that govern our social being.

> When survival stuff comes, and comes raw, and we have nothing else to fall back on, if someone is going to try to reason, try to talk to the cortex, about stuff that happens in the reptilian brain, it doesn't work.

Schachter-Shalomi continues here to describe how highly skilled technologists can show remarkable mastery in some areas but strikingly fail in others. When designing weapons systems, they take into consideration the full subtlety of pilots' reactions in combat. But when it comes to social problems, such as the poverty, decay, and crime of the urban ghetto, they fail to understand the dynamics of the problems there. Schachter-Shalomi says this is because of their own reptile brain responses to the perceived dangers to themselves of the crime and other violence that poverty is breeding there. The reptile brain then insists on "law and order" (more police, more prisons) as a solution.

I return now to Schachter-Shalomi's development in the second weekend. Continuing after he leaves Jacob and Esau amicably going their separate ways, Schachter-Shalomi moves into a broader consideration of the practicalities of amicable co-existence for our present day human family.

> Ardrey[96] points out that the urge for territory is a stronger urge than sex. Certain experiments have shown that when the sex drive goes down (in fish in tanks and so forth when the temperature is lowered) nevertheless territorial instincts still remain at that time. And here is where I feel we have been given an ethic that doesn't respect our side of things.

Schachter-Shalomi speaks about the relation between boundaries and loving. Real loving requires boundaries. Love is

---

96 **Robert Ardrey**, *The Territorial Imperative,* a book that Schachter-Shalomi recommended participants read in preparation for this weekend.

relationship, which pre-supposes boundaries and some level of separation: it is specifically in the softening and crossing of those boundaries that love consists.

Were there no separation it would not be love but a state of unity or nonduality—a different thing, the mere preaching of which does not seem to offer an immediately effective path to the solution of our human relationship difficulties.

> Let me speak about this turning the other cheek, for a moment. I'm not saying that this is a wrong thing to do. I'm saying that having learned first to have one's own space, then you go to turn the other cheek. If you turn the other cheek before you have learned to have your own space, then it isn't even appreciated. You do not come from a place you can be loving, you come like a *shmate,*[97] you come like a *shmegegge,*[98] somebody who is such a nothing that—!
>
> When you come to me and I turn my other cheek, in a loving way to you, then my boundary is still there, and I'm saying to you, loving you and accepting your anger at this point, I think I can absorb just a little bit more, here's my other cheek. But damn it, I'm not gonna give you my head and my nose and my eyes and so on.

But what if one could do more?

> That moment, if I can [manage to] not go into my knee jerk reflex... that is, how should I say, it's called *middat chasidut,*[99] it's like going way beyond the second mile at this point.

---

97 **Shmate** שמאַטע. Yiddish: A rag; someone you can wipe your feet on.

98 **Shmegegge**. American-Yiddish: A disdained, unadmirable person; a drip.

99 **Middat chasidut**. Hebrew: a noble deed worthy of praise; going beyond what one is obligated to do; expression of special piety.

It's more than that it is a level of saintliness that is a lot to ask of people. It has the practical problem that it won't *work* to ask it of people.

> Let's take a look what does it take to maintain one's own bailiwick. Because if that's not said, if I do not respect what is built into me, this program, it won't work. I may say it's time for this program to change, but what changes these programs?

Maybe whatever changes them is at work, part of the spiritual evolution of creation. But this takes time, a lot of time, perhaps more time than we have.

> You may remember this wonderful person, Itzhak Bentov,[100] *alav ha shalom.*[101] He pointed out that if you have all the time in the world for the genetic programming to change, that's to say if our technological reach hadn't gone so much faster, built up the speed with which it's going, then we would have a long long biological time to catch up.
>
> Let's take a look at how that goes. Teilhard de Chardin is teaching us. I'm using his teaching because it's easy and it's available. It's not different from what's found in the Kabbalah, it's not different what's found in the teaching about the *kalpas*[102] in India. It's the same teaching. It says this is how time goes.
>
> Remember when we talked last session about the seven days of creation, how each day came in another awareness

---

100 **Itzhak Bentov** (1923–1979). Scientist and consciousness scholar; author of *Stalking the Wild Pendulum*. Bentov's friends were shocked when he died in a commercial airliner crash in 1979.

101 **Alav ha-shalom**. Hebrew: "May peace be upon him."

102 **Kalpa**. कल्पः. Sanskrit: a very long age of time in Hindu tradition.

of how and what this planet is? Now planet is here, and needs life to fill it. And the *biogenesis*, that first phase where life begins to proliferate over the planet, it takes oodles and oodles and oodles of time—several million years before we get to the place where you can begin to speak of awareness in the way in which even the Neanderthal, the Cro Magnon, became aware.

Remember I read you[103] this thing about the film that would take a year from the beginning of the big bang, when everything was happening, the exciting stuff was happening December 31st, and the last few minutes of the film, and when there was one frame, then you begin to see what time it took for the *noögenesis*, the second phase, where consciousness, communication is being brought into the world. In comparison to the first period of time, the speed with which, from the time people learned to speak to each other to the time we have global communication that you can direct dial Timbuktu now on the telephone and you begin to see how fast that was in comparison to the other periods, how long it took.

I want to stay with this for a little. The next phase Teilhard de Chardin talks about. From the *biogenesis* we went to the *noögenesis*, consciousness. And then we get to what he calls *christogenesis*, which is the divinization of the planet. To take the planet and to make it divine.

Remember when we talked about how we are theotropic beings. As heliotropic beings grow towards the sun, we grow towards God. This is the *Atman* project that Ken Wilber[104] talks about. This is how Atman wants to become

---

103 In the Creation weekend Schachter-Shalomi had read a passage from the book *The Global Brain* by Peter Russell.

104 **Ken Wilber** (1949–). New Age thinker and teacher. He is the author of *The Atman Project: A Transpersonal View of Human Development,* among other books.

Brahman, in that language.[105] It is that which is coaxed, and what happens is that ever greater aggregates of mind-ness, of conscious-ness, of divine-ness, are brought into the thing.

So when we talk about that we are now in the new age, what has happened in Auschwitz, in Hiroshima, the moon walk, the computer technology, what's happened all around this shift is that we have moved at such a fantastic speed from a communication information thing to a place where we don't have enough space to put all the information that keeps coming in. It is stacking up. How do you talk about when too many planes are coming into an airport? You say they're getting stacked up.

Finding Balance

This greater consciousness moves beyond crude territoriality. But we still must balance apparently conflicting values. How is this done? How would we know how to guide the emergence of the next phases, while we are not fully there ourselves?

The territorial imperative in its pure form is limited. It wants everything for itself alone, but in fact no individual can survive alone. Cooperation is essential for survival. This brings in what could be called the amity imperative. But again, Schachter-Shalomi repeats, it can't be forced. The competing needs must be acknowledged and respected.

Territorial imperative, on the one hand, coming down to the single individual. The single individual cannot survive. So the amity principle says that several individuals combine so that they can go hunting together, so they can plant together, so they can midwife when somebody else gives birth, so there can be shared stuff. And in this sharing what

---

105 **Atman** आत्मन् **Brahman** ब्रह्मन्. Sanskrit, from the Indian Hindu tradition. Atman is the higher, universal Self. Brahman is the Absolute or ground of existence, the supreme Godhead.

is taking place is that the amity response and the territorial response get sometimes into a place where they create problems for each other.

What we have tried to do is to create an ethic without looking at the territorial response, or create laws that honor the territorial response without taking in sight the amity response.

Boundaries. It cannot be anymore that you should have disregard for Basques, for the Welsh, they all have to be recognized as people. So nationalism said small aggregates of specific people have to be recognized, their rights have to be given to them, you cannot ignore that.

Once this has been established, then we start looking and you see that we have blocs and alliances and now we're getting to the place where we are seeing that the boundaries are no longer there. What has happened is that whereas before it was just you and me and the clan that lives in this particular cave, it got to be federations of larger aggregates. It got to be larger aggregates, to states, larger aggregates, to the United States. It has gotten so people are talking about one of the solutions for the middle east is a United States of the Middle East.

It's not possible to keep on partitioning. How much are you going to partition? The *enantiodromia*[106] has happened. The pendulum has swung to the most minute possibility of splitting off individuals and now it is swinging back. How do we integrate larger units?

Now we're finding in transpersonal psychology and so on that we're working with unities that are larger, that we are participants in. That we want to contact who we are

---

106 **Enantiodromia**. Term introduced by psychiatrist Carl Jung for a principle that an excess of any force or tendency will produce a reaction back in the opposite direction.

part of. And that which we are part of needs us to have a membrane as an individual cell.

All ethics that are going to ignore my need for the space that I need won't work. The creation of an ethic that will honor self-boundaries is as important as the one that will say "That cell is part of an organ, and that organ is part of an organism, and that organism that we are is part of a larger aggregate."

When somebody says "Why do you want space for yourself?" The answer is "Because I want to participate in the larger thing. I want to participate in a healthy way in the larger thing. And I cannot be healthy unless that boundary of mine is going to be respected. If I respect it then someone else can respect it too."

Conclusions from the Genesis Weekend

The selection of transcripts included in this chapter had three main components. Schachter-Shalomi starts with some images and thought experiments about the relationship of male and female in the world. That brought out (among other things) the idea of a need to make space in the marital relationship. The image or meta-phor was the turning of the powerful but compact *yud* (י) into two *heh*'s (ה and ה) to make space in each partner. This space having been made, a child could be created for them.

Adam and Eve had the first wondrous human experience of creating a child. But their children didn't know how to share territory harmoniously, or how to cope with a limited resource in the form of an invidious comparison by God. A terrible result: the first death was a murder. God sends Cain away to find his own way and his own territory, and to develop other human skills beyond agriculture and animal husbandry.

The space of Rebecca's womb made a place for both Esau and Jacob to grow. But it became too tight, and they felt crushed, and struggled for more space. This physical competition in the womb continued to play out as they grew into very different sorts of people, and came to know that there was only one birthright and one primary blessing of the lineage. They separated, each became wealthy at a great distance from the other, then met again. Should they re-form a household together? Would that be like going back into the womb together? They choose separate territories.

But the world we live in has filled up. There is no longer unsettled territory waiting for members of the human family who can't, or don't want to, live together cooperatively.

And something else: we have seen the earth from outer space. It is one planet, one beautiful, living planet. Global communication means we know at least something about everyone everywhere. The narrow "us" and "them" models that were possible when we had only the vaguest sense about anyone beyond our clan and our nearest struggles—these models not only no longer work, they don't even seem believable.

How do we meet these challenges? Schachter-Shalomi is suggesting that we reach back into the collective memory codified in Torah to see what it can tell us about the dynamics of these things. The old way of understanding, in which Jacob stood for everything good and Esau for everything bad, is not going to help us solve our present problems living in one planetary family with too many people—including people very radically different from us.

Schachter-Shalomi is not trying to replace the old story with a new one just as rigid. He is inviting us to look into the source (the Hebrew Bible) for different lessons, ones that will help us now.

The lesson Schachter-Shalomi draws from Genesis in this retreat isn't that people need to get along and find a way to share this planet. We already know that. What he means to offer here is a way to look anew at Torah to find insights that will guide us to find workable ways to do what we know must be done and to discover ways to avoid pitfalls we've already learned yield unsuccessful or disastrous results.

Even mistakes can be learned from. Or perhaps it is especially mistakes that offer to thoughtful analysis the most useful lessons.

From the fourth weekend,
"Exodus"

6
Why Go to Egypt?

Why did God send the Israelites to Egypt? Did it just happen, or was there a purpose?

In the fourth session of the Primal Myths series, Schachter-Shalomi begins by taking participants on a journey that must have been a tour-de-force performance, sweeping them up and carrying them along in an immersion into his vision of what living in Egypt for those hundreds of years must have been like.

The way Schachter-Shalomi structured the presentation showed literary depth and imagination. (It may also have shown the influence or insight of his collaborator, Eve Ilsen, who has a reputation as a master of myth and ritual.) He doesn't just give us a slide show of Egyptian artifacts. He sets it all up as Abraham's dream, a vision God shows Abraham in the awe-filled and weird night sacrifice ritual in which God reveals to Abraham that his descendents will go to Egypt and be oppressed and enslaved there for four hundred years. The way this is done will be described below and Schachter-Shalomi's narration quoted.

The *mise en scène* of the slide show seemed important enough that I did not want to leave it out of this study. It shows a dimension of Schachter-Shalomi's understanding of the meaning of that central event of Jewish history, the sojourn in Egypt. What the Jewish people learned, and how that experience may have helped prepare them for their destiny, has major implications for a Jewish attitude towards other civilizations or cultures Jews find themselves living amidst.

But how do we grasp what that experience of Egypt was for the Israelites? Do we ever do the exercise of imagining the Biblical peoples *in* the Egyptian civilization? Or do we see the Bible stories in a Bible context and Egyptian civilization in a very different context—a world history textbook or a museum exhibit or a mummy horror movie?

The Reader's Imaginative Participation

Schachter-Shalomi has used the participants' experience of his re-enactment of Abraham's vision to convey a certain teaching. He set it up the way he did because the immersion in the experience allowed participants to learn in a way they might not have, or perhaps could not have, learned from a lecture.

Because I am conveying this here in writing, one of the leanest forms of communication, you as reader will not have the experience the participants had. There is no darkened room, no slide images. And there is not Schachter-Shalomi's expressive voice communicating so much more than the words he chooses. Only the bare words, spelled out on paper, are left, along with a few attempts of mine to suggest to you what I experienced listening to the audio files.

Consequently, I must make an appeal to you as readers. I invite you to summon up your sympathetic imagination to place yourself in that room, to permit yourself to come under the spell, to let Schachter-Shalomi's images and vision work on you. He is trying to undermine a limited and one-dimensional understanding of the sojourn in Egypt by bringing attention to a context that is usually not acknowledged. He is planting a seed that may suggest other dimensions, that may cause different things to be noticed in the future.

Slideshow

It was evening on the Friday night that was the first night they gathered together for this retreat. The room was darkened. At the front a screen was ready to display a slide presentation.

Schachter-Shalomi set the tone of awe and a sense of the faintly magical by beginning with what is in itself a spine-tingling episode in which Abraham makes a powerful and weird covenant ritual demanded by God and in which God makes a chilling prediction of the future to him. Here's how that goes in Genesis Chapter 15.

The word of YHVH comes to Abram in a vision, telling him again that his reward will be very great. Abram replies, asking disconsolately what God has to give him, since he is childless and his servant Eliezar is to inherit his house. He continues even more explicitly that God has given him no offspring. God replies that Eliezer will not be his heir; his own son will be. Then he takes him outside and shows him the stars. "'Look at the heavens and count the stars if you are able to count them.' And he said to him, 'So your descendants will be.'"

Abram has heard this sort of promise before. He has been told that his descendants would be as the grains of sand of the desert. But no descendents have come to him. Still, we are told that Abram had faith in YHVH and accounted him righteous. But some sense of lingering despondency may have been sensed, and God goes on: "'I am YHVH; I brought you out from Ur of the Chaldeans to give for you this land to possess.' But Abram says "My lord YHVH, in what shall I know that I shall possess it?' And God said to him, 'Take for me a three year old heifer and a three year old female goat and a three year old ram and a turtledove and a young pigeon.' And he took all of these for him and he cut them in the middle and he put each piece to be opposite its other. But the birds he did not cut."

As Abram sits with this macabre path before him, birds of prey come, but Abram drives them away. "And it happened as the sun went down, a deep sleep was falling over Abram. And behold, a terrifying great darkness was falling on him."

In this deep sleep, out of this terrifying great darkness, Abram hears a more specific prediction about his numerous offspring-to-be. "God said to Abram, 'You must know for certain that your offspring will be aliens in a land that is not theirs; and they will serve them and they will oppress them for four hundred years.'"[1] God promises that after that time he will bring judgment on the nation they serve and his offspring will go out again. And God momentarily softens the chill of the prediction with a promise that Abram himself will die in peace in a good old age.

But we are not finished with the awesome and dread-filled scene: it moves on to another striking and cinematic apparition. "And it happened the sun was gone and it was dark. And behold a smoking firepot and a flaming torch which went through between these half pieces."

The chapter finishes with the narrator stepping back out of the scene and informing us that on that day YHVH made a covenant with Abram that he would give to his offspring the land from the river of Egypt to the Euphrates, enumerating at length the peoples in present possession of that land (a qualifier on the enumeration that is, of course, itself ominous: this "gift" is one that is presently in the possession of others who no doubt believe it to be theirs).

Here is Schachter-Shalomi's *midrash* on this already-highly-theatrical scene. He enters imaginatively into Abram's state of mind as he sits between the halves of the animals, meditatively recreating Abram's thoughts. Schachter-Shalomi's voice, always rich and powerful and expressive, took on a particular depth as he narrated, carrying as well a slightly dreamy, hypnotic quality. (Ellipses in the transcription are Schachter-Shalomi's pauses in his re-creation of Abram's ponderings and appeals to God.)

> Promises, promises. Promises and promises and promises. God, I'm afraid. I'm getting older and it's dark. I have prepared for you sacrifices and I've set them up. And here's a fire for the sacrifice. ... Oh, what is this vulture doing descending on the sacrifice? AWAY! ... In this dark

---

1 Gen. 15:13: יָדֹעַ תֵּדַע כִּי־גֵר | יִהְיֶה זַרְעֲךָ בְּאֶרֶץ לֹא לָהֶם וַעֲבָדוּם וְעִנּוּ אֹתָם אַרְבַּע מֵאוֹת שָׁנָה

> night, in this terror, I hear a voice. "Abraham, go out, look at the stars. Can you count them?" … "*Nu*,[2] who can count the stars? … Yes, you mean to say I will have so many children? *Oy*, God, God, how do I know this isn't just a dream? Because there is something unpleasant awaiting them? These children that I will have will be slaves in a land that isn't theirs? … Oh, *Ribono Shel Olam*, what kind of land is that? Where they have to be slaves? You show me visions, show me that land."

Schachter-Shalomi, keeping the same deep and slightly dreamy voice now invites the participants to take chairs so they can see what's on the screen, "and you will find out what was shown to Abraham." As each slide appears, the images largely speak for themselves.

Schachter-Shalomi's narration is evocative, dream-like hints; hardly commentary, certainly not lecture. With virtuosity he creates the attunement of his intention to give participants a window into what he is casting as Abraham's vision in the strange darkness. Without having the slides we must, of course, imagine from the hints what the participants must have been seeing. (Ellipses are pauses in Schachter-Shalomi's narration, probably mostly between slide images.)

> The dimensions of the pyramids. … It is flat around there. Some of the stones were quarried far away. They had only light wagons in those days. The chariots on two wheels for the cavalry. … We get to see closer here, what a pyramid was made of. Lesser grave sites below. … For the laborer at the end of the day, a blessed moment when rest comes. … Water on this side and stark desert on the other; and the date palms that nourished people at the edge. … The gardens of an empire. … Akhenaten … not only the heart but the whole image made of stone. … In order for these circles

---

2 **Nu** נו. Yiddish: A protean word of immense usefulness. Meanings vary by context. Some are: So? Well? What about it? Well, then… .

to fit on top of one another, the precision with which they had to be hewn, woe the slave who would miss or spoil one of those stones. Always bigger than life, after that. ... Can you imagine what it took to put those transom stones on top of the columns? Make those columns stand up and not to break? Remember that obelisk in the storage city. ... And it looks as if the pharoahs are carrying the ceilings on their heads. ... Inside a tomb. ... So if there is a mountain, you don't have to build one. But if you build one, proportions have to be with great mathematical precision. ... What glorious design was behind all these buildings! ... Facing the desert, Colossi of Akhenatens protecting the lush valley of the Nile. ...

The goddess with a lion face, Sekhmet, powerful, gentle and fierce. Sekhmet glorious. ... Anubis with the key of life. Is he taking life out of the pharoah, or giving it to him? ... A jackal god. ... The falcon, Horus, a breast plate fit for kings. To make this, without the tools we have today. The labor that went into such a piece of jewelry. ... The pharoah, supported by his beast of burden, the whole face of the golden pharoah on the back of this piece. .... The scarabs, lowly beetles, making fertile the soil. ... Stories and pictures. Holy picture signs. Heiro-glyphics. ... Anubis again, over a dead pharoah. ... Those stylized beards. Hatshepsut. Queen, king of Egypt, wore a false one. ... Within that oval, a whole name, a whole story. Cartouche, these circles are called. ... Egyptian signs of the Zodiac, that might have inspired Maurice Sendak. ... Horus, the falcon and the king. ... Sarcophagus. ... The cover of that is heavier than one person can lift. Always amazed at the amount of muscle that was needed in the absence of machinery, or even beasts, to do this work. Labor intensive, slave intensive economy. ...

When people elsewhere ran around in bear skins and could hardly do more than grunt, here was a language and a philosophy. A high culture. …. The serpent, the pharoah, I don't know what story is behind this. … A domestic scene, a he and a she and a game on a board, just as we saw in the movie, Nefertari and her father-in-law. … Inlaid work, with such delicacy. … A preoccupation of a king to make sure that he had furnished his sepulchre during his lifetime. … The glory, now mummy. … The faces we see, both in the pictures and in this mummy remind us more of European than of African faces. … The mummy now shriveled and shrunk is not a good way to display the remains. … A gold cask, with a larger than life image of a king now at rest, still holding the insignia of office in his crossed arms. … Reminiscent of those Russian dolls that have inside of them dolls and inside of them dolls. …

The king, sits about in all his glory. I envy the elegance of their bodies. Look at those features. The nobility. Why are those hats so tall? Perhaps to indicate a cranial capacity beyond that of other human beings. When we mention the *shekhinah*[3] covering us with her wings, is the hat, the headgear the pharoah wears, not an approximation of that? … While here, statues are depicted with one leg ahead as if to step resolutely into the future, and with a noble consort at his side. … Again, protecting his empire. Proudly. Could you now see in his headgear the wings and the beak of the falcon? …

A couple. In all those pictures and images that we see, the woman together with the man. There is something to learn from each. … Here you can see them. …. *Nu*, so you don't have photographers, so you have sculptors, and they will immortalize you in slightly idealized mien. …

---

3 **Shekhinah**. Hebrew: the divine presence, indwelling or immanent in the world. Grammatically feminine. Sometimes personified as a protective or comforting presence, as the "Sabbath Bride," or even as the "divine feminine" with goddess-like qualities.

A headband that might remind you of American Indians. … And other features too, like Aztec, Mayan, and African busts, heads. … Ahhh! Would you appoint this man to be the major-domo of your household? He didn't quite rate a stone statue, he was just carved out of wood. But, competent! …

Ah, so what, so he's got short legs. But he's got some *kinderlekh*, and a loving wife who puts her arm on his, and he, the eager scribe of a king, ready to take down every one of his words. Scribe! This almost-wizard, to be able to make pictures that speak. A very honored profession. When we speak of our rabbis, centuries later, as the scribes. … Spinning, weaving. … Ahh. The bakers. Man who is bringing the baked goods to the pharoah. … Musicians. …

There is so much beauty there. So much appreciation of what is nice in life. … And in death. … Alabaster. … The aesthetic of beautiful things. … You don't buy such things for yourself. You commission them as gifts for someone special. … And this is how the vineyards worked … and the fields were hoed … Again, the baskets. The fish that is being brought, the yoke with which these things are carried. … The slaves, who in this position had to wait, and wait, and wait upon his master. That's where we got the word waiter from. That's a waiter. … All this is done with labor by hand. … Rich birdlife of Egypt is impressive. … Here, a pharoah's army. Often in the form of statues to protect him after death, as part of the sepulchre. … And here, someone who goes from or to the market. …

Leaving Egypt, for the desert, and the more you're there alone, the more you see things in rays and revelation. Could you imagine you stand before this one, and someone told you, "This is your God, O Israel"?

The slides are finished. His voice still holding the attunement, Schachter-Shalomi says:

> Staying in touch with what you saw, bring your chairs now to the front of the hall.

Schachter-Shalomi asks the participants to remember what they have seen as he goes through the story of the Exodus again. He quotes the admonitions from the Jewish tradition enjoining the telling of the story. But why is it that the telling of this story is so important? By telling the story, and keeping it vivid in our imagination, knowing that *we* were there, the lessons can be more fully realized.

> The way our sages say it, *"v'khol hamarbeh l'saper biytziy'at mitzrayim, harey zeh m'shubach."*[4] "Whoever will keep on talking about the going out of Egypt, the more praiseworthy it is to tell about it."[5] There is something that happens to us when we tell that story.

The School of Egypt

But what are the lessons? What was the point? Why did the Israelites have to go to Egypt, what did they learn there, why did it have to be just the way it was, and why did the exodus from Egypt have to happen the way it did? As he tells the story, Schachter-Shalomi reveals his vision of those matters.

Under the influence of the slideshow, one might start to think about the exposure to the high culture of advanced civilization.

---

4   וְכָל הַמַּרְבֶּה לְסַפֵּר בִּיצִיאַת מִצְרַיִם, הֲרֵי זֶה מְשֻׁבָּח:

5   This teaching appears in the Passover *Haggadah* at the point at which it introduces the retelling of the story. The Passover Seder is a celebration of the leaving of Egypt, with ritualized re-enactments of the events, and having as the central theme the re-telling of the story, with special emphasis on making sure children remain familiar with it. The *Haggadah* (Hebrew, "recounting") is the text that sets out the order of the service and includes readings, teachings, and songs. It also includes the Rabbinic injunction to remember the exodus as if *we ourselves* were going out of Egypt.

This might be a new thought in connection with this story, since from a surface reading of the Biblical account, one might well carry away a sense that Egypt was only exile, suffering, alienation. Josef had found favor and become rich and powerful, of course, but soon (so the impression is left) oppression followed. The image remembered most vividly is the slavery, being beaten by taskmasters, being forced to make bricks without straw.

Later, Schachter-Shalomi refers explicitly to this.

> So, while there has been up to now an emphasis on us telling the story about how we were in Egypt and how bad that was for us, I haven't yet seen the other side of that, of how much we learned there. What kind of a college that was for us.

But what does Egyptian high civilization have to do with us? one might ask. It is still an alien society with an alien religion. We were only sojourners there, and for the last part of it enslaved. There was even that attempt to kill all the baby boys at birth. This is, of course, a reasonable question. But consider, Schachter-Shalomi might say, what this people's trajectory seems to be.

Jacob, the sitter-in-the-tents, the manipulator within the family circle, goes to live with Laban and learns shepherding. He becomes so good at it that he manages, even with Laban's trickery and greediness, to make himself astonishingly rich in animal stock (as we see from his gifts to Esau) by the time he leaves Laban.

His son Josef is a lad not, apparently, old enough to be originally sent out along with his brothers and the flocks; he only joins them when his father sends him out to check on them. Josef is of a shepherding family, but he is a dreamer, and not yet even a shepherd himself. This boy is then abruptly sent to Egypt as a slave. What happens? He educates himself rapidly and learns to serve in the house of a high official of Pharoah so effectively that he is elevated to complete authority of that house.

Jacob's is a family, it seems, with a talent for learning, and for learning from new environments. But if they had remained as shepherds and sojourners in Canaan, what there might have been to learn would have been severely limited. But perhaps this family—the seed of Abraham—had a greater destiny. What would they need to prepare themselves for that destiny?

After the participants have moved their chairs:

> Threads I would like you to keep in your fingers, or at least in the fingers of your mind while we will tell the story again. …
>
> One of the threads is that Egypt is high culture. Where would I send my firstborn son[6] to the school of hard knocks? I wouldn't send him to the hinterland of the world. I would send him right there where the state-of-the art of being human is being lived, is being practiced. The highest culture available at that time.

But notice that they do not go to become Egyptians. Assimilation into the Egyptian culture is not the aim. Perhaps their destiny is even greater than—or at least different from—the culture and civilization of Egypt. So how can they live there and learn without assimilation? And what is the best way to learn?

> People say to me sometimes, "I want to come and learn with you. Can I come and learn with you?" And the answer is, "You come and learn with me? You'll learn… *something*. You really want to learn, come and work with me." When you come and work with me, ahhh, this is a different story. There is something that gets learned in the work that doesn't get learned in the learning. Learning still has a distance there.

Schachter-Shalomi now returns momentarily to the prediction God makes to Abraham on that terrible night recounted in Genesis

---

6   Schachter-Shalomi refers to God's statement, which Moses is instructed to carry to Pharoah in Ex 4:22, that Israel is his (God's) firstborn son: בְּנִי בְכֹרִי יִשְׂרָאֵל. In understanding what God might have wanted to bring to pass, Schachter-Shalomi asks himself what he would do with his own firstborn son.

Chapter 15. He quotes each phrase from the prediction in Genesis 15:13:[7]

> *Ki ger yihyeh zar'akha b'eretz lo lahem*: Your children will be strangers in a land that isn't theirs. *Avadum*: They will make them work hard. *V'inu otam*: And they will suppress them, they will give them pain. *Arba' me'ot shanah*: For four hundred years."
>
> Terrible! It's a long time! Will they be able to make their way out again?

This is not an easy school to which the Israelites are being sent. And success is no sure thing.

> Will they learn what they have come to learn, or will they be crushed by the oppression? If the oppression is less than everything it needs to be, they won't learn what they have to learn. If it is more than what it has to be, they won't be able to learn what they have to learn.
>
> What a difficult line this is, to create that learning challenge, that learning oppression, that learning *work*, slavery, situation that is necessary in order to become what one has to become!
>
> That's one thread that will go through the story.
>
> So every time when it looks like "*Oy vey!*" that's the school. That's the learning. That's the stress that's going to carve out the space on the inside so that there will be room for the learning.

Now Schachter-Shalomi considers how things may have evolved from the time of the first covenant with Abraham. Abraham had two sons. One, Isaac, got the line of blessing and the inheritance of the original covenant promise. The other, Ishmael, had

---

7 Gen. 15:13. וַיֹּאמֶר לְאַבְרָם יָדֹעַ תֵּדַע כִּי־גֵר | יִהְיֶה זַרְעֲךָ בְּאֶרֶץ לֹא לָהֶם וַעֲבָדוּם וְעִנּוּ אֹתָם אַרְבַּע מֵאוֹת שָׁנָה:

to go out and make his own way. Ishmael is also promised to be the father of a great nation, but it will be a different nation. In the next generation, Isaac has two sons. It is Jacob who gets the line of blessing and inheritance of the original covenant promise. Esau's line continues and prospers, but it is not the Israelite line, and it is at a distance, in his own territory. But in the next generation, Jacob has twelve sons, and they all end up together in Egypt. The tribes that descend from those sons leave Egypt together some centuries later; together they receive the revelation at Sinai; together they conquer Canaan and settle there. Each branch of Jacob's family brings something into the Israelite inheritance.

> So a covenant is made with Abraham, a covenant is made with Isaac, and is made with Jacob. Finally we have a family that does not have to have part of the family being outered, being culled away; all the members of the family are part of that family.

But how do they stay one family while in Egypt? If they are there for four hundred years, how could it be that they have not simply become Egyptians?

> Then they are being sent into a hothouse, into a situation where they are being kept together by a common need. You remember what happened with shepherds. Shepherds would like to go each on their own way. There wasn't enough room for Abraham and for Lot. So the shepherds fought. What did they say? They said "You take that side, I'll take this side."
>
> But you can't do that in Egypt. They don't like for people who are shepherds to run around on the other side of the Nile where people have their gardens that they have planted and where they grow with irrigation. "We don't want shepherds around these here parts!" So they have to be in their reservation in Goshen.
>
> They're doing, as a people, but their cohesiveness, not of their own choosing, is being created for them. At the time

when there is increase, "and the children of Israel, they were fruitful and they increased and they multiplied greatly and they became very strong,"[8] what would you have expected at that point? That they should disperse! That was the natural movement at that point.

And just at that point they can't disperse. They're being contained much closer, they're being contained in a much harder space. And now, when we learn that lesson, we begin to see that the containment that we experienced in Goshen at that time was that hothouse where they learned. Where we learned.

This being tied down changed the nomadic way of life. Into the fluidity enters some structure. Schachter-Shalomi will explore the relationship and balancing of fluidity and rigidity, of change and stability, later; this makes another major theme of the weekend, and will be taken up in the next chapter.

There is something fluid about being a shepherd. You're *landed* when you're doing agriculture. Year after year, this is your soil, this is your land. If you're a shepherd, you follow the seasons. You go where the pasture is. If one were to describe that one would say that a shepherd is a fluid being in comparison to the landed, anchored, farmer.

The Israelites, for their growth and learning, then, had to be in the culture school and the containment and slavery hothouse of Egypt. They had to be forced into a certain stability and cohesiveness. There was much to learn, but it wouldn't do for them to be too comfortable. Assimilation is not the goal; they needed to remain separated and separately-identified. Slavery ensures that separation, even as they labor at the crafts that teach the skills that will later allow the astonishing construction of the sanctuary.

Schachter-Shalomi now returns for a moment to the idea he had introduced earlier about the importance of the way that Jewish

---

8   Ex 1:7. This is the situation that aroused the concern of Pharoah that led to the enslavement of the Israelites.

tradition and practice take as a core image the experience in Egypt and the experience of the leaving of Egypt. This is evidenced in the annual retelling in the Passover Seder, the constant references in liturgy, and its centrality in the Biblical text.

> The memory of Egypt is so much more because we were in Egypt than had it been if we had not been in Egypt. Year after year the story is being told about the Exodus from Egypt and you begin to see that when Easter and Christianity builds on that energy that was released at that time in Egypt, you begin to see the fantastic power that is in such a person like Moses and such an event like the Exodus.[9]

At the end of the evening, Schachter-Shalomi picks up this thread again. Why Egypt? Why is the experience so very important?

> I would like to look once again at this picture of the hothouse of this people in this particular situation. The kind of learning that we did in Egypt. The kind of learning that gave us a script, that we would know of a God-script, that we would know of a people-script, that we would encrypt our insights and our experience in our story, that we would take from Egypt, from the prophylaxis of circumcision, to the way in which we name some of the people who have some of the best names in our history, Pinchas, Moses, if you go through the names that we have that are still being

---

9   Schachter-Shalomi does not expand on this intriguing observation that Easter and Christianity builds on the energy that was released at the time of the going-out of Egypt, but one can feel its plausibility. The energy of the liberation from slavery, the going forth to the promised land, happening at the time of Passover, is transformed into the Resurrection of Easter and the liberation/salvation of Christianity. This is one of the many startling, throw-away insights Schachter-Shalomi sprinkles through his teachings during these weekends.

used, Egyptian names. When you begin to look at what we
learned at that time.

You look at the story when Abraham went to Pharoah
first, and the whole story with Sarah and Pharoah, the
affair that's going on constantly, Egypt, Egypt, Egypt, the
flight to Egypt when Jesus is a child, what's going on there
with Egypt? What does Egypt have that's so fantastically
attractive? What is that that still lures us to visit the
pyramids, that makes us look for papyri, what is that thing
that makes us feel that when we go into the synagogue of
Maimonides[10] in the outskirts of Cairo in Fustat, and we
pray there, that something special is taking place in that
place.[11]

All this is something we want to incubate this night.

This magic of Egypt is being "incubated" this night. Schachter-
Shalomi has offered something that in some ways is still
embryonic, something that needs to be incubated in the participants' consciousness, or perhaps in deeper parts of their thinking.

The participants will incubate the images and suggestions over
the night, over the weekend, and over coming years of pondering
the meaning of the Egyptian sojourn. But as readers right now, trying imaginatively to re-create the experience Schachter-Shalomi
provided participants using the slide show, what do we have of
specifics?

This idea, that God sent his people, his beloved first-born son
Israel, to Egypt as a school, to learn what they needed to know
for their later destiny, or perhaps to prepare them to receive Torah
on Sinai, is a new one. We're trying to get our minds around it.

---

10 **Maimonides** (1135–1204 CE). Rabbi Moses ben-Maimon, also
   known as Rambam. Highly influential Jewish philosopher and
   scholar.

11 Indeed, one might ask why Maimonides himself chose to settle in
   and live out his life in Egypt rather than in the land of Israel.

Schachter-Shalomi gave some valuable insights with the description of the containment hothouse. He also mentioned the "culture school," and the slides were evocative clues to that; but he has said very little, trusting in the power of the experience and in the incubation process. What might *we* get from those slides that we are only imagining?

One such thing, I would suggest, is the origin of the crafts and technology of art and construction. When reading the instructions for design of the Mishkan, the portable sanctuary in the wilderness, and the account of its actual building, I have always been baffled as to where these people got all the skills to do that fine work. Before going to Egypt, they were shepherds. In Egypt they moved from shepherding to slavery and brick-making (or at least that is all we get in the narrative). But there seems to be quite a sophisticated knowledge and skill bank for working metal and textiles, both for construction and for ornamentation. Imagining the slides of impressive constructions and costuming and jewelry, I have the sense of a missing piece filled in.

Seeing the slides of the jewelry and other finery, one might also think of the jewels, the ornaments of gold and silver, and the beautiful clothing, that the Israelites had asked of their Egyptian neighbors as they were preparing to leave, and that they were given freely, and that they took with them.[12] Now we have pictures to go with that text.

Eve Ilsen, Schachter-Shalomi's collaborator in this series, makes another sort of connection with the jewelry and other finery shown in the slides. Later in the weekend, she led an experiential exercise in which the participants enter imaginatively into the process of walking out of Mitzrayim—walking out of their own familiar and perhaps comfortable but limiting past into freedom. In setting the scene for this, she quotes from the Biblical text and reminds participants of the slides of "stunning jewelry." She proposes that the gold and silver represent the treasure of Egypt,

---

12 Ex. 12:35–36.

the things of lasting value that the Egyptians gave the Israelites "because God disposed the Egyptians favorably towards them."[13] At a time when they are taking only the essentials, only what they can carry on their backs, the sandals on their feet and unleavened dough, they take these treasures.

> And what is the gold and silver that you take with you? It's very interesting, this gold and silver, because it is the wisdom, the enduring stuff, the stuff of value, it's the treasure of Egypt. It's what you have been able to gather of treasure in Egypt. And it is borrowed from the Egyptians. … Aside from that, you're taking only the essentials.

Another thing one might wonder about is the influence of the rich and developed religious culture of the Egyptians. On the one hand, it seems to have nothing to do with the Israelites then or later. By traditional Jewish perspective, the Egyptian religion is idolatry, worship of heavenly bodies and animals, most of the strains historically not even arguably monotheistic. Furthermore, there are references in the audio files for this weekend to the "desert culture" that Jacob's family brought with them—perhaps a simpler, purer faith that had something lacking in the Egyptian culture, for all its sophistication and complexity.[14] The Israelites clearly kept something of this through the centuries of living in Egypt: the religion covenanted at Sinai does not look like the religion of Egypt.

And yet, might some ideas, or some recognition of depth in certain new areas, have come into the religious understanding of the Israelites from this surrounding religious culture?

Inviting participants to contemplate the images from the slides, Ilsen added from her own knowledge of the religious dimensions

---

13 Ex. 12:36.

14 Unfortunately, if there was a presentation or more development of the exploration of the interaction of these religious threads in the Primal Myths weekend, it was not recorded or not preserved.

of the Egyptian culture, the culture that the Israelites were being exposed to in Egypt:

> One of the other things that we know is that Egypt at that time had developed a culture that esoteric and mystical sects are harkening back to.
>
> A great deal of what we have learned from those incredible tombs has to do with the search at that time in Egypt for becoming who you are past just the body. It's asking, "What is it that we are really? How many worlds do we actually live in? What survives? What is true, what is real? And how does one navigate this?" The *how* has to do with all the initiatory practices they had. And that truly must have been going on at some level. We know it because of the literature that has come out of there, and the art. …
>
> The Egyptian *Book of the Dead* has the journey of the soul after you die, involving the re-evaluating of your life, and the various aspects, the gods are various aspects. The places you are initiated through, and they are masculine and feminine and animal and human, there's a great deal of sophistication going on here in a realm of consciousness.

The interplay of the "desert culture," the religious understanding and sensibility that Jacob and his children brought with them, and the Egyptian culture, is something one would love to know more about. The Bible is striking silent on this, leaving us to our speculations and incubations.

Moses

As Schachter-Shalomi continues, another element emerges. Egypt is not the whole story. Part of the story is Moses.

What did Moses need in order to prepare him for the task of leading the people out of Egypt and through the wilderness to the Promised Land?

Just as the Israelites could not have accomplished their mission, and met their destiny, with what they learned as shepherds in

Canaan, Moses could not have been the great prophet and leader he was if he had grown up and lived as an enslaved Hebrew.

Growing up in the palace of Pharoah, the adopted son of the daughter of Pharoah, he not only absorbed the culture and education of the Egyptian nobility, but the character and demeanor of nobility. Perhaps he could imagine freedom, in a way the enslaved Hebrews could not. He could give up riches and privilege, as he did when he had to flee to Midian after killing the Egyptian task-master who was brutalizing Hebrew slaves, but he lived in Midian a free person.

When he sees the Egyptian striking the Hebrew slaves, his sense of justice flares up. Is this because he knows he was born of that tribe? Or is it just that his innate sense of justice rises up in indignation, a sense of justice that has not been beaten down by slavery, and flows directly into action?

Thus, despite all that is made of God's having to push him to take on the mission (and it is clear throughout the narrative that he is not an arrogant or power-hungry person), it's hard to imagine anyone else among the Hebrews who could have done what he did.

This child, adopted by the daughter of Pharoah, and at the same time raised at least in the neonate months [in his Hebrew family]—we don't know, did he grow up, did he know that he grew up in a Jewish home, or did he not grow up in a Jewish home, that's not so clear, neither from the text nor from the story.[15] He is known as Moses, he is drawn from the water, and it is not really let on as to what his parentage was. He is being raised in the palace. And he is seen as a very shining person.

So now we get to the place where he isn't there and he isn't here. There is something about his Jewishness that comes and spoils his Egyptianness and there is something

---

15 By "the story" Schachter-Shalomi evidently refers to Rabbinic midrash and other speculation as opposed to the Biblical text.

> about his Egyptianness that comes and spoils his Jewishness and he doesn't have a place there.
>
> But one thing that he does feel is that anger seeing that oppression when he finally sees it. To the point [that he strikes out]—and had he been raised among Jews, the anger that boiled up in him against the Egyptian taskmaster would never have reached the level of behavior. Do you know what I'm saying? If you have been a kid making your way to Hebrew School and being waylaid on the way and being beaten up by the *shkotzen* from next door, then you know, you already know that you don't act out, you don't become a *khukhem*[16] about that. You try and defend yourself by not hitting back the same way. It was the Egyptian that was in him that gave him the power to slay the Egyptian.

In the Torah Service Saturday morning, Schachter-Shalomi is reading from the Torah scroll with the cantillation and translating as he goes. For each section of the reading he calls certain groups of people from the participants to come up to the Torah scroll (this practice is termed an *Aliyah*, a going-up).

For the second *aliyah* Schachter-Shalomi calls "all who need to learn something from the enemy."

For this section Schachter-Shalomi leyns the account[17] of the daughter of Pharoah drawing the child out, and the child's sister offering (and then fetching) the mother to nurse the child, and the statement by Pharoah's daughter that she will pay the nurse's hire. And the child grew up and she took the child to the daughter of Pharoah. The question is left of how old he was at that point, what did he know. The Hebrew doesn't say; the implication is that he was old enough to be weaned. Schachter-Shalomi then pauses the reading for commentary.

---

16 **Khukhem** חכם. Yiddish. In Hebrew *chakham* is honored as a wise person, a sage. In Yiddish, as *khukhem,* it took on a sarcastic connotation to mean "wise guy,"

17 Exodus Chapter 2 Verses 5–10.

How much the child got consciously I can't guarantee. How much the child got unconsciously, that's a whole other story. The security to stand up to a pharoah later on, and to be able to— Where is it that I feel most weak when I have to stand up to someone who is against me? When I see them looking, when they are in a position of power and I am pleading for a little equity, for a little justice, and I feel at this point weak and empty inside, I feel the crying child that still is crying inside because the unconscious is timeless. So the deprived baby is still in me. And at such moments the deprived baby is what weakens me and makes me accept a dole instead of the rightful thing that I am asking for because I feel the worthlessness.

R'eh[18] Yokheved,[19] look at her, her name, יוֹכֶבֶד. Glory and honor of God. *Yah khuved.* She sees herself honored by being able to have this child. Honored that he is able to be alive and be nursed by her. Whether he got it consciously doesn't matter. The safety, the security he got from that in the first few years, and the mother, knowing that she was under the protection— Can you imagine if she had to worry about an Egyptian inspector is going to come and grab the baby, constantly? What would she have fed the child, insecurity? To know constantly, this is secure, under the protection, nothing is going to harm this child. A sort of regal free zone, as it were, for baby, because of Pharoah's daughter's security for whoever was watching over that child.

So, one might say, the Israelites needed Moses to take them out of Egypt, and Moses needed both the early nurturance at the

---

18 רְאֵה Hebrew: Look! Imperative of to see.

19 **Yokheved** is Moses's mother. Her name is not mentioned here, but it is given later in Exodus 6:20 when the line of descent from Jacob's son Levi is given.

Israelite breast and the the formative nurturance at the high culture of Pharoah's court.

The Israelites had things to learn in Egypt, but they had their own destiny. At a certain point the work had been done and it was time to go on to the next set of lessons. But they could not take themselves out. It had to be done by someone who had never been a slave.

Moses's special double inheritance did more, of course, than give him the strength and leadership to get them out (along with God's help, of course, according to the narrative).

Those forty years in the wilderness, a journey that could have been done in eleven days, were a time of learning from Moses how to replace slave mentality with a consciousness that could conquer and occupy the land that had been promised to their ancestors. It was a discipleship under the influence of a leader whom tradition has (since rabbinic times) called *Moshe Rabbenu*, Moses our teacher.

Despite continual difficulties and rebellions from people who still had much to learn, he left them a thoroughly structured religion, with a complete set of laws, with a complex set of religious and ethical principles, and with a social organization among and within the tribes that prepared them for the next phase. God, of course, is given credit for the instructions. But they had to come through a teacher and leader equal to their transmission and implementation.

7
Rigidity and Change

The first theme of the Exodus weekend was why God would send his "firstborn son, Israel"[1] to an alien land for four hundred years and what education or other development was taking place there. This was explored in the previous chapter.

The second major theme is fluidity versus rigidity, structure and stability versus change. That is the concern of this chapter.

This theme has been lurking, with occasional appearances in passing references, from the beginning of the weekend's unfoldings. The fluid, nomadic shepherds are being placed in a highly structured society. They are confined to one area, Goshen. As they multiply in numbers, they cannot disperse, but are kept together. They are still conscious of their individual ancestral identities as descendents of one or another of the sons of Jacob/Israel, but they remain very distinct from the Egyptians. They are so distinct, even after hundreds of years, that the pharaoh (a new one, we are told, one who doesn't know Josef) is concerned about them becoming so numerous and worries that they might aid an enemy should Egypt be invaded. He refers to them as they evidently called themselves: as a people descended from Israel (that is, Jacob): *am b'nei Yisrael*.[2]

More becomes explicit, and some new insights emerge, as the time comes for God's intervention. This is the time for the radical disruption of the status quo and the hierarchy of authority. When the Israelites leave Egypt there is the conflict between, on one

---

1 Moses is instructed to carry to Pharaoh God's assertion that Israel is his (God's) firstborn son: בְּנִי בְכֹרִי יִשְׂרָאֵל. Ex 4:22.

2 Ex. 1:9. עַם בְּנֵי יִשְׂרָאֵל

side, Pharaoh's rigidity and determination to not allow change, and on the other, that first proposed and then actual act of leaving.

Schachter-Shalomi leads into a more detailed exploration by asking what is going on when, as we are told, Pharaoh hardens his heart. For Pharaoh, what he has done determines what he will do. Like Ahashuverus in the book of *Esther*, what he decreed can't be withdrawn.[3] Pharaoh is contrasted with Moses who was put into the river, a symbol of fluidity.

Schachter-Shalomi then discusses in a general way fluidity versus being determined. He explores the idea of having one's path determined for one in terms of things we know from our own lives or present circumstances. He gives the example of one's "record" following one and limiting what one can do, such as not being able to be a supreme court judge if one was caught having "smoked a couple joints in college." What is the effect on people of being determined, locked into what happened in the past?

He continues:

> We cannot trust a change to have taken place because at one time this and this happened and it is part of the record. It is determined. That notion that we are *caught* brings us to despair.
>
> What was it in India, for instance? If you are born in a low-caste family, the best thing that you could possibly do is to finish this incarnation, being the best street sweeper that you can be, because only then is there a possibility that you would rise. That you will have another incarnation next time around that is going to be better.

---

3   In the Biblical book of *Esther*, the king Ahashuverus, influenced by a certain advisor, has issued a decree that all the Jews are to be killed on a certain day. When he concludes that the advisor has betrayed him, and sees that his queen is among those to be killed, he cannot withdraw the decree. He can only issue another, allowing the Jews to defend themselves.

The Disruption of a Rigid Social Structure

This story of the emergence of this group of people from Egypt, showing a disruption of the determined structure on a massive scale, demonstrates that not everything that looks determined has to be so. And the Torah, the Biblical narrative or parable that recounts this, challenges the ideology and promises a way out of the despair that comes when one's growth and freedom are cut off by rigid structure. It is a gift not only for the Jews but for all people who are, or experience themselves as being, in any sort of slavery.

> Imagine you are a slave now in the Egyptian situation. And here I want to draw a contrast [between the Biblical story and the Indian caste example]. There is something about this Torah that doesn't want us to be in situations where we don't want to be. That despair of constant slavery, of being determined once and for all, is what the Torah wants to free us from.
>
> In fact, if anybody puts us into such a situation—and I'm not only talking about us Jews—it *has happened.* Whatever happens in the world happens for all of us. The going out of Egypt not only freed us, it put out freedom into the world in a whole different sense.
>
> Look at how Blacks sang about that exodus from Egypt. Go down Moses! And everything that happened.

Schachter-Shalomi sings some lines from African-American slave spirituals that call on Hebrew scriptural images. Then:

> And so all of Bible was this thing of freeing, of freeing, and the songs that were there were the freeing songs.

Balancing Structure and Freedom

Later in the Exodus weekend Schachter-Shalomi takes up the exploration again. Structure is not always oppression. We need both structure and freedom, stability and change.

As was suggested earlier, one of the things that the sojourn in Egypt may have been doing for the Israelites was introducing certain sorts of structure that were needed for their evolution and development, to ready them for receiving Torah, for being a cohesive people in the promised land, and for their longer-term destiny.

> I don't want to build a house from water. I do want rigid materials that I can rely on. When I get into an airplane I want to make sure it's going to stay together, that I can rely on it. So there is that part that I want to rely on, that I want to secure. That's to say that the decisions that I make now, I want those decisions to be protected in the future. When I look back at the assets that I have accumulated for myself, I want to be able to say, "I look back into the past." So I have a future and I have a past, in which I want to have rigidity.

But it has to be balanced by fluidity. He continues:

> Yet, there is that moment in the *now* that I want to have the fluidity in. And if I begin to understand this, I see a certain kind of mystery. The mystery has to do with with *Kol Nidrei,* with the going out of Egypt, with that which gets revealed to Moses at the burning bush.

Schachter-Shalomi will look into these three examples in more detail shortly.

Exploring What Draws us towards Growth

Change is all around us, continuously moving us through life. And yet we need to establish stability in the midst of the change. But when we get some stability established, something pulls us again towards change. Schachter-Shalomi wants to explore this dynamic.

> What is it that we can count on that won't change? In a crazy way the one thing you can count on that won't

> change is that change is constant. The strange thing about that is that I can bet on change. I can bet on the truth of change. And at the very same time, every legal institution is based on making change not possible. When we are making a contract of pulling together, a covenant, pulling—*con-tract*—together. When we want to pull together two parties, party of the first part and party of the second part, we want to pull together the past with the future. We want to know what can we count on.

Schachter-Shalomi thinks about what drew Moses out of Midian. He recounts first how he got to Midian.

Moses has grown up and gone out and seen his Hebrew brothers and their burdens, and sees an Egyptian man striking a Hebrew man. After looking around and seeing no witnesses, he strikes down the Egyptian man and kills him and buries him. But word has gotten out, and he is not a hero of his people: when he tries the next day to remonstrate with two Hebrew men who are scuffling, they demand to know who made Moses prince and judge over them, and whether he means to kill them too. And in fact, Pharaoh does hear of it, and, we are told, seeks to kill Moses.

So Moses flees to Midian, where he settles and marries a daughter of the priest of Midian and shepherds the flocks of his father-in-law for many years—later tradition puts it at forty years.

> And here is Moses in a way having given up. Okay, he's got a wife and he's got kids. Egypt is behind him. …

Schachter-Shalomi describes a time in his life when he wished he could be a private citizen: "Enough already of being a rabbi, enough of being out there in the trenches."

What is it, he asks, that makes one move out of the easier path, to follow growth? What first impelled Moses to move out of the life as a shepherd in Midian? Why didn't Moses keep that up for the rest of his life? What made him receptive to God's challenge and assignment of the new mission?

> Whatever it is that says "You can't do that. You have to move." The thing that says you have to move.

"Teflon Moments"

Schachter-Shalomi had read in the Torah Service the passage in which the Israelites waited through the night for the final word to move out. He recreated in his account and commentary the awesome, magical feeling of that night in which they left Egypt. He drew attention to how everything seemed to go so smoothly: no confusion, no quarreling. He called it a "teflon" occasion; there were no sticking points. It was just happening, unfolding, as if God were orchestrating it and the people were just flowing with it.

This may be characteristic of the moments when divine will, or the divine intention, is moving through reality without hindrance. It may be something that occurs when the people, or the prophet, or when we ourselves, allow this to happen by getting out of the way—or it may be something that at certain times happens despite anything we might do to resist it.

The Burning Bush: *Mysterium Fascinans*

What creates those "teflon" openings? Schachter-Shalomi thinks about the moment in which Moses notices the burning bush.[4]

> For some it is fascination.
>
> I have a feeling that if I need a channel for an intellective process, if I need someone to bring that process down, to bring *mind*-full, to be aware, to bring an awareness down from one level where it is beyond, to another level where it gets specific and nitty gritty, whom would I pick?
>
> A curious person. I would pick somebody who wants to investigate.

---

4 Exodus 3:2.

When we are protecting ourselves from disruptive openings and changes, we put up barriers that shut out oddities that may threaten our working world-view, our "reality map." So, faced with the particular divine sign put out for Moses, the burning bush that was not consumed, some people might pass by without noticing that it was not being consumed, perhaps scarcely noticing it at all. Or they might just say, as Schachter-Shalomi imitates:

> "*Nu*, a bush is burning, let the bush burn. Doesn't belong to me!" Do you understand? It's like "*Yenem's* bush, a *goyishe* bush, leave it alone."[5]

This, however, is not Moses's response, and Schachter-Shalomi wants to explore more about what that was and why it was and what teaching there might be here for us.

> But when there's a fascination! And so here is that *mysterium fascinans.*[6] Yes, it's burning, and not consumed. Burning, not consumed. Burning! Not consumed! How come not consumed?
>
> Every scientific discovery comes through a serendipity of somebody asking "how come this anomaly is there?" It is like trying to lift up, as it were, the skirt of Reality to take a peek: what causes this phenomenon to be there?
>
> So if I needed to pick a somebody, I would pick a curious person. I would set up a curiosity there. [Imitates

---

5   **Yenem**. יענעם Yiddish: Somebody else, the other person, as in the Yiddish saying *Af yenems tukhes iz gut tsu patshn*, "Someone else's backside is easy to smack."

   Goyish. גוייש Yiddish: Not Jewish. In this context the meaning is similar to the previous phrase. A *goyishe* bush is a bush that doesn't have anything to do with us.

6   **Mysterium fascinans**. Latin: The fascinating mystery. Term coined by Mircea Eliade in *The Sacred and the Profane*. He attributes the idea to Rudolf Otto's *Das Heilege,* but the term does not appear in Otto's book.

the bush calling to Moses with body language and enticing voice calling] "Heeeyyy, yitz tza tza! Ya la la!"[7]

Something there is that is beckoning, that says "come hither." Now, it never was like this before. It always was before like it burned and then it stopped burning. That it should burn and continue to burn, that is not the way it was before. So there is something new. If you are going to be an innovator you have to have a certain kind of trust in that *new*, in that which is happening.

The Repudiation of Vows: *Kol Nidrei*

The next example Schachter-Shalomi ponders in exploring of the mystery that arises in the push and pull of balancing commitment and change is the *Kol Nidrei*[8] declaration. This emotionally charged piece of liturgy is for many the most treasured part of the Yom Kippur (Day of Atonement) services, although technically it is something made just before the Yom Kippur evening service begins. The declaration is not Biblical, but it is very old, going back at least to the ninth century.

The cantor on behalf of the congregation, or with the congregation singing along quietly, declares a repudiation of all vows made either in the last year or in the coming year. (Originally it referred to the past year. Now it is customary to consider it to apply to the following year.)

---

7   Part of chorus of a song that goes with a dance that, so informants tell me, was popular in Zionist youth movements of the 40's and 50's and at Modern Orthodox summer camps in the 50's and 60's. At one point the line of boys crook fingers at the girls and say enticingly "Heeyy, yitz-tza-tza" and the girls coyly reply "Yah-la-la" before the line of girls moves in the dance to join them. [Personal communications, Karen Roekard, Yoram Getzler, Yolie Bloomstein.]

8   **Kol Nidrei**, כָּל נִדְרֵי, Aramaic for "All vows," the opening words of the declaration. The declaration is entirely in Aramaic.

There is much discussion and controversy around the theological implications of this, of course, but for most congregants who are deeply moved by listening to it sung each year, the attraction is not in its message but in the ancient power of its melody[9] and the depth of feeling the cantor brings to its singing. The declaration is sung through completely three times, with the intensity increasing with each repetition. In many congregations the Torah scrolls are brought out and carried around the room to be touched or kissed by congregants during this special service.

A deep state of awe, perhaps with connection to ancestral and other-worldly experience, can be generated, launching the Yom Kippur service. The Yom Kippur process is itself, of course, plenty awe-filled when experienced by those taking the religious observance seriously. During the course of this day the faithful complete their repentance—the last chance to be written in the book of life before the heavenly gates of repentance close at nightfall.

Schachter-Shalomi is going to highlight what he proposes to be the intent of the repudiation rather than the musical or emotional dimensions, but by singing some of the melody he invites the participants to connect to the whole experience. There is a teaching here, in his view, and he wants the participants to see that it isn't just any casual teaching but one that the participants have already experienced as deep and ancient.

---

9   The melody is part of a body of music that arose in southern Germany between the 11th and 15th centuries. These melodies were and are known as *MiSinai*, "from Sinai," that is, given on Mt. Sinai with the Torah. This is not meant literally, but refers to the sacred emotional impact of these pieces: one might say, "straight from heaven." One of the touches of the Kol Nidrei melody specifically is described in the Jewish Encyclopedia as follows: "Instead of announcing the opening words ["kol nidrei"] in a monotone or in any of the familiar declamatory phrases, some ancient chazzan of South Germany prefixed a long, sighing tone, falling to a lower note and rising again, as if only sighs and sobs could find utterance before the officiant could bring himself to inaugurate the dread Day of Attonement." JewishEncyclopedia.com, Kol Nidre entry.

Let's take a look and see what happens in making vows. Kol Nidrei.

Schachter-Shalomi sings a few notes of the low, ancient, familiar melody, which sets an atmosphere in the room by calling up emotionally charged memories of deep and sacred time for most or all of the participants.

He then breaks in with the challenge:

Making vows. What are we saying? At the holiest day of the year we are saying "Vows, shmows. Forget it!" "I'll make a whole bunch of vows during the year and then they will be—"

He then quotes the words of the Kol Nidrei declaration[10] which specifies all the sorts of vows and promises and contracts and bindings and consecrations and oaths (and "equivalent terms") that are to be repudiated, abandoned, null, void, not firm or established, not valid, cancelled, undone. And also (for good measure, in the last lines of the declaration) that our vows are *not* ("*lo*") vows, our consecrations are *not* ("*lo*") consecrations, and our oaths are *not* ("*lo*") oaths.

Let them never take on a hold. I'm saying every vow I make where I want to bind myself totally, to set it in cement, at the same time I cross my fingers behind my back and I say, "On this holy Yom Kippur, *Ribono Shel Olam,*[11] please, whenever I make a vow, let that vow not hold. Let it not bind me."

---

10   כָּל נִדְרֵי וֶאֱסָרֵי וַחֲרָמֵי, וְקוֹנָמֵי וְכִנּוּיֵי, וְקִנּוּסֵי וּשְׁבוּעוֹת, דִּנְדַרְנָא וּדְאִשְׁתַּבַּעְנָא, וּדְאַחֲרֵמְנָא וְדְאָסַרְנָא עַל נַפְשָׁתָנָא, מִיּוֹם כִּפֻּרִים זֶה עַד יוֹם כִּפֻּרִים הַבָּא עָלֵינוּ לְטוֹבָה, כֻּלְּהוֹן אִחֲרַטְנָא בְהוֹן. כֻּלְּהוֹן יְהוֹן שָׁרָן, שְׁבִיקִין שְׁבִיתִין, בְּטֵלִין וּמְבֻטָּלִין, לָא שְׁרִירִין וְלָא קַיָּמִין. נִדְרָנָא לָא נִדְרֵי, וֶאֱסָרָנָא לָא אֱסָרֵי, וּשְׁבוּעָתָנָא לָא שְׁבוּעוֹת.

11   **Ribono shel olam** וֹנוֹבֵּר לֵשׁ סָלוֹע Hebrew: master of the universe, i. e. God.

So what can this mean?

> I need a time out. I need the possibility for making change. So that which says "I want to be able to rely" says "No change." And that which says "I want to be able to grow, to live, to change" says "Yes" for change.

Schachter-Shalomi sidesteps the complicated interpretive operations parsing what sort of vows can be repudiated under what circumstances, or (as argued by yet other commentators) how the Kol Nidrei declaration really is speaking about the sanctity of vows. These parsings are engaged in by those who struggle to understand this on a literal and rational level.

Rather, Schachter-Shalomi jumps to another level. He sees the message as a wake-up call, using a kind of shock or apparent contradiction of all one might expect, to jolt people out of the conventional sort of analysis, which seeks to explain the new or the odd in terms of the prevailing "reality map."

He sees in the Kol Nidrei a powerful assertion that there has to be room for things to change. Everything can't be completely determined, even if it is by a decree of Pharaoh, even if by the laws of physics that might say a burning bush should be consumed, even if it is by a solemn vow that was made.

Shatteringly, the Kol Nidrei strikes our consciousness. Wake up! At this awe-filled time, a message is coming through! There has to be room for change! Things don't have to go on just the way they have been going on, even if you thought that was the only possible way!

Going Out of Egypt

Moving on to his third example, the going out of Egypt, Schachter-Shalomi looks closely (as he unfolds the story over the weekend) at the details of the Biblical narrative, extracting significance from each element not just in relation to the story as a whole, but as a parable. Something that must have looked impossible from many points of view, not only proved possible, but actually occurred.

In the first place, how could it even be done? The Pharaoh's army had all the power. That the slaves of a god-like tyrant could just pack up and leave en masse should have looked like fantasy. And where would they go? Just march out into the wilderness? The wilderness was uninhabited for a reason: no water, no food. At first nothing is even said about the "promised land"; that begins to be mentioned later. But even if it had been offered as the plan, this was not an empty territory waiting for them; it was inhabited by others (people who could not reasonably be expected to obligingly move on when the Israelites arrive to claim their promised land).

In short, they were going into the unknown. And not an unknown full of likely possibilities, but an unknown with nothing but a promise that this God that Moses represents would be their God.

What about the logistics? We are told that 600,000 *gavrim* (generally, men of an age suitable for miliary service, possibly here just adult men), plus children and presumably plus women (they do seem to be present later).[12] Adding these in we have well over a million. Then we are told that "also" a "mixed multitude" (understood as non-Jewish Egyptians) went up with them.[13] Are these people also added to the number making the escape?

Regardless of where the arithmetic leads us, we have a daunting challenge for a midnight migration.

But there was another thing against this move, a difficulty more subtle and more basic. These people were slaves, not free. Furthermore, they had been locked into a fixed system that was severely hierarchical and carefully ordered long before they had become literal slaves. How could they think of leaving that highly

---

12 Gen. 12:37. כְּשֵׁשׁ־מֵאוֹת אֶלֶף רַגְלִי הַגְּבָרִים לְבַד מִטָּף

13 Gen. 12:38. וְגַם־עֵרֶב רַב עָלָה אִתָּם

structured and constrained life, everything they knew, the security however oppressive, the systems they had developed for getting by, the things they knew they could rely on? Leave it to just walk out into the wilderness?

Pondering this story as an adventure into the unknown, especially when recounted by a skilled story-teller, is absorbing, but providing a gripping story to the participants is not Schachter-Shalomi's primary purpose.

He sees it as a teaching story, and its teaching is that change is possible even when it looks most impossible. It teaches us about walking away from the Mitzrayim,[14] the slavery to habits or addictions in our own lives. And it teaches us about what it would take to be open to Revelation.

> Going out of Mitzrayim. Mitzrayim are those things that are fixed. The learning that we are getting when we want to get out from the fixed.

This story is a model for us, one that can be called upon whenever we are stuck in "the fixed." But the story gives us no instant solution, any more than the first night of departure was an instant solution for the Israelites. Leaving slavery behind is a long process; in fact it was a forty-year process in the Exodus case.

Perhaps we can learn about what we might face in our own process by studying the model given here. Schachter-Shalomi continues to follow through the story verse by verse; I will touch on a few of the teachings he extracts.

---

14 **Mitzrayim** מִצְרַיִם. The Hebrew name for Egypt. Widely taken in the tradition of Jewish Biblical commentary as being based on the Hebrew root צרר *tzarar*, verb, to bind, tie up, be restricted; *tzar*, adj., narrow, tight; and *tzar*, noun, distress. Thus Mitzrayim is taken as the narrow place, the bound-up place. The "*ayim*" ending is a dual ending, leading Schachter-Shalomi to declare it, in his preview of this session, the place of the "double bind."

Reality Maps

The narrative as Schachter-Shalomi has been tracing it has brought the Israelites to the edge of the Sea. The Egyptian army is behind them and closing; water is in front of them.

What has happened? Has God betrayed them?

As with the apparently impossible task of taking many hundreds of thousands, perhaps millions of people, including children and livestock, en masse out of slavery, again we seem faced with the impossible.

After bringing the participants to enter imaginatively into this impossible situation, Schachter-Shalomi and his co-leader, Eve Ilsen, offer a tag-team meditation on reality maps and the breaking-through of such limitations.

> **Schachter-Shalomi:** Unless a miracle happens, the gig's up.
>
> What stops a miracle from happening?
>
> I *want* reality *not* to shift. Imagine right now, if reality could shift, how would you know you aren't crazy?

> **Eve Ilsen:** In such a situation, if you're brought to the place where the miracle you require is precisely an irregularity in the unchangeables, how many of us are there who are totally unwilling to let go? Preferably we should die rather than to think that these unchangeables are actually mutable.

> **Schachter-Shalomi:** I feel the chills of people who [are] in situations where they know that if the disease that they have continues its course that they will die. And when they hear at the same time of extra-ordinary cures that might be gotten here or there and through means that are other than the means that they expect, they might still say "This is my reality. I'd rather die than accept the reality shift that would happen if I were to buy into that thing."

> **Eve Ilsen:** The things we think of as unchangeable, that I think everybody in this room would like to think are unchangeable, this is what we call a reality map. It's how we like to think we know the world is run. Certain things we think we know, and the more material they are, the more real we think they are.

Miracles: Budging Reality

What might be the state of consciousness that allows the shift, the disengagement from our reality maps, that allows us to move into a way out? What is the state of consciousness that allows us to move into what might even feel like a parallel universe? This is the question of what opens us to an apparent miracle. Because it requires us to step out of what we take for granted as possible, describing that state of consciousness requires words and images that begin to sound mystical.

> The reality has to budge. And there aren't any provisions for that. How is that going to happen? How are we going to enter into the world of the miraculous?
>
> I go back to the midnight in Egypt.[15] I go back to the burning bush.
>
> Something opens up at such a level of truth that when Sufis talk about that level of truth, like the absolute sense of truth, the true thing that is happening there, that *emes*[16] that is happening there, it is called *Haqiqat*.[17] *Haqiqat*. It is that world, the world we know as *Atzilut*.[18] It's the place of the

---

15 The "teflon moment" described on page 150 above.

16 **Emes** אמת. Yiddish (or Ashkenazi pronunciation of Hebrew): truth.

17 **Haqiqat** حقيقه. Arabic: divine truth.

18 **Atzilut**. In Qabala, the highest of the four spiritual levels of being, state of oneness with divine being. See also the earlier chapter on The Four Worlds.

great intuition, it's the place where there aren't two, *v'hu echad v'ein sheni.*[19] There are no two, all duality is over there. And it's in that place that in the passion of Krishna, he opens himself to Arjuna and says "look!" And as Arjuna looks into his heart, he sees universes there. He sees the whole picture. That's the way it is in the *Gita.*[20]

Ra'tah shifchah al hayom mah shelo ra'ah Yichazqel.[21] The maidservant saw at the sea what Ezekiel didn't see when he saw the great Merkabah, the wheel within the wheel. Just being there at the time of the splitting of the sea, which isn't only the physical sea, which is like a splitting of all that, so that that glimpse that comes from the not-two gets through.

And when we have time and eternity, we have two. But what is that one that transcends both time and eternity? Take that name again, Yud-Heh-Vav-Heh. *Hoveh,*[22] present. Yud *hoveh,* Yud present. The tiny point of the present. The one who causes the present to be. Present-maker. *Va'ani*

---

19 וְהוּא אֶחָד וְאֵין שֵׁנִי. Hebrew: And he is one, and not two. From *piyut* (liturgical hymn) Adon Olam.

20 In the *Bhagavad Gita,* part of the Hindu epic *Mahabharata.* The god Krishna reveals himself to the prince Arjuna in Chapter 11.

21 רְאתה שפחה על הים מה שלא ראה יחזקאל "The maidservant saw at the sea what Ezekiel did not see." This comment about the maidservant does not appear in the Biblical text. It appears in *Mekhilta deRabbi Yishma'el,* midrash to Exodus 15:2. *Mekhilta,* Jewish Publication Society, 1933, Vol. II, p. 24. Midrash commentary of the rabbinic sage Rabbi Ishmael (90-135 CE) on the line "This is my God and I will glorify him" (Exodus 15:2) from the Song at the Sea. The idea is echoed with variations in other midrashic texts.

22 **Hoveh** הוֹבֶה. Hebrew masculine singular participle of "to become, to be," the one who becomes or is or occurs. In modern Israeli Hebrew the form of the verb used for expressing masculine singular present tense. The tetragrammaton YHVH can be read as a *yud* followed by the verbal participle HVH, *hoveh.*

t'filati lekha Yah, et ratzon.[23] I am my prayer to you, Yud-Heh-Vav-Heh. This is to be a time of willingness, of *yes*, of divine approbation, saying "it's good." Divine affirmation.

The Pure Moment of Openness to Possibility

But Schachter-Shalomi has not departed into theological or mystical abstraction. His focus is still with what we can do to escape our own slaveries and impasses, whether they are personal or societal. This numinous *present* has a purpose. He is exploring a state of radical openness, of dropping all assumptions about what is possible, limitations based on what has been and what we have believed the future would have to be.

> I want that to happen at this moment. I want there should be a suspension of all that which exists in the before and that exists in the after, so that only this pure moment of now with all the possibility that's in it, for change, for shift, for all that, should be present here. And how do I do this?
>
> I don't know, but I want to describe something. "If I could I surely would stand on the rock where Moses stood." What I would like to do to be in that place at that moment is to say to every part of my body, "All programs except life maintenance are now suspended." The big *shabes*[24] box.
>
> Everything I have invested in future, which means to keep the same future going that brings me to this moment, all these investments I'm beginning to scrap. To give them up.

---

23 וַאֲנִי תְפִלָּתִי לְךָ יְיָ, עֵת רָצוֹן "I am my prayer to you, YHVH, at a favorable time." Psalm 69:14. Quoted in morning liturgy in the liturgical poem Ma Tovu. Schachter-Shalomi will close the weekend with reference back to this.

24 As the Sabbath (Yiddish form *shabes*) is a time out of time, a suspension of normal working-and-doing time, this moment steps out of normal activities and beliefs about past and future.

I'm prepared for my body to let go of every hold that I have. Of every face I want to make to impress other people. Of every muscle that I have in there that isn't where it wants to be at this moment by itself. I'm ready to let go of that.

Then, what other investments have I got? I will love all the people whom I love in such a wonderful way that my presence or lack of presence shouldn't make any difference to them. I will love all the people I care for in such a way that in a most generous loving way I want them to have the best in the universe that they can have and I shouldn't have to be there to give that to them. It shouldn't depend on my getting anything back for that. It should just be good. Can you imagine this kind of a giving up?

On the level of attitude, on the level of feeling, every grudge that I ever had, every satisfaction I wanted to have from vengeance at the end, my investment in the future, I'm prepared to give that up.

Schachter-Shalomi touches back on the stories and rituals the Jewish tradition offers that seem to describe and evoke that state.

I'm trying to see what is happening in that vision that the maidservant has at the Sea. That is at the burning bush. That is at the Yom Kippur *kodesh kodashim*,[25] the high priest going into the most holy moment to bring about atonement. It's that place where I get so drunk on Purim that I don't know the difference between "blessed be Mordechai" and "cursed be Haman."[26] I want to be able to get all systems into that neutral.

---

25 **Kodesh Kodashim**. The holy of holies, the innermost sacred part of the sanctuary, to which only the High Priest is permitted access. At the most solemn time of the most solemn day of the year, Yom Kippur, the High Priest enters to plead for atonement for the people.

26 On the holiday of Purim, the *Scroll of Esther* is read and all Jews are commanded to listen to that reading every year. Its story concerns the wicked Haman who plots to kill all the Jews and the hero

> In this situation, where I'm ready to let go, where I'm dying an emotional death, where I'm giving up, where equanimity is being found on the heart level. Where my heart *chakra*[27] enters *nirvana*.[28] In that very place where I'm saying all yeses and noes are equal to me, I can let go of any outcome that I want to have. This is this moment of this emotional truth.

Suspending the Reality Maps

The central problem is the reality maps (as Schachter-Shalomi is calling them) that lock us in to collusion or hold us in a place of suffering where growth cannot take place. How does one use that numinous present consciousness to transcend one's own, and the external world's, reality maps?

> And on top of that comes yet another real, powerful, look at how reality maps are really subjective. How what we call consensus reality is something we have bought into with other people so that we have a collusion going with each other. But this collusion is at this point a fatal collusion. If we hold onto this collusion we're going to be smack into the wall, we're going to die, we won't exist anymore. We have to give up the collusion that holds for

---

Mordechai who is given credit for saving them. The performance tends towards slapstick comedy, with congregants booing whenever Haman's name is mentioned. A rabbinical injunction is to become sufficiently drunk that one no longer knows the difference between Haman and Mordechai. Schachter-Shalomi cites it here as a moment of releasing judgment and investments in categories and dualities.

27 **Chakra** चक्र. Sanskrit: One of the set of subtle energy centers of the body, here referring to the one located near the physical heart. Literal meaning is wheel.

28 **Nirvana** निर्वाण. Sanskrit. In the Buddhist tradition, *nirvana* is the state of consciousness of having transcended cravings, anger, or other mental disturbances; experiencing perfect peace; no longer subject to human suffering.

this conventional reality in order to save the *élan* that lives in us. What a surrender that is.

I want to allow also for the reality maps to scroll by my head like a movie in which I suddenly see that if you have this reality, these will be the outcomes of this moment; if this reality the other outcome will be; if this reality another outcome will be. And I see 360 degrees for just a moment of all possibilities of outcomes coming.

And then those maps fall apart. And there is this one map in which the thing can happen the way in which it has to happen. And I can't be smart enough with my own smarts to find that map. I have to rely that as I am in the flow of this event, and as this event wants to realize itself, that I be in the right place for that event to realize itself, that this will be for the greater glory. … And there will be a tearing apart of all realities as known. as we had before, including the liquidity of water, which exists to this side and exists to that side but in the center water ceases to be liquid.

These reality maps fix us in circumstances that may be oppressive, harmful, or just stultifying. They are the perceived external limitations that prevent us from bringing change to our lives or our world, prevent us from growing. They may feel as impossible to challenge as the behavior of a liquid—for example, the behavior of the liquid that is making up the Red Sea that stands before the Israelites.

But belief in the impossibility of change in situations of "Mitzrayim," of "double-bind," of limitation, does more than prevent growth. It can lead to despair.

If I look at the law of *karma*, I find that the law of karma is so terrifying because of the bad karma that's built up. If every bomb that is available in the armaments now, if every bit of pollution that has seeped into the ground, if every thing that is around at this point were to have its expected continuity, there's no way out. Okay? That the karma that is set loose in the world, that if it were to be inexorable, I couldn't get out. We, living beings, couldn't get out. At the very same time, while all these dire predictions are being made about the fate of the world, while we are in this Mitzrayim and we can't get out, there's *A Course in Miracles*,[29] there's a Twelve Step Program. Every one of us is looking for "what is the way out?" We want a miraculous way out. [Schachter-Shalomi addresses the participants:] Why are you here? It's because you hope in some way you're going to find a way out.

To be able to discover where is the way out in [one's] self and in one's immediate surroundings in society is to try to find the place of healing. Healing is another one of those things that says "with everything that's going bad in the body, you'd expect an irrecoverable damage to be." How come there is healing possible? Because it seems to be the inter-vention, the coming in, the in-between the Mitzrayim, where it looks like it is rigid, it can't move, it is lost forever. If I look straight down the path, it looks like it's going to take us on a collision course, then why is it that as we go down the path there is something built in to nudge us, always, a little bit out of the path?

The obvious path laid out by our reality map seems to lead to a collision course, to disaster. And yet we fear being nudged out of the path. The deflection feels like a frustration of our attempts to deal with the situation within the terms of the reality map.

And so it turns out that the very same thing that we see sometimes as the frustrating thing, "how come we cannot

---

29 *A Course in Miracles*. A course of spiritual teachings written down between 1965 and 1972 by Helen Shucman based on a series on transmissions from an inner voice originally identifying itself as Jesus. It was subsequently edited and passed through various editions. Schachter-Shalomi sees this and similar phenomena as responses to people's desire for a way out of their binds.

> aim at what we really want without getting deflected," that
> the very law that makes for the deflection of our aim is the
> thing that saves us.

That deflection could be the sudden, unreasoned resolve to just walk out of Mitzrayim, out of the addiction, out of the stultifying situation. It could feel magical: a burning bush, a "teflon" midnight, an apparently parting sea.

The God of Becoming, the God of Change

Schachter-Shalomi finds in the naming of God in Exodus a powerful support for the importance of there being a way to open to change. He moves back to the moment when God approaches Moses to intercede with Pharaoh to release the Israelites, to Moses's response, and to the names God offers.

Moses speaking to God:

> I'm going to come to the children of Israel and I'm going
> to say "The God of your parents has sent me to you." ...
> "And they will say to me, "What's his name?" What should
> I tell them?
> Name....

Schachter-Shalomi stretches the word out. It's a big topic.

Jewish tradition post-Biblically has held that there is impiety in pronouncing the name of God YHVH. In reading Bible or liturgy aloud in a context of prayer, most traditionalists will substitute *Adonai*, "my Lord"[30]; in study or general discourse the orthodox will substitute *HaShem*, "the name." Desire for even greater care for piety may lead to further changes.[31]

---

30 The Bible also uses אֲדֹנָי *Adonai* as a name for God, and in those
   cases this is not a pious substitution. (This ambiguity only exists
   when the name is spoken; in reading one sees either אֲדֹנָי or יהוה.)

31 *Elohim* and *El* (both words for God) may be pronounced Elokim
   and Kel; even the substitute name Adonai may become Adokai.

This taboo on the speaking a name of God may seem puzzling to those outside the Jewish tradition who know how freely God's names, including the "personal" name YHVH, are used in the Bible. In Islam, all the many names of God are very precious and their use is an act of piety, even a spiritual practice. Christians often use the term "Lord,"[32] not out of recoiling from use of a personal name but because the personal name YHVH was translated into Greek as *kurios*, lord, in the *Septuagint*,[33] which influenced early Christian texts and usage. At other times in Christian texts, יהוה / YHVH is translated Jehovah or Yahweh.

However, for many who grew up under the influence of Rabbinical and later Jewish tradition, especially in the Orthodox practice, the sense of sacrilege in the use of the name can go very deep. Jewish earthiness makes it felt viscerally and Jewish scholarliness makes it explained rationally. Schachter-Shalomi shows both sides in the following when he discusses his own resistance to using a fixed name of God. He had been speaking of reading Bible translations that substitute Jehovah or Yahweh for YHVH.

> Whichever form they're putting out the name, it does something to my *kishkes*.[34] It doesn't feel right. It's like, I got the word now, I've got it in my control. Word, control, word, control. Word, rigid control. I have it, magic control. I can now coerce God.

But not only had this pious custom not come into use yet at the time of God's call to Moses and Moses' request for a name to tell the people, it would have been a problem if it had. Moses

---

32 By a common convention, printed LORD to flag it as a translation of יהוה / YHVH and not of אֲדֹנָי / *Adonai*.

33 **Septuagint**. Third century BCE translation of Hebrew Bible into Greek. The translation was done by Jewish scholars to help make the scriptures accessible to Hellenized Greek-speaking Jews who had limited familiarity with Hebrew.

34 **Kishke** קישקע. Yiddish: literally intestine. What one feels in one's *kishkes* one feels in one's guts: a deep, visceral response.

is not dealing with people sharing a mature developed religion whose conventions are known. This God has just "remembered" his people, perhaps after centuries of leaving them alone.[35] Who is he? They will want to know. What God is this? One of the Egyptian gods? A god of their ancestors, dimly remembered? Some Canaanite god, also perhaps dimly remembered?

> But [Moses] is saying "by what coin, how can I tell these people? They're going to ask who sent me." Do you understand, it makes a difference. If I were to come to a Moslem and say to him, *Yud-Heh-Vav-Heh* sent me to you with a message, I don't say *Allah* sent me with a message, it could be trouble. Come to an orthodox Jew, I have to say *HaShem*. I always have to be careful so the listener would be able to hear it. So Moshe's[36] question is not a foolish question. He's saying "Look, I've known God as *Atum*, I've known God as *Ra*. I've known God in the desert. In all kinds of forms and ways have I known God. But if I come and say "I come in the name of the God with a thousand names, with a million names, the un-named one, it's not going to help. So you gotta give me a name." Okay?

God Refuses to Give a Fixed Name

So God gives him a name. The name God gives him (in Exodus 3:14) is אֶהְיֶה אֲשֶׁר אֶהְיֶה, *ehyeh asher ehyeh*. The Hebrew contains a range of possible meanings not captured by any one English translation. The verb form is used for anything liquid, not solid or completed. Maybe future: I will be what I will be. Or optative: I might be what I might be. Or, I will be what I could be.

And the verb root itself is much more liquid than the formal and definite English "to be," with its baggage of European philosophical impositions. It is not so much "to be" as "to become, to

---

35 Exodus 6:5.

36 **Moshe**. Hebrew for Moses.

come to pass, to fall out, to happen, to befall."[37] I will become what I will become. I will come into being as I come into being.

What is clear is that there is fluidity and openness to change in this formulation.

> So [God] says to him, "I will be whoever I will be." "I will become who I will become." *Ehyeh asher ehyeh.* And he said, "Thus speak to children of Israel. The one who I am to become has sent me to you."

Schachter-Shalomi knows that this is a hard sell in the world.

> Now I want to tell you something. It is so hard to speak to traditional peoples in the name of the "becoming" God. It's so hard. Every people wants to be sure that when the final revelation is going to come that their bet has been covered throughout the ages. That their number has come up.
>
> Now why should we want to wait for a messiah if we have it all together now? Why should the Moslems have to await for a *Mah'di*?[38] Why should the Hindus have to wait for the next *Avatar*?[39] Why should anybody have to speak "We are waiting for *Mashiach*"[40] if we had it all now?
>
> We don't have it all now.
>
> And yet at the same time if you come to traditional people and you want to say "I speak in the name of the emerging God"….

---

37 BDB, p. 224.

38 **Mah'di** مهدي. Arabic: the prophesied redeemer of Islam who would rid the world of injustice before Judgment Day. "Guided one."

39 **Avatar** अवतार. Sanskrit: an incarnation of divine being in human form. "Descent."

40 **Mashiach** מָשִׁיחַ. Hebrew: the prophesied messiah who would gather all Jews into Israel and bring peace and justice to the world. "Anointed one."

Schachter-Shalomi will return to the problem with selling a changing God and to our own resistance to the idea of change on the part of the one we want to think of as our rock.

But he inserted a parenthesis at this point to note what he sees as a question that is in some ways closer to home. Names that don't have change built into them are a problem for people as well as for a deity.

> Do I allow for a person with whom I have a relationship, to allow them to be who they are emerging to be? Constantly? This is the rub in all relationships, when we want to *fix* them, and we want to make sure, I bind myself to you in such a way that you won't change and I won't change. We take each other by the breathing neck and say "I've got you." And I'm not going to let you change. I'm not going to let you breathe. This is what ruins relationships because there isn't breathing space there, there isn't a way of saying *"Ehyeh asher ehyeh."* Will you allow me to become in your presence who I need to become? If one were able to create marriage ceremonies around such: *Ehyeh asher ehyeh* , do you take *Ehyeh asher ehyeh* to be your...?

Schachter-Shalomi now indicates what we get instead of this desirable sort of relationship:

> "Lawfully wedded." "Wedlock." You get all these kinds of words [instead].

Closing the parenthesis, Schachter-Shalomi returns to the narrative of God's response to Moses's request for a name to tell the people.

> Can you imagine this conversation? Hear for a moment. God says to Moses, *Ehyeh asher ehyeh* is my name. Moses is puzzled, then God volunteers a little bit more. He says "Just tell the children of Israel *Ehyeh* sent you."[41] In

---

41 God shortens "I will become what I will become" (or however one

between Moses doesn't say a word. And God says further to Moses, "Thus say to the children of Israel: the lord the god of your forefathers, Abraham, Isaac, and Jacob, has sent me to you."

Evidently God realized that *he* had a hard sell as well, so he has to keep moving towards more familiar formulations. First he shortens it to *Ehyeh*, then tells Moses to identify him as the God of their ancestors, naming them.

Schachter-Shalomi continues God's statement to Moses and connects God's words here to spiritual practices of many traditions that work with divine names:

> "And this is my name forever. This is my *zikr*[42] from generation to generation." You see that word? *Zeh zikri l'dor dor.*[43] Do you see that? Usually translated "my memorial." Do you understand why I'm saying the word *zikr*? How do you use *zikr*? It's mindfulness. When I am mindful of Allah, and I say [intoning with intention and intensity as in the spiritual practice] "Allah, Allah, Allah…" paying attention and saying that word, I'm performing the *zikr*. *Zikr* is to be aware and to mention.
>
> "This is my name forever and this is my *zikr* for each generation. Every generation can say [chants repetitions of *Ehyeh asher ehyeh* as if it were a spiritual practice] *Ehyeh asher ehyeh, Ehyeh asher ehyeh, Ehyeh asher ehyeh.* Maybe we'll do some *zikr* with that so you'll get to see.

---

understands the Hebrew) to simply "I will become" אֶהְיֶה.

42 **Zikr** Persian pronunciation of Arabic word *dhikr* ذكر, cognate with the Hebrew word that appears here (זֵכֶר, remembrance). The Arabic word *zikr*, which also means "remembrance," is the central spiritual practice of the Sufis. It is repetition of names of God in ways that bring the practitioner into God-consciousness. It is to this tradition that Schachter-Shalomi is referring here.

43 זֶה זִכְרִי לְדֹר דֹר This is my remembrance/memorial from generation to generation. Exodus 3:15.

Schachter-Shalomi returns to the difficulty of accepting a deity that allows for process, one that is "slippery," not fully in our grasp.

> We want that God shouldn't change.
>
> [sings:] "O, thou who changest not, abide with me."
>
> You made a covenant with us, don't you dare to change. And this is what we're holding onto, we're going to hold God by the *gotcha*.
>
> And God is slippery that way.
>
> And at the same time, look how this comes. Because more and more there is a statement being made, "look, I'll give it to you. *Ehyeh asher ehyeh*. Don't want *Ehyeh asher ehyeh*? Okay, say *Ehyeh* sent you. It's also not good? I'm the same God [who was known to] Abraham, Isaac, and Jacob. Like I was *Ehyeh* for Abraham, for Isaac I was *Ehyeh*, for Jacob, and this is my name forever, I'm going to be *Ehyeh*. And every generation, *Ehyeh*. Okay, got it?"
>
> And at the same time he is putting it into the vessels that the people knew.

Learning and Change

The understanding that God put his name (or his description of the sort of God he is) into "the vessels that the people knew," leads Schachter-Shalomi into a much more radical notion that might seem a bit of a jump. We might have followed Schachter-Shalomi (despite it being a "hard sell") to an acknowledgement that God may be *hoveh*, a becoming-one or changing-one, and that he may indeed reveal successive versions of himself as the people are ready for it.

But Schachter-Shalomi segues from there to seeing the people themselves (which of course now at this time includes us) as part of the divine process of evolving. Our change, the changes to the vessels that are us, make possible more advanced revelations of divine being. Therefore in some way we can be seen as part of the functioning of divine being. Schachter-Shalomi continues from the previous quotation:

> And this insight, that we are the ganglia of the divine process, we are the nervous system for this planet at this point, we are the multi-modal possibility in which God expresses her/himself here now, at this point, do you understand how much one has to learn and grow in order to be able to see that everywhere? He couldn't come and say the Egyptians were also right. It wasn't the time. There is an issue of growth, you allow for change, you have to allow for the growth that's there too.
>
> That's the artificial intelligence issue that's happening in computers now. Is it possible to create a computer that will know how to learn.
>
> Well, this bio-computer that you are and I am is a computer that has been programmed to learn. Civilization is a program that is programmed to learn. Cultures are different programs that are being put into civilization. I have learned in my lifetime, when this hard disk, as it were, is wearing out, what's happening then? It gets put into the pool, into the network. And just understanding this, that we are each one a sensor, put out to find out, to learn, and to bring back the intelligence into that thing.

The "*omni omni*" God is the one who is omnipotent, omniscient, omnipresent, and so on. This sort of God is the one that would be an easier sell. But this sort of God, Schachter-Shalomi says, is ultimately a lie. This lie may need to be destroyed in every generation,

> Then I don't have to have an *omni omni,* but we're just coming out of the *omni omni* God. [Moses] would have had an easier job if he had just said "the *omni omni* sent me." The trumps sent me. Then he would have gotten right back into that place which would have been the *lie* that has to be destroyed in every generation.

Schachter-Shalomi doesn't want to over-simplify. There is a need for stability as well as change, and one statement, even in sacred text, that God is *Ehyeh asher ehyeh* isn't going to free people from wanting God to be a rock. People will still make temples and churches and religious institutions. But when the Mitzrayim of those rigidities is too limiting and too stifling, there will be a correction. And that correction may be God himself "busting out."

> You can't run a Church and you can't run an orthodoxy and you can't run a religion on a changing God. You just can't. So every once in a while, we domesticate the God so he'll fit the religion. And every once in a while God has to bust out of the domestication, go wild in a way.

"Busting Out" of Our Own Limitations

What applies to God applies to us as well. Who are we? What stable cosmology or reality map do we have to show to others so they can know who we are? Then there are the reality maps that society constructs for its own use. These are useful, even necessary—but when they pass their time we're stuck in a new Mitzrayim, and will have need of what we might learn from these ancient lessons to get back out.

> All of us are operating with some kind of cosmology. Because cosmology is that law that underlies everything else that we do. If someone were to say to me, "Who are you?"—in a way that is saying to me "What is your reality map? Show me your reality map and I'll be able to predict a little bit what your behavior is." But if I don't know the other person's reality map, how can I share? …
>
> It turns out by following the cosmology that was around in the last eon, in the last era, in the last century, what did we get?
>
> What we got, all these things were good. But when we followed out that reality map to the very end, we found

that it was inadequate. So as the old cosmology was found inadequate, we now are operating already on the new cosmologies. The trouble is our institutions, our systems, are still locked to the old cosmology. The penal system in the United States is old cosmology. The government is old cosmology. The state of the art of cosmological thinking is not incorporated here.

How do I get the old established cosmology to yield?

Rigidity in Ourselves

Schachter-Shalomi picks up another thread of the lessons of Exodus to try to answer this question of how we "get the old established cosmology to yield." He looks at what Exodus gives us of the process within Pharaoh—rare (for Bible) glimpses of psychological states—as Moses demands, negotiates, threatens, and calls down plagues. From Exodus 7:13 through 9:7 we hear five successive times about Pharaoh's heart becoming hard or stiffening, the last of those times (9:7) being fully explicit that he was causing his own heart to be hard or dull. Then the next five times, in Exodus 9:12 through 14:8, we are told that *God* strengthens or hardens Pharaoh's heart. (In addition we get two times that God tells Moses that he will do this.)

The first hardening of Pharaoh's heart is his own. Now when you watch that thing that says something about you take a position, how many times has it been in my life that I took a position, and having taken that position, although I regretted that position I had to stick with it. I wish that God would allow me to soften my heart. And to get away from the principle that I have established to be able to say [with emphasis on each word] "I changed my mind." Today when we start looking at a mind change, it looks like "fickle." It's such a lousy characteristic. A government cannot change its mind. What a terrible thing this is.

When Pharaoh at first hardens his heart, then we say later God hardens his heart. Then in a sense the position that he has taken is a position he cannot leave. The commitment that we sometimes make even to a wrong choice, and say I'm gonna see it through. And here again is where vindictiveness is coming in. We figure that as long as we have made that choice we have to. Our ego is not ready to let go of that.

And the digging in of position, the polarization that is taking place, that Pharaoh cannot get out of this stand to which he is committed.

Sinai: How Does Revelation Work?

The Biblical narrative takes us to the next stage after the crossing of the sea: the preparation for revelation at Mt. Sinai.

Schachter-Shalomi has been reading from the text and talking about the manna and the water. The people were hungry and threatening to go back to Egypt for better food; God provides manna morning and evening with a double portion on Friday so they should not have to gather on the Sabbath. Then they become thirsty and God has Moses strike a rock and sweet water flows.

Schachter-Shalomi is asking himself and inviting the participants to ask themselves what revelation can be. How does it work? What is it? How do I know if I have it? How do I know that something I get is true? How do I know whether it is of divine origin? How can we call upon revelation?

Suppose revelation does occur: if we stand on a mountain and there is thunder and lightning and the mountain trembles and a voice is heard, we may feel certain that something momentous has taken place. But do we understand the content of the message? Do we understand its meaning or its lesson? And what if it is not so dramatic as in the Sinai story?

One thing that we have to wonder is how the divine message can be translated through our limited human understanding. How would we know that we haven't distorted or oversimplified it? Perhaps the message doesn't come in words at all. We may need to work with a parable or a metaphor or even just an image.

If revelation is to tell me what I already know, I don't need it. If revelation is to tell me something that I don't know, how am I going to know it?

In other words, if revelation were to want to reveal to me something in a code that I don't understand, I wouldn't get a revelation. So I need to at least have the vocabulary for the revelation to reveal something. And if I don't have the vocabulary, then I have to reach for metaphor. But if I don't have the metaphor, I have to reach for symbol. I have to reach for something in order to be able to pour in what I need to pour in otherwise it's not gonna get there.

If the revelation is to be something beyond what I already know, I have somehow to be prepared to open to something that doesn't fit into my previous categories. And revelation can't be something I merely receive passively, an ornament to what I already was. In some sense I must be a participant, must be changed by the experience.

Now it turns out that not only does revelation want to reveal content, but revelation also has to create a revolution in the mind, so that the mind will be able to have the greater capacity to be able to hear on the extra dimensions.

The moment you start saying that God plays a game, and that God is both sides of the game, you get a picture of process.[44]

That is to say, most of the time when people talk about "the One" they see the One as a static One. If you see the One as a static One, then God means dead.

But if you say that there is a closed system but it's infinite, and everything happens within that system, and it keeps on flowing, and everything keeps on turning in that system, and becoming reworked in that system, and so the God who wants to know and the God who wants to

---

44 An idea had been put out earlier in the retreat that perhaps God was acting through Pharaoh as well as through Moses.

be known, both of them are God, but another world of that flow that's going on in that system.

And then the question is, how does this revelation appear? How does growth appear? Most of the time we speak of this as if it were quantity, and it increases in quantity. And we don't quite see the process.

Preparation for Revelation

Schachter-Shalomi steps back from the difficulties of what revelation is and how one knows it, to a more practical and perhaps more manageable topic: how one might prepare for revelation. He sees the Biblical text giving us a pattern for this.

> What do you think it is, that you're eating manna? If I were to want to re-make you so that a lot of your substance shouldn't be *treifener farshtunkener* [45] Egyptian stuff, but I want to make sure that you will have pure God-food for three months before I'm going to give you the revelation, can you hear that? A purification.
>
> And each time another dimension of that is brought in. Let us begin with taking you out of slavery. Let us then add to it the manna. Let's make sure you're gonna get pure water. Let's make sure you will live now by guidance seeing every day you are being reinforced into following the cloud, following the light, following the cloud, following the light. You're being entrained more and more following *"acharei adonai elohekhem telekhun."* You should walk after the lord your God.[46]
>
> You see, you're being entrained into this thing. The preparation that is being made for us, and what a lesson this is and when we are saying "we want revelation from God"

---

45 **Treyf** טריף. Yiddish: proscribed food, food which is not kosher.
Farshtunken פֿאַרשטונקען. Yiddish: stinking.
46 Deut. 13:5. אַחֲרֵי יְהֹוָה אֱלֹהֵיכֶם תֵּלֵכוּ

as to how we might entrain ourselves thereto. And you begin to see what an exciting journey this is.

A capacitor is a thing that charges up with electricity until it gets so charged that it *plotzes* [47] and then boom, it discharges. Get the sense? If we would be able to charge up the electrical capacitor, the spiritual capacitor like that, and then the charge builds to such a point that the theophany comes with the strength, the voltage, that we need to have.

Having Our Questions

Schachter-Shalomi then brings out another dimension to being open to revelation and prepared to actively integrate something from any revelation that comes. We have to have questions. Having questions means we aren't complete and satisfied with our current reality maps; it also means we are open and wondering.

Professor Heschel[48] put it this way. The Torah's the answer, what's the question? He said we'd lost the question. The reason why people can study Torah today and not be touched by anything that they study is because they're getting answers for which they haven't raised questions. When we come and ask for a revelation, when we make ourselves present to a revelation, what kind of revelation would it be if we didn't bring our questions?

The pockets we bring to the revelation get filled with the revelation. Very often in the shape in the pockets, do you know what I'm saying? You bring a filing cabinet and you have files for different things, and after the revelation you will file from the revelation in different categories. But what

---

47 **Plats** פלאַץ. Yiddish: burst.

48 **Abraham Joshua Heschel** (1907–1972). Prominent Jewish theologian and philosopher, born in Poland, lived in America from 1940 until his death. See the opening section of Heschel, *God in Search of Man,* pp. 3–4.

are the categories that you bring? What are the questions
that we need to have answered?

Because I know that otherwise we'll get there, we'll
have an experience, God will have said "I'm the lord your
God" and then someone will say "Are there any action
directives that derive from that?" "Oh, no, it was a very
high experience."

Schachter-Shalomi illustrates the problem with passivity using
a variant of the "how many [some category] does it take to change
a lightbulb" jokes.

How many people does it take to be at Mt. Sinai? Six
hundred thousand and one Moses. So that God would speak
and Moses would mediate and six hundred thousand would
say "yes." You get this kind of picture?

Then you can turn it around and say "What would be
the best way for truth to be captured at this moment of a
truth-burst to come through?" You know, a burst, like a data
burst? Now what does it take to capture a maximum of that
burst? [It would require that] each one of us comes with the
questions that are relevant for them.

The Need to Update Law

The weekend is drawing to a close. Schachter-Shalomi turns
his attention to how change affects Biblical law.

He begins by asserting that there is no "new" law, only a
"renewal" of "lawfulness" based on fresh encounter with the
divine reality. The law given by Moses was itself such a renewal.

Schachter-Shalomi is thinking about what we know most
deeply to be right, and how that same deep recognition in earlier
times was expressed—sometimes in timeless ways, sometimes to
earlier versions of laws that now call for "renewal."

> Moses got a renewal of the law. I don't believe there is
> such a thing as a new law. There is something that happens
> when we meet God that is a renewal of lawfulness.

Schachter-Shalomi brings an application of how openness
to change, fluidity, and the greater openness to revelation might
affect a societal question with a discussion of common law and
legislated law.

Some things, he says, are basic. These are the things we deeply
recognize as right, like not killing, and like being able to call on
truth in human interchanges.

> These are truths that strike us as perennial ones. That
> doesn't change too much.

Other things depend on circumstances. This is covered by laws
that address those circumstances. *Mishpatim*, he says, are like
common law.

> But when it starts coming down on how do we handle
> property, how do we handle indebtedness, how should a
> person who owes a debt deal with that debt? In the olden
> times it meant he became a bondsman, he worked it off.

> Statements such as "When you build a house, and the
> house has a flat roof, you are to make around the flat roof
> of the house a parapet, so that in case somebody's on top
> of that he shouldn't fall down." Safety devices are not
> optional; they're Torah-demanded. ...

> It's on this level that you get to see that many of the
> mitzvahs are not sacerdotal, that many of the mitzvahs,
> especially those that are called mishpatim, are simply the
> way in which we handle our secularity. The word *mishpat*
> comes from judgment.[49]

---

49 **Mishpat** is the noun from the root verb שָׁפַט to judge or govern.

Common law emerges from how people do things at a particular time. But changes in condition means the common law doesn't hold any more. So when that happens, a renewal of the law by revelation is needed.

> Mishpatim then represent an improvement in the state of the law. Each new generation demands that. The update....
>
> A new level of equity has to be established.

A Blessing to Move into New Growth: Kaddish for the Old Paradigms

Schachter-Shalomi gathers the participants for a closing circle, and offers a blessing. His blessing is that the things they are ready to leave behind really get left behind. It is this that will allow the participants to move ahead. But the blessing also explicitly asks for protection from a danger: the things the participants try to leave behind may cry out, even as the memory of good things in Egypt cried out to the Israelites in the wilderness. He asks that the participants not be moved by "false pity" for the cries of the old ways, and invokes the traditional prayer said when mourning the dead as a ritual to allow participants to reconcile to what must be released for new growth to emerge.

> In the moment of *et ratzon*,[50] of good will, of "yes" in you, that those things that we want to leave behind, we really left behind. That our guardian angels and beings that surround us protect us, so that the cries of the abandoned habits not move us to a false pity, but that we say over them a gentle *kaddish*. Let's say this *kaddish* right now.

Schachter-Shalomi leads the group, and all join in, reciting *kaddish yatom,* the prayer of praise of God that is is traditionally said by mourners.

---

50 עֵת רָצוֹן, time of good will.

8
"Renewal":
Does this Exploration of Rigidity and Change Help us Understand Schachter-Shalomi's Vision for Judaism?

Schachter-Shalomi did not connect the teachings he presents over the course of the Exodus weekend directly to his work of "Jewish renewal." However, the foregoing exploration of the sacredness of fluidity and change, when necessary, might help one see how he reconciles his obvious commitment to tradition with a vision that in some respects seems to depart from traditional interpretations.

Although he didn't make the connection during this weekend, he did address, in a session during the Genesis weekend, the contrast of his own approach to authenticity and the approach that seeks to to maintain the authenticity of tradition by exacting adherence to old patterns.

Schachter-Shalomi had been speaking about how we find our way in new times. We want to carry forward the values of the past, but in the past they have been couched in very different terms. How do we figure out how to apply them in our times? How do we still apply the old values and wisdom when we have learned so much more about certain things, such as (as was investigated in the Genesis weekend) the limitations and prices paid by territoriality?

I want that we should have values and morality and ethics. And we have to shape, form, the values and ethics and morality for the next age. It can't be the *alte kale mit a nayem shleyer*,[1] the old bride with a new veil. It has to be a renewed situation that deals exactly with our understanding. The state of the art of living.

These transformations have to be applied to religion as well. What worked for patriarchs and priests of ancient times may not be sufficient to guide us now. But the intent, the values, and the teaching being given, are all precious things not to be lost. We must bridge from them to where we are if we are to transport those teachings into the present and the future.

Schachter-Shalomi acknowledges that he has been accused of not being authentically Jewish because he has tried to make these bridges. But he says that the re-visioning/revisioning is exactly what he is undertaking to do.

So it is with religion. Some of the people who say to me, "Zalman, you're not authentic to *Yiddishkeyt*[2] because you're not repeating what was said yesterday." But my point is precisely that.

If we are to look to do what Abram and Malkitzedek[3] did, then there has to be a bridging into that next age. For all the values! I want to transport, make portable, every good value from the past. And take it into the future.

---

1 **Alte kale mit a nayem shleyer.** Yiddish: "Old bride with a new veil." The same old thing being passed off as something new.

2 **Yidishkeyt** ייִדישקייט. Yiddish: Jewishness, Jewish traditions, Jewish culture.

3 **Malkitzedek**, a priest not in the Jewish line. After Abram defeats some marauding kings, Malkitzedek blesses him in the name of the most high God. [Gen. 14:18–20]

> But it can't be transported without being transformed. The files of the CP/M won't read in DOS.[4] They have to first be transformed, there has to be a translation program they get filtered through first.

Schachter-Shalomi says that this is his vision for what he is doing with this Wisdom School. He is exploring together with the participants how to make the bridge, how to transform the teachings and the values so that they can be "read," understood and used, by us, and passed on to the future.

> And this is what we are creating here. We are shaping the template of Bible. We are trying to give a new order, as it were, to that membrane through which past midrash is going to flow into future midrash. Why wisdom schools? Because whatever we are doing here is to filter this thing through so that the great values that are here are *going to* cross and filter against the real understanding of the issues that we have today.

What some may have thought was being "authentic," he calls "importing it raw." That will not work any more than trying to open old computer files under the latest operating system.

Schachter-Shalomi sees his process of transformation or filtering as something that must be done, and something that in fact we do, in every area of learning. Medicine does not continue to rely on the teachings of Galen when there are MRI imaging machines whose evidence can be taken into consideration.

> So I'm not saying "Import it just as it was, raw." It has to be put through the process. And this is what is happening in

---

4　**CP/M and DOS.**　The earliest operating systems for microcomputers. CP/M: Control Program for Microcomputers. DOS: Disk Operating System.　Developed in the 1970's. This example refers to 1988 computer technology; in 2012 one might speak of Windows XP files not being readable under Windows 7.

> medicine, this is what's happening in science, this is what's
> happening in law. People are starting to ask the questions
> that say "What is necessary to take the good intent of the
> past and make it come out?"

Much as there is of a factual nature, and of changes in cosmology and social structures, there is also the matter of what we have learned about our own "instinctual stuff" (as he explored in the Genesis weekend). We can become aware of things that used to just happen, and then look back at the Biblical narratives and see why things worked out in the problematic ways they often did.

> And each time, something we were unconscious about is
> entering into our awareness. And we are learning not only
> about instinctual stuff, we are learning about games, we're
> learning about patterns we have in life, we are beginning to
> see set-ups, we're beginning to see the hot potatoes we pass
> on from generation to generation that we have to learn to
> be conscious about and to filter out. This is what this is all
> about.

A Cairn of Witness for Transition

Schachter-Shalomi takes a teaching from a growth process traced out within the Biblical narrative.

When God first speaks to Abram he does so in the place where Abram (along with his father Terach) had settled, in Paddan Aram (the field or country of the Arameans), the land of the Arameans. Later Abraham sends to Paddan Aram for a wife for his son Isaac, finding there the formidable Rebecca, sister of Laban.[5] Rebecca later sends her son Jacob back to Paddan Aram and Isaac orders him to take a wife from there; in Paddan Aram Jacob marries two

---

5   Gen. 25:20. When Abraham initially sends his servant Eliezer on
    this errand, he describes Paddan Aram as "my country and my
    kindred." (Gen. 24:3)

of Laban's daughters, Leah and Rachel.[6] Laban and his father Bethuel are both called Arameans.[7]

But in time, Jacob chooses to leave Laban and the Aramean territory, taking his wives and children with him. God has appeared to him and ordered him to go back to his original home in the south, in Canaan.[8] And when he leaves, the text says[9] "And God appeared to Jacob again, when he came out of Paddan Aram, and blessed him." It is time, God may be saying, for the Abrahamic line to leave Aramea for good and move on to their new destiny.

Jacob's descendents, the "children of Israel," will be the ones to sojourn in Egypt and be dramatically taken out again (now no longer a small family but as twelve large tribes); they will be the ones to receive Torah at Sinai and finally actually conquer and settle the promised land. They will have moved not just geographically but in terms of spiritual understanding and religious practice, away from the territory of the Arameans.

The transition, however, is not done without acknowledgment, marking, and sanctification. When Jacob first leaves Laban, he does so stealthily, and Laban pursues and challenges him, accusing him of stealing his daughters and tricking him. They come to an understanding, and make an uneasy covenant, and seal it by building a cairn of stones and placing God as witness to their agreement.[10]

> We also have to create between the old age and the new age this cairn and say "This is witness!" We have passed from the Arameans' territory into the other territory. The cairn of witness has to be set up. And we are saying "And we want God to be there. We don't want God not to look at

---

6 Gen. 28:2.

7 See, for example, Gen. 25:20 and Gen. 31:20.

8 Gen. 31:3.

9 Gen. 35:9.

10 See Gen. 31:44–48.

this. We want God to look at this transition, to be with us in this transition.

We too, Schachter-Shalomi is saying, need a "cairn of witness." If we are to make our own transition into a further stage of spiritual or religious growth, we need such a cairn of witness to ask God to guide us, stand with us, and be himself witness to sacredness of this delicate process.

God must be with us in all such transformations and transitions, not just so that it should be *Yiddishkeyt*, but so that it will be holy, spiritually harmonious, and viable. Schachter-Shalomi seals that with a prayer quoting scripture:

> And we pray, "Ribono Shel Olam, *Yehi adonai elohenu, imanu ka'asher hayah im avotenu; al ya'azvenu v'al yitshenu.* As God has been with our parents, so may God be with us. And not forsake us, and not leave us behind."[11]

---

11 1 Kings 8:57. יְהִי יְהוָֹה אֱלֹהֵינוּ עִמָּנוּ כַּאֲשֶׁר הָיָה עִם־אֲבֹתֵינוּ
אַל־יַעַזְבֵנוּ וְאַל־יִטְּשֵׁנוּ׃ May it be that YHVH our God is with us
as he was with our ancestors; let him not forsake us and let him not
abandon us.

From the sixth weekend,
"Deuteronomy and Ecclesiastes"

9

Deuteronomy and Ecclesiastes:
Finding a Balance

During this, the sixth of the seven weekends in the series, Schachter-Shalomi juxtaposes the text of *Deuteronomy*, tradition-ally attributed to Moses, and the text of *Ecclesiastes*, traditionally attributed to King Solomon. He explores what he sees as their balance of each other in their strikingly different approaches. This is no mere literary exercise: Schachter-Shalomi argues that the teaching of each text provides us in the present day with essential values and guidance, as well as having had an historical role in the formation of the Jewish people.

At the end of the first weekend, in his preview of the whole series, Schachter-Shalomi sketched the plan for this retreat as follows:

> The book of Deuteronomy says "Always do this; don't you ever do that." We know that voice. It is the voice of toilet training. It's the voice that speaks to a certain level of moral development. I'm not down on it, it's not a bad book, it's a very holy book. It's a book that has transformed the people, like The Little Red Book[1] of Mao has managed in twenty years to do something to bring an ancient civilization to the current century.
>
> So the book of Deuteronomy has *power.* It also is absolutist. The book of Ecclesiastes is not a good book to start teaching little kids. For everything there's a time and a

---

1   *Quotations from Chairman Mao,* published by the government of People's Republic of China from 1964 until about 1976. Usually known in the West as *The Little Red Book.*

season, sometimes you do this, sometimes you do that.[2] So you can imagine that we want to look at both books of Bible and the balance to be had.

A Sampling to Catch a Bit of the Flavor of These Books

The tone of Deuteronomy can be evoked by the following verses, variations of which are to be found in the latter four books of teachings given through, or by, Moses.[3]

A short statement:

"See, I am setting before you today a blessing and a curse: the blessing, which (will be) if you obey the commandments of YHVH your God, which I command you today, and the curse, if you do not obey the commandments of YHVH your God, but you turn aside from the way that I am commanding you today, to go after other gods that you have not known."[4]

And another passage that dwells at more inviting length on the rewards before naming the consequences of the disobedience:

"And it will be, if you really listen to my commandments that I command you this day, to love YHVH your God and to serve him with all your heart and all your soul, then I will give rain to your land in its season, early rain and later rain, and you will gather your grain and your new wine and your olive oil, and I will give green grass in your field for your livestock, and you will eat and you will be satisfied. Take care lest your heart be deceived, and

---

2 Schachter-Shalomi refers to Ecclesiastes 3:1: "For everything there is a season, and a time for every matter under heaven." לַכֹּל זְמָן וְעֵת לְכָל־חֵפֶץ תַּחַת הַשָּׁמָיִם:

3 That is, Exodus, Leviticus, Numbers, and Deuteronomy.

4 Deut. 11:26–28. רְאֵה אָנֹכִי נֹתֵן לִפְנֵיכֶם הַיּוֹם בְּרָכָה וּקְלָלָה: אֶת־הַבְּרָכָה אֲשֶׁר תִּשְׁמְעוּ אֶל־מִצְוֹת יְהוָה אֱלֹהֵיכֶם אֲשֶׁר אָנֹכִי מְצַוֶּה אֶתְכֶם הַיּוֹם: וְהַקְּלָלָה אִם־לֹא תִשְׁמְעוּ אֶל־מִצְוֹת יְהוָה אֱלֹהֵיכֶם וְסַרְתֶּם מִן־הַדֶּרֶךְ אֲשֶׁר אָנֹכִי מְצַוֶּה אֶתְכֶם הַיּוֹם לָלֶכֶת אַחֲרֵי אֱלֹהִים אֲחֵרִים אֲשֶׁר לֹא־יְדַעְתֶּם:

you turn away and you serve other gods and you worship them. The anger of YHVH will then burn against you and he will shut up the heavens and there will not be rain and the ground will not give her produce and you will perish quickly from on the good land that YHVH is giving you."[5]

In contrast, the tone of Ecclesiastes may be suggested in part by its famous lines "for everything there is a time and season," which I give here in Robert Alter's translation:[6]

"Everything has a season, and a time for every matter under the heavens. A time to be born and a time to die. A time to plant and a time to uproot what is planted. A time to kill and a time to heal. A time to rip down and a time to build. A time to weep and a time to laugh. A time to mourn and a time to dance. A time to fling stones and a time to gather stones in. A time to embrace and a time to pull back from embracing. A time to seek and a time to lose. A time to keep and a time to fling away. A time to tear and a time to sew. A time to keep silent and a time to speak. A time to love and a time to hate. A time for war and a time for peace."[7]

---

5   Deut. 11:13–17. וְהָיָה אִם־שָׁמֹעַ תִּשְׁמְעוּ אֶל־מִצְוֺתַי אֲשֶׁר אָנֹכִי מְצַוֶּה אֶתְכֶם הַיּוֹם לְאַהֲבָה אֶת־יְהֹוָה אֱלֹהֵיכֶם וּלְעָבְדוֹ בְּכָל־לְבַבְכֶם וּבְכָל־נַפְשְׁכֶם: וְנָתַתִּי מְטַר־אַרְצְכֶם בְּעִתּוֹ יוֹרֶה וּמַלְקוֹשׁ וְאָסַפְתָּ דְגָנֶךָ וְתִירֹשְׁךָ וְיִצְהָרֶךָ: וְנָתַתִּי עֵשֶׂב בְּשָׂדְךָ לִבְהֶמְתֶּךָ וְאָכַלְתָּ וְשָׂבָעְתָּ: הִשָּׁמְרוּ לָכֶם פֶּן־יִפְתֶּה לְבַבְכֶם וְסַרְתֶּם וַעֲבַדְתֶּם אֱלֹהִים אֲחֵרִים וְהִשְׁתַּחֲוִיתֶם לָהֶם: וְחָרָה אַף־יְהֹוָה בָּכֶם וְעָצַר אֶת־הַשָּׁמַיִם וְלֹא־יִהְיֶה מָטָר וְהָאֲדָמָה לֹא תִתֵּן אֶת־יְבוּלָהּ וַאֲבַדְתֶּם מְהֵרָה מֵעַל הָאָרֶץ הַטֹּבָה אֲשֶׁר יְהֹוָה נֹתֵן לָכֶם:

6   Alter, Robert, *The Wisdom Books*, pp. 354–355.

7   Ecc. 3:1–8:

א לַכֹּל זְמָן וְעֵת לְכָל־חֵפֶץ תַּחַת הַשָּׁמָיִם : ב עֵת לָלֶדֶת וְעֵת לָמוּת עֵת לָטַעַת וְעֵת לַעֲקוֹר נָטוּעַ : ג עֵת לַהֲרוֹג וְעֵת לִרְפּוֹא עֵת לִפְרוֹץ וְעֵת לִבְנוֹת : ד עֵת לִבְכּוֹת וְעֵת לִשְׂחוֹק עֵת סְפוֹד וְעֵת רְקוֹד : ה עֵת לְהַשְׁלִיךְ אֲבָנִים וְעֵת כְּנוֹס אֲבָנִים עֵת לַחֲבוֹק וְעֵת לִרְחֹק מֵחַבֵּק : ו עֵת לְבַקֵּשׁ וְעֵת לְאַבֵּד עֵת לִשְׁמוֹר וְעֵת לְהַשְׁלִיךְ : ז עֵת לִקְרוֹעַ וְעֵת לִתְפּוֹר עֵת לַחֲשׁוֹת וְעֵת לְדַבֵּר : ח עֵת לֶאֱהֹב וְעֵת לִשְׂנֹא עֵת מִלְחָמָה וְעֵת שָׁלוֹם :

What are These Books?

The Hebrew title of Deuteronomy is *Devarim*, and the Hebrew title of Ecclesiastes is *Qohelet*. Within the book of Ecclesiastes Solomon is not named. The author is referred to as Qohelet. The Hebrew root *Qahal* means to gather together into an assembly or congregation. (The translators of the *Septuagint* chose the Greek word *Ecclesiastes*, which means "one who assembles.")

Qohelet is the preacher, or teacher: one who gathers people together. The word has the form of a feminine participle, and by normal Hebrew grammar *Qohel* would be the masculine one who gathers people together and *Qohelet* a feminine gatherer of people. However, because of its use here for a clearly masculine author who identifies himself as having been a king over Israel in Jerusalem, it is treated lexically as a masculine noun.[8]

The author of Ecclesiastes uses the term appositively to *ani*, "I," in Ecclesiastes 1:12.[9] We understand that Qohelet, the gatherer or preacher or teacher, is the speaker or author of the book. Because Qohelet identifies himself as a "son of David, king in Jerusalem," he is traditionally understood to be King Solomon.

Schachter-Shalomi's Engagement with these Texts

One thing that comes out most strikingly in Schachter-Shalomi's teachings on this weekend is his ability—and willingness—to work with both the traditional pious level of reading these texts and the historical scholarly level. His breadth of intellect, and his imaginative breadth, makes him able to hold and honor and learn from both levels at once.

---

8 Another oddity of the grammar of this word is that one would expect it to be a causative: the one who causes people to be gathered or assembled. Instead it appears to convey more the sense of one who himself assembles. See discussion of this in Robert Alter, *The Wisdom Books*, p. 337.

9 Ecc. 1:12: אֲנִי קֹהֶלֶת הָיִיתִי מֶלֶךְ עַל־יִשְׂרָאֵל בִּירוּשָׁלָ͏ִם׃

Thus we will see him drawing teaching lessons from a view of Deuteronomy as proceeding from Moses recounting the history of the Exodus from Egypt and the forty years in the wilderness within the context of that time and environment. We will also see him drawing teaching lessons from an understanding of that text as being composed much later as part of King Josiah's reforms.

A major theme which emerges from the exploration of this juxtaposition is the need for us as individuals, and as the people of the Jewish tradition, and as a species, to develop judgment in order to be able to use discernment. But the process of this exploration takes on the question of how one develops that judgment, how one learns, and how one generation teaches the next to pass on its values and the truths it has come to know over a lifetime.

Evident also during this weekend is Schachter-Shalomi's interest in old age and what he was beginning to develop as "spiritual eldering." Both of these books (as traditionally understood) were written at the end of their authors' lives, giving the summary of what they had learned over those lives. Schachter-Shalomi has devoted himself since this Primal Myths series to working on distilling and passing on what he has learned, both in books and in-person teachings. Following his taste for using computer metaphors, he has described this in conversations (and indirectly in the previous retreat, p. 173) as downloading his hard-drive to his students and to the world—to the future generations.

> We have an opportunity [this weekend] of living with Moses and whoever Qohelet was.
>
> We begin to see two folks, two men in this case. They have gotten old. And each one finds himself in that place where he wants to leave a truth behind. We will hear[10]

---

10 Later in the weekend time is given for a participant to talk about Lao Tzu and Confucius and the similar juxtaposition of those two works: Lao Tzu on the way of the "Tao" (the "way" of aligning with the flow of the universe) and Confucius giving a set of duties and obligations meant to ensure an orderly society. As with Moses and Solomon, the historicity of Lao Tzu's [*continued overleaf*]

about another man who wanted to leave a country after he had served it for a lifetime, and the emperor says he can't go "until you leave your truth behind in the form of a book." Do you get that sense? With Lao Tzu it comes in the form of the *Tao Te Ching*. With Moses it comes in the form of the book of *Devarim*. With Solomon is comes in the form of *Qohelet*.

I want to go back and ask the question, prior to getting involved in details of what did Moses say and what did Solomon say, "Who are those people?" (If we have to say that,[11] "the Moses one" and "the Solomonic one.") Because both of them speak to us from a place of wisdom.

Schachter-Shalomi notes the very different imaginative experience of the two. Not only are their messages different, but, as we turn our attention to them, we experience their whole aura and affect as different. Both may be important to us, both may be loved, but our way of engaging with them will reflect the feelings they evoke.

And so we get these two mythic characters. We see a nimbus of imagination and fantasy around Solomon. We see a starkness around Moses.

---

authorship is debated by scholars, but tradition says that he is the author of the *Tao Te Ching*, and his name means "old master."

11 **"If we have to say that."** Schachter-Shalomi means that if someone insists that the supposed historical characters weren't necessarily the authors of these texts, we will just call whoever-it-was by that name.

10
Solomon and Solomonic Wisdom

We are very familiar with the character of Moses, the purported author of Deuteronomy. Most of us know from childhood Moses's story from his birth to his death, and we know his central role in the Jewish tradition. We know him as a monumental character, whether legendary or historical, and as the archetypical guide of his people from slavery to the brink of nationhood; we know that he is understood to be the one who brought all of the divine laws to the Jewish people. The previous weekend (the one on the book of Exodus) focused on Moses.

But we need to fill out our understanding of Solomon, the purported author of Ecclesiastes.

Solomon the Wise

Over dinner on the first night of the retreat, Schachter-Shalomi entertained the participants, and evoked a feeling for Solomon for them, by recounting folk tales featuring Solomon that emerged over the subsequent millenia. I will describe that material and its significance shortly.

At the first formal session of the retreat Schachter-Shalomi reviewed Solomon's story as told by the Biblical text.

> Let's take a look a little bit at Solomon and see who he is. He is the child of David and Batsheba, but not that first child.

Schachter-Shalomi reviews the story of David and Bathsheba and their first child, the one of the adulterous union, who died.[1]

---

1   2 Samuel chapters 11–12.

> So he is the legit child this time, it's all straightened out with David and Batsheba. Then the king his father dies.

Schachter-Shalomi reviews the story of David's last days and the competition among his sons for the succession.[2]

> It does come to Solomon that he is to be the next king.
>
> And then comes that beautiful moment in which he feels himself in the presence of God and he says, "I want to pray for wisdom. I have a task coming to me that I may not be ready for. I need every bit of guidance; I need your guidance every step of the way."
>
> God says to him, "You could have asked me for riches, you could have asked me for the lives of your enemies, you could have asked me for anything you wanted. How come you asked me for wisdom?" He says, "Because that's what I need so badly." So God says "I'll give you all of these and wisdom first."[3]

It's not just that Solomon happened to be wise. According to the Biblical account, he wanted to be wise; he prayed for it and sought it from God. And the wisdom that came (at least the surpassing dimension that comes after this time, after he becomes king) is a wisdom that is said to be given by God.

It might be appropriate, then, to consider the content of the wisdom he is offering to be God-given wisdom, something more than, or on a different level from, personal wisdom. Perhaps it wouldn't go too far, then, to understand the wisdom that Solomon expresses in Ecclesiastes to be divine wisdom.

> So watch this. So he builds a Temple. He prays for wisdom, he builds a Temple, he unites the kingdom.

---

2   1 Kings chapters 1–2.

3   See 2 Chr. 1.11–1.12.

Schachter-Shalomi notes (perhaps connecting this to the God-given wisdom) that Solomon conquers surrounding territory not by military conquest but by marriage alliances.

> And he makes love and not war to build an empire.
> In other words he conquers the surrounding territories in his harem, taking the daughters of the surrounding kings, marrying them by alliances, this is how he becomes the great king.

Wisdom's Resonance with the Feminine

Solomon represents wisdom, then, and this wisdom is a quality for which he prayed and which was given by God. But Schachter-Shalomi doesn't want to stop there. What other dimensions and connections need to be drawn to the idea of Solomon's "wisdom"?

> So what you get is he represents wisdom.
>
> Now let's go for a moment and see, how does wisdom usually get dressed up? Not necessarily as a male; in fact, as we will have occasion to find, She, *chokhmah*, is running around in the streets. "Wisdom cries out loud in the streets."[4] One is to say to Wisdom, "Be my sister."[5] You get the sense that here is Wisdom and the feminine, *sophia* [and the feminine], go together.
>
> Today we are going to look at Wisdom in two forms, two masculine forms, and we will look at these two males, as they stand before us prior to their death.

Schachter-Shalomi is engaging in some of the subtle weaving of themes of male and female that I find characteristic of his handling of gender issues. He is choosing to look at the way two male characters formulate and articulate the wisdom they have gathered

---

4   Prov. 1:20.

5   Prov. 7:4.

in their lifetimes; but wisdom itself, in the Bible and other traditions, is feminine. The Hebrew noun חָכְמָה, *chokhmah*, wisdom,
is feminine in grammatical gender and is personified as female in
the Wisdom books of the Bible, as is *sophia* is in the Greek pagan
and philosophical tradition. Schachter-Shalomi notes this in passing as he invites us into contemplation of the wisdom in the books
that these two men have bequeathed.

Holy Spirit May Speak in Female Language

Earlier, in introducing the word קֹהֶלֶת *qohelet*, Schachter-
Shalomi had digressed into recounting a discovery made in
the course of preparing for the weekend that had surprised and
delighted him. He first noted, without speculating on what it could
mean, that (as I mentioned above) the Hebrew word *qohelet* translates as "she who gathers." This perhaps reminded him of his
discovery and led into the digression:

> I was in the middle of preparing and I got this big "oh
> wow!" What was it that I had found? There in the middle of
> Rashi's[6] commentary—I'd like to read you this one so you
> can hear it because there will be times and occasions that
> you will want to use it, when there are people who will say
> something about male and femaleness of where we are with
> God.
>
> So I read you the line.[7] "*Qohelet*"—the name of that
> book—"*Lashon nekevah hu.*"[8] It is an expression of

6   **Rashi**, an acronym for Rabbi Shlomo ben Yitzchak, was an 11th
    century CE teacher of Torah who lived in southern France. He
    was recognized as the leading Torah authority of his time and is
    probably still in the present day the most influential, and widely-
    studied, commentator on Torah. His writings include extensive
    commentaries on *Tanakh* and *Talmud*. All printed editions of
    Babylonian Talmud have included his commentary, and many
    editions of Tanakh include at least portions of his commentary.

7   The line he quotes is from Rashi's commentary to Ecclesiastes
    Chapter 7 Verse 27.

8   *Lashon nekevah hu.* Hebrew: "It is female language."

the feminine, not of the masculine. You would expect
Ecclesiastes to be like "ecclesiastical" [in the Christian
tradition]: male, celibate, hierarchical. Rashi gives
us "*Lashon nekevah hu.*" It is the gathering, and "the
gathering" is female.

And here came that quote that I underlined and that
got me so excited, "Said Rabbi Jeremiah, son of Rabbi
Eleazar[9]—" We're speaking of someone who lives about
the third century of the current era. "*Ruach haQodesh,*" the
holy spirit: "*p'amin m'sichah b'lashon zakhar,*" at times
the holy spirit speaks in the masculine; "*v'fa'amin m'sichah
b'lashon nekevah,*" and at times she speaks in feminine
tongue.

I want to say how surprised I was to find an eleventh
century commentator quoting someone from the third
century saying that the holy spirit sometimes speaks in the
masculine form about himself and at times in the feminine
form about herself.

Schachter-Shalomi has discovered that Rashi was also struck
by the feminine form of the word *qohelet,* and he noticed that
Rashi was bothered enough by it to feel that it needed some commentary.[10] This commentary, as it generally does, takes the form
of quoting one of the Sages. Schachter-Shalomi identifies this
Talmudic sage as living about the third century common era. He
is struck, and brings these dates out, because neither Rashi nor

---

9   Rashi refers to a passage in Midrash Qohelet Rabbah, Chapter 7 (ז),
    paragraph 48 (מח).

10 Students of Rashi—which is to say, all students of the Jewish
    textual tradition—are enjoined in traditional learning environments
    to ask, about each piece of Rashi's commentary, "What was
    bothering Rashi?" This is because Rashi brings in explanatory
    material in response to a textual difficulty and one can work
    backwards from what may seem unrelated commentary to uncover
    the difficulty. This can then lead to one's own pondering and
    discussion. This phrase is even used as the title of a series of books
    about Rashi's commentary to Biblical texts: Avigdor Bonchek,
    What's Bothering Rashi?

the Talmudic rabbis are known for feminist views or even for any particular openness to honoring a feminine side of God.

What Schachter-Shalomi is seeing in Rashi's words is confirmation of his theological stance that divine being, as a being greater than particular gender personifications, should not be limited to the stereotypical characterization of one gender.

As he sees affirmed in Rashi's words, we need metaphors to speak about that which is beyond words and human images. Sometimes it is useful to use metaphors based on characteristics understood, in human terms, as male. But other times it is useful to use metaphors that bring to our awareness and understanding qualities that are associated in human terms as female.

The Bible, of course, relies heavily on conventionally male qualities, and these are not wrong, only limited. In the first weekend, in the context of the Creation, Schachter-Shalomi balanced this by highlighting and exploring divine qualities and processes that are conventionally female. Some of the images the Biblical text of Creation offers are powerfully masculine (at least according to conventional gender characterizations); others are unmistakably feminine (again, according to conventional characterizations), bringing out feminine images of gestation and nurturance.[11]

Rashi, in this commentary on the book of Qohelet, quotes a Talmudic rabbi as attributing the language to the Holy Spirit (*ruach ha qodesh*), who must speak sometimes in masculine language and sometimes in feminine language to convey the full reality. This gives Schachter-Shalomi "proof texts" in the tradition: instances of early, venerated teachers saying the same thing he is saying.

Solomon the Folk Archetype of the Wise

Painting a picture of how people through Jewish history thought about and imaginatively experienced Solomon,

---

11   See my earlier chapter Male and Female Images.

Schachter-Shalomi returns to folk tales and songs he began with at the first evening's dinner table.

> Solomon the Wise, that's how people spoke of King Solomon. "*Solomon der Weise hat gesagt....*"[12] In the German this is the form in which it was spoken. And all through the medieval period, people when they would quote something from King Solomon would say "He is the wise one." They have that beautiful song: What would be when the Messiah would come? There will be this great party. [singing:] "*Vos vet zeyn as Meshiach vet kumen? A sudenyu.* Who would speak wisdom at that party? Solomon, the great wise king. *Shlomo, ha melekh. Shlomo ha melekh* will tell us wisdom. *Af der sudenyu.*"[13]

Solomon as Genie of Imagination

The first recorded session of this weekend[14] evidently took place over dinner the first evening, as Schachter-Shalomi introduced Solomon and the tradition of Solomonic wisdom by telling stories about Solomon from ancient, medieval, and more recent authors. The stories were offered informally (interrupted by the business of dining and some cross-talk). Because they were offered not as formal teaching but with an intention of giving participants a flavor of some of what Solomon has represented in

---

12 German, "Solomon the Wise said...."

13 Jewish folk song in Yiddish language, entitled *A Sudenyu,* "a feast." "What will be when Messiah is come? A feast. ... Who will say words of wisdom for us at the feast? King Solomon will say words of wisdom ... at the feast." The song also describes the wine we will drink and what we will eat, and says that Moses will explicate Torah for us and King David will play for us and the Prophetess Miriam will dance for us, "*af der sudenyu,* at the feast." A performance by Betzalel Edwards of Jerusalem, Israel, can be found at http://youtu.be/DKC4HuJiBQI (accessed 12 September 2012).

14 This audio file was erroneously cataloged in the archive as the last in the series.

the Jewish tradition (much of that flavor having elements of the fantastical), it has not seemed useful to transcribe the full stories for this presentation. However, some of his remarks made in passing between stories help illustrate Schachter-Shalomi's own views about Solomon and the contribution that Solomon as a character and as a teacher made to the tradition.

One characteristic Schachter-Shalomi recognizes and is struck by is something he calls "indirection." He sees this in at least one Biblical account as well as in later and folkloric tales.

> One of the wonderful things about Solomonic wisdom is how indirect it is. That's to say, he did not judge, he created a sort of billiard move. You know what I mean?

To illustrate, Schachter-Shalomi relates the Biblical story[15] of Solomon and the two women with one dead and one live baby, each claiming the live baby as her own. When Solomon presents as his solution the proposal to cut the live baby in half and give half to each mother, one mother acquiesces and the other withdraws her claim to the living child rather than have it killed. Solomon's conclusion, recognized (the narrative tells us) by "all Israel" as displaying "divine wisdom," is that the true mother is the one whose love for the baby made her willing to give up the baby to save its life.

The "billiard move" is to aim not directly at the pocket that is the intended destination but to bank the ball off the side wall of the table so that it changes direction to reach the pocket, perhaps avoiding undesired collisions that would have occurred had the ball been aimed directly.

In this case, Solomon may not have known who the real mother was; or perhaps he did know, but the "divine wisdom" lay in causing the mothers themselves to reveal the truth.

Schachter-Shalomi then recounts a long tale whose purpose was to explain the Biblical verse "Cast your bread upon the face

---

15 1 Kings 3:16–28.

of the waters, for in many days you will find it."[16] In this tale, as Schachter-Shalomi presents it, Qohelet's advice in the book of Ecclesiastes is given a back-story of a literal throwing of flour on the sea, albeit in this case an act that was unintentional—in fact an act carried out by the wind to the dismay of the owner of the flour.

The indignant owner of the flour comes to King David's court to complain of the robbery. Solomon, with his magical powers, is able to call the wind to court to account for its actions, and so he, his father King David, and the others learn why the wind blew away the man's flour. The wind, it turned out, was responding to a distress call from a foundering ship, and the flour served to glue the ship back together long enough to save the crew and its cargo.

Then we hear the happy ending that the saved ship later makes it back home and in gratitude for the flour that glued it back together awards the man who lost his flour a third of the value of the cargo.

These events are gradually unfolded, with a young Solomon quietly orchestrating them, while a more straightforward and practical King David goes about his normal and direct king business.[17]

> So, this sentence is one sentence, "Cast thy bread upon the waters for in the long run you will get it back." … So you could see how the imagination of our people was totally involved in trying to understand the background to all these statements in the book of Ecclesiastes.

---

16 Ecc. 11:1.

17 See Ginzberg, *Legends of the Jews*, p. 956 n27, for the gist of this story about the man and his sack of flour. (The cited note also discusses traditions and popular tales that bring out Solomon's superiority of wisdom over that of David, including stories of Solomon correcting his father.) See also bin Gorion, *Mimekor Yisrael*, Vol. 1, p. 127–128 for a similar tale from the Arabic tradition of Solomon bringing the wind to trial over theft of the flour.

Schachter-Shalomi sees in this, and even more so in some subsequent tales that carry Solomon's magical powers to yet more fanciful extremes, a testimony to the way this character in particular has sparked the imagination.

The next tale Schachter-Shalomi recounts undertakes to explain how Solomon decided where to build the Temple. It involves a story of two loving brothers living on opposite sides of a mountain, each so filled with compassion for the other that each brings a gift of rice one night over the mountain to the other. They meet at the top of the mountain, and their loving meeting is observed by birds, who tell Solomon about it;[18] he honors and commemorates this amity by building the Temple there.[19]

Solomon is credited with the ability to talk not only to winds and birds, but to demons and other elements of creation with whom we (in ordinary reality) do not converse. He has the ability to ride around the world on a carpet, to instantly be transported here and there, to possess a magical ring that gives special powers, and so on. These all make for wonderful, long, rambling tales.

Schachter-Shalomi next begins a very long and elaborate tale that could have served Scheherezade well—and perhaps did so serve her: a long struggle between Solomon and the King of the Demons. It features a kaleidoscopic unfolding, filled with adventures, twists and turns, impersonations, magic carpet rides, stealing the magic ring, losing the ring by dropping it in the sea

---

18 The birds report to Solomon because, as is well known to the tellers of and listeners to such tales, Solomon speaks the language of the animals. This popular belief is based on I Kings 5.13 וַיְדַבֵּר֒ עַל־הַבְּהֵמָה וְעַל־הָע֔וֹף וְעַל־הָרֶ֖מֶשׂ וְעַל־הַדָּגִֽים׃ ("and he spoke on/concerning beasts, flying things, creeping things, and fish"). For a tracing of this idea of Solomonic ability to talk with animals, and Midrashic attempts to ground or rationalize it, see Ginzberg, *Legends of the Jews*, p. 957, n34.

19 See Ginzberg, *Legends of the Jews*, p. 956. Ginzberg tells a similar story but instead of the birds carrying the story of the two brothers to Solomon, a heavenly voice directed Solomon to go to a field where each brother was secretly adding to the other's store of grain.

while on a turbulent carpet ride, finding it again inside a fish, and so on.[20]

Imagination, Creativity, and Flexibility

In the recorded talks Schachter-Shalomi does not spell out the connection between the imaginative richness that was triggered by the character of Solomon and the old man of wisdom who wrote the pensive words of the book of Ecclesiastes. Perhaps the connection could be traced to the line of thinking Schachter-Shalomi brought out explicitly in the material of the Exodus weekend included in my chapter entitled Rigidity and Change.

There is a certain rigidity (or at least stability and clarity, if "rigidity" sounds too pejorative) in the presentation of the laws in Deuteronomy. By contrast, the message of the book of Ecclesiastes is freer, showing flexibility and indeed, according to the teaching Qohelet wishes to transmit, a *need* for flexibility. This is what Qohelet calls wisdom.

Perhaps something about this unconventional approach to right living, combined with Solomon's "billiard move" solutions to problems as represented in the canonical text (at least in the case of the decision regarding the disputed baby), served to trigger this rich imaginative flow.

And how has this served the Jewish people, one might ask? Aside from providing the delight of the stories, we might again turn to the more theological thinking Schachter-Shalomi was doing during the Exodus weekend about the need for flexibility, indeed *change*, to balance stability and rigidity.

Keeping the tradition alive and fecund may require a certain admixture of magic carpet rides.

---

20 See Ginzberg, *Legends of the Jews,* pp. 973–978. Most of these elements in Schachter-Shalomi's telling are mentioned and documented there.

11
Book of Deuteronomy

Deuteronomy as Transformative Heritage

Schachter-Shalomi's first major piece of work for this weekend is to represent the contribution of Deuteronomy to the Jewish heritage. In doing this he wants to account for the full complexity of the issues.

On the one hand, he sees Deuteronomy as having certain limitations, or perhaps it would be more accurate to say that its application may have limitations.

On the other hand, he is aware that there can be a tendency (one that, he has reason to believe, is shared by some of the participants in this weekend of his Wisdom School) to treat these limitations as intrinsic flaws that invalidate the whole. He wants the participants to fully appreciate the importance and the power and, indeed, the indispensability of Deuteronomy's *torah*, its teaching, including the value of its *way* of teaching.

His first assertion is that Deuteronomy (which in a way is standing in here for all the books of Mosaic law, of which this is a summary) has had an essential formative role for the Jewish people, transforming them from a confused, rebellious, mixed multitude of former slaves into a nation.

> That book [Deuteronomy] transformed something for our people at that time. It did a job. And you begin to see the results of that job over a period of time.

Later in the day he adds to this, finishing with a pointed warning to participants to take Deuteronomy's contribution seriously, and not lightly dismiss it as not being to their taste.

And within a few generations, it transforms the people. It becomes as Heinrich Heine[1] called it later, the portable fatherland. When you are no longer able to be in your country, this is your portable homeland.

Now, give this seriousness, okay? It is like creating a culture.

Schachter-Shalomi takes up this theme again a little later.

I don't know what happened in the Cultural Revolution in China, and the troubles that were there, but Mao's Little Red Book was responsible for China being now with us in the same century. That much credit has to be given. *The Little Red Book* was the *Deuteronomy* of China.

If you begin to recognize the power that a book has that becomes shared, that is a traffic control that says "On this day, all of us do this. At this time all of us do that." That behavior is something to which we can give a kind of consent.

The nature of this process of creating a culture, its power of transformation, was tied to its clarity and certainty:

The [assertion] keeps coming up: "Don't change anything, don't add, don't subtract." That's what we hear in Deuteronomy.[2]

---

1   **Heinrich Heine** (1797–1856), German poet: "A book is their [the Jews'] fatherland, their property, their ruler, their good and evil fortune. Within the boundaries of this book they live; here they can exercise an inalienable right of citizenship, here they cannot be expelled or despised, here they are strong and admirable." Cited in *Cultures of the Jews* (ed. David Biale), chapter by Richard J Cohen, p. 772.

2   For example, Deut. 4:2 לֹא תֹסִפוּ עַל־הַדָּבָר אֲשֶׁר אָנֹכִי מְצַוֶּה אֶתְכֶם וְלֹא תִגְרְעוּ מִמֶּנּוּ and Deut. 13.1 לֹא־תֹסֵף עָלָיו וְלֹא תִגְרַע מִמֶּנּוּ . See also Prov 30:6.

> And it keeps on saying, "This is forever. This book is
> forever." It says *"ki mei ha shamayim al ha aretz,"*[3] as long
> as the sky is over the earth. That's how long this is going
> to be. Remember Chief Seattle? … He said "As long as the
> sky is over the earth, these things are the things that will be
> true, that we hold to be true."

But this very clarity and certainty in Deuteronomy is what
some of the participants balk at, perceiving it as rigid and
spirit-crushing. Schachter-Shalomi addresses this directly, using
one of his computer analogies.

> Well, it turns out that we cannot see the same kind of a
> thing anymore, and so we have to take a look and see: do
> we install Deuteronomy into ourselves? Say I have a hard
> disk and there's only a limited amount of space that I have,
> even though it can take many many megabytes of memory.
> But remember here I have to take a whole big chunk of
> Deuteronomy onto my disk, take up memory for that, and
> do the same thing with Ecclesiastes, does it pay for me to do
> that?

He does want us as a people[4] to do just that. The book of
Deuteronomy is not just of historical value, to be honored for what
it did in the past, but now perhaps simply transcended. There *is* a
place for having it on our hard drives now. But it is important that
we make use of it intelligently, knowing how it functions and for
whom or what it is appropriate. Continuing:

> And I would like to make a case for that at this point,
> "yes" that it pays, *provided*. And this "provided" is the key.
> When you say "you must take it without a *provided*, you

---

3   Deut. 11.21. כִּימֵי הַשָּׁמַיִם עַל־הָאָרֶץ׃, literally "like the days/
    duration of the heavens over the earth."

4   He wants this at least of Jews, and as usual the teaching or invita-
    tion seems cast in the form of a rather wider net than one designed
    only for that particular tribe.

> must take it as you get it, uncooked, we run into trouble.
> But if you get the "provided" straight, something happens.
> So let's take a look once again.

Historically, this book helped a disorganized collection of slaves grow into a responsible nation with social organization, national cohesion, and structures of governance, worship, and judiciary.

But even now, and perhaps necessarily in all ages for the human psyche, there are times when we individually find ourselves in the psychological state of the freshly-freed slave: confused, unmoored, in need of security, ready to grasp at things that are not in our interests as full human beings. Then we need this book, or something very much like it. Continuing:

> The task of Moses is to bring us out from Egypt. Every time I get into the possibility of being unfree, every time I get into the situation where I would like to yield to the easier slavery, to the tacky hold of slavery on me, I need to have a Moses to kick me in the behind and to start saying "You have been set free, you cannot go back into that place."
>
> Now let's take a look and see. When you are in a situation where you say "*Gevald, gevald,*[5] how am I going to get out of this. I'm overwhelmed; there are so many things in my life that are making claims on me. I don't feel that I have a chance to live for myself. Everything is biting in and taking chunks out of my life. *Gevald, gevald!* When will I be able to live?"
>
> And then somebody says, "I will serve you as traffic control. I will show you the cumulative possibility that is available for you, bit by bit. You do a little of this, if every

5　**Gevald!** גוואַלד. Yiddish: In usage, an exclamation of alarm, a cry of distress, a call for help, a wail of sorrow. Literally, force or violence.

day you do a little of this, you do a little of that, and you
see here I will build such behavior in for you, and it will get
you out. It will install for you the possibility of being able to
achieve, you're going to get to the promised land.

After a brief digression (which we will pick up in a moment),
Schachter-Shalomi returns to the usefulness of structure when we
are at loose ends feeling our own lack of discipline.

I need a law-giver for myself. How many times have you
said to yourself "I need some discipline. I wish to be able to
find a discipline in my life that's really going to straighten
me out because if I'm going to continue to flounder like I've
been going up to now, this is not going to work. I need to
have the discipline."

When somebody begins to show you that discipline is
possible, show you that you can do 613 commandments
and you can have, every day of the year, you can have the
right thing; all you have to do is get your calendar together.
Mark down the things you are going to do every day.
[quiet laughter from participants] We are laughing together
because what we're trying to do, we're trying to reduce the
chaos of our lives right now by being able to apportion for
ourselves.

Leaving Wisdom Behind for the Next Generations

Besides the historical process of building a nation out of
slaves, and besides clarity in managing the practical difficulties
of life, there is the matter of the next generation. This brings
Schachter-Shalomi to the third major theme and function and
value of Deuteronomy. He begins this by returning to the idea of
old men writing down their wisdom for the benefit of the future
generations.

We do have to manage to feed and house us and the
people that are connected to us and we have to wonder, how

is this next generation going to be able to do it too. Because if what I'm learning the hard way cannot be distilled in some form to give the next generation the distillate of that so that they don't have to go through and make the same mistakes and learn like we did, the hard way, everything that we learned, then there's a futility, there's *havel havelim*,[6] then what's the use of it all.

Look at Solomon for a moment. His father is not the one who is going to build the temple.[7] It is Solomon who builds the temple. If Solomon had to do the same thing that David did, he too would be a "bloody man." He too would not have been able to build the temple.

So there is a difference between generations. There is a way of something that we can leave behind. It isn't so futile for him despite the fact that he says later on, "There's no end to making books. Be careful, my son, don't make books because there's no end." And then he sits down and writes a book himself. ...

So what you get is the recognition that it won't help and at the same time the fantastic urge that I must pour back into the pool of society what I've learned in my life. That urge is a very strong urge, and the older you get the stronger that urge comes. It says "Can I make order?"

---

6 **Havel havelim,** הֲבֵל הֲבָלִים Hebrew: insubstantial of insubstantials; breath of breaths. The phrase has also been translated "vanity of vanities" following King James Version. Robert Alter translates it "mere breath." Ecclesiastes 1.2 and subsequent.

7 I Chronicles 28:3: King David speaking: "And [*or* But] God said to me, 'You will not [*or* may not] build a house for my name, because you are a man of war and have shed [*lit.* poured out] blood.'" This is the explanation why the Temple was not built by David and had to wait to be built by his son, the wise Solomon who, as Schachter-Shalomi says, "made love not war."

Now here follows that bit of digression Schachter-Shalomi wanted to note in the midst of talking about our need for structure to help us when we are floundering. Even while making the very real case for that need for structure, a case that he and evidently (judging from the laughter) the participants as well could recognize, he has to acknowledge that the Biblical text itself may be giving us a clue about the limitations of this blessing and gift, however much it may be needed for certain times.

> But notice here, Moses brings us to the promised land, but he doesn't take us into it…. Moses will not enter the promised land despite the fact that he is *shray gevald,*[8] he is crying[9] "I pray to God please let me in, please let me in, please let me in."[10] "You mustn't go in."[11]
>
> You begin to see the recognition that somehow that Moses cannot live the children's life. That Moses can give all the instruction and all the teaching and all the very valuable commandments, and yet at the gates of the land he has to say "And now, *kinderlekh,* you go by yourself. I cannot accompany you. I cannot come with you at this point. Now the power is yours."
>
> When you begin to recognize the entraining, that Moses is an entrainer, and that his task ends at a particular time, then you begin to see the value of Moses. I want you to get the mythic picture so that whatever we're going to hear of Moses, it's going to fit into that myth.
>
> We have a Moses, we are a Moses, Moses is in us.

8 **Shray gevald** שרײַ גוואַלד. Yiddish. Crying out loudly in distress.
9 Deut. 3:23. *Etchanan.* וָאֶתְחַנַּן אֶל־יְהוָה בָּעֵת הַהִוא לֵאמֹר
10 Deut. 3:23–25.
11 Deut. 3:26–27.

Incisively Impress it upon your Children

Schachter-Shalomi now develops a central thread of the third area he opened up, that of the need to have a teaching that will be for future generations, looking at what will be effective for teaching the children specifically. What language, what mode of teaching, will reach children, will make sense to them, will meet them on their own level?

> Now, why am I doing this? *V'shinantam l'vaneykha v'dibarta bam.*[12] I have to have something that can be put into such language such that the kids will hear it, again, and again, and again, and it will give the kids an outline of behavior.
>
> "So if I do that, God is going to like me?" "Yes, God will like you." "Will I succeed if I do that?" "Yes, you will succeed if you do that." "Will heaven and earth bless me, will I get rain in due season?" "Yes, you will get rain in due season." This is the way it works. You must not go after other gods no matter how many blandishments you are being offered. This is not where you have to go. *Acharei*

---

12 Deut. 6:7: וְשִׁנַּנְתָּ֣ם לְבָנֶ֔יךָ וְדִבַּרְתָּ֖ בָּ֑ם בְּשִׁבְתְּךָ֤ בְּבֵיתֶ֙ךָ֙ וּבְלֶכְתְּךָ֣ בַדֶּ֔רֶךְ וּֽבְשָׁכְבְּךָ֖ וּבְקוּמֶֽךָ׃ Impress them ("the words that I command you today") incisively upon your children and speak to them when you sit in your house and when you walk on your way and when you lie down and when you rise up. These lines are part of the central declaration and affirmation of the oneness of God that begins "Sh'ma Yisrael," Hear, O Israel. Schachter-Shalomi is quoting a passage familiar because it is recited morning and night every day. (The word translated sometimes as "teach them diligently" [English Standard Version] or, as I had it, "impress [the words] incisively on them," literally carries a meaning something like "bite them sharply." The verb שׁנן *shanan* is to whet or sharpen, related to the noun שׁן shen, tooth. A vivid image.)

adonai eloheikhm telekhun. "You must go after the lord your God and to him you shall cleave."[13]

You get all those statements. It isn't a far-away book. You want to get inspiration, you want to get spiritual? *Vedanta*[14] you aren't going to get. Okay? I'm not going to give you anything from the high place, you're going to get it right here, right now, this is what you have to do, every day. It's all very very clear. It's close to your heart, it's close to your mouth,[15] you really got to do it, you *can* do it.

Teach the Lad

Later he carries this further, looking at teaching and learning as applied to people, civilizations, and cultures at different stages of development. He calls on a verse from the Biblical book of Proverbs.

> *Chanokh lana'ar al pi darko; gam ki yazqin lo yasur mimenah.*[16] Teach the lad according to his way, even when he gets old he will not turn away from it.

Schachter-Shalomi is going to use this verse in two ways. First, he will take the first half to explore implications of teaching a child "in his way." Schachter-Shalomi understands this to mean, as do most of the traditional ancient Jewish commentaries and

---

13 Schachter-Shalomi seems to be referring to Deut. 13:5. אַחֲרֵי יְהוָה אֱלֹהֵיכֶם תֵּלֵכוּ וְאֹתוֹ תִירָאוּ וְאֶת־מִצְוֹתָיו תִּשְׁמֹרוּ וּבְקֹלוֹ תִשְׁמָעוּ וְאֹתוֹ תַעֲבֹדוּ וּבוֹ תִדְבָּקוּן׃ "You will/should/are to/ walk after YHVH your god and you are to fear him and his commandments you are to keep and you are to listen to his voice and you are to serve him and you will/are to cleave to him."

14 **Vedanta** वेदान्त. Sanskrit. Vedanta is a particular spiritual path within Hindu tradition. Most often now refers to a path of realizing a single ultimate reality as ground of all being.

15 Deut. 30:14.

16 Prov. 22:6. חֲנֹךְ לַנַּעַר עַל־פִּי דַרְכּוֹ גַּם כִּי־יַזְקִין לֹא־יָסוּר מִמֶּנָּה׃

most present day traditional Jewish educators, to say that it must be in terms a young person can understand.

Then Schachter-Shalomi will take the second half of the verse to explore what will happen when the child is older and can, perhaps, see things from a more informed understanding. In this, Schachter-Shalomi's perspective is at least partly different from most of the traditional commentaries, which seem to take the meaning to be that the teachings will stick if they can be comprehended by the child initially.[17]

The first part of the proverb may usefully be compared to Deuteronomy and the second part (at least in Schachter-Shalomi's understanding) to Ecclesiastes. Or, alternatively, the first part might be seen as corresponding to the position of the Israelites on the run from Egyptian slavery and the second part to a later stage of psycho-spiritual development, a stage of maturity or wisdom.

In the extended unfolding of what Schachter-Shalomi sees in the application of the verse from Proverbs to the situation with Deuteronomy and Ecclesiastes, we have a particularly rich interweaving of ideas, bouncing off one another and then returning in sometimes surprising ways. This may have operated on consciousness in a more organic way in a retreat setting with oral teachings being woven into a full, integrated program. Reading the written word in a book is a different experience. I have tried as much as possible[18] to organize the material in the more logical

---

17 But, of course, a question immediately arises: one must wonder just what is sticking. Would that imply that all one's Torah learning and theology are to be stuck at the "Sunday school" level? Much of Schachter-Shalomi's work in Jewish Renewal is addressing the problem that many of those whose Jewish education ended at that level are alienated from the religion. More on this will come out when he discusses the second half of the verse later in the retreat.

18 That is, as much as possible consistent with my wish to retain the effect of the retreat immersion context and the effect of Schachter-Shalomi's artistry as a weaver of ideas.

way one expects of written exposition. But to some extent you, the reader, must place yourself into the retreat consciousness and follow the twists and the layers of investigation and the returns.

Schachter-Shalomi begins with a nod to something like what we understand in the present day about the ways children learn (which perhaps Solomon, in writing the Proverbs, already knew).

> After Piaget[19] and all the other folks we are clear that if I'm to teach somebody I have to look first at who is it that I am teaching. I have to understand what their needs are and then address the needs of that person in that situation. When that happens, there is a take, there is an absorbing, there is a taking-in of the teaching that is so strong and so real and so powerful that it can grow later on. … This child needs to be taught in a way that is person-specific to that being, and the entry to that teaching has to be on the level where that child is. Then there is growth possible. But if I ignore the person-person, I can train somebody into a veneer of behavior and put it on top. …

What if we needed to do for a people, or the world, something like what Moses did for the Israelites?

> Now let us say that we are Moses. Let us say that we are the instrument for teaching a people. Let us say that we look around and see, even from our 20/20 hindsight, where we are in the late twentieth century, on the eve of the twenty-first century,[20] what do we know about education, what do we know about value-teaching?

---

19 **Jean Piaget** (1896–1980), psychologist and philosopher of epistemology and children's cognitive development. Studied and theorized about processes of learning and thinking.

20 This is, of course, spoken that weekend in 1989.

We have found in the attempts to teach our own children that when we try to hand over our own values just as we experience them, given our life experience, given our level of development, it doesn't work.

> One of the things we have learned is that when we attempt to teach our children values from the point where we embrace the values, in other words from our level of development, it somehow doesn't take. It's a pity but that's the way it is.

The same may be found when we try to impose our world view and values on other peoples in the world.

> When we get addicted to a world view and we say that the world view that fits our moral development is the world view that fits everybody, then when we have to go and talk to other people who are not on the same level of moral development, and want to impose the moral development that we have, it seems to them so totally arbitrary, so totally crazy.

Schachter-Shalomi then gives an example very close to home of trying to give over a moral world view to people who are not ready for it.

We cannot avoid knowing, of course, that there are limits to what a child can understand and process and follow, and Schachter-Shalomi will return to say more about that presently. The child may need and feel reassured by clear demarcations and simple explanations of cause and effect.

The adolescent, however, is old enough to start seeing the cracks in living with those pious simplifications.

> "I don't understand" says an adolescent. "How come you're such a hypocrite?"

Faced with these cracks in the absolutist dicta, the adolescent may then feel that his birthright, the promise made to him that things will be clear and simple, is being threatened. His experience isn't broad enough, his judgment not honed enough, to yet discern a new, more complex, ethic. So he strikes out at those whose life must (necessarily) be lived according to some more complex principles of decision-making.[21] These may be the very people who told him what are now starting to look as if they may be lies. But in this turbulent adolescent time, rather than give up those principles on which one has relied, maybe it is safer to accuse others of hypocrisy.

> Adolescents talk very often to parents: "You're such a hypocrite. You're saying one thing, you're saying another." And the parents say "Come on, you have to judge the situation. You can't make a hard and fast rule." And so on and so forth. But they are going to be saying "Come on, that's hypocrisy. You're cutting corners when it suits you."

Growth of Humanity

Now Schachter-Shalomi extrapolates from the teaching parents must give to the growth or spiritual evolution of humanity.

> So what you see is that where an adolescent is, is one level, and where a child is is another level, and in recognizing that there is a project, and this project is in phylogeny. Phylogeny means in the development of humankind through history. We see that in phylogeny we

---

21 It must of course be acknowledged that some of the adults being so rudely assaulted by their offspring are guilty as charged. Or, to put it more compassionately, their way of dealing with the situational complexity is to throw up their hands in the face of the challenge of devising a new more comprehensive moral reality—the challenge, in short, of wisdom. Indeed, it is not a small challenge to know, as Solomon suggests we must, when it is a time to be born and a time to die, a time to fling stones and a time to gather stones in, a time to embrace and a time to pull back from embracing. (Ecc. 3:2–5, in Alter translation.)

have grown. That is, what the *zeitgeist* is today, it is beyond the level of what we call mutual contracting.

He returns to the moral world view of Moses and Deuteronomy to look at it from another angle.

> What we see is what Moses sets up [which] is very much talking physical reward and punishment. He is saying, "If this guy doesn't behave, if the kid doesn't behave, if he eats more than he should,[22] he curses his parent, kill him, erase that."[23] You get that? The draconic punishment.

Schachter-Shalomi anticipates an objection—not to what might seem lack of compassion, but to the effectiveness of this system.

> What you get is, what you start saying is, "This is behaviorism.[24] Behaviorism can't work." And this answer is it *can* work, but for a certain level of behavior.

---

22 Deut. 21:20: וְאָמְרוּ אֶל־זִקְנֵי עִירוֹ בְּנֵנוּ זֶה סוֹרֵר וּמֹרֶה אֵינֶנּוּ שֹׁמֵעַ בְּקֹלֵנוּ
    זוֹלֵל וְסֹבֵא Then they are to say to the elders of the town, our son,
    this-one, is a stubborn-one and a rebel—he does not hearken to our
    voice—a glutton and a drunkard! Deut. 21:21: וּרְגָמֻהוּ כָּל־אַנְשֵׁי עִירוֹ
    בָאֲבָנִים וָמֵת וּבִעַרְתָּ הָרָע מִקִּרְבֶּךָ וְכָל־יִשְׂרָאֵל יִשְׁמְעוּ וְיִרָאוּ׃ Then
    all the men of the town are to pelt him with stones so that he dies.
    So you shall burn out the evil from your midst and all Israel will
    hear and be-awed. [Everett Fox translation]

23 Ex. 21:17: וּמְקַלֵּל אָבִיו וְאִמּוֹ מוֹת יוּמָת and Lev. 20:9 כִּי־אִישׁ אִישׁ
    אֲשֶׁר יְקַלֵּל אֶת־אָבִיו וְאֶת־אִמּוֹ מוֹת יוּמָת. Whoever curses his father
    or mother shall surely be put to death.

24 **Behaviorism.** A school or philosophy of psychology that treats
    all organisms as collections of behavior. This behavior could,
    according to the theory, be modified by adjusting the environmental
    stimuli—rewards and punishments. It was seen by its proponents as
    more scientific than other theories because it didn't need to involve
    (supposed) inner states. It emerged through the 19th and 20th
    century (influenced in the 20th by Ivan Pavlov and B. F. Skinner)
    but fell out of favor in the second half of the 20th century.

Now we consider the situation of a child again, and how we find we must present our values not whole but in appropriate stages.

> In the beginning you say to your child "You must not cross the street under any circumstances." It takes a long time until you can trust your child enough to say that at three o'clock in the morning you could cross even against a red light.
>
> That kind of situational ethic you cannot entrust right from the start. What you have to get to is recognizing that you cannot learn to be at the level of situational ethics if you haven't had at one point the very very severe thing that says "under no circumstances do you cross against the light."
>
> When you hear that language constantly in the Torah: "always," "never," "go to the right," "go to the left," "do it precise," "keep it that way." And "what's the reward in this world," and "what's the punishment in this world." And you don't see any postponement of that.

Schachter-Shalomi notes that the rabbis of the Talmud, who were in a position of having to apply Biblical law to a later time and place, were hard-pressed to take the laws as harshly or as free of consideration of situation as they sometimes seemed to be expressed in the Torah text.

> As you find out later in Rabbinic language, they have to say "wait a minute, it's possible…"[25]

This greater complexity required to make sense of the life people find themselves actually living is also dealt with in *Tanakh*, of course.

---

25 The final chapter of this book cites examples of what Schachter-Shalomi has in mind here.

Next weekend we're going to look at Job.[26] "How is it possible that the righteous suffer, how is it possible that the wicked prosper? That's not what you taught us in Deuteronomy. In Deuteronomy you said…." You know?

And this is where we got to the conflict between where King Solomon is and where Moses is.

And I would want to press right now that Moses's greatest gift to us was the he was able to meet us where we were at that time coming out of Egypt. And that he was able to take the big vision of God and put it into a language that would fit that time and that period.

"For Their Generations": Blessed Routines

And what Moses did is not just a good thing that came to undo the effects of slavery. Because Schachter-Shalomi is exploring the parallels of that training with the way children need to learn, we are recursively back to using this story and its laws to give something that will flow from generation to generation.

What we are getting here is very much a book that can be read year after year after year after year and can serve the communication of generations. I want to talk about this for a moment. The communication of generations.

"And the Lord spoke to Moses saying, Speak unto the children of Israel and let them make for fringes on their garments *l'dorotam*,"[27] remember that? For their generations. And in the translation that I set out this morning is "So they might have generations to follow."

---

26 The last retreat of the series takes up the stories of Ruth, Esther, Jonah, and Job.

27 Num 15.38. דַּבֵּר אֶל־בְּנֵי יִשְׂרָאֵל וְאָמַרְתָּ אֲלֵהֶם וְעָשׂוּ לָהֶם צִיצִת עַל־כַּנְפֵי בִגְדֵיהֶם לְדֹרֹתָם. "Speak to the children of Israel and say to them, they will make fringes/tzitzit on the corners of their garments, for their generations.'"

Tzitzis are ways so that generations can follow afterwards. There is a concreteness given to that.

Schachter-Shalomi invites us into an experience of this connection of generations in action by painting a picture of children learning, and coming to identify with being Jewish, and coming to their own pleasure in and appreciation of the Jewish tradition. His voice usage as well as his words call on the participants to remember, or re-experience, their own childhood, or that of their own children, with such routines.

> If you've gone to a kindergarten of a Jewish Community Center, a day care center, and you look what they're doing on Friday. There is [here he drops into a gentle, loving, kindergartenish sing-song with his voice] the lighting of the candles, and the stuffed Torah, kid walks around with the Torah, and gets a piece of *challah*,[28] and gets a little grape juice for wine. Okay?
>
> These kinds of things are the routines, are the blessed routines that can be expected by which the kids punctuate time, by which they have a notion [of Shabbat]. And the skills that they learn—"I want to say the blessing tonight!" "I want to say the blessing tonight!" The vying for who is going to say the blessing and so on and so forth, because there is something that I can contribute.
>
> When you begin to watch this in children, and you start looking back at the book of Deuteronomy, you begin to see what kind of fantastic *tour de force* for the education of a people that book was.

---

28 **Challah**. Hebrew: A special braided bread made with eggs and fine flour and eaten on Shabbat. First called this in Europe in the Middle Ages (Yiddish *khale* חלה). In the Pentateuch, a kind of cake used in offerings.

Learning: Two Views Held in Tension

Schachter-Shalomi had early introduced the question of learning, using it as one of the prisms through which he invited participants to examine what is going on with the two approaches he is juxtaposing in this retreat.

But there are some difficulties in the questions about learning, and Schachter-Shalomi is not going to rush to a convenient mechanism that sweeps any pesky misfitting pieces under the rug, nor does he want the participants to be too quick to feel they had a resolution.

The primary difficulty is this. You can't take responsibility for your own learning when you don't know what you don't know. And you can't make yourself into something that you aren't yet when you don't even know what that would feel like or whether it could work. From this point of view, one needs a teacher who will take on the vision and the responsibility and do whatever combination of threatening, coaxing, bullying, and inspiring it takes.

But is this situation desirable? Is it even tenable? Learning is such an inward process—in all cases, perhaps, but especially when it is character that we are wishing to develop. We can learn, but can someone else *cause* our learning? Would the infantilizing of the process undo the value of what the (perhaps well-meaning) teacher was trying to do? Can any human being turn himself or herself over to be worked on like clay? Would any human being be willing to do that?

Schachter-Shalomi offered the following challenge on Saturday morning as a lead-in to the Torah reading from Deuteronomy.

> On the one hand you have someone saying "You cannot, until you have become enlightened, take on responsibility for your own learning." How do you know how you have to teach yourself? You don't.
>
> If you had become what you are intended to become, you would then be able to take on the responsibility of teaching yourself to become that. But you haven't become

that yet. And you are a bundle of impulses that are warring with each other and you haven't got anything sorted out for yourself. How dare you to think you can take on the responsibility of your own education?

Do you hear that? This is the Moses position. "You guys, backsliding, if it was up to you, you would have gone back to Egypt a whole bunch of times already. You'd be right back in the clay pits where you were before. Because you haven't seen the vision. Therefore I have to, in a way, infantilize you and paternalize you. I have to take on the responsibility for your education because you can't handle it yourself."

Let's take another point of view for a moment. Nobody but the learner knows what the learning costs them. Nobody but the learner knows what he actually has learned. It is not an external thing.

Who says I can actually learn anything other than what I already know? If I were to go to the place where the Rabbis put that, it goes like this. The angel teaches the child in the mother's womb the whole Torah before the child is born. Then you forget it because you are hit over here on the soft part under the nose.[29] Then, having had this amnesia you get back into life and everything that you learn, you re-learn that which you had already known. Anything that you want me to learn that isn't mine to learn I'm going to lose anyway. …

So one might take the position and say "You cannot be a teacher of mine if you want to paternalize me, if you want to infantilize me. You can become my teacher only if you treat me as an adult who wants to be a learner. You can help me learn, you cannot teach me."

The myth from the Rabbis to which Schachter-Shalomi refers parallels the myth that Plato gives for that same difficulty. Plato's

---

29 *Babylonian Talmud*, Tractate Niddah, Folio 30B.

myth also has us learning everything before birth and then passing through a river of forgetfulness on the way to being incarnated. But Plato has another, more pragmatic way to trigger learning (recollection)—*aporia*.[30] Dig so deeply into the difficulty that you feel completely baffled and give up the easy but inadequate or fallacious answers. Then you are ready to learn. Intentionally or not, Schachter-Shalomi seems to be leading the participants to this *aporia*.

Schachter-Shalomi doesn't have a resolution to offer here. But he doesn't want to fail to acknowledge both sides, and he *does* want to urge the participants to struggle with the question.

> Do you see these two points of view? Look at your threads.[31] These two points of view are warring with each other. Which one is true? Well, unless you see them side by side and see the limits of truth of one and the limits of truth of the other, you get stuck there.
>
> Please hold this in tension. I'm not saying you should let go of the tension. Holds these points of view in tension in you so that throughout what we will be doing today and tomorrow, this tension can be there. I don't want this tension to be resolved at this point. Within the tension I want you to hear the Torah reading that I'm about to read.

The Torah Service

Having urged participants to hold the questions that have been raised "in tension," Schachter-Shalomi moves into the reading from the Torah Scroll. For this service, he read selections from Deuteronomy.

---

30 **Aporia** ἀπορία. Greek: Complete bafflement. Literally, state of no way or means of achieving, accomplishing, discovering, etc. [Liddell and Scott, p. 1451.] .

31 **Threads**. Schachter-Shalomi directs participants' attention to the *tzitzit*, fringes: bundles of threads affixed by knots to the corners of their prayer shawls. The threads below the knots lie separately side by side.

The Goals of the Torah Reading Selections

In his selections for this reading, Schachter-Shalomi had two purposes.

He wanted to give an overview of the flow and feeling of the whole book, to the extent that was possible in brief selections, and to touch on a few passages that connected to some of his themes for the weekend.

He also wanted to make sure that participants heard and felt its valuable moral insights and compassionate sensitivity to people in difficult situations or circumstances—as well as some firm drawing of the lines of social justice that we could no doubt stand to be reminded of today.

The Reading

As is his frequent practice, his reading consisted largely of simultaneous *ad hoc* translation as he followed the Hebrew in the Torah scroll. The English was done with the cantillation pattern for the Hebrew. Occasionally he interspersed a bit of commentary on the text or on one of the Hebrew words or phrases. But for the most part through this reading he is just selecting, reading Hebrew, and translating.

Through this section he frequently substitutes the divine name Yah (used in the later Psalms) for יהוה / YHVH instead of the more conventional translation substitute name Lord.

The Content of Deuteronomy, Moses's Contribution, and Gratitude for it

Schachter-Shalomi begins with Moses's injunction to treat these teachings as clear and certain: Pay attention. Stick to just what I am saying; don't add or subtract. Guard what I'm commanding you today. These are the commandments of your God.

> "And now Israel, harken to the statutes and to the judgment which I am teaching you to do, in order that you

might live and come and inherit that land which Yah, the God of your parents, is giving you. And do not add to this thing which I command you this day and do not subtract thereof, and to guard all the commandments of Yah your God which I command you this day."[32]

Dangers of Complacency

Schachter-Shalomi now moves to verse 22. A warning: When things go well in the new land, the people may forget whose blessing this is, and start to set value on objects which are not God, and they may do evil. If so, they will lose the land.

"For I shall die in this land. I shall not cross over this Jordan and you will cross it over and you will inherit this good land.

"Be careful lest you forget the covenant of Yah your God which he makes with you. And you might then, forgetting, make for yourself a hewn image, a depicting of that which Yah your God had commanded you not to do. For the Lord your God is a consuming fire, a zealous God. You will have children and grandchildren and you will get to be old in the land. And you will then get spoiled. And you will make for yourself an idol, a depicting of something, and you do that which is evil in the eyes of the Lord your God, and cause anger.

"I am calling today as witnesses the heavens and the earth that this will be your destruction, quickly from this land which you are crossing over the Jordan there to inherit. You will not have long life in it, for you will soon be destroyed. And the Lord will spread you among the nations and you will remain very few of you among the nations which the Lord your God will lead you there."[33]

---

32 Deut. 4:1–4:2.
33 Deut. 4:22–27.

What the Children Must Hear

Schachter-Shalomi says that he will again skip ahead slightly to the place in the Deuteronomy text "where your child begins to ask the question." He starts reading at Deuteronomy 6:20.

> "When your son will ask you tomorrow" (tomorrow, this coming week; this is the *pesach haggadah*[34]) what are the testimonies, the statutes, and the judgments which Yah our God commanded you, and you will tell your son, 'slaves we have been to Pharaoh in Egypt and Yah took us out from Egypt with a strong hand, and Yah sent therefrom signs and miracles that were great and that were bad for the Egyptians and for Pharaoh and for all his household, and this was all in front of our eyes. And us he took out from there in order to bring us out from there in order to give us this land which he has sworn to our fathers.
>
> "'And he commanded us to do all those statutes in order to be respectful of Yah our God for our good all our days. To give us life as we are alive today. And it will be a righteousness for us if we will keep to do this commandment before Yah our God as he commanded us.'"
>
> You see this part that keeps on repeating: and you shall teach your children diligently. Constantly there is that repetition of how the teaching has to be. We are still very much in the rhetoric of that for quite a number of chapters here, and we now go to chapter 10, sentence 12.
>
> "And now, O Israel, what is it that Yah your God is asking of you? But that you respect Yah your God, that you walk in all his ways, to love him and to serve Yah your God with all your heart and with all your soul and to keep the commandments of Yah and his statutes which I command you this day for your good."

---

34 The Passover Haggadah features questions by children about the history and the answers their parents should give, quoting this text.

Okay? Once again we are still with that, nothing much
is being asked of you, what you need to do is very clear.
You have to be respectful of God, you have to follow the
commandments, and as you do that you will see how your
life is going to be in order, things are going to be clear, you
will be able to live.

Who Can Speak for God?

We are getting all these instructions through a prophet. Moses
is transmitting the words that YHVH speaks and tells him to say to
the children of Israel. They do trust Moses, trust that he speaks for
their God. But what about later? What about when Moses is gone?
Will they still get guidance from prophets that comes reliably from
YHVH? Can there be false prophets? How would one know?

We continue a little bit farther down. Chapter 13. Sentence 2 is really where this section begins.

Now here comes the question, who has the right to speak
for God? Because he is now dealing with this. People are
anxious. When you are gone, who will be speaking to us
for you? And here we get to "how do I know that this is the
voice of God? Of the real God? Of this God who took us
out of Egypt?"

The people are right to be anxious. What Moses has given them
will not cover all situations that arise and will arise in the future.

The Jewish people will need further guidance after Moses is
gone, and Jewish tradition has generated vast amounts of oral
and written guidance to fill this need. Interpreters, commentators, explicators, makers of *responsa*[35] to apply *Halakha*[36] to new

---

35 **Responsa**. Rabbinical rulings on the application of *Halakha* to
specific situations or questions.

36 **Halakha**. Hebrew: literally, a way of walking. The set of
commandments or observances that define Jewish obligation for the
orthodox; Jewish law as traditionally and currently interpreted.

situations—these have followed one after another, in choruses and in conversation and in argument with one another, responding and revising and at times leaping to rulings that would have astonished Moses.[37]

How do we know whether these are true prophets and dreamers of dreams? How do we know whether they should be listened to?

> So following with sentence 2:[38]
>
> "If there will arise in your midst a prophet or a dreamer of dreams, and he will give you a sign, or he will give you a signal, and that sign or signal which he has given to you will come, and he will say to you, 'ah, you saw the sign came, now let us go and serve other gods whom you did not know, and we will serve them.'
>
> "Don't listen to the words of that prophet or the words of that dreamer! For Yah your God is testing you to know if you are still loving the Lord your God with all your heart, with all your soul. You are to walk after the Lord your God; him you are to respect, his commandments you are to fulfill, his voice you are to listen to, him you are to serve, to him you are you cleave."

We are being told here how we will know a false prophet. It won't be by whether he or she has a sign or a signal, perhaps a prediction that comes true. Rather, we will know by the content of what that prophet or dreamer of dreams has to give us for instruction.

Do those words help us to be still loving YHVH our God with all our heart and all our soul? Does it help us to walk after the one we made a covenant with? Does it help us know how to listen to his voice and cleave to him? Then we will have a true prophet; we should listen.

---

37 The final chapter of this book deals with such cases, including one Rabbinic story in which Moses's astonishment is trumpeted.

38 Deut. 13:2.

If he or she tells us to walk after other gods, we can know that we should not listen. This is a test. If it separates us from the God we have known, if it diminishes our ability to love that God to our depths, if it prevents us hearing his voice and cleaving to him, then we should not listen.

Schachter-Shalomi is giving us Torah's instructions for knowing true guidance in the future, whatever its source. He does not apply it to his own teachings, and probably had no such thought at the time.

However, listening to him, or reading the words he quotes from Moses, it may naturally occur to *us* to put him and his teachings to the test. What sort of dreamer of dreams do we have here, in Schachter-Shalomi and his dreamed up re-visioning of Judaism?

Some of his vision is certainly at odds with prevailing institutionalized tradition. But human interpretation may be mistaken and the detailed applications can become sclerosed. We have been given a test that goes to the root of the matter. Although Schachter-Shalomi is not a Biblical prophet, we can use Moses's principles, to ask these same questions of Schachter-Shalomi's teachings.

Do these teachings help us love YHVH our God with all our heart and all our soul? Do they help us cleave to divine being? If so, we should listen. Or do they diminish our ability to love God to our depths, or do they prevent us from hearing his voice and cleaving to him? Then we should not listen. Moses, or God speaking through Moses, has provided for later generations a test for whether new guidance is authentic Jewish teaching.

Social Relations Built on Justice

Schachter-Shalomi pauses in his Torah reading at this point. After a break he picks up what is a crucial theme for him in this book, namely what he appreciates as deeply humane, compassionate, just, and advanced laws that form a basis for the community's human social obligations to one another and their economic relations. Resuming with Chapter 15:

[Moses] has gone through the holy days, he has told again about the place to which we are going to come.

And now tells us about the laws of the sabbatical year, interpersonal relationships, how one is to deal with debt and avoid one of the terrible things that happens to people, namely feudalism, a place where the rich get richer, the poor get poorer, and before long the poor are in such a position that if they want to have something to eat they are indentured forever. How does one deal with that? Is there a way out of that?

He has just spoken before about the Levites, that they are to get their tithe, and so set up a taxation for public weal, in a sense, because that's what the Levites were doing, what the priests were doing. The healing and the reconciling of people to God. And having set up the polity in which the people were to be governed, he now talks about the agricultural rest, again. And follow:

"At the end of seven years, you are to make a year of sabbatical, and this is the way in which that has to happen. Any one who has a debt over his neighbor, he must not pursue his neighbor, and his brother, for it will be a rest year for the Lord."

And then he goes on and says, "The one who is not one of your neighbors, one who is a stranger, him you can dun for the debt, but your brothers you have to let go of. And this is the way you can prevent that there will be abject poverty. For the Lord your God will bless you in the land which the Lord your God gives you as an inheritance to inherit it. Listen to the voice of the Lord your God to keep all these commandments which I command you this day. The Lord your God has blessed you as he has spoken to you. You will get the pawns of many nations but you will not have to pawn your own. And you will thus rule on many nations and they will not rule on you.

"And if it will happen that there will be a poor person in your gates, one of your brothers in your land which the Lord your God gives you, let your heart not be hardened against him, let your fist not be tight against your brother the pauper, for *open* your hand to him, and the pawn that he brings you, give him enough for it, for his need which he will need.

Be careful lest there will be in your heart the nasty thought—" בְלִיַּעַל *b'li ya'al* is a way of saying that, someone that has no lift, someone so low-life there is no lift in him. There is no rising up there.

"If you will have such a low-life thought, saying 'The seventh year is coming, the year of remittance, of letting go of debts,' and thus your eye is going to be bad against your poor brother, and you will not give unto him, and he will call out to the Lord your God and then you will have a sin.

"So give him again and again, *naton titen,*"[39] do you see the doubling in the Hebrew? "Give him again and again, and let your heart not be bad as you give it to him, for this is why the Lord your God has given you a blessing in all your actions and everything you set your hands to. For there will never be a time when there won't be any poor in the land. Therefore the Lord your God commands you saying 'Open again and again your hand to your poor and to your abject poor in your land.'

"And if your brother, your Hebrew brother or your Hebrew sister, will be sold to you, and they will serve you for six years, and in the seventh year you are to send them free from your land. But when you send them free—" remember how it said before in Exodus, he came with nothing, let him go with nothing,[40] remember?—that's the rule.

---

39 Deut. 15:10. נָתוֹן תִּתֵּן These are two forms of the verb *natan*, to give ("giving, you will give").

40 Exodus 21:2–4.

Now Moses is saying, "When you send him free from you, don't send him empty-handed. Hang things on him. Lay things on him."[41] *Anaq* is like a necklace. So as he's about to leave, give him some dates, a string of figs, hang things on him. "And from your sheep and from your threshing floor and from your wine cellar which the Lord your God has given you you will give to him.

And you will remember that you were slaves in the land of Egypt and that God has redeemed you and therefore I command you this thing today.

And what will be if he says to you 'I don't want to go out' because he loves you and your household and it is good to be with you? Then you are to take the awl and make him a hole in his earlobe near the door and he will then serve you for a long time." The word says *olam*; "forever" is the usual translation but it means only to the fiftieth year.

"And also to your maidservants you do the same. Let it not be hard in your eye as you send them forth free from you. For double the time of hire, he has served you during these six years, and the Lord will bless you and all that you will do."

Participants had come into the weekend with criticisms of verses that may have seemed rigid or harsh, and Schachter-Shalomi himself had spoken of its limitations in such regards. But while one wants to acknowledge such truths, and not deny or ignore them,[42] it would lead to distortion of the whole to let discomfort with some passages cause one to miss the vision and perspective and moral sensibility that leads to the many instructions of consideration and

---

41 Deut. 15:14. הַעֲנֵיק תַּעֲנִיק. *Ha'aniyq ta'aniyq*. Again, repetition creates emphasis.

42 **Not denying or ignoring**. Schachter-Shalomi addresses this explicitly later in the retreat. See Chapter 14, "What Do We Do with Difficult Passages?"

kindness and fairness—to one's neighbor, to strangers, to slaves, and even to animals.

Gratitude to Moses

Earlier, Schachter-Shalomi had engaged participants in an experiential exercise that they did in pairs. Within their dyads, participants took turns speaking as themselves to their partner, who was witnessing as Moses, to tell Moses what they were grateful for from him.

At end of this Torah reading, with the scroll still spread, Schachter-Shalomi offers a blessing giving his own thanks to Moses.

> We thank you, Moses, for a teaching that considers the poor. We thank you for a teaching that says that there is no absolute winner, [such] that he wins so that everyone [else] has to be an absolute loser. That having to give tithe, having to share your income, having to share your blessing, is exactly why you got the blessing in the first place. So that the poorest need not be so poor that their life is a burden on them and that the richest need not be so absolute that they harden their heart. For such teaching, and if this is the element to which Moses wants to bring us in all those commandments, saying "If you eat the right kind of food, it will make it easier for you. And if you rest on the Sabbath, it will make it easier for you. And if you keep all these commandments, it will be easier for you." For this we thank you, Moses.

Insights from Another Side: Deuteronomy from a Less Traditional Perspective

Just as Schachter-Shalomi sees and makes use of multiple levels of meaning in the Biblical text, he will take teachings from alternative ways of understanding the provenance of that text.

He finds the traditional understanding (as given by God through Moses) rich and useful. But he can also see and work with the understanding of the text as emerging from a much more historical and human process. That view too can yield insights in understanding and making use of Deuteronomy.

In the view that Schachter-Shalomi suggests here, Deuteronomy was written at a time when reform was needed and the people were having hard times. The diagnosis was that they had ceased following the Mosaic commandments; they had, perhaps, even lost them. A new book had to miraculously appear, summarizing the old story and the commandments, so that it could be a basis for reform and to save the people from divine destruction.

Tanakh recounts that King Josiah was brought a scroll by the priest Hilkiah, supposedly discovered in the sanctuary during repairs. Josiah tears his clothes because he realizes that these are laws that he and his people have not been following. He calls on the prophetess Huldah to interpret it; she says in God's name that God is indeed enraged against them because they have forsaken him, and plans to bring destruction on them. Josiah then under-takes reforms to return to the teachings of this newly-discovered scroll of Law.[43]

> So here is Josiah and in his day, and around Hezekiah's time, that book is written, so we're looking at about the seventh century before the common era, the time that Deuteronomy is written.
>
> So what you get is a retro-myth, do you hear what I'm saying? You speak sometimes of a retro-fitting. Here's a retro-mything. It is taking the story of the Exodus from Egypt and casting it now as a great motivator for why we have to follow this law.
>
> What is that first commandment saying?

---

43 2 Kings 22:3–23:3.

"I am the lord your God who took *you* out of the land of Egypt." I'm not introducing myself as the one who created heaven and earth and all that stuff. That would make me also make demands on other people. I'm coming to you particularly, you especially, and I want you to hear that story. This is how I brought your forefather Abraham, this is how I followed this whole thing through, I brought you into Egypt, took you out of Egypt.

"And here was Moses the lawgiver, and he was up with me for forty days and forty nights and he prayed for your existence because if it wouldn't have been for him you would have been destroyed. He gave up being the one from whom a new nation could have been spawned, and didn't want to be that; he said 'Erase me from the book that thou hast written'…"

Do you understand how Moses grows in stature at this point, to a fantastic place?

Furthermore, because Deuteronomy is a summary of the story and the laws, Schachter-Shalomi also describes it as particularly useful to Ezra and Nehemiah when they come back from Babylon to teach Torah to the people of the land of Israel.[44]

It accompanies the people later on to Babylon. This is the book that they bring back from Babylon in the time of Ezra and Nehemiah who are reading it again. And it's a restatement of the law, it's a digest of the law. If I can't read the whole Torah, what do I read? Deuteronomy.

Gratitude to Redaktor

Alongside a welcoming acceptance of the teachings in the Biblical text taken in a traditional way as divine instruction, Schachter-Shalomi is also prepared to take teachings from the text viewed as having passed through an historical development. This

---

44 Ezra 7.

came out most strikingly in a statement of acknowledgment and gratitude for the redactor of the text,[45] and was expressed in a parallel statement to the expression of gratitude he had made earlier to Moses for Deuteronomy.

One is struck by his ability to hold both views at the same time, and his comfort with that. His sincerity and comfort come across especially when listening to the audio. One hears a depth of real appreciation in both versions; neither version seems to undermine or vitiate the other.

> Now who is the person who finally puts together—
> When we hear a priestly code, a J and an E, the whole thing gets put together and Deuteronomy seems to be a complete book by itself, and you have J, E, P, and D, and they are being put together as a code from which the Five Books of Moses are being stitched, as it were. Each one is a fragment. And then when all these fragments are stitched together, you get a whole *sefer Torah*, a whole scroll of the Torah, which then can be held together and read as one piece.

Schachter-Shalomi's voice softens and deepens; one feels even through the limited bandwidth of the audio file the awe and love he is experiencing in that moment as he goes on to say:

> Can you imagine the person who sits and writes this stuff, who does the final editing job? We don't know who he was. Likely that he was a priest. Very likely that that person was inspired.

---

45 Schachter-Shalomi refers to the Documentary Hypothesis, developed by Biblical scholars in the 18th and 19th centuries to explain inconsistencies in the Biblical text. Four main sources were identified, termed J (the Yahwist), E (the Elohist), D (the Deuteronomist), and P (the Priestly writer). According to the hypothesis, these independent narratives were combined or woven together by redactors or editors, whose contribution is labeled R. See, for example, Friedman, *Who Wrote the Bible?*

I want to say something about that inspiration. Some people would feel that if God didn't dictate it, beyt, reysh, aleph, shiyn, yud, tav—*b're'shiyt*[46]—you know, every letter in every one of the tittles and the jots that are on top of that, that this would be somehow false.

But if you begin to see all the nuances that are in that book! the way in which these things match! the way in which you can get insights from taking one sentence from here and another sentence from there, the numerical values that you can stretch from one sentence to another, how exciting it gets to be! And then you start saying, isn't it amazing!

I want to honor the person who is the editor of that. And this is what Franz Rosenzweig[47] said. When the Bible scholars were marking, this is not J or D or E, but this is R, what did R stand for? *Redaktor.* It stood for the editor who put this stuff together. And Franz Rosenzweig says, "This is the *Rabbenu.*" The *Moshe Rabbenu,*[48] the real teacher whom we have to honor, is that *Redaktor.*

And when you say "Is this a divine Torah?" here's where we run into this problem. Is it a divine Torah? If you say it has to be forever, we run into a problem. If you start saying it is a strategy for a certain period of history, it's a different story.

What this book [Deuteronomy] was trying to do was not only trying to incorporate the common law understanding

---

46 Schachter-Shalomi is spelling out the first letters of the Bible, the letters of the first word בְּרֵאשִׁית in Genesis.

47 **Franz Rosenzweig** (1886–1926). German Jewish philosopher and theologian.

48 Moses is traditionally called *Moshe Rabbenu,* "Moses our teacher," because he is understood to have brought us the written Torah (the five books attributed to him).

that you had in Hammurabi,[49] for instance, but it also was a reworking of all the law codes of the Ancient Near East, it was a reworking of all the practices that were around for the sacrificial practices that the Phoenicia and other people had. The business that you can't sell land forever didn't originate here.

This is where I want to give credit and unburden Moses of the burden. The credit I want to give to this Rabbenu, this nameless *Redaktor* of this text and say "What a marvelous job you did in a summary of the common law, placing it under your vision of what God desires from human beings, setting it up in a do-able, replicable, generation-transmittable form! and having done this—*this* I want to say is God's word."

Simultaneous Paradigms

Something very interesting is happening here: it seems that Schachter-Shalomi is shifting his sense of gratitude and piety already expressed for Moses Rabbenu to Redaktor Rabbenu. He has not dropped his deeply religious attitude to embrace a secular view, but rather subsumed certain facts considered in other contexts to be secular, into his religious and theological system. It is still the divine word, the divine Torah, descending and delivered through human vessels. He addresses this apparent strangeness:

Now it's strange that I'm making this big humanistic statement and then I'm coming back and saying this is God's word, okay? *V'zot ha Torah asher sam Moshe lifnei*

---

49 **Hammurabi.** Babylonian king, ruled 1792–1750 BCE, first king of the Babylonian Empire, known for having written or at least promulgated one of the first written codes of law in recorded history.

b'nei Yisrael—al pi Yah b'yad Moshe.[50] It came through God's mouth, as it were, but in the hand of Moses.

The other striking dimension here is that he hasn't abandoned the paradigm of the descent through Moses. Both paradigms are precious, and they carry different kinds of truths.

Applying the Torah Teaching to Present Practice

Schachter-Shalomi continues directly from his statement just quoted about the Torah having been placed before the children of Israel, from the mouth of God through the hand of Moses. He carries that thought forward into an examination of how one might continue the process.

> [What came through the hand of Moses] is that teaching, that gets so condensed—what has been considered to be the equitable *Zeitgeist*[51] of that time. How one best is to live in the world. And connects that with a vision.
>
> Now let's say, what happens when we grow past that? *Gam ki yazqin lo yasur mimenah.*[52] So how do we deal with that?
>
> And I find that each time when I have to go and check when somebody asks me a question and when I ask myself a question, what would be the right way to deal with it?

---

50 Line of prayer sung as Torah scroll is raised from the table at the end of the Torah Service and held aloft open to the words just read. וְזֹאת הַתּוֹרָה אֲשֶׁר שָׂם מֹשֶׁה לִפְנֵי בְּנֵי יִשְׂרָאֵל, עַל פִּי יְיָ בְּיַד מֹשֶׁה. "And this is the Torah that Moses placed before the children of Israel. From the mouth of YHVH by the hand of Moses." The musical setting most often used is grand, momentous, anticipatory, noble, processional.

51 **Zeitgeist**. German. Spirit of the age.

52 The second half of Proverbs 22:6, the part about what will happen when the child grows up. "Even when he should grow old, he will not turn aside from it." גַּם כִּי־יַזְקִין לֹא־יָסוּר מִמֶּנָּה׃

Schachter-Shalomi gives an example of looking to Deuteronomy to answer a question of present day practice. Deuteronomy says that when you build a house and the house has a flat top you must have a guard rail on the roof so that if someone falls from the roof you will not be guilty of their blood.[53] This situation, while rarely applying directly now, is a paradigm for other situations, perhaps completely new situations, that do exist. The paradigm is that one must take care when building something even for oneself to see that the safety of others is not compromised.

> In other words, the precedent for the application for my life situation, if I look enough, with open eyes, with an understanding that is not hard but pliable, if I see the text organic rather than a strait-jacket, what keeps coming is instruction, instruction, instruction. It may not tell you what to do in the 21st century, but what you need to do in the 21st century, the thread of that, can be picked up and applied.

The fact that the book describes situations that no longer exist, or reflect practices we feel that civilization has moved beyond, doesn't invalidate the teaching. Rather, we can find the teaching not in the specifics but in the spirit and intention behind the commandment.

Graduating and Going Beyond

Schachter-Shalomi shifts the language again slightly, and proposes another term for this progress, or development, or growth, or re-visioning to meet changing circumstances and evolution of social conditions and human consciousness. He proposes calling it graduating. That has the advantage of emphasizing how one has been educated and enriched by the teaching that went before, and indeed prepared by it to move on to that to which one graduates: the many graduate schools that life unfolds for us.

What went before was the necessary—the valuable and valued—preparation for the next stage of one's gradual unfolding,

---

53 Deut. 22:8.

allowing the organic evolving of ever-deeper and subtler levels of spiritual understanding.

> I wanted to share this because I want to get out of the sense that in order to live as a moral being today I have to break this. I want to say the other way around: in order to live as a moral being today I have to "graduate" from this. What a difference this is!
>
> When people say to me, "What is the conflict between you, Zalman, and Lubavitch?" And my answer is "I've graduated." I'm not against! I've graduated. What a difference it makes.
>
> And you can see what I would like to be able to say to fundamentalist brothers and sisters is the same thing. "We are not out to break the source of your values and inspiration and guidance. We're there to help you live it in such a way that you can learn it, graduate from it, learn it and apply it in the given situations of your life."

Other Levels of Interpretation

Perhaps partially because, in the time he had between Friday evening and Sunday afternoon, Schachter-Shalomi could not deal with Deuteronomy and Ecclesiastes in full depth, he limited himself to the simple, surface level of meaning, the *p'shat* level.[54] That is, he took the statements and instructions at their surface meaning.

> We have not addressed more in our talking about Moses than the level of simple, manifest meaning. We haven't yet begun to speak about *remez, drash, sod,* the higher levels

---

54 The *p'shat* level is the plain meaning in terms of the system of four levels of interpretation. This system, whose acronym is written PaRDeS, emerged by the thirteenth century of the common era. Schachter-Shalomi does not use these hermeneutical categories explicitly in the presentations that are the subject of this study. A footnote in the last chapter of this book glosses these levels.

of interpretation. At the higher levels we see patterns, there we have insights and a lot of other stuff, but that doesn't lead to behavior. Or at least it leads to behavior only in the long run. The immediate form of behavior, the limits on behavior, is what you get described here in the book.

Although he is deliberating limiting most of his teaching this weekend to the *p'shat* meaning, Deuteronomy and all the Torah texts can be understood on other levels, as clues, metaphors, allegories, and pointers to mystical levels of experience.

For example,[55] the "Promised Land" could be understood as God-consciousness, or a spiritual state of union with the divine. The various adversities the Israelites met could represent various spiritual blockages to be overcome on the way to the "promised land." The crossing of the Red Sea could be the passage through the birth canal as the Israelites emerge from Egyptian gestation into nascent peoplehood.

The different characters could be understood as parts of our own soul or psyche or ego: we might have within us Moses, Miriam, Aaron, the frightened spies and the courageous spies, the rebellious Korach, Aaron's sons who offer "strange fire" and are consumed by the fire that issues from God out of the sanctuary. And each of the other characters that appear could be explored as recognizable parts of ourselves. Myriad levels of insights and teachings could come out of these sorts of interpretations. Then the interactions of these characters could have teachings: the inner Moses struggles with the inner Pharaoh or with the backsliding parts of ourselves, and so on.

Then the various archetypes could be seen playing out: Miriam's special relationship to water could represent the soul-watering of

---

55 Although such interpretations are not offered very often in the Primal Myths sessions (and explicitly avoided in this particular weekend), in other unpublished oral teachings he has done so more freely over the years. My examples are typical sorts of interpretations from these other levels that I have heard from him or from his direct students.

spirituality: if that should die, we will go thirsty as the people did after Miriam's death.

Schachter-Shalomi has chosen not to open up those levels of understanding at this time, through this weekend's exploration of the text. He chose this despite the fact that for many of the participants those levels of understanding would have been more palatable than the black and white, "my way or the highway," "choose either blessing or curse," simple level of the text.

One might suppose other reasons for this besides time limitations. Schachter-Shalomi had certain points to be made about the simple *p'shat* level, and he wanted to spell them out at sufficient length that the participants came to appreciate what was there, how it had functioned over the millennia forming and transforming the Jewish people, and what even today there is to be grateful for. Jewish tradition insists that all the levels of understanding are true simultaneously.

To present a "higher-level" interpretation, even one that was more congenial to the spiritual evolution to which his participants prided themselves on having attained, ran the risk of making some dismiss the *p'shat* level and not respect its value and legitimate (or even necessary) use now.

Furthermore, it is primarily this simple level that was developed in Rabbinical Judaism into the *Halakhah*, the set of observances that define Jewish obligation for the orthodox. Even for those who do not observe all the obligations, the tradition has a power. Most Jews who are not strictly observant still choose to follow a subset of the Halakhic requirements. The subset might include circumcision of sons, attending synagogue on the High Holy Days, participating in a Passover Seder, perhaps lighting candles for the Sabbath or avoiding pork or shellfish.

These observances may be thought of more as customs than as laws, but some core practices from the tradition feel necessary if one is to experience oneself as Jewish. And these come from the Mosaic law; they are not emerging from allegorical psycho-spiritual dimensions, however deep and true these may be in their own realm.

12
Transition to Ecclesiastes

Why Do We Need Ecclesiastes?

Included in the process and rhythm of the weekend are the usual Sabbath services. On Saturday evening, when the Sabbath itself comes to a close, there is a service called *Havdalah*,[1] separating the sacred time of Shabbat from the ordinary time of the six days of the week. Schachter-Shalomi included in his leading of this service (which was not recorded) some words of transition between exploration of, and teachings about, Deuteronomy, and the upcoming more detailed consideration of Ecclesiastes. In opening the Sunday session, he refers to this.

> We now move, shift, *havdalah*. The likelihood is that there will still remain residues and I hope you will be aware that we will use them as grist for our mill.
>
> Now when I made the *havdalah* and had in mind that we are moving from Deuteronomy to Qohelet and that we have to say that there is a division between them, that they are not identical, that what happens in Deuteronomy is one kind of thing and what happens in Qohelet is another kind of thing.

It may be true that in the natural course of things following in God's path, "walking after God," may lead to blessing, and that acting counter to the good counsel of the commandments leads to

---

1   **Havdalah**. Hebrew. Literally, separation, the thing caused to be divided or separated.   249

trouble, and the natural equivalent of curses, if not direct divine retaliation.

However, there may be levels of complexity not covered here. Recognition of these levels of complexity, and of special situations, is of course what led the Rabbis of the Talmud to expand and restate the commandments.

Furthermore, there is a theological difficulty with assuming that we can control the divine dispensation of blessing by our behavior. Are we really in control? Can we force God's hand? What if God's purpose requires matters to unfold in a way that may bring suffering to a good person? This question is taken up and addressed in the book of Job.

Schachter-Shalomi looks at it from a more organic point of view. Some things have to unfold in a certain way and can't be forced. All our attempts to force them to go the way we think they ought to go seem to be thwarted. On the other hand, we have to do our best to do right; we must try to see what the responsible act would be *as if* we were in charge.

But there may come a point when we find that there are things that will not yield even to our most responsible moral choice.

> For every thing there is a time and there is a season and when the time comes for that to happen it begins to happen and it attracts to itself forms in all kinds of ways in which it must manifest. In the situation where everything is either a duty or a transgression of a duty, that's to say, in the place of Deuteronomy, in the atmosphere of Deuteronomy, you want to teach responsibility. You want to teach the kids diligently, you want to repeat to them before they go to sleep, when they get up in the morning, *sh'ma' yisrael,*[2] these are the rules, this is the way in which you're gonna learn.

---

2   All these phrases are from the central part of the prayer service, the section that begins "שְׁמַע יִשְׂרָאֵל, Hear O Israel." *The Complete ArtScroll Siddur*, 2001, pp. 90–94 for the weekday morning service (and at corresponding parts of other services). The words *sh'ma*

So then you say the following: the world is poised between life and between death. I'm quoting again: "Behold, I set before you life and good, evil and death. Choose life."[3] And as it is poised in the center of the scale, you and the act you are about to perform will either topple it to the side of the good or to the side of the evil. Your act is the next act.

You get that sense of responsibility? That's the way we talk to each other when we want to say "And now you're gonna be *bar mitzvah* and you have to take this on. Whatever you will do is going to create a difference in the universe. You're a person whose acts take on meaning and have consequences."

Well, how else should you be talking to a young man who can make babies already, can make babies happen? You want to be able to say to him, consequences and what you will do, all this will go together, and you have to take responsibility.

Then you start looking at a situation and you say—

[The audio file breaks off at the end of tape; there is a short gap while the new tape is inserted, then:]

---

yisrael is taken from Deut. 6:4. The part about impressing the teaching upon the children is taken from Deut. 6:7.

3   Deut 30:15–19: See, I set before you today life and good, and death and ill: in that I command you today to love YHVH your God, to walk in his ways and to keep his commandments, his laws and his regulations, that you may stay-alive and become-many and YHVH your God may bless you in the land that you are entering to possess. Now if your heart should face-about, and you do not hearken, and you thrust-yourself-away and prostrate yourselves to other gods, and serve them, I announce to you today that perish, you will perish, you will not prolong days on the soil that you are crossing the Jordan to enter, to possess. I call-as-witness against you today the heavens and the earth: life and death I place before you, blessing and curse; now choose life, in order that you may stay-alive, you and your seed. [translation by Everett Fox]

Can't Force the Sun to Rise

> ...and no matter how much I push and how much responsibility I take to make it daylight right now I can't make that happen. It's not the time for that to happen. Okay? That sense that something does not depend on my volition and my moral choice, but it depends on whether it's the right time.

To deal with the complexity of life we need wisdom: that is, we need discernment and judgment, which come only with experience. Before we have accumulated the experience, and learned to exercise discernment and judgment, we need clear guidelines that try to eliminate any room for poor choices. But could that time of training lay the groundwork for good judgment later? Might it be like practicing scales to lay groundwork for improvisation later?

Finishing the Proverb: "When He Becomes Old"

Schachter-Shalomi uses a verse he had introduced earlier to show how Bible might show us how the teaching value of Deuteronomy could transition into the teaching of the Biblical Wisdom literature.

He had been working with the verse Proverbs 22:6 that said *Chanokh lana'ar al pi darko; gam ki yazqin lo yasur mimenah.* חֲנֹךְ לַנַּעַר עַל־פִּי דַרְכּוֹ גַּם כִּי־יַזְקִין לֹא־יָסוּר מִמֶּנָּה׃ "Teach the lad according to his way, even when he gets old he will not turn away from it."

Schachter-Shalomi had used the first part of the verse, "Teach the lad according to his way," which he explored as "according to the child's way," that is, appropriate to his level of understanding, experience, and moral development.

Now Schachter-Shalomi turns to the second half of the sentence, the assertion that, if one does teach the child in that way, as he grows older he will not turn away from those teachings, or that path.

> But now let's go to the other part of that sentence....
> *Gam ki yazqiyn.* As he grows older there has been enough
> of the absorbing, of that fitting that life situation, that when
> that child grows through a whole series of moral dilemmas,
> in other words when the old solutions don't work....

The child is served up to a certain point. But when the old solutions don't work, will he even then not turn, *lo yasur*, from what he has learned?

> Remember in this picture you have: this bad guy comes
> and whispers in your ear "go serve an idol," remember? Kill
> him. The guy talks to you "do good," listen to him. So what
> you get is a very clear black, white, black, white, very very
> clear, hardly any shades of grey in Deuteronomy.
>
> By the time you get to King Solomon you start looking
> around and you see there's all shades of grey, there's hardly
> any blacks and whites left.

The differences in this particular respect are striking: no greys, almost nothing but greys. What do we do with that? Do we have to throw one system out? Or can the right kind of teaching in the first part of life allow us the bravery and the breadth of imagination and intellect required to ask the right questions? Can it lead us to ask what this *Torah* of apparent paradoxes is being offered to teach us?

> When you get to see these two things side by side, it's
> like saying "why did God give us two eyes?" Why did these
> two documents appear about the same time? Then I must
> say it's because they are mutually enlightening each other.

Punctive and Durative

Over the course of the weekend, this tapestry that Schachter-Shalomi weaves has been the work of many different threads. One of the threads is a trope that Schachter-Shalomi brings out from time to time, and develops particularly on this weekend. It is a contrast—and balancing—of two approaches he calls punctive and durative.[4] He will use this distinction to give a way of looking at the complementary approaches of Deuteronomy and Ecclesiastes.

He had first introduced the punctive and durative distinction in the Creation weekend, connecting it initially to the Biblical Hebrew verb forms of *qatal* and *yiqtol*, sometimes translated as verbal tenses "perfect" and "imperfect," that is, completed and not completed.[5] Schachter-Shalomi will go further to follow out the idea of punctive and durative beyond the verb forms into understandings of life and the workings of the universe.

In the first weekend he introduced it as follows.

> Punctive, taking one point in time; and ongoing, durative.
>
> *B'reshiyt bara elohim et hashamayim v'et ha aretz.*[6]
> In the beginning (punctively! remember, big bang), God created.

---

4   Schachter-Shalomi attributes these ideas to the American linguist Benjamin Lee Whorf who, Schachter-Shalomi says, found that verb tenses in a native American language was a better model than perfect and imperfect; Schachter-Shalomi says that they had two tenses, the punctive and the durative. Whorf did publish a grammar of the Hopi language, and his book *Language, Thought and Reality* develops these ideas using similar words but in a slightly different way. Schachter-Shalomi's usage, while inspired and influenced by Whorf's insights, is best understood as its own discourse.

5   This classification acknowledges that Biblical Hebrew does not have the modern European sense of past, present, and future However, most grammarians recognize that the division into "completed" and "uncompleted" is still an inadequate approximation of these forms and many prefer to speak noncommittally of *qatal* and *yiqtol*. See my footnote on *qatal* and *yiqtol* on page 16.

6   Gen. 1:1. בְּרֵאשִׁית בָּרָא אֱלֹהִים אֵת הַשָּׁמַיִם וְאֵת הָאָרֶץ׃

Vayomer elohim y'hi or, vay'hi or.[7] And God proceeded to say "let there be light" and he's still saying let there be light. Get it? It's in the durative.

So when you hear punctive, durative, you begin to realize that the masculine tendency to see events in the world is a punctive tendency. And the feminine is a durative. Making a child for a man is a punctive thing. For a woman it is a durative thing. Once you begin to see these two tenses, and you notice them in the Hebrew, every once in a while something very refreshing comes.[8]

As he takes up the exposition in the Deuteronomy and Ecclesiastes weekend, he describes it in this way.

Punctive, it happens and it is done. Durative carries with itself that notion of time.

But more is at issue here than one-time and on-going. There are kinds of on-going activities or states that may be being understood with a punctive state of mind.

However, when we (men, at this point—I, Zalman[9]) think of something having duration, we say "And the Lord shall reign forever and ever, as it was in the beginning, so it

---

7 Gen. 1:3. ‏וַיֹּאמֶר אֱלֹהִים יְהִי־אוֹר וַיְהִי־אוֹר:‏

8 Schachter-Shalomi refers to certain usages of the *yiqtol* verb state in Hebrew (such as his example ‏יְהִי־אוֹר‏ "y'hi or"), which, if understood as *durative* in his sense, he finds more interesting than if understood simply as a future tense (as it often is in the European past-present-future model).

9 Schachter-Shalomi would like to connect a dimension of this punctive-durative distinction to something he sees as gender-associated, but he is sensitive to overstepping into stereotyping. So here and later he interrupts himself when generalizing about male tendencies to emphasize that he is speaking about himself.

is now and ever shall be, world without end,"[10] and you get that thing? The condition of *now* has frozen. That is to say the punctive, the snapshot of now has been extended for all time and all space. Okay? Now, that is *not* durative.

A little later Schachter-Shalomi explains more. Durative is not only not the snapshot extended for all time and space, it is also not a whole lot of little *puncts* lined up one after the other. There has to be a shift in the conscious experience to see life as a durative process, organic, with its parts continuously flowing.

There may sometimes be a usefulness to describing things with punctive language. It may be rhetorically useful or it may even be the most accurate description of something. But lining up a lot of punctive moments and thinking that the result is life could lead to the feeling that "life is one damn thing after another."

Every durative period could be divided into an infinity of punctive points along the way. But the flow, the movement that is going through in the durative is more than the sum total of all the points along the way.

The people who are complaining that the CD is not the best kind of music, that they would rather have music recorded in analog, are complaining that the digital version is chopped out, punctive digits of musical stuff and it doesn't have the continuation of the sound. I don't know the difference, but there are some people who can tell you, this is digital music, this is not analog music. Because it seems to be made of punctive stations rather than durative flow.

Schachter-Shalomi connects this to experiencing life as process.

---

10 In Latin: *Sicut erat in principio, et nunc, et semper, et in saecula saeculorum.* This phrase as quoted here appears in the Catholic liturgy. Called the Gloria Patri, and sung at the end of recitations of psalms and canticles, it invokes the Trinity and then finishes with the quoted words in Latin or vernacular.

> "If you harken to the lord your God, you will start such a process in your life"— this is not the language of Deuteronomy. The language of Deuteronomy is "If you listen to the lord your God you will do this and it will be done."
>
> The understanding is that each time, 613 discrete commandments, you do it, it's done, one down, one down. You operate with checklists rather than saying "How do you fulfill yourself as a person in the service of God? You live a whole year in the process of it."

Here Schachter-Shalomi gives the example of people who want to explore Judaism who, when they come to a *frum* (orthodox religiously observant) community, are told that they have to start by doing all the *mitzvot* (observances, commandments). It is a problem, he says, that they are not invited live with the *mitzvot* while adding them gradually, so that they have a chance to come to understand the meaning of each one in their own authentic experience. He continues:

> That sense of where the cycles are in a person's life, … that's the durative sense, that gives that extension through time, and that is time-friendly.

Schachter-Shalomi now gives a personal example and talks about frustration he has felt when he gives a task to his secretary and finds that "she needs time to do it." He's handed it over, he says, so in his mind it's finished. He goes on to larger examples where this sort of thinking may lead to premature sense of closure. Sometimes after the (perhaps satisfying) punctive moment, the real work has just begun.

> The way in which in Israel it's "*gemarnu*!" We're finished with it. What do you mean, you're finished with it? "We got the territories, *gemarnu*, we're finished." You're not finished! … It takes time to finish. [One needs] to know that even when you think you are finished you aren't finished yet.

So the Germans have a saying, *"Vater werden ist nicht schwer. Vater sein dagegen sehr."*[11] To become a father is very easy, takes only a punctive moment. To be a father is the durative part.

So I'm saying that this is hard for us because we don't have a sense of time and season.

Both Aspects are Part of Reality: Figure and Ground

Schachter-Shalomi doesn't want to oversimplify this, however. It is not, and cannot be, that one is right and the other wrong. We must live both, and must understand both; to balance properly, one must discern appropriate applications. Thus (he alerts the participants), in his teachings he will be mixing the approaches.

We couldn't understand punctive if we only lived punctive. It takes durative living to understand punctive. And so my language is a mix of these things as we are talking.

As one image for the interplay and coexistence of the two approaches, he uses the trope of figure and ground.

Punctive becomes the figure in the durative ground. Durative in a sense becomes durative only in contrast to the punctive of it.

He had brought out the figure and ground metaphor a little earlier, developing it this way:

Hold this for a bit in how one speaks about morality. In a durative situation it isn't only the figure that we are addressing, it is how the figure sits in the ground. So when,

---

11 German. To become a father is not hard; in contrast, to be a father is very (hard).

for instance, we are hearing from someone like Tillich,[12] when Tillich says God is the ground of all being, what we are hearing at this point, we are talking about that feminine aspect of God. The ground in which there arises the figure. What we are aware of is the figure and not the ground. And sometimes it switches around, like the two faces becoming a goblet; figure/ground switches around sometimes.

The context in which a statement is being made is the ground of the statement. The same statement in a different context may have an altogether different flavor. When we start getting to ethics from a contextual point of view, you cannot make the statements that Deuteronomy is making. Get it? Deuteronomy is setting up a situation in which you are constantly surrounded by those who are going to deflect you from the way; you're going to be back-sliding. [Moses] does not believe that people will have it in themselves to do it right unless they are governed from the outside, unless they are led.

Whereas, on the other hand, you get—it's not anarchy that comes out from Ecclesiastes. It is a recognition that you gotta do what you gotta do, but you can't take it that seriously.

Circumstances

Another way to think about the difference between Deuteronomy and Ecclesiastes is to look at the way things that at one point seem very definite can shift with circumstances.

That something should turn into its opposite is something that the punctive mind cannot understand.

"Will you love me forever?" is the kind of thing that says, "will you keep this punctivity extended forever?"

---

12 **Paul Tillich** (1886–1965). German-American Christian theologian. See *Systematic Theology, Vol 2: Existence and the Christ* (1957), p. 10.

> But if I were to say "Will you keep on loving me?" notice how the context has changed, so that when all the changes are going to happen, will you love me appropriate to the changes that will happen? And what a difference it is!
>
> If I say, will you love me the way you loved me when I was eighteen when I'm sixty four, you know, then I think *"Ikh hob nisht keyn koyekh!*[13] I don't have any energy for that!" If I can get to the place where I can say "Will you love me in a way that's appropriate for then, *oy!* this is what I need."
>
> This is not what you get in Deuteronomy, and this is the flavor that keeps coming out from underneath of Qohelet.

Is there a Progression?

So does this mean that Qohelet has replaced Deuteronomy for our time because we have evolved spiritually or because situations are different now?

No: Schachter-Shalomi circles around again. It's not that simple. We have different aspects at work simultaneously.

The approach of Deuteronomy would need to be updated for our times. But it would not turn into Qohelet. And Qohelet itself would need to be updated if it were to be brought into full usefulness for our time.

Deuteronomy gives a kind of "traffic control" (as Schachter-Shalomi called it earlier) that is of value at any time; it just needs to be adjusted for the sorts of vehicles and intersections and road construction that are encountered now, as well as for conventions and attitudes we may have in our driving and in our interactions with others on the road.

> At this point I think we're all agreed that what we need to do in order to boot the Moses software today is to make

---

13 Yiddish expression, meaning as Schachter-Shalomi translates.

adjustments for the new hardware that we have for the new conditions, the new environment in which we are operating.

That still doesn't mean that Moses would be identical with where Qohelet is. It only would mean that in our day Moses would give us different traffic control than he would give us then. And Qohelet in our day would give us what is addressed to us.

Consonants and Vowels

Schachter-Shalomi now tries yet another analogy to the way we need to use both these approaches simultaneously. In speaking, we articulate words using both the hard momentary sounds of the consonants and the shaping of breath that forms the vowels.

Without preparatory introduction, he utters a string of unintelligible sounds. Although he only explains later, he is pronouncing a version of some sentences using only the vowels of the words. There are intonations, but we can't identify the words or catch the meaning. Then he utters the same statement using only consonants. Again, we can't understand what he is saying.

> I've made the same statement both times, once with consonants without vowels, once with vowels without consonants. You do understand me when I speak vowels and consonants together. [Suppose] I were now to say that Ecclesiastes is vowels, the Wisdom literature[14] is vowels, the right hemisphere is vowels, that the durative is vowels. And that the punctive is consonants, like stops: glottal stops, labial stops, and dental stops. And it needs to have the breath to carry it.
>
> And how would you say "breath"? *Havel.*

---

14 Schachter-Shalomi presumably refers to the Biblical "wisdom books": Job, Psalms, Proverbs, Ecclesiastes, and Song of Songs.

To further underscore or illustrate the idea of Qohelet as the vowel-like approach, he sings the line: *Havel havelim amar Qohelet.*[15] He sings this line with the traditional Qohelet musical trope,[16] in a way that seems to him to show that the Qohelet words, especially with that musical trope, come out as mostly vowels.

Pulling back to the original teaching image of the vowel-less and consonant-less sentences, he continues:

> The sense is not made by the vowels alone; the sense is not made by the consonants alone. It is this interplay of vowel and consonant that we are dealing with.

This image or metaphor asserts the importance of drawing on both approaches. One or the other by itself will not serve the purpose of giving guidance for life to human beings, just as vowels or consonants alone would not serve the purpose of conveying intelligible discourse.

Schachter-Shalomi Challenges his Model of Deuteronomy for the Children

Earlier, Schachter-Shalomi had explored the idea of Deuteronomy as suitable for the stage of intellectual development and limitations of experience and judgment found in children, as well as a means of passing tradition on through the generations. This stage might also be that of a group of ex-slaves, or perhaps of other peoples who had not had any experience of self-government.

But as we so frequently see, Schachter-Shalomi seems more committed to deepening the questions than to providing answers. So, lest we start down another path of over-simplification, Schachter-Shalomi now undermines the idea that the Deuteronomy approach is good for children. Even for them, we now hear, it may

---

15 הֲבֵל הֲבָלִים אָמַר קֹהֶלֶת from Ecc. 1:2.

16 Chapter 13 has more material on Qohelet's musical trope.

be a problem. Having put out his teaching metaphor of the consonants and vowels, he says:

> Once we get a little handle on this, then we see that to take and teach children an education that will only be consonantal education is going to lead to the fundamentalism that's driving religious people crazy.

Teaching children with the Deuteronomistic version, the consonantal version, is teaching fundamentalism, which he sees as a source of problems.

So perhaps it is the case that even children need some broader context? Or, if children are natural fundamentalists, maybe we need to work the "vowels" in gradually as they become ready for them, before they either become self-righteous grown-up fundamentalists or, on the other hand, start seeing things for themselves and rejecting the tradition that offered only the consonantal teachings.

If we have been following Schachter-Shalomi as he unfolded things this weekend, it seems a tricky business.

> This is the reason why today we find that "religion" is out and "spirituality" is in. But spirituality without religion doesn't have the next generation. Religion without spirituality doesn't have *this* generation. [participant laughter] So if you want to bring the two of them together, how are you going to do that? You need to have the vowels and the consonants together. You need the spirituality and the religion. You need the two sources from which we are nourished.

And, presumably, we need Deuteronomy and Ecclesiastes.

13
Book of Ecclesiastes

Having discussed a number of dimensions of Deuteronomy, and considered the need for balance, Schachter-Shalomi turns his focus to the Biblical book of Ecclesiastes.

Schachter-Shalomi acknowledges that some have dismissed Ecclesiastes as cynical or as mere "conventional wisdom." Perhaps at least in part because Schachter-Shalomi identifies with the old man Qohelet who wishes to pass on his wisdom from a lifetime, he tunes in sympathetically and sees a different tone and some different messages. He would like to evoke that same sense in the participants of this weekend.

> In a way you might read Qohelet as conventional wisdom. If you do that you will give it one reading and you won't get the other possibility from it.

Havel Havelim

Much of the reputation of Ecclesiastes for cynicism probably comes from the lines "Vanity of vanities, saith the Preacher, vanity of vanities; all is vanity" (as King James Version famously has it).[1] Schachter-Shalomi will be thinking about this line, and the meaning of the Hebrew words, as he attempts to delve deeper into the consciousness of this (reputedly) wisest of men.

> And here is where I need to come to the business of
> הֲבֵל הֲבָלִים *havel havelim*, those words—vanity of vanities,

---

1   Ecc. 1:2. הֲבֵל הֲבָלִים אָמַר קֹהֶלֶת הֲבֵל הֲבָלִים הַכֹּל הָבֶל׃

> emptiness of emptiness, breath of breath, futility—all these
> words that are being used [in English translations], and they
> don't translate [the Hebrew] well.

Schachter-Shalomi tries to think what translation would better capture the sense of the Hebrew. Failing, at least for the moment, with English, he recalls reading a Hebrew translation of *Bhagavad Gita*[2] done by a scholar of both Hebrew and Sanskrit. Schachter-Shalomi found that this translation into Hebrew added to his understanding of the Sanskrit text. Similarly, he speculates, suppose one went the other way and Ecclesiastes were translated into Sanskrit, and the word *havel* were translated as *maya*.[3]

> When I hear for a moment, if someone were to say,
> "*Maya* of *mayas*, everything is *maya*." Could you hear
> what a difference it would make in how we would read
> Ecclesiastes?
>
> *Maya* doesn't only mean illusion. It means that
> wonderful play that is going on in the universe, that makes
> you think you are the chief actor, when in reality you
> happen to be the audience of your own play. When you
> get to catch on to the flip that is going on here, then you
> wouldn't say the old man, Solomon, is a cynic. Then you
> begin to look at the book from a different perspective.

Cantillation—Use of Sound, Musical Modes, and Melodic Patterns

For another angle from which to approach insight into the spirit of Ecclesiastes, Schachter-Shalomi talks about and illustrates the cantillation patterns used for reciting Biblical texts within the

---

2 ***Bhagavad Gita***. A central and treasured spiritual text of the Hindu tradition, part of Sanskrit epic *Mahabharata*.

3 **Maya माया.** Sanskrit: a term in Indian religions for the apparent external world. It has various shades of meaning in different Indian traditions; Schachter-Shalomi's own understanding follows.

Jewish tradition. The effect of the musical mode, tone, and setting affects our understanding of the words.

Schachter-Shalomi sings an example of one cantillation pattern, or musical trope, that is conventional for Deuteronomy and then one that is conventional for the books of the Prophets. Then he sings the musical trope for Ecclesiastes. His melody for Qohelet is reflective, somewhat melancholy, somewhat poignant, but perhaps also conveying a certain serenity.

> I wanted you to hear: melody creates context, just as inflection creates context.

Here Schachter-Shalomi gives an example of saying in Yiddish "Oh, you little fool (*oy, narele*)!" in a loving way and then in an angry way.

> The tone of voice, the melody, the inflection, all of this has something to say. And when you begin to hear it from that perspective something else happens.

Using the Breath

One way Schachter-Shalomi draws the participants into another level of listening is to incorporate a practice many or most of them have experienced, and some of them may do as a regular spiritual practice. This is meditation practice using the breath, specifically that of watching the breath.

In one classic form, thoughts are allowed to arise and then allowed to pass on by like clouds drifting through the sky. In a variation of this, one thinks a word or phrase with each phase of the breath, perhaps one on the inhalation and a different one on the exhalation.[4]

So here he begins consideration of Ecclesiastes, and sets up his own reading of it, by asking participants to do an exercise of

---

4   *Mantra on the breath* in the Hindu traditions; *fikr of the wasifa* in Sufi traditions.

breath-watching meditation (noticing but letting punctive thoughts go, letting them drift on by) while he reads from Ecclesiastes.

> You were often involved in meditation practices in which you were invited to let there flow in the mind what flows in the mind. And to pay attention to your breath. And as you are breathing, whatever there arises in your thought, you let it arise, you don't become attached to it, and you let go of it.
>
> What would be a good way of saying, "Okay, let me not get involved in that. I've checked this one out. This too is chasing after the wind. I can let go of that. It arises in my mind, I'm aware of it and I release it, I relinquish it, I return back to my breath." Okay?
>
> I will read some of Ecclesiastes now and I will want to read it in such a way, from the Hebrew. And you pay attention to your breath. Let the words come in and go. And as you pay attention to your breath, think of "*havlei*" as you breath out, and "*havelim*" as you breath in. Think of it as [makes "ha" breath sounds out and in] almost hearing your breath as you are breathing in and out.[5]

Schachter-Shalomi's Translation and Recitation

Schachter-Shalomi reads in a gentle, ruminating tone, pausing a moment between thoughts and elements of thoughts, taking verses from the first two chapters. He translates from the Hebrew text using his voice to convey the meditative, contemplative, exploratory, and open feeling of a thoughtful person of wisdom

---

5 The words he gives them to put on the breath are "*havlei havelim*" which literally translates as "breaths of breaths" with both words plural; the text makes the phrase a singular breath of breaths. Schachter-Shalomi doesn't seem to be making a point here of the first plural. Perhaps it is euphonic; the flow of the words is more wavelike as he gives the practice.

turning over what he has learned and sharing it. It is Schachter-Shalomi channeling Qohelet.

The verses are not strictly in order, but are fairly closely translated, not paraphrased. Perhaps Schachter-Shalomi is recounting from memory, or perhaps reading from the Hebrew text and translating as he goes with a bit of skipping around. It begins at Chapter 1 verse 12.

> "I, Qohelet, was king over Israel in Jerusalem. I gave over my heart to search and to witness in wisdom all kinds of things that happened under the sun. That can be a bad thing that God has given to people to busy themselves with. And there I saw all the activity that happens under the sun. Busy, busy. Herding the wind. Straighten up a twisted wire. You can't get it straight.
>
> "So I spoke to my heart and said, 'I, who have grown big, and who have accumulated wisdom, maybe more awareness than all of those who were in Jerusalem before me.'
>
> "And I saw my wisdom with my heart and my awareness. And I set my heart to know that wisdom, and to know what is in folly. And I saw that that too was herding the wind. A lot of wisdom, a lot of frustration, a lot of knowledge, a lot of pain.
>
> "So I decided, let me pour joy into me. Let me look at goodness. This too is breath. I laughed, and then thought it was silly. So what are you so happy about?
>
> "I sought out to find out what it's like to be drunk. So I put all my wisdom into checking out folly. So I might get to see which one of these is good for people to do under the sun, as they count the days of their life.
>
> "I did many great things. I built me houses, planted me vineyards, gardens, orchards, all kinds of fruit. Wonderful irrigation canals to give those trees water. Servants, maidservants, even those born in my house. Lots and lots

of cattle. Richer than anyone else prior to that time in Jerusalem. Whatever my eyes desired, I gave them. I did not withhold anything from my heart. And I said, let this be my exertion and let this be my reward.

"I did find out that wisdom is so much better than folly, as light is better than darkness.

"Breath. Maya. *Havel havelim, amar Qohelet.*"[6]

At this point, after a moment of silence, Schachter-Shalomi ends the meditation exercise. After another pause, he concludes with his overall sense of the book:

If one were to say "this is the only world we got, and we're happy being in this only world we got, and we don't need anything beyond what's in this moment, and this is enough reward for all the work we have done, and it's okay."

Translations keep making it a pessimistic book, and I felt a kind of wry humor.

Then he finishes with a blessing for the book, parallel to the blessing he gave after the reading from Deuteronomy at the Torah service.

And I wanted especially to say:
Baruch ata adonai, elohenu melekh ha olam,[7] who allowed this book to be part of our holy canon, text of the Bible, to give us a window, another possibility, that makes us feel as adults, and allows us to take somehow the captaincy over our souls. Amen.

---

6 הֲבֵל הֲבָלִים אָמַר קֹהֶלֶת "Breath of breaths/merest breath/vanity of vanities, said Qohelet."

7 "Blessed are you, YHVH, ruler of the universe...." Opening words of Hebrew blessings.

14
What Do We Do with
Difficult Passages?

It is all very well to look at the beautiful passages in Deuteronomy and Ecclesiastes, and to consider the morally advanced social principles, and appreciate the theological and cultural contributions made by Biblical texts. But for all one's appreciation of what is worthy of appreciation, it can be hard to get past the passages that do not seem beautiful *or* morally advanced.

Some people, including, of course, some participants in this series of weekends of Schachter-Shalomi's Wisdom School, are put off, or even deeply distressed, by passages that seem to be heartlessly, or even genocidally, advocating killing off the native inhabitants of the "promised land"—killing all the men and taking women, children, and other plunder as spoils to be made use of (the word *v'akhalta,* "and you will eat/consume," is used in Deuteronomy for the use to be made of the women and children[1]). The frequent commandment of capital punishment for offenses we might not consider worthy of the death penalty (the adulterer, the wife who cannot provide public evidence that she was a virgin on her wedding, the defiant child, the inviter-to-idol-worship, the carrier of wood on the Sabbath) strikes some as harsh and not life-affirming.[2]

And then there are the statements ignoring or demeaning women, or otherwise demonstrating a misogyny that one may not

---

1 Deut. 20:14.

2 The Talmudic rabbis also found this too harsh, and used their talents of commentary and interpretation to argue that in fact this death penalty was almost never actually carried out. See *Babylonian Talmud*, Tractate Makkot, Folio 7A.

like to connect with sacred text or word of God. (There are also beautiful woman-affirming passages in the Bible, including ones in Deuteronomy and Ecclesiastes. These are appreciated, but do not help with the painful passages.)

Schachter-Shalomi does not end the weekend without addressing this question. The example he gives in his discussion of an apparently misogynistic line in Qohelet is not the worst in that book, and there are other worse passages in Deuteronomy. But Schachter-Shalomi's discussion, and his recommendation, create a paradigm for thinking about, and perhaps dealing with, all such passages. To develop this paradigm, one need not dwell on the most distressing or inflammatory wordings.

> When we looked at the stuff that came out from Qohelet and from Deuteronomy, there was a certain element that had to do with misogyny. "I haven't found one woman among thousand," remember? "One man I have found, not one woman among a thousand."[3] You read in Deuteronomy and you see situations of discrimination that make you sometimes wonder, *make you wonder,* not "sometimes," make you wonder. What's this? could this have been the divine will, is that the way it has to go?

But what can we do? We can't just go cutting out pieces of the Bible we don't feel comfortable with. For one thing, there may be a teaching here for which this is only a parable.

If we had a story about a king who sends out his son to hunt for a precious pearl, and the son gets lost and forgets he is the son of a king, and the king sends messages to try to remind him of his true home, and so on, we don't throw the story out because monarchies

---

3   Ecc. 7:28. אֲשֶׁר עוֹד־בִּקְשָׁה נַפְשִׁי וְלֹא מָצָאתִי אָדָם אֶחָד מֵאֶלֶף מָצָאתִי וְאִשָּׁה בְכָל־אֵלֶה לֹא מָצָאתִי׃ [7:27] Behold, this have I found, saith the preacher, *counting* one by one, to find out the account: [7:28] Which yet my soul seeketh, but I find not: one man among a thousand have I found; but a woman among all those have I not found. [King James Version]

are no longer in favor with us. We understand that this is a parable of something else (our coming into incarnation and forgetting our divine inheritance, and so on, perhaps).

For another thing, where would we draw the line? And different people may be uncomfortable with different things. Who gets to say? And in the end, what would we have? A modern book, the book we would have written, but no longer a book that can teach us something we didn't already know.

> To some extent we have touched on these things yesterday, and all I wanted to bring to our attention at this point is that the *ouch* places cannot be—how should I put it? You cannot re-do Bible in such a way that we're gonna take them out. "We don't like them, we're gonna take them out." We find stuff that is written there that we don't like. Not only we don't like it personally, we know that the Spirit today does not approve of these things in the same way in which it was. We know that a statement like "One man in a thousand I have found, one woman in a thousand I have not found," that this is the kind of statement that we cannot give the consent of our higher self.
>
> What are we going to do with a text like this? To say that the next edition of the Bible is going to take that sentence out, you know, isn't going to be fair. It's not going to be fair because then there is no end to what somebody is going to want to take out, and I could imagine reading a Bible that we would take out all the *Halakhah*, all the laws from the Bible.

An Inner Act

Schachter-Shalomi is ready to say what he would suggest doing instead, but participants are feeling, uncomfortably, their own difficulties with, and mixed feelings about, the text. The discomfort in the room is making participants want to interrupt and discharge their discomfort.

> So I want to say, whenever you come across a piece that speaks to you and says "Ouch!" what I would like you to do—

Here Schachter-Shalomi is interrupted by a participant comment (inaudible, but evidently some sort of wisecrack) followed by participant laughter. Schachter-Shalomi doesn't let himself be derailed. He waits, then he says, "No, I'm going to wait until this settles; this is important." Then when they are quiet and seem able to listen again, he resumes.

> The work that we have been doing this year, part of that is to redeem the text. To make the text nourishing rather than something to beat people over the head with. So whenever we come across something of this sort, an inner act has to be done. I want to describe to you *one such act*.

Censoring the text, or re-writing it, might be thought of as an external act. Schachter-Shalomi is proposing that we need an inner act. These might take different forms; he gives an example of one that was simple, done with integrity and dignity.[4] Schachter-Shalomi was evidently impressed that it was done without a felt necessity to either reject the sacredness of the text or to make excuses or justifications for the difficult bit. It perhaps helped that the example was not from a text of the Jewish tradition, even though it involves a passage that has been the excuse for hostility and worse directed to Jews.

> I am in Vancouver with a colleague of mine, Paul van Buren who taught at Temple University,[5] a professor of religion teaching Christianity, [who] has written some

---

4 The example follows.

5 Schachter-Shalomi was a professor of Jewish Mysticism and Psychology of Religion at Temple University from 1975 until his retirement in 1987; van Buren was also on that faculty.

remarkable books about the Dual Covenant theory[6] from a Christian perspective. We are in a church. We had a weekend together so on *Shabbes* he was with me in the *shul* and this is Sunday morning and he is celebrating Mass. He's an Episcopal minister and he is celebrating Mass at this point. He comes to the place where the Gospel of John is read, and he reads: "And he came unto his own, and they knew him not." Jesus comes to his own, meaning the Jewish people, and they don't accept him.

And [van Buren] stops for a moment, and he says to all the people in the church at that time, "And this is not a fact. To whom did he come, but his own? Who were his early disciples, but his own? Who spread his word and his gospel if not his own?" Then he continued to read.

The painful thing, or the morally problematic thing, may need to be acknowledged. It might be wrong to gloss over it. One could witness it, but then move on. One could take the view that it is one truth that the statement is morally problematic, and another truth is that this is a holy book and an important book.

Do you understand? I am holding this in front of us at this point that, if there is a witness from time to time, that has to be said, so that as you might read "One man in a thousand and one woman in a thousand I did not find," then you might want to say "Too bad for you, Solomon, too bad for you, Qohelet." And then to read on.

I'm not stopping reading this book, because it is holy and it is important and yet, yes, I am dissociating myself from this particular aspect, this particular sentence, until I can lift

---

6 **Dual Covenant Theology**, proposed by some liberal Christians, holds that God's original covenant with the Jews has not been abrogated or superseded by the covenant given through Jesus Christ, and that therefore Jews following their own laws can enter heaven without converting to Christianity.

it, until I can have insight, a way of raising this so it becomes something better. [If so,] fine, but if I can't, then—okay?

Insight that Lifts

In addition to the inner act of dissociation from a particular aspect of the text, we also need to keep open the possibility that in some cases other meanings may arise and give one a different perspective on the difficult passage. That different perspective might come from a better understanding of the Hebrew grammar, it might come from work of textual criticism or insight from more recently discovered texts or translations, or it might come from interpretations on one of the other levels than the simple literal surface level. But if we don't hold this possibility at least tentatively, we lose the chance of meaning filling in.

> So I would just want to say, keep in mind whatever we dissociate ourselves from, it may not fill itself with meaning immediately, but keep it there. With the help of God, meaning will start filling in.

Declining an Inheritance

Finally, Schachter-Shalomi uses a personal story to illustrate, vividly, that one can be grateful for heritage and still reject some of it. He tells the story of learning of his father's death when he was teaching at Naropa University. Driving after leaving from his days of sitting *shiva,*[7] another car cuts him off in traffic and he finds himself cursing the other driver in Yiddish. Shaken, he pulls over and realizes that this voice is not his, but his father's.

> I said, "Papa, thank you so much for all the things that you have given me as a heritage. But some of these things you can keep."

---

7   Seven days of mourning, done at home, with visitors paying calls.

In the end, for all our gratitude, it may be that "not everything do we want to keep."

> I want to mention this because there are times when we are going to get to a heritage of this sort and get the sense of a gesture, a way of talking or something, that we recognize doesn't belong to us and they come to us in our heritage and be able to say "This is not what I want to keep." And to let go of that. And I know that this is going to be useful information to all of us, that when we recognize, as we have done with these books, not everything do we want to keep.
>
> "Moses! What we find in Deuteronomy, wonderful heritage! There are some things we don't want to keep. Qohelet! there are some things we don't want to keep."

Although we want to do such winnowing with sensitivity, delicacy, and even, at times, with the humility to leave a tentativeness, Schachter-Shalomi will not say that everything can be justified or defended. When our spiritual immune system, our deepest moral sensibility, recoils from something, that must be honored and acknowledged.

The final chapter of this book will show some things that the Rabbis of the Talmud did when their spiritual immune systems recoiled from explicit Torah commandments. In several cases the conclusion was drawn that the offending commandment was put there in order to test the moral sensibility of the Sages—so that they could "recognize that it was never meant to be applied."

Some of these passages, Schachter-Shalomi might say, could be there to test our own moral sensibility. When they inflame our sense of justice, we are brought to think about the issues and they become more clearly and more passionately defined for us. In arguing with a text that we must take seriously, we are impelled to think through the matters at a deeper level and consider all dimensions. When we clarify for ourselves what our position must be, we are truly owning it.

Schachter-Shalomi might also say that the part of us that is objecting to the perceived injustice could be the part implanted in us *b'tzelem elohim*, in the image of God. Perhaps it is actually our God part that is protesting the written Torah injunction. In the complexity of human-divine reality, and in defiance of the simple blessing-or-curse paradigm, Torah may have encoded its own tests for us.

All these considerations, all necessarily speculative, enjoin us to hold open the possibilities even as we remain sensitive to, and honor, our responses and our moral judgments and sense of truth.

15
Questions This Weekend Leaves for Us

In the material of this weekend, Schachter-Shalomi has taken on some of the largest issues with which a tradition based on sacred scriptures must engage.

What if some portions of the sacred scripture don't seem to apply anymore? What if the whole context of the faith community and its world view have changed? What if it seems useful on some levels but distasteful or even morally repugnant on others?

How far are members of that faith community, or its leaders or institutions, willing to go to make excuses or justify? How many things can be simply ignored, and what price is paid for that?

If an attempt is made to say that the apparent meaning isn't the true meaning, and the true meaning is something that the leaders or institutions know through their particular wisdom or holiness (or, perhaps, privileged communications from God passed along orally from Sinai), how much schizophrenia can the community handle while still honoring both the original text and the apparently contradictory interpretation?

Schachter-Shalomi uses Deuteronomy, as a relatively coherent summary of the Mosaic law, to represent the Mosaic system of teachings and that approach. It has much that is precious and impressive, even inspiring and beautiful. But it has an apparent flaw: it seems not to allow sufficiently for the complexities of circumstances.

The central paradigm is that if the specific commandments are followed, blessings and prosperity will flow, rain will come in due season, the promised land will remain with the Israelites, God will bring ruin to all their enemies, and all will be well for the faithful. If the Israelites fail to walk in God's ways and fail to keep all the commandments, curses and disaster will come upon them, droughts will dry up the land, and they will be driven into exiles by their enemies. On the surface, this system keeps God's actions firmly within a very simple two-compartment version of human thought.

But it doesn't take very much living of life to start feeling the limitations. Naturally, the ever-resourceful human mind can find a way around almost anything, and some of the most practiced and resourceful minds of the human species have been at work on this problem within the Jewish tradition. The problem may be thought resolved when it is asserted that if disasters come, there must have been some transgression, in action or thought.[1]

If a cause can be found—we failed or transgressed—it is still a simple system and we are in control. If only we repent and stop the transgressions and bring ourselves back into alignment with God's law, we can win back the promised blessings.

But the limitations lead to alternative theologies even within the Hebrew Bible. Schachter-Shalomi chose here to counterpose Deuteronomy to Ecclesiastes, perhaps drawn to the spirit of the old man Qohelet wishing to set down his wisdom to harvest the fruits of his life to leave to future generations. But he might also have chosen Job, another book included in the "Wisdom Literature"

---

1   Why was the land of Israel destroyed by the Romans? Because, according to Rabbi Yehudah in the name of Rab, the people had failed to say the prescribed blessing before studying Torah. (*Babylonian Talmud*, Bava Metzia 85B.) If it were known that they had never failed to say the blessing, it could be understood that they hadn't said it with enough reverence. (In other places Talmudic sages find other ways to place the fault for the destruction of the Temple with us.) This system, like the systems of celestial mechanics that could explain any anomaly by adding more epicycles, is "doomed to succeed." But, like its celestial mechanics counterpart, at some point it can begin to lose its persuasiveness.

of the Bible.[2] In that book, Job's friends counsel him with the message of Deuteronomy: if disasters have befallen you, you must have sinned. Job, while steadfast in his faith, denies wrong-doing.

After these conversations between Job and his friends and accounts of Job's sufferings have gone on for many chapters, God himself makes an appearance, speaking out of the whirlwind. In some of the most dazzling and thrilling language in the Bible, God spends four chapters[3] essentially castigating all the human interlocutors for presuming to know anything about God's intentions and the reasons why anything happens. Our human theology and theodicy are puny, ridiculous, and presumptuous. Where were we when God created the heavens and the earth? The power, the mystery, the magnificence of Creation are so far beyond our own power and understanding that to try to hem God into the confines of our own mental constructs deserves the devastating contempt that is God's "answer" to the problem. Job bows to this, as we later readers must as well. There is really no denying God's position, no refutation of the powerful rhetoric he employs.

And yet, even if one is going to live out one's life in radical awe, doesn't one still need to know (as Job surely must have, when his wealth is restored at the end of the book) whether to build a parapet when one makes a new house? Whether it's a good plan to have a day of rest after six days of work? How long a period of mourning to give a captive bride?

---

2   Schachter-Shalomi does discuss Job in the final retreat of this Primal Myths series, but he does not use the Job material to make this point at that time. Rather, in the section on Job in that weekend (which also covered Ruth, Esther, and Jonah) Schachter-Shalomi first summarizes Job's story, then leads participants through an experiential exercise, including a night vigil in which they re-live Job's trial in their own deeply imagined experience. At one point Schachter-Shalomi does refer to the advice of Job's friends as "religiosity"—a term that is another sort of comment on the view that, if one is righteous, blessings and prosperity necessarily follow and its converse, that ill fortune proves transgression.

3   Chapters 38–41.

It does seem that we need both sides. Maybe we could make up our own rules for living, but for the most part Deuteronomy offers a pretty good set, or at least a good way of thinking about the process of living among people and with the land, a way of thinking that we can use as a first approximation to make good rules for ourselves.

But we must ask, as this exploration of Deuteronomy and Ecclesiastes has drawn to a close, whether Schachter-Shalomi has managed to come up with a way to reconcile the two approaches in terms of his own sets of argumentation.

We have had a proposition that Deuteronomy (in its clear injunctions, and in its assurance that if one follows these clear commandments that things will work out well) is what is needed for children and those at certain stages of development.

Judgment is honed both with developing brains as the child grows into adulthood and with slow years of experience. It is unrealistic to expect people to have discernment and judgment before they have had considerable experience of life, of actions and consequences, of the different sorts of situations and circumstances that people can find themselves in, and of ways that people can feel things and react to things that may not be entirely rational. Until the child has had these experiences in the world, it will not work to ask him or her to discern whether it is a time for this or a time for that.[4]

Other simplifications also break down when one has more experience. For example, in Deuteronomy, if a woman is raped out in the countryside, it is assumed that she cried out in vain for help, and she is not punished for unsanctioned sex. But if the act takes place in town, it is assumed that if she objected she would have cried out and been heard, and therefore, if no one heard her cry out, that she was willing, and she is punished.[5] This may be an understandable first approximation if one has no experience of the

---

4 The times referred to in Ecc. 3:1 and following.

5 Deut. 22:23–25.

sorts of force and intimidation that are typically brought to bear in situations of rape. But it is entirely inadequate when one does.

At this point the wisdom of Ecclesiastes will have to be invoked. One can understand that there is a time when the sexual congress is voluntary, and a time when it is not, whether in the town or in the countryside. But more information and consideration of other factors, besides the rather simple determination of whether the act took place in town or country, must be brought into play. These might be more difficult to ascertain. What restraint or threats were present? What future retaliation might be brought against a woman who accused the man publicly by crying out, or even one who mounted sufficient resistance to thwart his intentions? Whose story is to be believed?

Including these complexities makes the matter not nearly as clear, not as simple to determine, and thus confusion and instability are introduced into the smoothly operating gears of implementing social order and morality.

A question left by the weekend's exploration of the two books is how, and perhaps whether, the child versus adult dichotomy actually works (and, if similar, the more-primitive stage of spiritual or political evolution versus the more-evolved stage).

Can we, following the application of Proverb 22:6,[6] learn the Deuteronomy version of reality first and then with that as foundation, combined with experience, come to judge with discernment to know when times are right for what? Is it like the example I gave earlier of practicing scales so that later we have a foundation for improvising?

Schachter-Shalomi has offered the idea of weaving both Biblical approaches together with the metaphor of the vowels and the consonants making up comprehensible verbal communication. How do we put these two systems of wisdom together? Jewish tradition would insist that both, as part of the scriptural canon, are

---

6   See Chapters 11–13 above for Schachter-Shalomi's exploration of this verse.

holy wisdom and word of God. If this is true, somehow they must fold together into a whole to give guidance for our lives.

Has Schachter-Shalomi made a persuasive case as to how to do this? Can anyone make a persuasive case without doing some adjustment of one or the other? Schachter-Shalomi does seem to have explored some adjustments. At one point he says that it pays to download Deuteronomy onto our hard drives "*provided*," provided we don't have to "take it uncooked." At another point he says that there may be some things in the inheritance that we don't want, just as there were things in his own father's rages that he, for all his gratitude, wished to decline.

Schachter-Shalomi has opened up some broad avenues and some twisting by-ways. Exploration of these, while perhaps not leading to immediate answers, certainly has deepened the questions. In his "Wisdom School," perhaps it is his goal to leave the participants pondering the questions. We recall that he has urged the participants to "hold both in tension," saying "don't try to resolve it now," and to treat the difficult material as "grist for the mill."

Schachter-Shalomi's Method of Learning: Engaging with the Words of Torah

The blessing one makes before studying Torah ends with the phrase "(who charges us) to engage with words of Torah."[7] The verb, la'asoq לעשוק, in the Hebrew of the Rabbis who formulated this blessing, invites us to busy ourselves with the text, to *engage* rather than merely read it, to *engage* rather than study it merely to learn what it says.

Biblically, the root עשק had to do with contending.[8] Its Arabic cognate, however, was about clinging with love. We are invited

---

7   *La'asoq b'divrei Torah* לַעֲסוֹק בְּדִבְרֵי תוֹרָה.

8   BDB p. 796. Used in Gen. 26:20 where the Gerar hersmen contended/quarreled/strove with Isaac's herdsmen over the wells Isaac has dug.

to dig through the levels of Torah, to turn it and turn it,[9] to argue with it, to explore and delve into it like a lover wishing to know the depths of a beloved, to transform ourselves with it.

According to the pious understanding, according to the working hypothesis, this text was given by God to teach us how to live. But it is only a key. It must be applied to our own lives, our own psyches, the world we ourselves live in.

We must bring living questions if we are to get a living wisdom back.

Implicit in this multi-millennial tradition of Jewish engagement with Hebrew Scriptures is a notion—a principle—a faith. That notion is that this is a holy text that has encoded into it the wisdom and the lessons needed for every age. The lessons needed for our age are there. But we need to tease them out and make them our own by turning and turning, immersing ourselves, contending, and exploring with openness to the possibility that we may be transformed by it.

That is the method of learning Schachter-Shalomi is engaged in, and Schachter-Shalomi's method of teaching is to show that by his own example, and to urge and incite and inspire his students to do that for themselves.

When I said that I undertook in this project to show how Schachter-Shalomi uses interpretation of Biblical narrative to support his vision of a living Judaism to be the guide for our time, I did not mean to promise that I would extract a static set of teachings that would be his proposed credo.

Neat and convenient as such things are, they quickly become limiting. And then, as Schachter-Shalomi said earlier, God has to "bust out"[10] with a correction.

---

9   *Hafakh bah v'hafakh bah; d'kolah bah.* הפך בה והפך בה. דכולא בה. Turn it (Torah), turn it; everything is in it. *Babylonian Talmud, Mishnah,* Pirkei Avot 5:26.

10 See page 174.

So Schachter-Shalomi does not provide a new dogma, a new Thirteen Principles[11] to which every Jew must hew.

Rather, each person must think through the complex questions of human life for himself or herself. It is not an academic exercise. Rather, the reading of this text leads to self discovery and self understanding.

Engaging with the words of Torah, as the commandment phrases it, is something ongoing and requiring developing levels of understanding.

The questions into whose depths Schachter-Shalomi has led us cannot be answered with simple formulae, but they *can* draw us deeper into the engagement that will continue through a lifetime, as the tree of Torah continues to bear its figs year after year.

---

11 **Maimonides** asserted Thirteen Principles of Faith, *Shloshah Asar Ikkarim*, which he said were required to be believed by all Jews or they would not be Jews. These were spelled out in his commentary on the *Mishnah* (tractate Sanhedrin, chapter 10). See Twersky, *A Maimonides Reader,* pp. 402–423 and Kellner, *Dogma in Medieval Jewish Thought.* But Jews have never been able to leave static interpretations alone, and Maimonides's principles, though enshrined and still recited as part of liturgy, were roundly challenged since before his ink had dried. See Kellner, *Must a Jew Believe Anything?*

Schachter-Shalomi's Context
in Jewish Tradition

16
Continuous Re-Visioning as an Essential Feature of Jewish Tradition

Section 1: Introduction

Schachter-Shalomi might be seen as a radical innovator, breaking with Jewish tradition; yet he comes from a traditional background and is deeply knowledgeable about the traditions. Can his trend of thought, his apparent departures, themselves be seen as springing from the tradition itself?

In the course of this chapter I will show how Schachter-Shalomi's approach in his teachings on the Biblical text, and his use of that text to ground and suggest scriptural authority for his re-visioning of Judaism for the present day, fall fully and deeply within Jewish tradition.

I make use of certain lines of thought from the scholarship of Jewish traditional Biblical interpretation to provide an overview sketch of the larger picture from within Tanakh itself, through Second Temple and Talmudic times and through the successive generations of subsequent commentators defining the Jewish tradition.

I then take more time to touch particularly on one older example of a re-visioning of Judaism that, like Schachter-Shalomi's, is referred back to readings of the Biblical text. This will be a more detailed survey of the practice of interpretation by the Rabbis of the first half millennium after the destruction of the Second Temple.[1]

The Rabbinic transformation is a crucial and very striking case of a past re-visioning of Judaism that took place when the old paradigms no longer held.[2] My sketched case study is offered to illustrate the continuous re-visioning process and to allow us to appreciate how deeply its roots are drinking the living water in traditional Judaism.

The process of applying Bible to meet the needs of contemporary people has been a primary purpose of commentators within the Jewish tradition. I offer the observations of this chapter to support my claim that Judaism has survived and remained a vital, living religion precisely because it incorporated a powerful commitment to re-visioning itself for each age.

Understanding the Biblical Text within Jewish Tradition

My interest in this process has been in the way it has played out within tradition itself, that is, within pious Jewish tradition based in Bible but interpreted through the Rabbinic tradition and the later traditional authorities.

But what is that pious Jewish tradition? Have the various commentators within that tradition, with such varied circumstances and approaches, shared some common assumptions about working with the Biblical text?

---

1   The scope of this project will necessarily limit even this more thorough survey to the gathering of suggestive elements that indicate directions of thought, strategies, and patterns. It will not attempt to fully engage the complex and even contradictory threads, motivations, goals, and process of this Rabbinic transformation of Judaism.

2   Many more case studies could be taken from later commentators, of course. One thinks of Maimonides and his monumental effort to re-vision Judaism as a coherent, systematic body of law based in rational principles.

These commentators range from Rabbis in Babylon in the first millenium of the common era, to Spain and Egypt and France and Germany in the early part of the next, to Eastern Europe in the latter part of the second millennium, from the Land of Israel to America. Could there be anything that they share, and if so will Schachter-Shalomi be found to share that as well?

In fact, it has been argued that there are a set of assumptions shared through the millennia, by traditional Biblical commentators, from the late Biblical era through the present day.[3]

First, the Biblical text is taken not as a collection of legends or an historical record but as a sacred teaching being given as a gift from God. Its purpose is instruction. It is complete and harmonious; everything within it has a purpose, something to teach, and all of it given by God (not just parts in which God is directly quoted).

But interpretation is needed, since it might look in places like a collection of stories or laws whose time of applicability is past; since it appears on the surface to have mistakes, inconsistencies, and even contradictions; since it offers examples of characters and practices that may seem at best unevolved and at worst repellent; and since some of the declarations are obscure or incomprehensible. It is interpretation that brings through the originally-intended divine message.

That interpretation comes in part from the Sages of the tradition. But it is also understood to arise afresh through divine guidance of particularly wise righteous ones throughout time.

There are some who, with Schachter-Shalomi, develop the idea that there is an imperative for individual interpretation to renew the teaching—not just for every age but within every soul. In this way, in the words of the blessing used before studying Torah, we "engage with Torah."

---

3   These have been succinctly laid out by Biblical scholar James L. Kugel. I will look at his formulation, and consider how Schachter-Shalomi's approach fits with it; see pages 304ff, below.

That "interpretation" is part of the process of coming to understand what is being taught through the sacred text.

The prudent student will, of course, attend most carefully to the interpretations of the past sages. But just taking in the words of others, however well one equips oneself to parrot them back, does not constitute real learning.

The Rules of the Game

We might look at this process as a deep game. What if the rule in this game is that we treat Scripture as instruction given by God in its entirety, without mistakes or historical tampering, encoded with the teachings and wisdom needed by each generation in its particular time and place? We would have to honor the text as if it were God speaking directly to us.

But we would have to take this same text as also providing teaching and wisdom to shepherds, Egyptian slaves, desert wanderers, warriors conquering an already-populated territory, bringers of animals to the Temple for sacrifice, monarchs and subjects, exiles in Babylonia and Persia, rabbis choosing to remain in their academies in Baghdad, Jews scattered to the four corners of the earth. What a great number of levels of meaning there would have to be! Is this even plausible?

And as we re-interpret, how do we justify our presumption? How would we maintain our pious faith that we are unpacking and decoding God's intentions? How did the Rabbis who re-visioned Judaism wholesale after the destruction of the Second Temple justify offering a new set of laws, claiming that they are consistent with those presented in the written Torah, but applying to very different conditions?

And yet this is more than a game, or so it must be to a traditional Jew. In interpretation, whether in small details or wholesale re-visioning, we are reading the mind of God. We are letting God speak his instructions to us. *Ruach haQodesh*, the Holy Spirit, is working through us, as it did through the prophets. When we discover teachings that apply in our present circumstances, and guide and inspire us in our immediate challenges, we have the thrill of seeing divine intention reveal itself.

This is a game with very high stakes. We don't want to get it wrong, and that makes us cautious. It might well seem that the prudent path is to let the sages of old, or the rabbinic authorities of our own time, tell us what the instructions of Torah are for us.

On the other hand, to read the words of scripture seeing the divine intention coming through would be like standing on the top of the mountain with Moses.

Let me use Schachter-Shalomi's own words to present his view of letting God speak his instructions to us as if we were standing with Moses at Sinai.

Schachter-Shalomi's Metaphor for the Descent of Torah

Each year the Jewish tradition celebrates a day as the anniversary of the giving of Torah on Sinai. The day is called *Shavuot*, and it is observed fifty days after Passover, after the going-out from Egypt, when Exodus says that the Israelites received the theophany at Sinai.[4]

It is customary to stay up all night that night studying Torah. I had the privilege one year of participating in this all-night study with Rabbi Schachter-Shalomi. Among other teachings he gave that night, he said the following:[5]

> So how would God want to communicate with us? ...
>
> Now can you imagine what the problem would be if the place where there's a great generator, would be directly wired to this bulb [pointing to overhead light fixture]? It

---

4   Ex. 19:1.

5   This is my transcription from a recording made of his teachings that night in June, 2008.

> would blow out right away, it would explode. So what does
> it have to have? It has to have transformers. And when
> they talk about the transformers that are necessary, they're
> called *sod*, *drash*, *remez*, and *p'shat*[6] (going from the top
> one which is the secret and then coming to the *drash* level
> of interpretation and then comes down to *remez* and then
> comes to *p'shat*.) So it goes through these transformations in
> order to reach us.

There are really two levels of this "transformer," as Schachter-Shalomi tells it. The first is the Biblical text itself, which puts the divine intention into human language. The second is the four dimensions of interpretation that he mentions, *P'shat, Remez, Drash,* and *Sod.*

Schachter-Shalomi speaks about the level of the Biblical text itself. The Biblical text speaks in human language, which is a start.

> So now comes the question "how would God send us
> messages?" They depend a great deal on our alphabet. In
> other words, *dibrah Torah k'lashon b'nei adam.*[7] The Torah
> speaks in human language.

But it must go beyond that original, perhaps, to reach each individual.

---

6 These four dimensions of understanding for Jewish traditional of reading Scripture could be briefly characterized as follows. *P'shat* is the surface level; it means interpreting the words in their own context using normal word meanings, grammar, history, and so on. *Remez*, meaning "hint," is catching philosophical or spiritual truths in the words; it may take allegorical or symbolic meanings. *Drash* is textual inquiry and creative exposition, seeking out additional layers of meaning. *Sod*, meaning "secret," is the mystical kernel beyond words.

7 Schachter-Shalomi is referring to a rabbinical doctrine in the Talmud, דברה תורה כלשון בני אדם, Torah speaks in human language. There are twenty instances of this in Babylonian Talmud; see Bava Metzia 31b for two of them.

> So that means that if God wants to give me something
> as a *m'lamed*,[8] not as an imposer, not making a zombie or a
> robot out of me, but if he wants to give this Zalman with his
> history a Torah, he has to use the language that Zalman will
> understand. Otherwise it won't come to me.

Our understanding can go beyond the words that were used
at the time of the Biblical characters. A larger "vocabulary" of
life experience, breadth of imagination, and perhaps even spiritual evolution will allow us to understand more of what is coming
through.

> … [N]ow the more letters of the alphabet we have—you
> remember the typewriters that used to be before? Now take
> a look at the keyboard and you have so many more buttons
> to do things with. That gives you a greater capacity of being
> able to do things. So if I bring a primitive keyboard to the
> *Ribono shel olam*,[9] I'm going to get a primitive message.
> Do you understand? I have the sense that when we speak
> about fundamentalists, people who only read the *p'shat* of
> the thing, and they sometimes don't have a sense of what
> an oriental language is, that it uses metaphor and is not so
> literal, is not to be taken so literally.
>
> So I need to have a rich vocabulary, I need to have a rich
> ability for God to impress nuance to me. You know black
> and white is one thing, color is something else, 3D is still
> something else. You understand what I'm getting at? The
> more capacity we have for the revelation to start coming
> down [the more we can receive].

---

8   **M'lamed** מְלַמֵּד. Hebrew: teacher. Schachter-Shalomi had begun
    the talk with the question "Is God a good teacher (*m'lamed*)?" A
    good teacher wants the student to want to learn. A good teacher isn't
    just imposing something on the student.

9   **Ribono shel olam** רִבּוֹנוֹ שֶׁל עוֹלָם Hebrew: master of the
    universe, i. e. God.

Another thing we can bring to getting the fullest message from the text, from the revelation, is clearing out noise, static that is obscuring or distorting that message.

> When you look at the description of how Eliahu, who was a teacher of Elisha, had to travel until he comes to Sinai, and then he climbs up on the mountain, and then there's a noise and there's the earthquake, and there's a fire, and there's a storm, and then finally, what comes then? "A small, still voice," yeah, I don't like that translation. I want to say, *qol d'mamah daqa,* the sound of subtle stillness.[10] *Qol,* the sound, *d'mamah* the stillness, *daqa*, thin: the sound of subtle stillness.
>
> And in that sound of subtle stillness, there comes to him the word, the revelation. So can you imagine how, if that was the way to go about doing this, to cut out the noise, to cut out the quaking, just make it so quiet, so that there is now *no noise* and the signal can be clear. Do you understand, noise and signal? When there's a lot of static on the radio, there's a lot of noise. When there's no static, then you get clear sound and you have the signal. So how do you do that? By stilling the noise and allowing for the signal to come in.

We also have to engage ourselves actively. We will not get a true revelation from Scripture by experiencing it passively or (as it were) as a consumer. We will not get it by accepting whatever doctrine and interpretation we have been given by the authority of tradition.

> But if I ask myself, in those places when I can't sleep and I want to know "what is the whole purpose of life and what am I doing here" and so on and so forth, at that point

---

10 I Kings 19:12. ‏קוֹל דְּמָמָה דַקָּה׃‎

what I need to know in order to live better isn't necessarily another interpretation that Rashi[11] gives me.

And we have to bring our questions, real questions, as he emphasizes in exploring how prophecy happens in the sixth Primal Myths retreat.[12]

> What I need to know at that time is something that has to do with my life. What is my current question? What have I been working on, you know? If I get it from God, if I get it as a revelation, that's what comes down for me, that is going to be wonderful. And if I get only more fancy words and so on and so forth, and nothing that will help me with the real issues in my life, then Shavuot came only to bring me blintzes.[13] Blintzes are good, but if I don't get answers to my questions I'm going to be in trouble.

Section 2: How Has This Process Unfolded over Time? How Scholars Have Seen It

The Authority of Scripture

All traditional religions with a scriptural basis rely on those writings to carry authority, sense of sacredness, and the teaching that makes this religion's particular contribution to spiritual understanding, the teaching that conveys the unique flavor and

---

11 **Rashi**, an acronym for Rabbi Shlomo ben Yitzchak, was an 11th century CE teacher of Torah who lived in southern France. He was recognized as the leading Torah authority of his time and is probably still in the present day the most influential, and widely-studied, commentator on Torah.

12 See the section "Having Our Questions" on page 179 above.

13 Cheese blintzes and other dairy treats are traditionally served and eaten on Shavuot.

destiny of the people to whom it was given. Thus, as long as these followers remain identified with the religion, those scriptures will have a special sanctified place as the source of the wisdom and the authority of the teachings.

And yet, all religions evolve with time and circumstances, and must do so or they will cease to be meaningful to their followers.

Michael Fishbane introduces his study of inner-biblical interpretation by making a similar point. He then discusses the importance that interpretation and commentary come to have within the scripture-based traditions.

> One of the most remarkable features of the great world religions is the emergence to independent dignity of traditions and commentaries which supplement the original authoritative teachings—be these latter the product of divine revelation or human wisdom. ... [I]n the classical expressions of Judaism, Christianity, and Islam on the one hand, and Hinduism, Buddhism, and Confucianism on the other, that interpretation has become a cultural form of the first magnitude—transforming the foundational revelations of the first group and the metaphysical insights of the second, and determining the fateful historical paths of both.[14]

Isaiah Gafni, Professor of Jewish History, The Hebrew University of Jerusalem, puts it this way:

> Religions commonly refer to a corpus of writings as their sacred scriptures. These works serve as the basis for that faith's principle beliefs and practices and thereby render that religion distinct from all other religious systems. All religions, however, continue to develop. But at the same time, they go to great lengths to show how these new manifestations of their faith are nevertheless grounded in

---

14 Michael Fishbane, *Biblical Interpretation in Ancient Israel*, p. 1.

those same scriptures produced centuries and even millennia ago. This is no less true of Judaism.[15]

This determination to insist that the manifestations of the faith are grounded in the same scripture makes it difficult to find explicit acknowledgment within the tradition that they have returned to the well to find new wisdom in the old words. "Innovation" becomes an accusation, heresy. Rather, the understanding needed for the new circumstances must be discovered to have been the original meaning, intended at the beginning.

The determination that teachings must be grounded in Scripture leads to returning again and again to those texts, and digging through the layers of meaning and interpretation, thus, in fact, finding treasures that might otherwise have been lost. Schachter-Shalomi's way of seeing the meanings for each generation all encoded within the text, with interpretations "backward compatible" so that a later interpretation does not invalidate an earlier one, follows this imperative.

Looking ahead to post-Biblical exegesis, Fishbane identifies two factors as the necessary historical components:

> …on the one hand, authoritative texts or teachings whose religious-cultural significance is fundamental; on the other, conditions to which these texts or teachings do not appear to be explicitly pertinent.[16]

In their introduction to the first volume of *A History of Biblical Interpretation,*[17] editors Alan J. Hauser and Duane F. Watson (looking at the matter historically) see the start of interpretation with the incorporation of the biblical traditions into the first biblical text.

---

15 Isaiah Gafni, *Beginnings of Judaism, Part 1*, p. 8.

16 Fishbane, *Biblical Interpretation in Ancient Israel*, p. 3.

17 Alan J. Hauser and Duane F. Watson , eds., *A History of Biblical Interpretation: Volume 1, The Ancient Period.*

What is selected in this creative process will be a direct
result of the perspectives, social mores, religious beliefs,
hopes and fears, and political and economic needs of the
person or community that does the creating. ...

After the canonical text has been established through this
selection process, changes in the circumstances of its people continue, and so re-visioning must go on.

The next step in the creative process comes when
these created units are passed on from one generation or
group to another. ... [E]ven in clearly neutral contexts for
transmission, where there is no conscious desire to alter
or emend the tradition(s) received, the transmitters will
nevertheless place their own, or their group's, particular
perspective onto the material being transmitted, often without
being aware that such a shift in perspective is occurring. ...

Sometimes, particularly if more radical changes in circumstances have occurred, a more radical change in perspective
is needed; we will see such a case when we look shortly at the
Talmudic re-visioning. Houser and Wilson continue:

Furthermore, those transmitting the traditions were, in
many cases, quite intentionally altering the material they
had received to make it suit their own purposes. ... It is
only human nature for any person receiving and conveying
important traditions to view them from a perspective that
most clearly makes sense in the context of that person's
particular religious, cultural, social, economic, and
intellectual milieu, which often will not be the same as the
milieu presumed earlier by the person or group that created
or previously transmitted the tradition(s).[18]

---

18 Hauser and Watson, *A History of Biblical Interpretation,* Vol. 1. The
preceding quotations all from pp. 1–2.

They then give examples of this from within the Biblical canonical text and then from each later phase (Septuagint,[19] Philo of Alexandria,[20] the Dead Sea Scrolls,[21] Targumim,[22] Rabbinic Midrash, and the noncanonical Jewish literature), continuing into Christian interpretation.

Daniel Boyarin affirms:

> The text of the Torah is gapped and dialogical, and into the gaps the reader slips, interpreting and completing the text in accordance with the codes of his or her culture.[23]

Shai Cherry, in his book *Torah through Time*, describes how he learned to interpret the Biblical text. He describes how he was introduced to Jewish biblical interpretation while studying at the Pardes Institute of Jewish Studies in Jerusalem:

> My teachers…presented the world of Torah commentary not as the literary analysis of a static text, but as the

19 **Septuagint**. Translation of the Hebrew scriptures into Greek, by Jews for the benefit of Greek-speaking Jews in the Diaspora, done over a period of time but begun in the late 3rd century CE.

20 **Philo of Alexandria** (20 BCE–50 CE). Hellenic Jewish philosopher and biblical exegete whose vision leaned toward allegorical interpretations and reconciliation of Jewish tradition with Greek philosophic traditions.

21 **Dead Sea Scrolls.** Scrolls dating from 250 BCE–50 CE found at Qumran on the shore of the Dead Sea. The product of a community of a Jewish sect. Provides what is presently the earliest manuscript versions of biblical texts as well as other documents.

22 **Targumim**. Rabbinic translations of Hebrew biblical texts into the vernacular, usually Aramaic. Sometimes less translations than paraphrases, explanations, and interpretations, but of course even the most conscientious translations will carry interpretive choices.

23 Boyarin, Daniel, *Intertextuality and the Reading of Midrash*, p. 14. Quoted in Shai Cherry, *Torah through Time*, p. 3.

unfolding of Jewish thought through the matrix of the Torah."[24]

Cherry goes on to describe his subsequent experience reading Torah with students, initially imagining the Bible would be a "familiar base text":

> As we delved into the commentary on selected biblical episodes, it was clear that the earliest commentators, both Jewish and Christian, were reading the Torah beyond its plain sense. That is not to say they were misreading the Torah; rather, they were generating a "deep reading" of the Torah by connecting the Bible's ancient words to the current reality of their own lives.[25]

We can immediately recognize Schachter-Shalomi's endeavor here. The understanding that it was the "deep reading" that allowed the ancient commentators to connect the words of Scripture to the current reality of their own lives reflects the spirit of Schachter-Shalomi's approach. Schachter-Shalomi invites us into a deep reading in which we immerse ourselves in the text with respect and sympathy and openness, allowing the fullness of the intention to unfold its wisdom.

In discussing the Biblical roots of Judaism, Isaiah Gafni asks how it is that the beliefs and practices of Jews today appear to be so radically different from the major guidelines of the faith as set out in the Bible. He gives a series of examples, such as the biblical mandate that worship be conducted through an elaborate system of animal sacrifices, even though that has not been done for almost 2000 years; that decentralization of the biblically prescribed cult

---

24 Shai Cherry, *Torah through Time*, p. xi. *Torah through Time* then proceeds looks at case studies of many levels of understanding that traditional commentators through time have brought to understanding Biblical text, illustrating this process by its fruits.

25 Cherry, *Torah Through Time, p.* xii.

was expressly prohibited, and that the worship was to be conducted exclusively in the temple in Jerusalem, and yet for 2,000 years Jews have worshipped in synagogues over which there are no geographical restrictions; and that the most visible form of religious leadership among Jews today is the rabbinic model, despite the fact that nowhere in the Bible is there mention of rabbis or the rabbinic model.[26]

> These innovations, and countless others, found their way into the Jewish religion during the centuries, and indeed the millennia, that followed the original emergence of the biblical corpus. Nowhere, however, would they be branded as innovations. Such an admission would challenge the central belief of traditional Jews whereby every seemingly new practice or belief was in essence already incorporated in the critical moment of divine revelation to Moses at Mt. Sinai. So you have an interesting tension: a belief in constant continuity of an ancient tradition, and yet constant innovation.[27]

Schachter-Shalomi's way of working with this tension between the belief in constant continuity of the ancient tradition and yet the need for updating the understanding of the received wisdom lies in his view of the continuous descent of Torah, the continuing new dispensations of wisdom, in proportion to our capacity to receive, and directed to the needs of our times.

And yet the ancient traditions are never displaced; for Schachter-Shalomi they are "transcended and included." Using his ever-ready computer analogies, he speaks of the Halakhah we need for today as being "backward-compatible" with the old

---

26 Gafni, *Beginnings of Judaism,* pp. 9–10.

27 Gafni, *Beginnings of Judaism*, p. 10.

Halakhah.[28] By understanding the intention behind the laws in their older form, we can still cherish them even while moving to ones that are appropriate to radically different circumstances or more-evolved ideals.

Gafni continues:

> The Bible, from its earliest appearance, never ceased to be reread and reinterpreted by all subsequent generations of Jews. … New challenges, brought about by an ever-changing world, constantly required new interpretations or induced new insights into the biblical texts. People would find solutions to new realities in the Bible, even though the Bible doesn't even hint at them.[29]

It is important for Schachter-Shalomi that this is not a matter of Bible being a revelation adequate for its time and place but needing to be supplemented to apply to our time and place.

Rather, his phenomenally close and careful reading of the original Hebrew text makes it clear that he is looking for insights and guidance for our time and place *in and from that original revelation*. There is a continuous descent of Torah (Torah in the sense of divine "teaching"), but that Torah doesn't replace the original revelation (i.e., the canonical Bible); rather, it *helps us read* the original revelation.

Four Assumptions in Jewish Biblical Interpretation

Biblical scholar James L. Kugel identified a set of assumptions[30] shared by "ancient interpreters." In discussing these assumptions Kugel is concerned with interpretation within the centuries just before and just after the start of the common era—the three

---

28 See Zalman Schachter-Shalomi and Daniel Siegel, *Integral Halachah: Transcending and Including*. This is a collection of a number of Schachter-Shalomi's teachings on this subject.

29 Gafni, *Beginnings of Judaism*, p. 11.

30 James L. Kugel, *The Bible As It Was*.

centuries in which, as he puts it "Israel's ancient library of sacred texts were becoming *the* Bible."[31] I would extend this and say that these characterizations are recognizable in the approaches of almost all traditional Biblical commentators from the late Biblical era through the present day. Indeed, Kugel is particularly interested in the principles of interpretation that emerged during the formative period because the overall interpretive methods themselves became "canonized," along with individual interpretations, "no less than the scriptural texts that they explained."[32]

The first assumption is that the Bible is, as Kugel puts it, a fundamentally cryptic document. That is, it requires interpretation. It is esoteric. It is is God's word in some sense encoded. Or, that it is symbolic, as, for example, Philo of Alexandria has it. Or that it is outside time such that one Biblical character represents another character of a later (even post-Biblical) time. The actual interpretations may vary, but Kugel says that the principle (that things are implied or hinted at beyond the apparent plain meaning of the text, and that their deeper or truer meaning requires interpretation) is shared, Kugel says "universally," by the ancient interpreters.[33]

Schachter-Shalomi would probably not call the Bible "cryptic." But he created his wisdom school because without processing the biblical text through our own understanding, it will not yield its wisdom.

And Schachter-Shalomi would say that because it is divine *teaching*, engagement with heart and imagination as well as mind is necessary. The narrative stories are there to learn from, but we have to see the intent behind the teaching: these are parables. Even commandments such as the detailed description of the building and ornamentation of the sanctuary may be teaching by metaphor. The elaborate details of the sacrificial cult may have lessons that do not become irrelevant after the destruction of the temple. We bring to our interpretations attention, mind, and openness to emotional and spiritual resonances, and without these the text may

---

31 Kugel *The Bible As It Was*, p. 46.

32 Kugel, *The Bible As It Was*, p. 46

33 Kugel, *The Bible As It Was*, p. 15.

shrivel into dry, sometimes apparently implausible, tedious, or even repellent recitation.

The second assumption identified by Kugel is that Scripture is relevant to all times and places, that is, to its original audience, to *us* as its present-day audience, and to all who receive its teachings in between. It is a book of instruction, not (merely) an historical document. It is the responsibility of the interpreters to translate what looks like material of only antiquarian interest to bring out its present day relevance as guidance for living our lives and for our own relationship to God. Everything in the Hebrew Bible, Kugel says, contained an imperative for adoption and application to the readers' own lives.[34]

It is clear that Schachter-Shalomi considers the text fundamentally "relevant," and that its purpose throughout is *instruction*. It is on this basis that he brings loving attention to every word. To fashion my source material into case studies, it was necessary to select particular passages from the weekends. But the whole of the weekend typically involved many hours of extended discussion, passage by passage, phrase by phrase. The goal was always to take Torah to heart, to make it relevant, to see what its teaching offered for us to apply to our own challenges of life—whether those are the same universal human issues that the Biblical characters were facing or whether they are new challenges that would have been unimaginable to those characters.

The third assumption is that Scripture is perfect and perfectly harmonious. It doesn't have mistakes. Apparent mistakes or apparent inconsistencies have deeper meanings whose interpretations themselves yield other teachings. Furthermore, it is one unified whole. Each part illuminates and comments on other parts, and it is all one message. The effort to resolve inconsistencies is a rich source of commentaries.

---

34 Kugel, *The Bible As It Was*, pp. 15–16.

That Scripture is complete and harmonious, with its different parts commenting on, elucidating, and completing one another, is implicit in the way Schachter-Shalomi weaves the lessons together.

Does Schachter-Shalomi believe that every word and every squiggle and every apparent grammatical error in the received text has a divine message? On one level, he is too sensible and too well educated to deny the existence of scribal errors or emendation in the received text.

But there is something more interesting to him than what can feel like a process of historicizing away all the spirituality. If we look for the divine truth behind the words we may find an insight or teaching that would have been lost if we were too quick to dismiss things based on apparent contradictions, suspected tendentious redactors, or scribal errors.

I would suggest that something like this project of seeking the divine truth behind the words is Schachter-Shalomi's starting point. This practical pedagogical technique cannot, of course, be separated from the piety and deep faith that makes the religious power of the text and the traditions around it feel so precious and holy.

Kugel further says it is an extension of the "third assumption" of perfection of the text that led the rabbis in particular to justify the conduct of the Biblical heroes.[35] They too must be perfect,

---

35 This extension is not universal. There are instances of Talmudic and midrashic and medieval commentators criticizing some of the "heroes" of the tradition. For one example, Nachmanides says that Sarah sinned in her harshness towards Hagar (as recounted in in Gen. 16:6) and that Abraham sinned in sanctioning it. [Ramban, *The Torah: with Ramban's Commentary*, Vol. 1, p. 373.]

even if it required words to be understood as meaning the opposite of their plain meaning.[36]

Schachter-Shalomi would say that this sort of modification of the text in line with the principle of perfection, however pious the intent, errs when it "corrects" the divine revelation. The holy Torah has something to teach us when it shows our patriarchs missing the mark, or trying out solutions that may seem plausible at the time but with hindsight reveal their flaws and unintended consequences. By studying their stories, their paths, we may learn to avoid similar false leads and mistakes ourselves.

Kugel also points out that the traditional defense of perfection is filtered through the concepts and values of the interpreter:

> Scripture's perfection, in other words, ultimately included its being in accord with the interpreter's own ideas, standards of conduct, and the like.[37]

Schachter-Shalomi is not critical of this, even though it may lead to interpretations that limit the divine revelation to the prejudices and limited vision of the world-view of the interpreters of earlier times. Those limitations and some of the resulting understandings may be unfortunate, but the reality that all interpreters will bring their own values to understanding the text is ineluctable.

And, because he believes that there is a spiritual evolution of humanity, interpreters also evolve and learn from experience,

---

36 Kugel (p. 21) gives the example that when the Bible (Gen. 34:13) says that Jacob's sons speak deceitfully to the men of Shechem, "*deceitfully* really means 'with wisdom,'" according to ancient interpreters. Similarly, Hillel Halkin ("Law in the Desert," Jewish Review of Books, Spring 2011) gives the example of Isaac who, when he realizes that he has been tricked by Jacob, says to Esau "your brother came in deceit and took your blessing." *Targum Onkelos,* a translation into Aramaic from about 110 CE, translates the Hebrew *be-mirma,* "in deceit," as the Aramaic *be-chukhma,* "with wisdom." Rashi repeats this as the meaning here.

37 Kugel, *The Bible As It Was*, pp. 17–18.

leading to the application of better discernment of the divine intention and application of more advanced standards of conduct. It is to be celebrated that today we can bring these fresh deeper interpretive understandings as tools to reading the text.

Schachter-Shalomi would urge that it would be wrong to limit ourselves to the results of readings of the text by older interpreters who are applying their "own ideas, standards of conduct, and the like." To do so would be to deny the on-going flow of revelation, to freeze divine meaningfulness, and to limit God to the paradigm of a particular time and social order.

The fourth assumption is that all Scripture is divinely inspired and sanctioned, and not just passages that are quoted as being said directly by God to Moses or other human beings, or as reported in the Creation story. This includes, Kugel points out, passages such as praises to God in the Psalms, or other other passages attributed to human characters.[38]

This view of Scripture is Schachter-Shalomi's reason for turning to Bible at all. He finds divine presence and divine guidance in all these holy words. Therefore believing in their divine provenance is something more like direct personal experience than it is a matter of merely taking this assumption as a starting point and working hypothesis, more like personal experience than like blind faith in the authority of tradition.

I say it is *not merely* taking this assumption as a starting point and working hypothesis. In the second Primal Myths retreat, Schachter-Shalomi was challenged by a participant to say how we know that Tanakh is the source of values that should be resifted and reformed for the future. Schachter-Shalomi in responding said that he couldn't give a final answer, but he called it a "working hypothesis" that Hebrew scriptures (and, he says, "other holy writ documents") come into being as divine teachings.

This may be partially an unwillingness to be dogmatic about something that cannot be known for certain. It may also be (and

---

38 Kugel, *The Bible As It Was*, pp. 18–19.

this is how I hear it) a case of Schachter-Shalomi's willingness to hold both reality maps at the same time. He feels the *Ruach haQodesh* coming through the text: that is direct personal experience, which he will not deny. But he is also aware that whether or not that is ultimately true, he can take it as a working hypothesis to see what it yields.

In summary, Schachter-Shalomi seems to hold at least in spirit to all of the assumptions Kugel identifies.

Scripture, Interpretation, and Life: Two (or Three?) Torahs

The Jewish tradition recognizes an interplay between Scripture and interpretation.

We have the Written Torah, *torah she-bikhtav*, תורה שבכתב, the torah (teaching) which is written. This is the Hebrew Scriptures as they have been passed on to us: the Five Books of Moses, the other historical accounts and wisdom writings, the prophetic writings.

Then there is the interpretation that has been passed along or come through since the written torah was canonized. This is called the Oral Torah, *torah she-be'al peh.* תורה שבעל פה, the torah which is by means of the mouth or in the mouth or passed from mouth to mouth.

In the narrowest and most restrictive sense it is the teaching that, according to Rabbinic Judaism, was given to Moses on Sinai by God's mouth rather than written on tablets, or perhaps was given to be passed along by mouth and never written. It was then (according to the rabbinical tradition) passed along until it came into their possession.[39]

There is a broader, still traditional, application of *torah she'be'al peh,* which allows for authentic interpretations to be

---

39 This will be discussed at more length in the section Rabbinic Re-Visioning, page 332 below.

brought through even after the time of the complete body of rabbinic doctrine, that is, after the time of the Mishnah, Gemara,
rabbinic halakhic midrash, and so on. It would include Geonic
responsa[40] and the teachings and formulations of later sages such
as Rashi, Rambam,[41] Ramban,[42] and (depending on one's own
leanings and affiliations) various more recent teachers and rebbes.

Michael Fishbane brings in another dimension in his book
Sacred Attunement.[43] He goes beyond those two categories of
Torah and describes a third, the divine reality that precedes the
written Torah, calling it *torah kelulah,* "Torah of the All-in-All."
This is something he says we can read for ourselves in all of
existence.

There is something experiential here. To learn from this torah
we must be attuned to the divine presence. This is not something
to read in a list of laws, whether in the written torah or the oral
torah or the later codes of law from Maimonides or Josef Karo[44]

---

40 **Geonim**. Between 589 and 1088, these successors to the Talmudic
   Rabbis headed rabbinic academies in Babylon and were the
   generally accepted spiritual leaders of the Jewish community
   world wide in the early medieval era. They played a prominent and
   decisive role in the transmission and teaching of Torah and Jewish
   Law, deciding issues on which no ruling had been rendered during
   the period of the Talmud (particularly regarding questions raised
   about new circumstances for Jews living in far flung reaches of the
   Diaspora). These decisions are called (as are similar decisions of
   leading rabbinical scholars today) ***responsa.***

41 **Rambam**. Acronym for Rabbi Moses ben Maimon (Maimonides)
   (1135–1204). Author of *Mishneh Torah*, which was the first
   complete classification and codification of all the Mosaic and
   Rabbinic laws.

42 **Ramban**. Rabbi Moses ben Nachman (Nachmanides) (1194–
   1270), medieval Jewish scholar, physician, kabbalist, and biblical
   commentator.

43 Michael Fishbane, *Sacred Attunement: A Jewish Theology.*

44 **Josef Karo**. (Toledo, 1488 – Safed, 1575). Author of *Shulchan
   Aruch*, authoritative codification of Jewish law, finished 1555.

that undertake to condense and systematize the corpus of rabbinic doctrine.

But, with the appropriate attunement, the *torah kelulah* has a very practical element. It is learning from the interaction with one's own life experience.

> Hermeneutical theology grounds religious thought in texts (scripture) and in life (the *torah kelulah*). ... The relationship between the received text and life-situations unfolds in the course of interpretation. The teachings of scripture become known only through exegetical engagement with their concrete expressions—not through any abstract deliberation or reflection. ... It is only when the textual content is humanly appropriated as a living truth of existence that our own life fills out its exegetical spaces, and its linguistic features infuse our consciousness with challenge and possibility. Then the scriptural text offers models of theological living, of life lived in the context of God, and we live a citation-centered existence.[45]

I would suggest that, in the case studies that form the core of this project, Schachter-Shalomi may offer us an example of Fishbane's picture of letting text inform life and life inform text. The result is that then text is brought to more vivid life by the process, leading the practitioner to a "life in the context of God" and a life illuminated by Scripture.

Authority Comes from the Community

Another version of seeing Torah that comes from the living truth of Jewish existence is represented by theologian Judith Plaskow. Plaskow recognizes that feminist re-interpretation of Scripture and Halakhah raises the question of the authority of the

---

45 Fishbane *Sacred Attunement*, p. 63.

texts. She asks, considering that the Bible itself seems to offer grounds for differing interpretations,[46]

> When one element of a text is declared true or normative, where does authority actually lie? Do biblical texts themselves provide a sure basis for judging between their conflicting perspectives?"[47]

Plaskow has described both changes that the tradition has evolved over the millennia, and also different versions of interpretation and custom in diverse Jewish cultures. How did these changes unfold, without undoing Judaism? What was the authority for the process of evolution?

She answers this way.

> The contrary uses to which the Bible has been put suggest that the needs and values of a community of readers are as much a source of norms as the texts themselves. Different communities have different stakes in maintaining and defending the authority of the Bible, but the selection of particular texts or passages as central or normative can seldom be justified on purely textual grounds.[48]

Plaskow sees Scripture itself as a product of community.

> It may be revelatory or communicate lasting values, but revelation is communally received and molded.

Furthermore, when revelation is put into language, some enduring experience has been put into the limitations of words.

---

46 Some feminists, she notes, have cited passages of Biblical androcentrism and others have cited passages that can be used to argue that the "true" meaning is woman-affirming.

47 Judith Plaskow, *Standing Again at Sinai*, p. 19.

48 Plaskow, *Standing Again at Sinai*, p. 19.

Not only must it suggest rather than chronicle the revelatory experience, it does so within the cultural framework that language itself inscribes.[49]

Any new vision of Judaism will also be grounded in the community out of which it rises.

When the rabbis said that rabbinic modes of interpretation were given at Sinai, they were claiming authority for their own community—just as other groups had before them, just as feminists do today.[50]

How does the authority of the community both support needed change and also preserve what is "Jewish" in the tradition? Plaskow considers the way rabbinic Judaism replaced Temple sacrifice with study and prayer as the dual foci of Judaism.

This profound change was perceived as a transition rather than a break only because the Jewish community willed it so, and undertook to reinterpret the past to meet the needs of a radically different present.[51]

Plaskow addresses anxieties some have felt that feminism, in transforming thousands of years of historical development, may destroy Judaism. She says that such anxieties misunderstand the nature of fundamental religious change. Religious traditions have their own inertia and resistance to being manipulated. The process of change depends on acceptance of the community, and the community accepts and authorizes the change because it meets the needs of the community and feels true to the Jewish experience.

The Jews of the past, drawing on the religious forms available to them, created and recreated a living

---

49 Plaskow, *Standing Again at Sinai*, p.20.

50 Plaskow, *Standing Again at Sinai*, p.21.

51 Plaskow, *Standing Again at Sinai*, p. xviii.

Judaism, reshaping tradition in ways consonant with their needs. What determined the "Jewishness" of their formulations was not a set of predetermined criteria, but the "workability" of such formulations for the Jewish people: the capacity of stories and laws and liturgy to adapt to new conditions, to make sense and provide meaning, to offer the possibility of a whole life.[52]

Changes that endure will be ones that "speak to felt needs within the community and ring true to the Jewish imagination." Others "will fall by the wayside as eccentric, mechanical, or false."[53]

Schachter-Shalomi's work appears to share this understanding of change within the tradition. He is concerned that some of the traditional ideas no longer work for us, and consequently are no longer providing meaning or offering the possibility of a whole life (to use Plaskow's words). Schachter-Shalomi sees that our spiritual immune systems have rejected some of our tradition. If more "workable" forms and formulations are not created, or re-created, the result could be a withering away of the tradition itself.

But the new must prove itself as well. It must not only sound good—ring with a tone of our human ideals—but it must sound Jewish. It must ring true to the Jewish experience and imagination, to use Plaskow's words again.

Schachter-Shalomi's deep immersion in traditional Judaism no doubt makes him eminently sensitive to many of the nuances of that tone—its textures, its overtones and undertones. But it must be tested by the community of Jews.

Here one appreciates the lengths to which Schachter-Shalomi goes to draw the Wisdom School participants into the process of thinking through the re-visioning. He resists giving the answers. Where answers seem to emerge, he deliberately challenges them, deepening the complexity of the questions, forcing participants to

---

52 Plaskow, *Standing Again at Sinai*, pp. xviii–xix.

53 Plaskow, *Standing Again at Sinai*, p. xix.

engage with the problems inherent in what they might be trying to grasp as a solution.

He has a vision of where Judaism needs to go, but he knows that it isn't something that one person can impose based on his personal vision or his authority. Where Judaism goes will be where the whole Jewish people takes it. What he can do is to bring his deep commitment, his feeling for the tradition, his erudition, and his creative imagination to helping make that process one that will yield a result workable for the future.

Feminist scholar Rebecca Alpert makes a point similar to Plaskow's in response to Biblical and Rabbinic commandments that are misogynistic or in other ways limiting of human diversity.

> If we assume that those laws and practices are fixed for all time, then we may reject the religious perspective in its entirety. If however we assume that Judaism has undergone radical change over time and that it is in fact the flexibility and dynamism of the tradition that has sustained it, then we may see an opportunity to reinterpret and transform these rules and prohibitions as well as to reject specific ones if necessary and build on a new foundation.

She goes on to argue that "there is no one monolithic Judaism nor was there ever such a phenomenon." Jewish communities have existed in all parts of the world over millennia, being influenced by the host communities: "Judaism has flourished for many thousands of years in no small part because of Jewish communal adaptations to living among different nationalities, races, and religions."[54]

Schachter-Shalomi, of course, makes this same point—most dramatically in this Primal Myths series in his exploration of what the Israelites were learning in Egypt. He often notes that we have always learned from host cultures and other religions, and

---

54 Rebecca Alpert. *Like Bread on the Seder Plate*, p. 13.

he makes no secret of what he personally has learned from other religious and spiritual traditions.[55]

Section 3: Re-visioning as an Essential Part of the Jewish Tradition: Within the Biblical Canon

If the Jewish tradition has seen continuous interpretation and re-visioning, we should find it in our foundational texts as well as in later commentaries. Let's look at whether that is evident in the Bible and the Rabbinic corpus. In looking at evidence for inner-Biblical development, we will rely on scholarly opinion and on our own reading of the Biblical text. When we look at Rabbinic tradition, in the next section, we will find much more explicit support in the Talmud itself for the idea of continuing interpretation to meet changing circumstances (although the Rabbis will not, of course, call what they are doing re-visioning).

Within the Canon

If different times and circumstances require different understandings of Revelation, we might expect that it would be so over the course of the received Biblical text. What worked for the first humans in the Garden of Eden would not be suitable for people spread over the earth, living in cities, having technology. What worked for nomadic shepherds like the Hebrew Patriarchs would not work for a people who have spent hundreds of years in Egypt, or for a people forging themselves into a nation. The first conquerors and settlers in the land of Canaan, living under Judges, would be different from the people living under a monarchy. A great shift

---

55 References to many of these are found through his talks presented in this study. See also some of the experiences mentioned in the Biographical Sketch in the appendix.

of circumstance and world view must have taken place between Jacob and Solomon.

The patriarchs certainly practiced sacrifices—for that matter, even the first-born human, Abel, sacrificed a sheep to God. But what a change of world view there must have been between Abel's offering and the complex, detailed, and highly-ritualized sacrificial cult and role of the priesthood as detailed in the books of Exodus and Leviticus!

The prophets of the time of the Monarchy and of post-Exilic times called upon the old stories and laws. But we would expect that they would understand and use that material rather differently. Their need was to exhort a people in a later historical time to mend their ways, turning from practices in which they were engaged in those later times. They were trying to avert threats that were looming in those later times.

And indeed we do see the stories and the laws and the teachings change, in emphasis, in focus, and even in specific content.

ॐ••ॐ

Interpretation of Bible to meet the needs of the people (or to convey the teachings the exegetes thought they needed to hear) begins, then, within the present canonical text of the Bible itself.

One may wish to understand "exegetes" in this case in the broadest sense. It could include God himself, delivering sequential revelation to fit changing circumstances. It could include prophets conveying what they have heard (or understood that they were hearing) from the divine mouth (*al pi Hashem*). Moses himself appears to re-fashion his instructions as circumstances change. His recapitulation of the laws in Deuteronomy differs from what Exodus tells us God speaks to him when God tells him what to say to the Israelites.

Michael Fishbane, in *Biblical Interpretation in Ancient Israel*,[56] makes an exhaustive scholarly study of the inner-Biblical

---

56 Fishbane, Michael, *Biblical Interpretation in Ancient Israel.*

exegesis. A careful tracing is also done in Antony F. Campbell and Mark A. O'Brien, *Unfolding the Deuteronomistic History.*[57] See also Emanuel Tov, *Textual Criticism of the Hebrew Bible.*[58] In her essay "Inner-Biblical Exegesis in the Tanak"[59] Esther Menn also traces the evidence within the books of the canonical Bible for the exegetical process.

Exhaustive marshalling of examples or detailed analysis is beyond our scope here, but a few points may be made and a few examples may be mentioned.

One category of inner-Biblical exegesis includes changes attributed directly to God by the text. An example of this would be the change after the Flood to permit the eating of flesh. In Genesis 1:29,[60] God says "Behold, I have given to you all seed-bearing vegetation which are on the face of all the earth; and all the trees which bear seeds in their fruit. To you it will be for food." But in Genesis 9:3,[61] God says "Every moving thing that lives will be for food for you, As I gave green plants to you, (I now give you) everything." There are also instances where commandments given by God in the book of Exodus are restated by God in the book of Numbers in different form; and even instances of the form of the commandments changing between repetitions in the same book.[62]

Then there are cases where prophets attribute to God exegetical and innovative commands. If we assume that God has spoken

---

57 Antony F. Campbell and Mark A. O'Brien, *Unfolding the Deuteronomistic History: Origins, Upgrades, Present Text.*

58 Tov, Emanuel, *Textual Criticism of the Hebrew Bible.* See especially pages 262–275 for examples of exegetical changes to the text.

59 This essay appears as Chapter 2 in Alan J. Hauser and Duane F. Watson, Eds., *A History of Biblical Interpretation, Volume 1.*

60 Gen. 1:29.| וַיֹּאמֶר אֱלֹהִים הִנֵּה נָתַתִּי לָכֶם אֶת־כָּל־עֵשֶׂב זֹרֵעַ זֶרַע אֲשֶׁר עַל־פְּנֵי כָל־הָאָרֶץ וְאֶת־כָּל־הָעֵץ אֲשֶׁר־בּוֹ פְרִי־עֵץ זֹרֵעַ זָרַע לָכֶם יִהְיֶה לְאָכְלָה׃

61 Gen. 9:3. כָּל־רֶמֶשׂ אֲשֶׁר הוּא־חַי לָכֶם יִהְיֶה לְאָכְלָה כְּיֶרֶק עֵשֶׂב נָתַתִּי לָכֶם אֶת־כֹּל׃

62 Fishbane, *Biblical Interpretation in Ancient Israel,* 530–531.

through the prophet, God has emended or expanded the original law. If we consider that the prophet has referred his own under-standing or exegesis to the divine voice, we would place this in a category of prophetic exegesis.

For example, the prophet Jeremiah, or God speaking through him, adds new elements to the original Sinaitic laws of Sabbath observance. God uses the justification "as I commanded your fathers" although no such command is recorded previously.[63]

In the case of Deuteronomy, Moses recapitulates the narrative of the exodus and the years in the wilderness, including com-mandments originally given by God in earlier books. In Moses's retelling the story, and his restatement of God's original com-mandments in his own words, there are omissions, additions, and changes of emphasis. If we suppose (with the religiously tradi-tional view and as the text itself asserts) that Moses is the narrator of this retelling, then either Moses had additional revelations to supplement or explain the earlier ones, or he himself chose to bring the new emphases and new material.

Fishbane follows the scholarly opinion that Deuteronomy is a later composition. He categorizes this with "introducing exegeti-cal revisions in the course of a total rewriting of received materials under the auspices of a prestigious name (like Moses in the Book of Deuteronomy) or omniscient narrator (like the Chronicler)."[64]

But whether this is pseudepigraphic exegesis, or Moses's own exegesis, or, indeed, God's emendation, need not be determined for our purposes; the point remains that the narrative account, and the statements of the laws, has shifted. The canonical Bible, *Tanakh*, is not without its own inner process of interpretation; indeed, not even the Pentateuch escapes the need for continuous re-visioning as circumstances change.

---

63 Jer. 17:21–3. Compare Jeremiah's version to YHVH's words in Deut. 5:12 and elsewhere.

64 Fishbane, *Biblical Interpretation in Ancient Israel,* 530.

Emanuel Tov mentions a number of categories of textual emen-
dations that appear, which he identifies by comparison among
texts. He uses both variant texts of the canonically Biblical books,
including Qumranic texts, and other sources such as translations
(for example, Septuagint and Targumim[65]). A few of the many
categories of Tov's examples are the following.

There are anti-polytheistc alterations, where words or passages that would seem to suggest either specific rival gods or more
generally the existence of many gods, are changed to avoid that
implication. There are examples of changes to passages that might
be confusing, such as saying that God completed his work on the
seventh day, when it was understood that he rested on that day; this
was changed to say that he completed the work on the sixth day.
Words or characterizations that sound critical of the Patriarchs,
or of King David, are softened. Passages that are uncomfortable
because they seem to cast disrespect onto God (phrasings such
as "curse God" or "scorn God"), are altered, leaving it unclear
whether or not one is supposed to understand the substitute wording to be euphemistic.[66]

Esther Menn gives a detailed study of the inner-Biblical legal
codes in Tanakh, showing the ongoing process of exegesis as the
Israelites dealt with different situations in different historical periods and also, Menn points out, as experience with the application
of earlier versions revealed a need for revision or clarification.[67]

> Despite this depiction of commandments and law as the
> eternally valid stipulations of the covenant with YHWH,
> there is clear evidence in the Bible that legal traditions did

---

65 **Targumim**. Translations or paraphrases of Biblical text into
vernacular, mainly Aramaic. Composed in late Second Temple
times, originally oral but later written down.

66 Tov, *Textual Criticism of the Hebrew Bible.*, pp. 271–272.

67 Or, to take the traditional pious perspective that these codes were all
presented by God, we would make God the one who modified the
details of the codes to fit changing circumstances.

indeed develop and change, as cases were tried, judicial
precedents were set, and social conventions evolved. The
legal codes in the Pentateuch (the Covenant Code in Exodus
20:22–23:33, the Holiness Code in Leviticus 17–26, and the
Deuteronomic Code in Deuteronomy 12–26) themselves
stem from different historical periods, and many of the
laws they contain bear signs of application, adaptation,
and substantive revision. Outside the Pentateuch as well,
in prophetic and historiographic writings, evidence points
to the intentional study and reworking of laws in legal and
judicial circles, as well as possibly in more scholarly and
speculative contexts.[68]

Menn continues with a close and careful reading of the texts
illustrating the adaptation and development taking place over the
course of the canonical biblical text.

᷿•᷿

But is it anachronistic to treat the Bible itself as a text being
interpreted through the course of its development and process of
revelation? Is exegesis not something that came later, after an text
came to be established as canonical?

Menn sees interpretation of Scripture as "an ancient and native
Israelite phenomenon."

> Intentional study, exegesis, and revision of authoritative
> works emerged as common practices long before the
> completion of the written works ultimately included in
> the Jewish biblical canon…. The glosses and explications,
> expansions and revisions, allusive responses and creative
> constructions of new works in relation to more ancient ones
> found throughout the Tanak indicate that a text-oriented
> religion predates the closure of the biblical canon.

She describes a process of working on received texts to make
them relevant to succeeding generations as taking place throughout

---

68 Menn, "Inner-Biblical Exegesis in the Tanak", pages 64–65.

Tanakh, providing a model for the ensuing exegetical cultures of Judaism and Christianity.

> Tanak models in itself various approaches to Scripture that attempt to extend historically the divine voice discerned through received texts and to preserve these texts as the preeminent focus of religious intellectual endeavors, while at the same time ensuring their relevance for contemporary communities (Fishbane 1986:25). In this broad project of addressing present generations through the medium of texts from the past, and thereby honoring these texts even while transforming them, inner-biblical exegesis shares much with scriptural exegesis throughout the ages.[69]

Menn argues that the preoccupation with written texts that later characterized Israelite society and Judaism was projected far back in Israel's early history.[70] Such an early example would be the writing of commandments on stone tablets, first by God and then (apparently) by Moses, and the placing of these tablets in the ark to connect the people to the covenant at Sinai.[71] According to Menn, the book of Deuteronomy and the books of Joshua through 2 Kings show a process indicating a substantial increase in the "dependence on written texts for religious guidance." She notes that Deut 17:18–20 presents Israel's ideal king writing out and studying a copy of "this Torah" as his most important duty. In Ezekiel's call narrative, God gives the prophet an actual scroll. Zechariah depicts a giant scroll flying through the air. These and other examples lead her to say:

> Once certain traditional writings were perceived as holding an honored and even, in some cases, revelatory status, various types of hermeneutical activities emerged

---

69 Menn, "Inner-Biblical Exegesis in the Tanak", 55–56.

70 Alternatively, one might understand the antecedents of that preoccupation already being present in the early history.

71 Ex. 25:16, Deut. 10:1–5, 1 Kings 8:21. See Menn "Inner-Biblical Exegesis in the Tanak," p. 58.

in different sectors of Israelite society to keep these texts comprehensible, applicable, and relevant to audiences of successive generations.[72]

At times these hermeneutical activities were responses to difficulties in the text itself, such as obscure wording or grammar or paucity of detail, but at other times it came from sometimes radical changes in the circumstances of those for whom these texts were a sacred inheritance. As Menn puts it:

> ...at other times they were motivated by broader changes in the historical or cultural situation (such as the crisis of the exile, the emergence of rival political parties, or innovations in theology) that required adaptation or reauthorization for the present.[73]

This process has continued ever since, keeping the texts comprehensible, applicable, and relevant to audiences of succeeding generations, as their historical and cultural situations change. It is within this ancient tradition that Schachter-Shalomi must be placed.

Menn's conclusion is particularly applicable to Schachter-Shalomi's work of re-visioning, as he understands it.

> The presence in the Tanak of multiple strata—of texts and interpretive materials that revise, actualize, and reauthorize the traditional literature of the past—establishes through example the fundamental importance of scriptural interpretation as a religious activity. The sacred corpus of Israel represents revelation and interpretation as part of a continuous dialectic process in which successive

---

72 Menn, "Inner-Biblical Exegesis in the Tanak", page 60.
73 Menn, "Inner-Biblical Exegesis in the Tanak", page 60.

generations contribute to the received tradition through exegesis….[74]

This ideal of continuous interpretation and re-visioning as "religious activity" seems to describe Schachter-Shalomi's sense of his own reading of Scripture for present-day circumstances and state of spiritual evolution of humanity. He sees the exegesis as living Torah, as Torah descending for us in our time. Schachter-Shalomi might say that it is not we who are changing the old and obsolescent text to fit our needs, it is Torah itself which is revealing itself to us in the form that brings the divine intention and will to bear on our circumstances. These circumstances are themselves an unfolding of divine intention and will.

Section 4: Re-Visioning as an Essential Part of the Jewish Tradition: Within the Talmudic Corpus

Schachter-Shalomi's re-visioning for the present day looks to traditional Jewish texts and practices as the source of the wisdom we need now. This project has focused on Schachter-Shalomi's use of the Biblical text. That these same passages could have different teachings for different ages supposes that the passages embody an intention, and principles, which play out in specifics that are needed for particular situations. It supposes that there is a richness of meaning encoded in the text.

One might liken the text to dreams which must be interpreted. The same outward form of a dream might mean different things to different people, and embody different messages or wisdom, or express different truths depending on what that individual needs for his or her life.

---

74 Menn, "Inner-Biblical Exegesis in the Tanak", page 76.

This sense of multiple levels of meaning within a received text is not new; it appears in the Rabbinic corpus and throughout Jewish tradition.

The Jewish tradition has unfolded from its beginnings in a process of self-re-visioning. The Bible itself, as the last section showed, illustrates a process in which God's vision for humanity and for the Israelite people underwent radical shifts—or perhaps it was the people whose idea of God's vision had to change.

After the closing of the Biblical canon, this process continued. This section will trace this with a few examples from the Second Temple period (586 BCE–70 CE) through Talmudic times (up to approximately 600 CE). Again, as in the previous section, my goal will be to be suggestive rather than demonstrative.

Second Temple Shifts

The most radical re-visioning that Judaism has ever had, or is perhaps ever likely to have, occurred after the destruction of the Second Temple in 70 CE, when the sacrificial cult that was the center of religious practice for the Israelite people, and the center of their worship, came to an end.

Judea, the ancestral home land, was in Roman hands. The Temple in Jerusalem was destroyed, and Jews were banished from Jerusalem. The people were largely in exile. The religion that had centered on the Land, and on the Temple in Jerusalem, and on the hereditary priesthood and its sacrificial rituals, was gone.

Either Judaism would cease to exist, with its people assimilated into Hellenistic culture, or it would have to be re-invented. The Sages after 70 CE accomplished that radical re-invention.

Much groundwork had already been laid, however. The efforts of Ezra, who returned from Babylon to set up Torah readings and lectures interpreting the texts, and the activities and developing philosophies of the Pharisees during the time of the Second Temple, introduced an institution and a power base that complemented and in some ways competed with the priesthood and the Temple sacrificial cult and rituals.

The first Temple was destroyed by the Babylonians in 586 BCE, but Babylon was in turn conquered by the Persians and in 538 the Persian king Cyrus invited the exiled Jews to return to their homeland and rebuild the Temple. The rebuilt Temple was completed and consecrated in 516/515 BCE.

Many of the original exiles still remained in Babylon all through this period and indeed all through the time of the Second Temple. But in the middle of the 5th century BCE there was a sort of religious revival in Babylon, and some Jews from there came back to the Land of Israel to instruct the people who had remained there in what they saw (or had developed) as the proper practice of the religion.[75]

In 458 BCE Ezra, a Jewish leader, of a priestly family but traditionally called "the scribe," arrived in Jerusalem in time for the festival of Sukkot.

As Gafni describes,

> It was during that festival that Ezra had the entire Torah read and explicated publicly for seven days. This public reading of the Torah may have laid the foundation for the reading of scripture on a regular basis on Sabbaths and on holidays, one of the earliest and universal practices carried out in Jewish synagogues from the Second Temple period until the present.[76]

Nehemiah 8:8 describes the scene with these words: "And they [Ezra and his colleagues] read in the scroll, in the Torah of God,

---

75 One feels at least an irony here. Jews who had chosen to live in Babylon for generations after they were allowed by Cyrus to return to Israel, and generations after the Temple was rebuilt in Jerusalem, now presumed to cast themselves as the authorities of legitimate Judaism. They came to remonstrate with, and instruct, those other Jews who had remained in the ancestral homeland, and those who returned promptly to it—the ones who had rebuilt the Temple.

76 Gafni, *Beginnings of Judaism*, Part 1, p. 42.

interpreted, and putting insight (*or* sense) (*or* meaning), and they [the people] discerned (*or* understood) what was in the reading."[77]

As Ezra read, it was translated from Hebrew into Aramaic, the vernacular of the people, and explained. Rabbi Stephen Wylen says of the explication part of this reading:

> [T]he people needed an explanation because even in translation the words of the Torah were not directly understood. There was discontinuity between the cultural, social, and scientific assumptions contained in the Torah and the culture and worldview of the Judean populace who now listened to these words from the mouth of Ezra the Scribe. The Torah presumes a world in which Jews live independently in small agricultural villages. But the Jews who gathered in Jerusalem to listen to Ezra lived in an extensive empire, and many Jews were now engaged in urban commercial activity. Even the conditions of farm life were quite different from what they had been in ancient Israel. Furthermore, the worldview of the Jews had been transformed by intimate contact with the cultures of Babylon and Persia. The translators had to explain the Torah of Moses to the people, translating ideas into terms to which they could relate in their current life.[78]

Gafni sees this reading and interpretation of Torah as moving Judaism towards being a "religion of the book." The act of publicly reading the book, and delivering the "explanation," that is, its interpretation, becomes "no less vital to the religious activity of Judaism than the offering of sacrifices."[79]

This practice spread throughout the Diaspora all through the Second Temple period.[80] The *synagogue*, Greek for "gathering

---

77 וַיִּקְרְאוּ בַסֵּפֶר בְּתוֹרַת הָאֱלֹהִים מְפֹרָשׁ וְשׂוֹם שֶׂכֶל וַיָּבִינוּ בַּמִּקְרָא׃

78 Stephen M. Wylen, *The Seventy Faces of Torah: The Jewish Way of Reading the Sacred Scriptures*, p. 4.

79 Gafni, *Beginnings of Judaism*, Part 1, pp. 42–43.

80 See Gafni, *Beginnings of Judaism* Part 2, pp. 86–96.

place," was a center for reading and explaining the Law, as described in literary evidence, including the testimony of Philo[81] and the New Testament.[82] It was led by persons knowledgeable in Torah rather than the caste of priests.

The explanation given along with Ezra's reading of the Torah was, of course, necessary, so that people of different historical and cultural situations could understand it and find relevance in it. Ezra realized that this was true even for those who had never left the land of Israel, and it became even more urgent as centuries went by and as generations lived not only in Babylon but in Alexandria and even Rome.

This meant that when the Temple was destroyed in 70 CE, there was already an alternative form of worship being practiced: the study of Torah. It also meant the institution of the interpretation (the "explanation") of the meaning of that text, by people whose credential was their learning and their preaching, was established.

The Contribution of the Pharisees

The Second Temple period also saw the rise of the political force termed Pharisees. All sources we have about these people are from much later, and have their own perspective. The Rabbis, who carried on the Pharisaic line, had investment in honoring their antecedents. The New Testament sources used them as a foil to contrast their own approach. Josephus[83] seems to have been trying to describe the different sects of this period in categories that corresponded to Greek philosophies.[84] However, despite these limitations in the trustworthiness of the reports, some major effects of their philosophies and activities can be identified.

---

81 Philo, *Hypothetica*, 7:11–13. *The Works of Philo*, p. 744.

82 Luke 4:16–21, and the book of Acts.

83 **Josephus**. Titus Flavius Josephus (37 – c. 100) was a Jewish historian and one of our primary sources for Jewish and Jewish-Roman history in the second temple period.

84 See Gafni, *Beginnings of Judaism*, Part 2, pp. 9–11.

First, there was a political opposition between the Pharisees as a teaching and interpreting power base and the hereditary priesthood controlling sacrifice in the Temple. There were direct struggles with the priesthood regarding the way rituals were carried out in the Temple. But more important was the Pharisees' claim to speak for the Jewish people, and indeed, to speak for God. They claimed to present the understanding of Torah given through a divinely transmitted oral tradition, the "traditions of the elders."

Wylen says "The Pharisees and their successors, the Rabbis, evolved into an ideologically motivated party that challenged the priesthood for leadership of the Jewish people." Part of this challenge was to assert "an ideal of the priesthood of all Israel, which made the professional hereditary priests of Judaism extraneous."[85]

Based on the promise in the Sinai covenant (Exodus 19:6) that Israel would be "a kingdom of priests," the Pharisees took it upon themselves to behave like priests, following the Torah injunctions originally given for the priests only. They also promoted literacy and knowledge of the Torah text as a universal ideal, not limited to the hereditary priesthood.

By making the priesthood less central, groundwork was laid for Judaism to survive the destruction of the Temple and the consequent elimination of the function of hereditary priests.

A second piece the Pharisees put in place was a practice, and rationale, for interpreting Torah in as radical a way as necessary to make its words and commandments relevant to emerging situations and needs.

Wylen describes the Pharisees, in contrast to the other major party, the Sadducees, as freer in their interpretations. He says that they "initiated the new approach to Torah"; that is, their interpretations were less strictly tied to the text. The Pharisees came, in

---

85 Wylen, *The Seventy Faces of Torah*, p. 65.

time, to deny that they were innovating, claiming that they were following "an ancient tradition going back to Moses."[86]

In the New Testament *Gospel of Mark*, Jesus condemns the Pharisees for their violations of Torah-based Jewish law, which the Pharisees attempted to impose on all Jews based on the authority of their "traditions of the elders."[87] At that point, evidently, the Pharisee power base in Jerusalem did not extend effectively into Galilee.

The Rabbis Institutionalize the Oral Torah

Gafni discusses how the Rabbis developed the authority of this oral tradition.

> It is the rabbis who took this a step further, and stress that these are not just additional oral embellishments of the Torah, but in fact a parallel Torah that was also given to Moses on Mt. Sinai. Indeed, the post-Temple rabbis considered themselves to be the contemporary links in that ongoing chain of tradition, and their moral and legal authority would rely heavily on that assumption.[88]

The chain of transmission, according to the Rabbis (asserted in *Mishnah, Pirkei Avot* 1:1), went from God to Moses to Joshua, Joshua to the tribal elders, elders to the prophets, prophets to the "men of the great assembly" (the early sages, who taught the great Pharisees, who taught their successors, the Rabbis). This claims a direct and unbroken line from Sinaitic divine revelation. (Wylen

---

86 Wylen, *The Seventy Faces of Torah*, p. 51.

87 *Mark* 7:1–23. See Daniel Boyarin, *The Jewish Gospels*, pp. 103–126, for a thorough exploration of this. Boyarin speculates that some of the innovations about which Jesus protests emerged in Babylon. Galilean Jews who had never left the land were finding their Torah traditions being violated and insulted when the Pharisees came up from Jerusalem attempting to impose these innovations.

88 Gafni, *Beginnings of Judaism*, Part 2, p. 14.

also points out about this: "Note that the rivals of the Rabbis, the hereditary priests, are bypassed in the chain of transmission."[89])

This claim of being in possession of divine instruction allowed the interpretive freedom for the process of re-visioning that was necessary to keep Judaism alive and vital—albeit in a form so different that without this insisted-upon continuity it might have looked like a different religion.[90]

Rabbinic Re-Visioning

In 70 CE, following a rebellion against Roman rule, Rome laid seige to Jerusalem. When it fell, the Romans destroyed the Temple in Jerusalem. If God not only could not defend his people, but could not even defend his own Temple, what claim did he have? Would this not prove that the Roman gods were more powerful?

There would no longer be a centralized Temple worship or a sacrificial cult, so unambiguously commanded in the written Torah. Without the ritual of Temple sacrifice, there was no provision for atonement for wrong-doing.

This was a crisis on all possible levels. That Judaism should have survived this disaster, in any form, defies all reasonable expectation.

What was needed was more than incremental interpretive explanations of how the Torah commandments applied to changed circumstances. Judaism itself had to be re-invented. That was the work of Rabbinic Judaism, of the Sages of the first centuries of the Common Era. Their work, as it was in time written down in the voluminous texts of the Talmud, re-made a religion while powerfully asserting that no innovation was taking place, and claiming a sanctity for their reformulation equal to, or greater than, the sanctity of the original written Scripture.

---

89 Wylen, *The Seventy Faces of Torah,* p. 30.

90 I will shortly quote Wylen asserting this very thing; see page 333.

Jacob Neusner, translator and and pre-eminent scholar of the Talmud, describes this as the creation of a whole civilization:

> [T]he Talmud carries out in its own way the task of civilization. It does so by showing how intellectuals wrote down details of law, theology, and scriptural exegesis in such a way as to form a coherent, cogent, and critical construction. It conveys a vision of the social order subject to God's dominion.[91]

Wylen asserts:

> The rabbinic form of Judaism, which arose after the destruction of the Second Temple in 70 CE, is a different religion from that described in the Bible. The biblical religion is a religion of sacrifices presided over by priests. The rabbinic religion is a religion of worship, study, and *mitzvot*, presided over by wise men called rabbis. For centuries, in the last years of the Second Temple and in the years that followed the destruction, priests and rabbis were rivals for leadership of the Jewish people. That struggle is reflected in the conflicts between priestly Sadducees and the rabbinic Pharisees recorded in the Talmud and in the New Testament. The rabbis ultimately prevailed, and the rabbinic Talmud established the agenda for Judaism ever since.[92]

Gafni uses these words: "The destruction caused a total reshaping and redefining of Judaism as we had encountered it up until that event."[93]

The Oral Torah tradition is cited as the authority for these re-visionings of the stories and commandments. Yet it is understood, or assumed, that there is a unity of Written and Oral Torah. Neusner, for example, argues that "the writings of the ancient

---

91 Jacob Neusner, *The Babylonian Talmud: A Translation and Commentary,* Volume 1, General Introduction, p. xxiii.

92 Wylen, *The Seventy Faces of Torah*, p. 99.

93 Gafni, *Beginnings of Judaism*, Volume 2 p. 136

sages present, in written form, the oral part of that cogent and one whole Torah of Sinai that defines the way of life and world view of Israel, the Jewish people, the people of the God who revealed the Torah to Moses at Sinai."[94]

The apparent meaning of the Written Torah, and the Rabbinic assertions of proper interpretation of the passages, and the expostulation in the *midrashim*—these may be seen as different parables expressing a single Teaching (*torah*). This suggests an implicit understanding that different interpretations may exist together within the text.

"Seventy Faces": Multiple Meanings in Other Talmudic Formulations

Midrash Bamidbar Rabbah 13:15/16 says "There are seventy faces of/within Torah."[95] Every word, phrase, or passage can yield multiple meanings, multiple interpretations. (Biblically, "seventy" typically stands for *a very large number*.)

These various interpretations may seem to contradict one another, and yet all may be true each on its own level, all may all have something valuable to teach. Like the apparently contradictory teachings of Hillel and Shammai, they may all be the word of the living God.

Mishnaic sage Ben Bag Bag is quoted in *Mishnah, Pirkei Avot,* as saying: "Turn it and turn it, for everything is in it." He continues "Look deeply into it; grow old and worn with it; and from it do not budge, for you can have no better portion than it." Ben Hei Hei then says "In proportion to the exertion is the reward."[96] We may look to Torah for whatever wisdom we need. If it doesn't

---

94 Jacob Neusner, *The Oral Torah: The Sacred Books of Judaism: An Introduction*, p. ix.

95 יש שבעים פנים בתורה, *yesh shivim panim batorah.*

96 *Babylonian Talmud, Mishnah, Pirkei Avot* 5:26 בן בג בג אומר הפך בה והפך בה. דכולא בה. ובה תחזי. וסיב ובלה בה. ומנה לא תזוע. שאין לך מדה טובה הימנה. בן הא הא אומר לפום צערא אגרא:

appear immediately, or make sense in the previously-understood interpretation, turn it and turn it some more. The wisdom that is needed is in there to be searched out.

Schachter-Shalomi's close, careful, tireless, tender turning of the words of Torah prove him an attentive *chasid* of Ben Bag Bag.

These and These are the Words of the Living God

The Rabbinic tradition offers us numerous explicit supports for multiple perspectives and interpretations even within the ideology of the divine transmission of the Oral Torah as presented by the Rabbis themselves. The text of the Talmud, especially of the Gemara, consists of a dense tapestry of opinions of different rabbis, expanding, explaining, arguing, disagreeing, and re-interpreting Mishnah and one another.

That words and verses inherently possess multiple meanings, Shai Cherry terms pluripotence. He says that pluripotence did not attain full expression until the mystical writings of the Middle Ages but that the elements of a pluripotent view of the Torah are found already within Rabbinic culture. He sees it in the commitment to multiple interpretations of a single biblical verse and in promotion of the value of innovative readings of Torah.[97]

Debates between first century BCE Pharisees Hillel and Shammai, whose schools continued into the Rabbinic Period, are extensively cited and studied within the Talmudic and later tradition. These two early Sages are presented as taking opposing views on most matters, and study of the differing perspectives is considered instructive. The perspective of the school of Hillel proved more congenial to the Rabbis and their rulings were adopted as Halakhah when some directive was required, and eventually the school of Shammai ceased to exist. But the recorded perspectives of Shammai's school were, and still are, honored and studied.

---

97 Cherry, *Torah through Time*, p. 14.

This created a tradition and explicit teaching that two apparently contradictory principles and interpretations, two contradictory readings of Scripture, can both be true. The phrase is recorded: "These and these, both are the words of the living God." *Eilu v'eilu divrei Elohim chayyim hein.*[98]

Babylonian Talmud, Eruvin 13b, represents this with a story purporting to document divine judgment, and with a moral flattering to the school the Rabbis favored. In Neusner's translation:

> For three years there was a dispute between Beit Shammai and Beit Hillel, the former asserting, "The law is in agreement with our views." and the latter contending, "The law is in agreement with our views." Then a *bat kol* (a voice from heaven) announced, "these and those are the words of the living God, but the law is in agreement with the rulings of Beit Hillel." Since, however, "both are the words of the living God," what was it that entitled Beit Hillel to have the law fixed according to their rulings? Because they were kindly and modest, they studied their own rulings and those of Beit Shammai, and were even so humble as to mention the words of Beit Shammai before their own.[99]

According to this account the law sided with the house of Hillel *because* they were respectful of their opponents in the debate, studied their rulings, and made sure that those arguments had a hearing.

---

98 אלו ואלו דברי אלהים חיים הן *Babylonian Talmud*, Eruvin 13b

99 אמר רבי אבא אמר שמואל: שלש שנים נחלקו בית שמאי ובית הלל, הללו אומרים הלכה כמותנו והללו אומרים הלכה כמותנו. יצאה בת קול ואמרה: אלו ואלו דברי אלהים חיים הן, והלכה כבית הלל. וכי מאחר שאלו ואלו דברי אלהים חיים מפני מה זכו בית הלל לקבוע הלכה כמותן - מפני שנוחין ועלובין היו, ושונין דבריהן ודברי בית שמאי. ולא עוד אלא שמקדימין דברי בית שמאי לדבריהן.

There has to be one law to follow. When the Sages disagree about that law, a decision is made to follow one and not the other, and this is done by majority vote. But both interpretations have the force of the divine word, and the tradition even includes the assertion that although in pre-Messianic times Hillel's ruling is most often adopted, in Messianic times (when our consciousness has been perfected) Shammai's rulings, which are said to be deeper and truer, will hold.[100]

Something similar is supported by the careful Talmudic documentation of the conflicting perspectives of Rabbi Akiva and Rabbi Ishmael, who taught a little later than Hillel and Shammai and are in the earliest generation of the Rabbinic sages.

Rabbi Akiva taught that there is no extraneous word, letter, repetition, or oddity of grammar or phraseology or style in Scripture. Everything was placed there by God to teach a particular lesson.

By contrast, Rabbi Ishmael read the text as if it simply meant what it seemed to be saying. Where Rabbi Akiva might build an elaborate interpretation on a certain colloquial or metaphoric turn of phrase, Rabbi Ishmael would say that "The Torah speaks in human language"[101]: We read the passage as it appears. We don't need to make something out of every superfluous or odd word. Take it as meaning what it seems to mean.

This common sense approach may seem more persuasive than the sometimes outlandish-seeming readings that Rabbi Akiva and others who followed his approach made of textual words and phrases, readings that at times seem to flatly contradict the obvious (at least surface) sense of the Scriptural narrative.

But Rabbi Akiva's approach has a powerful payoff. If all these things have meaning, a meaning other than the obvious

---

100   Isaac Luria, 16th century mystic and kabbalist, said that in messianic times Shammai's views would prevail. See, for example, Cherry, *Torah through Time*, 153.

101   דברה תורה כלשון בני אדם. Torah speaks in human language. As previously noted, there are twenty instances of this in Babylonian Talmud; see Bava Metzia 31b for two of them.

common-sense meaning, then that true meaning must be explained. And Rabbi Akiva (or a later Sage following his principles) will explain it. And this gives a very wide field for re-interpreting the text in a way that will apply to contemporary situations and beliefs. The new interpretations, new lessons, and new divinely-supplied requirements for living can be set out and promulgated—all putatively based on the original written Scripture.

Although Rabbi Ishmael's teachings are carefully recorded, honored, and studied, including his view of treating many of the stylistic or grammatical idiosyncrasies of the text as being natural human language, Rabbi Akiva's approach has been favored in Talmud and later tradition.

❧•✍

The changes in our present-day world situation are certainly transformative and, in Schachter-Shalomi's characterization, paradigm-shifting. On the one hand we have the threat of global extinction through ecological disaster or nuclear war, and on the other hand global connection through technologies of communication and travel and through seeing the planet from outer space.

But radical as these changes are, they do not require so complete a re-invention of Judaism as did the destruction of the old Israelite religion. The Talmudic Rabbis faced a challenge that (at least as they evidently saw it) required a very free hand in making texts mean what they needed them to mean.

Schachter-Shalomi, by contrast, is extraordinarily careful and true to the text. His interpretations never contradict the plain meaning, or substitute words that would better suit his purposes, or take phrases out of context to make pedagogical points that are inconsistent with other given facts of the narrative. He may point out resonances, or metaphorical or mystical possible dimensions, or etymological connections that yield insights for him, but never at the expense of the plain meaning. One senses that his own scholarly and personal integrity, as well as his respect for the text as sacred, would not permit him to do that.

He does, however, live fully in the breadth of understanding of "these and these." He is comfortable with "both…and"; indeed with all "seventy faces of Torah." Both the vowels and the consonants, both the punctive and the durative, both Deuteronomy and Ecclesiastes, both divine word and working hypothesis.

Evolving Halakhah: Applying the Written Text to Living Human Needs

Eliezer Berkovits[102] represents the Oral Torah as the guidance for the necessary process of application of principles provided by the Written Torah to the myriad situations of the life of the people throughout history. This includes, in every age, circumstances that had never before existed. The work of the scholars, he says, beginning with the Rabbis in the centuries after the final destruction of the Temple, is to decide and set and evolve *halakhah*, the way the Jewish people are to walk. Halakhah provides that transition by interpreting Tanakh, thus making it *Torat chayyim,* living teaching and relevant law.

Berkovits independently echoes the view of Schachter-Shalomi, and of course others, that our present day presents a particular need for living teaching that can speak to our needs. Berkovits says, "Our generation has witnessed probably the most radical transformation of the conditions of Jewish existence since the destruction of the Second Jewish Commonwealth in 69-70 CE." He cites first the destruction of European Jewry and its traditions and institutions of learning in a disaster of horrifying and traumatizing inhumanity, and second the appearance of a national state in the ancient homeland. "There has never been greater need for halacha's creative wisdom in applying the Torah to the daily realities of human existence than in our day."[103]

---

102   Eliezer Berkovits (1908–1992), a leading Talmudic scholar, philosopher, and theologian. The views cited in this section are from *Not in Heaven: the Nature and Function of Halakha.*

103   Berkovits, *Not in Heaven*, pp. xx–xxi.

But how did the Talmudic Rabbis go about applying the Written Torah to situations that, because of their multiplicity, it could not have addressed?

Berkovits gives three Talmudic principles that the Sages used when the written Torah did not give explicit guidance; or when it gave commandments that suggested different, even contradictory, decisions; or when the surface level meaning of the written text seemed unacceptable.

The first is the principle of *sevara*,[104] something arrived at by reasoning or common sense. "In a number of talmudic passages it is taken for granted that the *sevara* is no less authoritative than the biblical text itself."[105] He says that it is effective in every area of talmudic law, and he gives a wide range of examples, including extensions of Torah law and one case where the ruling arrived at by *sevara* contradicts the plain meaning of the text (despite the talmudic rule that the plain meaning may never be disregarded).[106] By the principle of *sevara,* a new law may also depart from a prevailing ruling where consequences of that ruling would be unacceptable.[107]

The second principle is *efshar*,[108] what is possible or feasible.[109] Halakhic rulings must take into consideration what is

---

104 סברא

105 Berkovits, *Not in Heaven*, p. 4.

106 Berkovits, *Not in Heaven*, pp. 6–7. Deut. 24:1–4 says that if a man divorces a woman and she marries another man and the second husband dies or divorces her, the first husband may not take her back because she has been defiled. It seemed unacceptable to the Rabbis that a properly married woman could be "defiled" by that marriage, so they decided it only applied in the case of the woman's adultery. *Babylonian Talmud* Yevamot 11b.

107 Berkovits, *Not in Heaven*, pp. 7–9.

108 אפשר

109 Berkovits, *Not in Heaven*, pp. 11–28. The full principle is
היכא דאפשר אפשר, היכא דלא אפשר לא אפשר
Heicha de'efshar efshar; heicha delo efshar lo efshar.

feasible for human beings, given their nature, their situations, and their needs.

Lo efshar (not feasible) can range from objectively impossible, to very difficult, to practically or morally infeasible: inconvenient or undesirable enough that the average Jew isn't going to do it or shouldn't be required to do it.

This leads to another principle. No edicts may be issued if the majority of people cannot obey them, because this will lead to transgression. The edicts lose their validity immediately.[110] In some places this is even applied to Biblical commandments. The Talmud says, "Leave Israel alone; it is better that they should transgress in ignorance than that they should do so intentionally."[111]

Berkovits cites examples of practical or moral feasibility decisions. Sometimes the extra month of Adar was added, not for aligning the solar and lunar calendars, but because the roads and bridges were in bad repair due to winter rains and more time was needed before the pilgrimage festival of Passover, and because travelers from Babylon had been delayed and would have been disappointed to miss the festival.

Another example was making an exception to the Biblical commandment not to bathe on Yom Kippur: a new bride was allowed to bathe for thirty days after her marriage even if Yom Kippur fell in that time, so that she should remain beloved of her new husband.[112] Her feelings created a moral feasibility issue in the minds of the Rabbis.

The feasible is most strikingly invoked for economic issues. For example, the Biblical commandment to remit all debts every seven years creates hardship both for lenders and for those needing to borrow (since lenders become loath to make loans as the

---

"If it is possible, it's possible; if it isn't possible it isn't possible." See *Babylonian Talmud*, Chulin 11b for an example.

110   *Babylonian Talmud,* Avoda Zera 36b.

111   *Babylonian Talmud*, Beitza 36b, Bava Metzia 60b.

112   *Babylonian Talmud,* Yoma 73b.

sabbatical year approached). Deuteronomy 15:9 is aware of this, and exhorts and threatens,[113] but the Rabbis recognized that this highly idealistic idea was economic disaster. There had to be recourse. So Hillel introduced the regulation of *prozbul*. By this device, creditors could transfer promissory notes to a rabbinical court, which was not bound by the injunction to release debts, and could demand payment, which it then transferred to the lender.[114]

Another economic difficulty arose from the Biblical require-ment to let the land lie fallow every seven years. The poor, who had the right to glean the fields (including the corners that were required to be left unharvested), suffered the loss of those glean-ings. Nor could they hire themselves out as laborers in those fields while the fields lay fallow. Based on the economic (and moral) "unfeasibility" of this, the Rabbis arranged for many areas to be set aside from the sabbatical requirement by formally excluding from the "sanctity" of the land of Israel.[115]

The third important way Berkovits describes that Halakhah interprets the intention of the written Torah for all areas of Jewish existence he calls the "priority of the ethical."[116] These are Torah principles such as "And you shall do what is right and good in the eyes of the Eternal,"[117] "Its ways are ways of pleasantness and peace,"[118] and "That you may walk in the way of good people, and guard the paths of the righteous."[119] Berkovits gives examples

---

113 Deut. 15:9: "Take-you-care, lest there be a word in your heart, a base-one, saying: The seventh year, the Year of Release, is nearing—and your eye be set-on-ill toward your brother, the needy-one, and you not give to him, so that he calls out because of you to Yнwн, and sin be incurred by you." Translation by Everett Fox.

114 *Mishnah* Shvi'it 10:3; *Babylonian Talmud* Gittin 36a–b.

115 *Babylonian Talmud,* Yevamot 16a.

116 Berkovits, *Not in Heaven*, p. 28.

117 Deut. 6:18.

118 Prov. 3:17.

119 Prov. 2:20.

of Rabbinic decisions that were based on these principles, ones that in some cases even counteracted or contradicted other explicit Biblical commandments.[120] The principles are invoked explicitly and implicitly in various places, but summed up in these words: "The Torah in its entirety exists for the sake of the ways of peace."[121]

Berkovits's examples of innovation based on this priority include cases where the application of the plain, literal meaning of the Biblical commandment would lead to humiliation of a woman in relation to her husband; where the punishments seems out of line with the offense; when the poor or the ignorant might be shamed; to eliminate quarrels or hatreds between people that might be brought on by the application of Biblical laws as stated, including property law and marriage laws; and when the punishment (especially in the case of flogging) insults the dignity of a person (*kevod habriot*). Berkovits cites as a Halakhic principle the Talmudic assertion "Great is the importance of a person's honor, for it over-rides a biblical commandment."[122]

Application of one principle (e.g., "Its ways are ways of pleasantness") over other injunctions is one way to explicitly contravene a biblical commandment about which the Rabbis were uncomfortable.

Another way used logic to back the situation into a corner until it could be proved that the situation could never occur and therefore the law would never be applicable.

For example, Bible stipulates that a "stubborn and rebellious son" is to be put to death.[123] Rabbi Shimon of the Mishnaic period simply asserted that it never happened and never could happen, because no parents would hand over a child to be stoned to death

---

120 Berkovits, *Not in Heaven*, pp. 28–69.

121 *Babylonian Talmud,* Gittin 59b.

122 גָּדוֹל כָּבוֹד הַבְּרִיּוֹת שֶׁדּוֹחֶה אֶת לֹא תַעֲשֶׂה שֶׁבַּתּוֹרָה
Examples of Talmudic usage of this principle include *Babylonian Talmud*, Tractate Eruvin 41b and Tractate Brakhot 19b.

123 Deut. 21.18–20.

for the child's excessive eating and drinking.[124] Rabbi Yehudah, also of the Mishnaic period, took a more ingenious approach. He notes that the Biblical text says that the parents are to appear before the elders and declare that the child does not hearken to their voice.[125] "Voice" is singular. But it is impossible that their two voices should be so identical in every way as to be a singular voice; therefore it could never happen.[126]

Why, then, in such cases, was the original commandment written? Rabbi Yehudah asks the same question. His answer is "To interpret it and to receive divine reward (d'rosh v'qabel sakhar)."[127] Berkovits explains that the interpretation the Rabbis are supposed to be making here is that it was never meant to be applied.[128] He comments, "It is as if it were a test of the intelligence and conscience of the student and the teacher."[129]

Another Torah law the Rabbis could not allow to stand was that if a city was led astray into idolatry by some of its inhabitants, the whole city was to be destroyed and burned, all its inhabitants and all their property.[130] Here again the Rabbis proved that it never was and never could be; in this case it was impossible to burn the city as commanded because at least some doors would have

---

124 *Babylonian Talmud*, Sanhedrin 71a.

125 Deut. 21:20: וְאָמְרוּ אֶל־זִקְנֵי עִירוֹ בְּנֵנוּ זֶה סוֹרֵר וּמֹרֶה אֵינֶנּוּ שֹׁמֵעַ בְּקֹלֵנוּ

126 *Babylonian Talmud*, Sanhedrin 71a.

127 *Babylonian Talmud*, Sanhedrin 71a. The principle is cited for both the impossible execution of the rebellious son and the impossible destruction of the idolatrous city.

128 Artscroll adds in its translation the vaguer statement that the could-not-be-applied law was given to reward those who study it.

129 Berkovits, *Not in Heaven*, p. 47.

130 Deut. 13:17.

mezuzot[131] on them, which contain the name of God, which cannot be burned. And here again it is explained that the commandment was given so that it could be interpreted and that they be rewarded for recognizing that it was never meant to be applied.[132]

This is a bold answer to the question Schachter-Shalomi left us with in considering what we do with difficult passages.[133] The Rabbinic reasoning is saying, according to Berkovits, that we are meant to be disturbed by some of the commandments, to protest from our moral sense, and to think about the implications of that. This inflames, and develops, our moral sense; it clarifies for us what is right and wrong. One might say that the part of us that protests and cannot accept is put there as part of the *b'tzelem elohim,* the image of God within us.

For the Rabbis, many of these difficult passages had to do with transgressions for which capital punishment was ordered and with laws regarding corporal punishment. Others had to do with marriage and divorce laws whose implementation resulted in cruelties, especially to women. Another commandment that needed re-visioning was that regarding the *mamzer*, or "bastard," who according to biblical law was not permitted into the family community of the Jewish people.[134] The Rabbis found many ways around the simple commandments that led to these distressing results.

---

131 **Mezuzot**. Pieces of parchment with with certain Hebrew verses (part of the *shema* recitation, "love your God with all your heart and soul and might," etc.) attached to doorposts in fulfillment of the Biblical command in Deut. 6:9.

132 *Babylonian Talmud* Sanhedrin 71a. Cited by Berkovits *Not in Heaven*, p. 48.

133 See Chapter 14, "What Do We Do with Difficult Passages?"

134 In *Babylonian Talmud*, Kiddushin 72b, it is noted that it is taught in a Baraita that *mamzerim* will be pure in the "future to come" (the Messianic era). R' Meir disputes this, but Rabbi Yose argues for it; the Gemara decides the law according to Rabbi Yose.

Thus, we see that the Sages of the Talmudic times had not only to apply biblical commandments to situations not originally spelled out, but they had to deal with their own difficulties and discomfort with some of the commandments as originally stated in the Written Torah.

When they had to set aside the plain meaning of some texts, they made a practice of finding some wording somewhere else that, as they represented it, explained the meaning of the difficult text. This came out in sometimes in reading into the words a meaning different from the plain meaning (with the words of the other verse or phrase providing the key to understanding the difficult text). Other times it was done by finding a higher principle that took priority over the one that had to be set aside. Other times it was understood that the biblical commandment was there to emphasize the importance of the matter at hand, but was not something that could happen, or that could lead to the commanded punishment.

Schachter-Shalomi seems to share the sense that the divine will must be consistent with our inner sense of what is right and just—an inner sense that must have been put there when we were created *b'tzelem elohim*. He would not assert that the words of the Written Torah must be interpreted in ways that seem to contradict the plain sense. But his support of our protesting what seems unjust is in this tradition.

In discussing what we do with the difficult passages, he muses that he must hold those passages in abeyance, "until I can lift it, until I can have insight, a way of raising this so it becomes something better...." He recognizes that knowing the deeper meaning may be beyond him at the moment in the case of some passages, but until he is able to see the divine intention, he must still have the inner integrity to dissociate himself from that particular aspect.[135]

---

135 See page 275,

The Rabbis' use of the image of an Oral Torah can be seen as metaphor for an inner spiritual guidance in the application of the teachings set down in the Biblical text to our lives in every generation. By describing it as having been given to Moses on Mt. Sinai along with the text that was written down, they declare that guidance to be as sacred and God-given as the biblical text. The concept of the Oral Torah provides a grounding for necessary re-visioning.

Act for God

The Rabbis developed and asserted a principle that at times it was necessary to "act for God" by nullifying previous principles of the Temple practice, tradition, and even commandments of the written Torah. This allowed them to consolidate their authority, establish some of the principles of the Oral Torah as they were conveying it, and to modify received practices and command-ments as necessary for the new circumstances.

Psalm 119:126[136] says "It is time to act for YHVH; for they have violated your Torah." The plain meaning of this verse is that the speaker feels a call to act for God by defending Torah. The Rabbis, however, needed a proof text to support necessary modi-fications of received commandments and traditional practice, and the first half of the verse offered a rousing call.

So, in the first tractate of the Babylonian Talmud, Tractate Brakhot, page 54a, the Sages of the Mishnah quote this verse to support such a position. There a larger principle that they say is surely God's will requires that a Biblical law should be negated. Rabbi Natan (still in the Mishnah section) proposes a general interpretation of the verse by reversing the parts and inserting a Mishnaic Hebrew word *m'shum* "because" to re-state the verse

---

136: עֵת לַעֲשׂוֹת לַה' הֵפֵרוּ תּוֹרָתֶךָ

"They [now the Rabbis] make your Torah void *because* it is time to act for YHVH"[137].

Having established this principle (to their own satisfaction, anyway), they have much-needed leeway to modify principles and commandments that are impractical, or, in their view, too harsh, or no longer applicable in these later, post-Temple times.

Changing Halakha with a Shofar Blast

Another way of "acting for God" was demonstrated famously by Yochanan ben Zakkai. Before the destruction of the Temple in 70 CE, it was permitted to sound the Shofar for Rosh HaShanah on Shabbat in the Temple, but not outside it. After the Temple was destroyed, it seemed that the law would be that it could not be sounded anywhere on Shabbat.[138] Gemara gives the account of how Rabbi Yochanan handled the problem:[139]

> Our rabbis taught: It once happened that Rosh Hashanah fell on the Sabbath. Rabban Yohanan ben Zakkai said to the sons of Beterah, "Let us sound the shofar." They said to him, "Let us discuss the matter." He said to them, "Let us first sound the shofar and then discuss the matter." After they sounded the shofar, they said to him, "Now let us discuss the matter." He said to them, "The shofar has already been sounded in Yavneh, and one does not undo that which as been done."

Some startling innovations become unquestionable foundations of Judaism, while others, like this one, continue to be returned to and argued millennia later.

---

137 רבי נתן אומר: הפרו תורתך משום עת לעשות לה'

138 Furthermore, some of the Rabbis saw blowing the shofar as falling under the Biblical prohibition of work on Shabbat. Others wished to prohibit it as leading to the Biblically prohibited transgression of carrying on Shabbat. (See discussion in *Babylonian Talmud*, Tractate Rosh HaShanah 29b.)

139 *Babylonian Talmud*, Tractate Rosh HaShanah 29b.

Growth of Interpretive Principles

The Rabbis developed and over time increasingly formulated interpretive principles. These principles allowed them to re-vision Biblical laws into what they needed for their purposes. Wylen notes that in addition to recourse to the "traditions of their teachers," the Oral Torah,

> … the Pharisees had another way to determine Torah law. They had rules of logical interpretation by which they could derive new law from the written Torah. The Pharisees used their loose reading of the Torah, along with their line of authority and their rules of interpretation, to apply the Torah to the new conditions of life in the Hellenistic world—the world of Greco-Roman culture.[140]

Wylen describes the development of this tool.

> The earliest set of logical rules for interpreting Scripture are ascribed to the great Pharisee leader Hillel. Jewish tradition records the Seven Principles of Scriptural Interpretation of Hillel. Tradition ascribes Thirteen Principles to Rabbi Ishmael, a first-century CE Sage. The thirteen include Hillel's seven. Thirty four principles are attributed to the second-century Rabbi Yose the Galilean. We note a trend here: in each succeeding century the logical principles for deriving new law from Torah expand. The oral Torah expands in form as it grows in content.[141]

Local custom: *Minhag Ha Medinah*

Another way in which the tradition of Talmud supported change (in principles of living or halakhah, at least) is the recognition of custom, *minhag*, as halakhah. A social custom that has

---

140 Wylen, *The Seventy Faces of Torah*, p.52.

141 Wylen, *The Seventy Faces of Torah*, pp. 52–53.

established itself (even one that establishes itself in opposition to a rabbinic interpretation of the law) eventually acquires the force of law.

Allowance for local custom in determining application of halakhic principles, and even the principle that custom can over-ride halakhah, shows a thread of the fluidity that Schachter-Shalomi speaks about.[142]

The Babylonian Talmud speaks of *Minhag HaMedinah,* customs of the locality, as determining proper practice in dealing hours or work and provision of food for hired laborers.[143] *Mishnah* says, in the name of Rabbi Shimon ben Gamliel, "Everything is in accord with local custom."[144]

The Jerusalem Talmud goes farther in its discussion of that same Mishnah to say that common custom can trump law: *Minhag mevateil halakhah,* custom cancels/overrides Halakhah.[145]

Wylen: "The social customs of the Jewish people are a source of Torah; custom is one way that the voice of the living God continues to speak in the life of the Jewish people."[146]

Midrash: Reading Current Practice Back

One of the tools that emerged for the re-visioning of Judaism from the old Israelite religion into Rabbinic Judaism is the tool of Midrash. The word *midrash* has as its root the verb דָּרַשׁ *to seek*

---

142   See chapter Rigidity and Change.

143   *Babylonian Talmud,* Bava Metzia 83a, Mishnah.

144   The Mishnah being commented on says: הכל כמנהג המדינה

145   *Jerusalem Talmud,* Bava Metzia 7:1. המנהג מבטל את ההלכה
The Rabbinic discussion in the Gemara delves into the application of this principle; the Sages did not, of course, consider it to be absolute. Historically, however, custom *has* over-ridden Rabbinic decree, regardless of rabbinic ideas about what should be allowed. Where segments of the Jewish people have determinedly followed their customs in opposition to Halakha, the Halakha has given way.

146   Wylen, *The Seventy Faces of Torah*, p. 84.

(here to seek out meaning in the text). *Midrashim* are re-tellings of the Biblical passages with different emphasis, with explanations of potentially obscure elements of the passages, with expansions of the passage with additional material, and with inserted imaginatively constructed stories whose pedagogical intent and conclusions suited the needs and teaching purposes of the rabbinic authors. A midrash begins by citing the source text in the canonical Bible text, but then may take great liberties in not only expanding on the text but in some cases apparently contradicting the stated facts of the source text.

An extensive literature arose in Talmudic times and continuing into Byzantine times using these expansions and re-tellings to convey the lesson the Sage or teacher wished to promulgate, or to change the previous understanding of the passage.[147]

Aside from using these expansions and re-interpretations to present the original narratives and teachings in terms relevant to later times and changed circumstances, the Rabbis used them to legitimize changes that became necessary with the destruction of the Temple.

The Rabbis had created a new Judaism, and they needed to avoid appearing as innovators and to establish their authority and the authority of the new laws and institutions. One technique to help with this was to read the practices of this new Judaism back into the Biblical stories. Thus, the Patriarchs were shown to be studying in Rabbinic *yeshivas*, praying according to the rituals the Rabbis had set up, eating according to the laws of *kashrut*[148] the Rabbis had established, and so on.

---

147 Wylen analyzes a number of traditional Midrashim showing the lessons drawn. For example, in one he shows how "The rabbis discovered in the Torah a precedent for the preference of rabbis over priests." (Analysis of *Mekhilta*, Bo, Pischa 1.) Wylen, *The Seventy Faces of Torah*, p. 99.

148 **Kashrut**. Hebrew. The laws of *kashrut* are the rabbinic dietary laws.

Moses Not Recognizing Akiva's Torah

Babylonian Talmud Menahot 29b[149] tells a story meant to illustrate both the superiority of the Rabbis (or at least of Akiva, one of their pre-eminent exemplars) over Moses, and at the same time show Moses's acknowledgment of Akiva's superiority. Moses's acknowledgement testifies to the legitimacy of the teachings of the Rabbis, despite their seeming departures from Moses's Written Torah. Part of the interest and charm of this story, however, is the wry awareness that Akiva's teaching does seem to have departed radically—to the point of being unrecognizable to Moses himself.

The set-up of the story has Moses asking God about some little crowns on some of the letters in the written Torah scroll. He has "gone up on high" and found the Holy One affixing crowns to the letters. He inquires why these letters weren't already perfect without the crowns. God replies that there is a man named Akiva who will arrive after many generations who will interpret on the basis of each point of the crowns "heaps and heaps of laws."

Moses wants to see this man, so God transports him to Akiva's study hall. Moses takes a seat in the back, but can't understand what the people are saying; he feels faint. At a certain point one of the disciples asks Akiva how he knows something he is asserting, and Akiva replies "It is a law given to Moses from Sinai."[150]

One imagines a beat here, a moment for the student of Talmud to experience the almost-dizzying mixture of humor and seriousness. One might feel faint oneself, trying to see where this is intended to come down.

But Moses is portrayed as having the opposite reaction. He now regains his composure.[151] Even though he doesn't recognize

---

149 *The Babylonian Talmud,* Menachot 29b.

150 הֲלָכָה לְמֹשֶׁה מִסִּינַי

151 נִתְיַישְׁבָה דַּעְתּוֹ

the teachings, the assertion that they came from him from Sinai establishes for him their legitimacy. He is awed by Akiva's superiority to himself. He returns and comes before the Holy One and says "How is it that you have someone like that and yet you gave the Torah through me?"

This story allows a rare peek at the Rabbis acknowledging how much has had to change. But circumstances themselves change, and Torah must move on to accommodate that. The original transmission requires deeper and deeper interpretation, or it may lose its power to inspire and guide later generations.

Majority Rule

The Rabbinic re-making of Judaism required some astonishing assertions. The Rabbis needed the authority to over-rule any previous laws. In the future, decisions about law would be made by the consensus, or just the majority rule, of the Sages. But to make the principle as strong as possible, they established it with a story that the majority can over-rule even heaven itself. Here is the account in the *Babylonian Talmud*, Tractate Bava Metzia, 59b.

This incident involves a group of early Rabbis, ones who were alive at the time of the destruction of Jerusalem and the Second Temple in 70 CE.[152] The incident recounted here would have taken place some years later as the new Rabbinic form of Judaism was being worked out and put in place.

---

152 Rabbi Eliezer had witnessed the destruction of the Temple and smuggled his teacher Yochanan Ben Zakkai out of Jerusalem in a coffin as the city was being destroyed. [Four rabbinic sources: Avot de Rabbi Nathan A Ch. 4, Avot de Rabbi Nathan B Ch. 6, Lamentations Rabbah 1:5 #31, and Babylonian Talmud Gittin 56 a–b. Thanks to Rabbi Jack Shlachter for these sources.]

In an argument with his rabbinic colleagues over the susceptibility of ritual impurity of a certain kind of oven,[153] Rabbi Eliezer is said first to use "all the arguments in the world"[154] (that is, he argued as powerfully as could be done). But his colleagues did not accept his arguments and maintained their position.

Rabbi Eliezer then begins calling on heaven to support his position. "If the Halakhah is in accordance with my position, let this carob tree prove it" and the carob tree uproots itself and moved a hundred cubits away. Even though God has demonstrated his agreement with Rabbi Eliezer's position by performing this miracle, Eliezer's colleagues refuse to acknowledge God's instruction/torah as having authority. They say "Proof cannot be brought from a carob tree."

Eliezer then calls on a channel of water to reverse its flow, which it does, with the same response: "Proof cannot be brought from a channel of water." Then he calls on the walls of the house of study to prove his position, and they begin to fall. Rabbi Yehoshua rebukes the falling walls with the challenge "If Talmudic scholars argue with one another about the Halakhah, what affair is it of yours?" The walls remained leaning, but did not fall.

Finally, Rabbi Eliezer says "If the Halakhah is in accordance with me, let it be proved directly from Heaven." A heavenly voice[155] went forth and said "Why are you disputing with Rabbi Eliezer? The Halakhah is in accordance with him in all circumstances!"

Even this is not taken to carry any weight. Rabbi Yehoshua rose to his feet quoting part of a verse from Deuteronomy 30:12, "The Torah is not in heaven!"

---

153   "Oven of Akhnai," one made of pieces of a broken vessel rather than by shaping mud. On the principle that, although ovens and unbroken vessels generally are ruled able to transmit impurity, broken vessels do not, Eliezer argued that an oven made of broken pieces cemented together could not transmit impurity to the food.

154   כָּל תְּשׁוּבוֹת שֶׁבָּעוֹלָם

155   A "bat qol," בת קול

Yehoshua's implication, of course, is that Torah is no longer God's but is now theirs. This, however, was not the original meaning of the phrase he quotes. Rabbi Yehoshua has re-interpreted the Biblical text to suit the needs of his re-visioned Judaism. Deuteronomy 30:12 is part of Moses's closing exhortation to the Israelites before his death. He is urging the people to take the divine teachings to heart, not to consider them beyond their understanding, as something that one had to send someone up into the heavens, or over the sea, to return with its meaning.[156] Moses, in fact, is denying the need for interpreters, perhaps even the need for rabbis.

The Gemara's account of this incident is now interrupted as the interlocutors ask what this means. Rabbi Yirmeyah said, "Since God already gave the Torah on Mount Sinai, we do not pay attention to heavenly voices. For you [God] already wrote in the Torah at Mount Sinai 'After the majority to incline.'"

One is struck anew at the extent of the arrogation here. This interpretation of the Torah proof text not only contradicts the plain meaning, it reverses the sense. Exodus 23:2 says *Lo tihyeh achareiy raba'im l'ra'ot*[157] "You shall *not* fall after the many to evil." Rabbi Eliezer was following the original commandment in not falling in with the majority to a conclusion that contradicted heaven. For his pains he was excommunicated.[158]

---

156 Deut. 30:11–14. כִּי הַמִּצְוָה הַזֹּאת אֲשֶׁר אָנֹכִי מְצַוְּךָ הַיּוֹם לֹא־נִפְלֵאת הִוא מִמְּךָ וְלֹא־רְחֹקָה הִוא: לֹא בַשָּׁמַיִם הִוא לֵאמֹר מִי יַעֲלֶה־לָּנוּ הַשָּׁמַיְמָה וְיִקָּחֶהָ לָּנוּ וְיַשְׁמִעֵנוּ אֹתָהּ וְנַעֲשֶׂנָּה: וְלֹא־מֵעֵבֶר לַיָּם הִוא לֵאמֹר מִי יַעֲבָר־לָנוּ אֶל־עֵבֶר הַיָּם וְיִקָּחֶהָ לָּנוּ וְיַשְׁמִעֵנוּ אֹתָהּ וְנַעֲשֶׂנָּה: כִּי־קָרוֹב אֵלֶיךָ הַדָּבָר מְאֹד בְּפִיךָ וּבִלְבָבְךָ לַעֲשֹׂתוֹ:

157 לֹא־תִהְיֶה אַחֲרֵי־רַבִּים לְרָעֹת

158 Rabbi Eliezer, one of Rabbinic Judaism's greatest scholars, prize pupil of Yochanan ben Zakkai and teacher of Rabbi Akiva, was excommunicated for opposing the majority in this incident. Making an example of him stressed the importance of this new principle.

The men are arguing about an oven made out of broken pieces; the question is whether it counts as a "vessel." This rare or perhaps even hypothetical example seems an odd matter for these eminent sages to be arguing so passionately about. Perhaps importance in the specific halakhic decision they were debating would have distracted from the principle of the authority being with the majority.

The majority rabbinical opinion is asserted here to be the determining factor, over-ruling direct commandment of God. This seems very puzzling if the dedication to the punctilious determination of the potential of an object to render food impure (the matter about which they have been arguing) is for the purpose of following divine instructions and commandments.

But perhaps what we have here is a recognition that these laws and customs have their primary purpose in the creating of a community knit together by shared practice. That practice cannot depend entirely on Biblical injunctions, because they are incomplete and can be rendered inapplicable or irrelevant by changes in circumstances and technology. So there must be a ruling authority that can follow every twist and turn. God may have set a certain tone with the initial commandments, but now Torah is no longer in heaven. The cohesiveness of the community will come from the rabbis: those of the Talmud and their successors.

To seal this, the Talmudic story adds an account, said to be reported to a certain Rabbi Natan generations later by the Prophet Elijah. Elijah was understood to have been at the Heavenly Court at the time that Rabbi Yehoshua had refused to heed the heavenly voice. Natan asked Elijah what God had done when that happened. The Gemara relates that Elijah reported that God had smiled and said "My sons have defeated me, my sons have defeated me!"[159] Thus the decision to place their majority rule above even direct divine testimony is represented by the Rabbis as having God's sanction.

---

159 This whole story with its epilogue appears in Bava Metzia 59b.

This may seem disturbing if one views it as a shameless assertion that the institution has taken over, governing through its ruling clique, so that God is no longer needed.

However, it does leave room for the community, through its most learned rabbis, to act on their own inner flow of Torah. This fresh flow can come through with wisdom for the emerging challenges. It can free the community from the old commandments formulated for circumstances long gone, and tailored for stages of spiritual evolution it has moved beyond.

I offer the Talmudic passage as another piece of evidence that Rabbinic Judaism makes many sorts of room for change.

The Inherent Interpretability of Torah

In *Jerusalem Talmud*, Sanhedrin, Chapter 4, Halakha 2, Rabbi Yannai says: *Iylu niytnah hatorah chatukhah, lo hay'ta l'regel amidah.*[160]

Jacob Neusner translates this as: "Said R. Yannai, "If the Torah were handed down cut-and-dried [so that there were no possibility for disagreement in reasoning about the law and no need to make up one's mind], [the world] would not have a leg to stand on."[161] His translation interprets the thing which would not stand as the world. Cherry follows this, giving the translation "Rabbi Yanai said, 'Had the Torah been given in an unequivocal way, the world could not endure.'"[162]

In contrast, Artscroll's translation and commentary understands the implicit subject to be the Sages, who would be deprived

---

160   אילו ניתנה התורה חתוכה לא היתה לרגל עמידה

161   Jacob Neusner, ed. and trans. *The Jerusalem Talmud, A Translation and Commentary*. Bracketed words are added by Neusner.

162   Cherry, *Torah through Time*, p. 13. He introduces his reference to this passage with: "[I]t is worthwhile to appreciate the extent to which [the Rabbis of the Talmud] gloried in the inherent interpretability of Torah."

of freedom to make it mean what they need it to mean: "[The Sages] would not have a leg on which to stand (when deciding halachic questions. God therefore constructed the Torah in a way that allows several legitimate conclusions regarding these questions, so the Sages may decide the halachah in accordance with their judgment.)"[163]

Cherry adds his own comment on this, stepping back slightly from the endurance of the world to point to the necessity of Torah interpretation for our continued existence as a people: "The very future of our existence depends on the ability of the Torah to be interpreted."

Many Voices ("Including Ones Not Yet Created")

There may be one Written Torah, and one eventually-written-down body of texts of the Oral Torah coming through the Rabbis of Babylonia and the land of Israel in the first five or so centuries after the destruction of the second Temple. But the legacy is hardly univocal.

Not only does the Talmud carefully record the voices of many conversants, sharing differing perspectives and even flatly disagreeing with one another, but the Bible itself presents differing principles and regulations, which can in some situations be at odds.

Beyond that, there is the impediment that what is put into words is limited, and is inevitably received by different people differently, due to their individual life experiences, situations, and state of mind. When very different geographic, cultural, and historical circumstances are figured into this, the way the same words are received may vary widely.

---

163 Artscroll Schottenstein Edition *Jerusalem Talmud* Sanhedrin p. 26A4. Bracketed and parenthetical words are added by the Artscroll commentators.

And yet, if this Torah is divinely given, it is intended to speak to each of these people as they receive it (or at least takes into consideration that it will be differently received).

Midrash Rabbah, *Exodus*, addressing the passage in Exodus in which the people receive the covenant on Sinai, says that the message on Sinai is to all people then and in the future: each person received a Torah unique to that soul's capability.

The covenant at Deuteronomy 29:14, before the Israelites enter the promised land, is understood by this Midrash as recapitulating Sinai. Moses says in Deuteronomy that this covenant is not just with those who are standing there with them that day, but with the ones who are not there that day.[164]

The Midrash explains this as meaning that the messages that the later prophets would prophesy were received on Sinai; and not just the prophets but all the Sages—Rabbis—that would arise later: "all the Sages of later generations." And not just them, but all the souls that would be one day created,—each received his share of Torah (as ones that were "not there that day").

And "one voice divided itself into seven voices, and these into seventy languages."[165] Citing Psalm 29:4, "The voice of God is with power,"[166] the Midrash then glosses "that is, according to the power of each individual, according to the individual power of the young, the old, and the very small ones."[167]

Oral Torah through the Whole Jewish People

If all of us, all the souls that would one day be created, have received our share of the Torah as it was given on Sinai, then the Oral Torah is not limited to that which was written down by 500

---

164 כִּי אֶת־אֲשֶׁר יֶשְׁנוֹ פֹּה עִמָּנוּ עֹמֵד הַיּוֹם לִפְנֵי יְהֹוָה אֱלֹהֵינוּ וְאֵת עִמָּנוּ הַיּוֹם:

165 Yitro, 28:6, *Midrash Rabbah, Exodus*, p. 335.

166 חֲכַב הֲוָהִי־לוֹק ִ

167 Yitro 29:1. *Midrash Rabbah, Exodus*, p. 337.

360 ~~Schachter-Shalomi's Context

CE. Just as the Rabbis in those early centuries were developing Oral Torah for their understanding, conscience, sensibility, and circumstances, the Jewish people must continue the study, conversation, debate, and development of a halakhah, a *praxis*, a way of walking in the Jewish path, in order to test and bring to fruition the Oral Torah that was passed to them at that time of covenant.

This seems to be similar to the understanding that Schachter-Shalomi brings to his mission. He phrases it a little differently at different times to bring out the fullness of divine workings and the complexity of human spiritual experiences, as well as recognizing the different covenants which God has made with the world, humankind, and Jews throughout the unfolding of time and creation. So he brings attention to the imprinting and covenant of God's creating human beings in his image, the breathing of God's breath into human nostrils, the many phases of explicit covenants, which in fact don't end at Sinai but continue through to the end of Deuteronomy and beyond.[168]

Rather than focusing, as this midrash did, on a single incident of a torah put into every soul at Sinai, which might be taken as a static thing, Schachter-Shalomi prefers to speak of a continuous descent of Torah, which, by computer analogy, allows for continuous software updates.

---

168 In 2 Sam 23:5, King David, dying, claims that God made an
    everlasting covenant with him. כִּי־לֹא־כֵן בֵּיתִי עִם־אֵל כִּי בְרִית
    עוֹלָם שָׂם לִי עֲרוּכָה בַכֹּל וּשְׁמֻרָה. In 2 Chron. 7:18, YHVH speaks
    to Solomon about the covenant he made with David regarding
    the monarchical succession. In 2 Kings 11:17, Jehoiada makes a
    covenant between YHVH, the king, and the people. King Josiah
    makes a covenant with YHVH for himself and his people in
    2 Kings 23:3.

Torah is a Tree that Bears Figs for Every Generation

Babylonian Talmud Eruvin 54a–b was quoted in the epigraph to this book.[169]

The Rabbis are commenting on a verse of the book of Proverbs, 27:18, which says "The one who tends a fig tree will consume her fruit."[170]

Jacob Neusner's translation of the Talmudic passage is:

> Said R. Hiyya bar Abba said R. Yohanan, "What is the meaning of this verse of Scripture: 'Whoso keeps the fig tree shall eat the fruit thereof'? How come words of the Torah were compared to a fig? Just as the fig—the more someone examines it, the more one finds in it, so words of the Torah—the more one meditates on them, the more flavor he finds in them."[171]

Shai Cherry gives the passage as: "Just as one finds new figs on a fig tree each time one searches, so too does one find new meanings in the Torah each time one searches."[172]

The fig imagery also illustrates for Cherry the reason that Rabbi Akiva could explain things (and attribute them to Moses) that Moses himself couldn't understand. He says:

> Akiva, living a thousand years after Moses, understands not only Moses' Torah, but some of its implications, as

---

169 *Babylonian Talmud*, from Eruvin 54a–b: אמר רבי חייא בר אבא אמר רבי יוחנן: מאי דכתיב (משלי כ"ז) נצר תאנה יאכל פריה, למה נמשלו דברי תורה כתאנה - מה תאנה זו כל זמן שאדם ממשמש בה מוצא בה תאנים אף דברי תורה: כל זמן שאדם הוגה בהן - מוצא בהן טעם.

170 Proverbs 27:18: נֹצֵר תְּאֵנָה יֹאכַל פִּרְיָהּ

171 Neusner, Jacob, ed. and trans. *The Babylonian Talmud, A Translation and Commentary,* Vol. 3, p. 266.

172 Cherry, *Torah through Time*, p. 32.

well. Akiva has the advantage of time of seeing how the
words of Torah, like ever-ripening figs, have revealed
their latent meanings in the intervening centuries between
Sinai and Akiva's Israel. … Every generation has followed
Akiva's example and generated fresh insights from Moses'
message.[173]

Similar imagery to the ever-bearing figs is evoked in Rabbinic
commentary on Proverbs 5:19. That lovely verse of Proverbs
says "A deer of love and a doe of grace. May her breasts saturate/
satisfy you at all times. May you be intoxicated continuously by
her love."[174] The Babylonian Talmud (Eruvin 54b) follows its
gloss on Proverbs 27:18 and its figs with comments on this verse.
After an explanation of the deer and the doe, they go on to the
second half of the verse, the phrase "Let her breasts satisfy you at
all times." That this follows so directly the discussion of the significance of the figs indicates the Rabbis' sense that this continuing
satisfaction with the breasts continues the theme begun with the
fig tree, the theme of Torah's on-going yielding of her treasures.

Cherry had discussed this passage earlier. He translates the
Talmudic passage[175] as:

Why were words of Torah compared to a breast? Just as
a nursling who returns to the breast continues to find milk,
so does the person who meditates on Torah continue to find
new meaning therein.[176]

---

173 Cherry, *Torah through Time*, pp. 33–34.

174 Proverbs 27:19:   אַיֶּלֶת אֲהָבִים וְיַעֲלַת־חֵן דַּדֶּיהָ יְרַוֻּךָ בְכָל־עֵת
בְּאַהֲבָתָהּ תִּשְׁגֶּה תָמִיד:

175 *Babylonian Talmud*, Eruvin 54b: דדיה ירוך בכל עת, למה נמשלו
דברי תורה כדד? מה דד זה, כל זמן שהתינוק ממשמש בו מוצא בו
חלב - אף דברי תורה, כל זמן שאדם הוגה בהן - מוצא בהן טעם.

176 Cherry, *Torah through Time*, p. 13.

Cherry continues:

> [T]hese early Rabbinic statements point to the assumption that new interpretations will continuously be brought forth from the Torah of Sinai. The Rabbis were the midwives bringing forth new interpretations of Torah, a Torah pregnant with Divine meaning.[177]

The Rabbis were bringing forth new interpretations, but they are not the end of the flow of the wisdom from Sinai. The Oral Torah is a deeper stream than one set of statements and laws. It continues to bear its fruit, or let down its milk, or give birth to its divine meaning, through all the generations.

---

177 Cherry *Torah through Time*, p. 13.

Epilog

The process of applying Bible to meet the needs of contemporary people has been a primary purpose of commentators within the Jewish tradition. I have argued that Judaism has survived and remained a vital, living religion precisely because it incorporated a powerful commitment to re-visioning itself for each age.

Schachter-Shalomi is deeply immersed in the Jewish tradition. He knows the Hebrew Bible. He knows the texts of the Rabbinic and later traditions, and the thinking behind them. And he knows the traditions of interpretation and re-interpretation that have kept the text and the religion living waters for the Jewish people.

He is re-visioning Judaism for our present age, and he finds guidance for that re-visioning in the Hebrew Bible.

Proverbs 3:18 says that Torah is a tree of life for those who strongly take hold of her. The series of retreats of the Primal Myths Wisdom School, to which all the participants committed themselves for the duration, for a winter of weekends of immersion in the Biblical text, was a dedicated exercise in grasping this tree and drawing upon its life-giving wisdom.

Proverbs 27:19 and its Talmudic commentary speak of Torah as breasts that satisfy the nursling whenever it returns to them. The nourishing milk of Torah descends at the baby's cry.

And Talmudic commentary on Proverbs 27:18 says that, just as the keeper of the fig tree will find that the more he or she examines, or searches, or handles, or rummages into the figs, the more flavor will be found, so the more one meditates on Torah the more flavor and wisdom will be found.

Schachter-Shalomi shares these ways of seeing Torah with his Talmudic predecesssors. He approaches the Biblical text as if to breasts whose milk flows whenever the nursling returns. He approaches that text as if to a tree of successively-ripening figs, with new figs and new wisdom being offered for every generation of keepers of the tree—provided that the keepers of the tree will lovingly gather the figs and take the time to intricately and thoughtfully examine them.

Life, Work, and Contribution of Rabbi Zalman Schachter-Shalomi

This chronology is based on information in the Yesod Foundation web site[1] and the Reb Zalman Legacy Project web site.[2] I have included some of the commentary given on the Yesod site verbatim (with minor editing and corrections of typos).

Meshullam Zalman HaKohen Schachter was born on August 17th, 1924 in Zholkiew, Poland (now part of the Ukraine) to Shlomo and Hayyah Gittel Schachter. In 1925, his family moved to Vienna, Austria where he spent most of his childhood. His father, a Belzer *chasid* with liberal tendencies, had him educated in both a socialist-Zionist high school, where he learned Latin and Modern Hebrew, and a traditional Orthodox yeshiva, where he studied Torah and Talmud.

In 1938 his family began the long flight from Nazi oppression. Leaving Vienna, they went first to Antwerp, Belgium, then were in an internment camp in Vichy France, before finally escaping to Africa, the West Indies, and finally to New York in 1941.

Yesod:

> While still in Belgium, Schachter became acquainted with and began to frequent a circle of Chabad Chasidim who cut and polished diamonds in Antwerp. This association eventually led to his becoming a Chabad *chasid* of the Lubavitch branch, in whose yeshiva he enrolled after his

---

1 **Yesod Foundation.** Nonprofit Jewish foundation based in Boulder Colorado, listing Schachter-Shalomi as Spiritual Director. www.yesodfoundation.org.

2 **Reb Zalman Legacy Project.** A collaborative effort of the Yesod Foundation and Naropa University to preserve, develop and disseminate Schachter-Shalomi's teachings. www.rzlp.org.

family arrived in New York. Having been excited by the intense mystical piety of the Chabad-Lubavitch movement, Schachter (he would add Shalomi to his name in the early 1980s) attended the central Lubavitcher yeshiva in Brooklyn.

Schachter received his rabbinic ordination from the Central Lubavitch Yeshiva in 1947 while under the leadership of the sixth Lubavitcher Rebbe, Yosef Yitzchak Schneersohn. He taught and served as a congregational rabbi at various Lubavitch synagogues including Fall River, Massachusetts (1949–1952). In addition, in 1949 he began traveling to college campus with his friend Rabbi Shlomo Carlebach at the direction of the Lubavitcher Rebbe.

Yesod:

"Having been saved from the Holocaust. . . I felt something was needed from me to give back," he recalled. "I saw what was happening to our tradition, that it was being diminished. That the best and most advanced of our people had been decimated. So I was moved to think about creating a Noah's Ark for our tradition." In other words, he was looking for forces within Judaism that would re-energize it and make it self-confident again.

Already Schachter was showing signs of an iconoclastic temperament. In his congregations, he allowed women to take part more fully in worship and introduced guitars into the liturgy.

He also entered a graduate program in the psychology of religion at Boston University (including a class taught by Howard Thurman), where he experienced an intellectual and spiritual shift.

He earned an M.A. in psychology of religion at Boston University in 1956 and obtained a post teaching in the Department of Religion, University of Manitoba, in Winnipeg, Canada. He was on the faculty there from 1956–1969.

He was also instrumental in the founding of the Department and Clinic of Pastoral Psychology at United College (later University of Winnipeg).

Yesod:

> When he joined the Near Eastern and Judaic studies department of the University of Manitoba in Winnipeg in 1956, Schachter was still looking for ways to restore Jewish traditions, not change or "renew" them. He felt that the Jewish Essene monastic tradition revealed by the Dead Sea Scrolls, the vigorous spirituality of the Hasidim, and the treasures of Kabbalistic mysticism were pre-Holocaust resources that could give Jews hope and energy after the great European disaster.

> But he was also pushing the frontiers of his experience. In 1959, under the guidance of Timothy Leary, he took LSD. ... Through the 1960s, Schachter and a small group of like-minded colleagues began experimenting with liturgical changes, meditation, and new modes of prayer.

In 1963 Schachter began work for a doctorate in Hebrew Letters at the Hebrew Union College in Cincinnati. He received the Doctorate in 1968.

In 1968–1969 he spend a post-doctoral year at Brandeis University, teaching and taking courses.

Yesod:

> "In 1968, I had my sabbatical from Manitoba," he said, "and I came to Brandeis University to do some study for myself—I studied Arabic, Syriac, Akkadian, Ugaritic—all those ancient Near Eastern languages, because I was interested in what had happened to our people prior to the patriarchs. That was when a lot of stuff about the goddess religion was coming up; there was so much happening around rediscovering the ways of nature and wicca and so on. I wanted to see what pre-patriarchal Judaism was like, what our roots were in these areas."

During this year in Boston he was involved in the first year of Havurat Shalom, a small cooperative congregation, with Rabbis Arthur Green and Barry Holtz, in Somerville, Massachusetts.

Yesod:

> During his sabbatical, he took part in the founding of
> a havurah—a small Jewish study group—in Boston. "We
> did remarkable things with liturgy;" he says. "Having seen
> how people sat and meditated on cushions, we did it too. We
> used a lot of body movements and dance in what we were
> doing, and that was part of the delight. And gradually I was
> moved from restoration to a whole other idea that had to do
> with renewal."

During this time the separation from the Lubavitch Chabad
organization occurred. As Yesod characterizes it, while grateful to
the Lubavitcher movement for initiating him into the mystical tradition of Judaism, Schachter was becoming discontented with the
movement's parochialism and insistence that it alone possessed
spiritual truth.

In 1969 he founded his own organization, B'nai Or, inspired
by Havurat Shalom, Christian Trappist spirituality and the Dead
Sea Scrolls.

Yesod:

> Schachter founded the B'nai Or Religious Fellowship
> (now ALEPH: Alliance for Jewish Renewal) with a small
> circle of students. These were among the first stirrings of the
> Jewish Renewal movement, an effort to re-energize Jewish
> piety by making it more emotionally satisfying, inclusive,
> experimental, experiential, and compelling. For Jews
> who were alienated from the sometimes tepid rationalism
> of the Reform movement and the stern ritualism of the
> more traditional denominations, the brilliant neo-Hasidic
> writings of Martin Buber and Abraham Joshua Heschel
> were a call to embrace the living fire of a slightly different
> traditionalism—the great tradition of ecstatic union with
> God carried by the Hasidic mystics. At the same time it
> was a call to link themselves to the world of the moment,

its pains, possibilities, and lessons, its psycho-spiritual breakthroughs and political changes.

Schachter, with his superb traditional training, omnivorous mind, and personal warmth, was a natural leader of the movement. Back at Manitoba, he began an intense inquiry into what to keep and what to alter in a vital Judaism. He corresponded with the Catholic monk and mystic Thomas Merton and visited the Trappists at the St. Norbert Abbey outside of Winnipeg, observing the process of *aggiornamiento* (bringing up-to-date), the modernization of liturgy, language, doctrine, and the role of lay people that had been mandated by Pope John XXIII and Vatican II. He talked to Sufi mystics, Indian gurus, and Native medicine keepers. In two books, *The First Step* (1983) and *Fragments of a Future Scroll: Hassidism for the Aquarian Age* (1975), he laid out his dynamic conceptions of Jewish prayer, meditation, and observance.

In 1974 he gave his first *smikhah* (ordination) to Rabbi Daniel Siegel of Boston (one of the current leaders of ALEPH), and help found the Aquarian Minyan of Berkeley, California.

Also during 1974 Schachter met the Sufi master Pir Vilayat Inayat Khan and in 1975 he was initiated as a *sheikh* of the Chishti-Inayati Sufi Order by Pir Vilayat Inayat Khan.

The same year he obtained a post as Professor of Religion in Jewish Mysticism and Psychology of Religion at Temple University in Philadelphia where he stayed until his early retirement in 1987, when he was named professor emeritus.

Yesod:

> When he moved to Temple University in Philadelphia in 1975, Schachter-Shalomi put his Jewish-renewal activities into high gear. With the B'nai Or Religious Fellowship (later called P'nai Or, and finally ALEPH: Alliance for Jewish Renewal) as a base, and lectured, taught, ordained

rabbis, visited Jewish renewal groups as they sprang up, translated psalms and prayers into vigorous new English.

In 1980, he and two other rabbis ordained one of the early influential women rabbis, Rabbi Lynn Gottlieb. This was part of the pioneering of rabbinic ordination of women.[3] Rabbi Gottlieb was Schachter's first; ordination of many other women rabbis followed over the years.

In 1985 Schachter (now Schachter-Shalomi) took a forty-day retreat at Lama Foundation in New Mexico. On this retreat he meditated deeply on aging and the role of elders in society. This line of thinking led to the Spiritual Eldering movement and the book, *From Age-ing to Sage-ing*.

In 1987, taking early retirement from Temple University, he taught full-time at the Reconstructionist Rabbinical College in Philadelphia (1987–1990) and also taught at the Academy of Jewish Studies in New York (1987–1990).

In 1988–89, he conducted the Primal Myths Wisdom School whose teachings are the foundation of the case studies in this book.

In 1989 he founded the Spiritual Eldering Institute in Philadelphia.

In 1990 he met with the 14th Dalai Lama, Tenzin Gyatso, in Dharamsala, India.

Yesod describes that occasion this way:

> Always sensitive and sympathetic to Jewish involvement in eastern traditions, in 1990, Schachter-Shalomi was invited to a meeting in Dharamsala, India between the Dalai Lama and Jewish leaders to discuss how Tibetan Buddhists might "survive in exile," as Jews had done for almost 2000 years. This dialogue, and Schachter-Shalomi's remarkable influence upon it, became the focus of a best-

---

3   The Reform and Reconstructionist movements had begun slowly ordaining women in 1972 and 1974; the Conservative movement would ordain their first in 1984.

selling book by Rodger Kamenetz, called *The Jew in the Lotus*. Immediately, the book became a catalyst for Jewish-Buddhist dialogue and the sensitive issue of why so many American Jews were involved in so-called "Eastern" spiritual paths.

Yesod summarizes some of this other ecumenical involvements as follows:

> From the earliest days of Schachter-Shalomi's career, he has been involved in ecumenical dialogue with leaders and practitioners of other spiritual paths, from Trappist monks to Sufi sheikhs. These frequent forays into what was then "forbidden territory" led Schachter-Shalomi to describe himself as a "spiritual peeping-Tom." But, far from being a mere browser, Schachter-Shalomi became deeply learned in the most minute aspects of the theory and experiential practice of these traditions, praying matins with the monks and performing dhikr with the Sufis.
>
> This deeply personal approach to "dialogue" led to significant friendships with many of the world's great spiritual teachers, including Father Thomas Merton, Reverend Howard Thurman, Pir Vilayat Inayat Khan, Ken Wilber, and the 14th Dalai Lama.

From 1995 to 2004, he held the World Wisdom Chair at the Buddhist-oriented Naropa Institute (now Naropa University) in Boulder, Colorado, moving to Boulder in 1996. According to the Yesod chronicle, he had found a home from which he could teach contemplative Judaism and ecumenical spirituality in an accredited academic setting.

Yesod:

> In 1995, Schachter-Shalomi was invited to take up the World Wisdom Chair at Naropa University, the only accredited Buddhist-inspired university in the Western hemisphere. The World Wisdom Chair holder is an exemplary scholar-practitioner of a world religion or

humanistic discipline, serving as special guide and elder to the Naropa community, providing for the integration of world wisdom traditions with modern culture. Thus, Naropa University in Boulder, Colorado became home to Schachter-Shalomi and a new phase of his teaching career. By the time of his retirement from Naropa in 2004, he had influenced thousands of students and spiritual seekers of all backgrounds, inspired a new Contemplative Judaism program, and donated a permanent legacy of archival material to the university.

Among this material was the set of audio tapes that are the source material for the case studies of this book.

In 2004, Schachter-Shalomi retired from Naropa University.

That same year, he founded a spiritual order he named The Desert Fellowship of the Message with Netanel Miles-Yepez. This order combines the lineage of Sufi master Inayat Khan (based on his initiation into that line from Pir Vilayat Inayat Khan) with a Hasidic line Schachter-Shalomi traces to Avraham the son of Maimonides. He calls it a Sufi-Hasidic, Inayati-Maimuniyya Order.

Yesod concludes their chronicle with the following:

Today, he is retired and living happily in Boulder, Colorado with his wife Eve, and his two cats, Mazel and Brakhah.

Works Cited

I. General Works by Author

Alter, Robert. *The Five Books of Moses* (New York: W. W. Norton, 2004).

———. *The Wisdom Books* (New York: W. W. Norton, 2010).

Alpert, Rebecca. *Like Bread on the Seder Plate* (New York: Columbia University Press, 1997)

Ardrey, Robert. T*he Territorial Imperative* (New York: Atheneum, 1966).

Bentov, Itzhak. *Stalking the Wild Pendulum* (New York: E. P. Dutton, 1977).

Berkovits, Eliezer. *Not in Heaven: the Nature and Function of Halakha* (Jerusalem: Shalem Press, 1983).

Biale, David, ed. *Cultures of the Jews* (New York: Schocken, 2002).

bin Gorion, Micha Joseph. *Mimekor Yisrael: Classical Jewish Folktales*, ed. Emmanuel bin Gorion. 3 vols. (Bloomington: Indiana University Press, 1976).

Bohm, David. *Wholeness and the Implicate Order* (London: Routledge, 1980).

Bonchek, Avigdor. *What's Bothering Rashi?* (Jerusalem: Feldheim Publishers, 1997–2005).

Boyarin, Daniel. *Intertextuality and the Reading of Midrash* (Bloomington: Indiana University Press, 1994).

———. *The Jewish Gospels* (New York: The New Press, 2012).

Campbell, Antony F. and Mark A. O'Brien, eds. *Unfolding the Deuteronomistic History* (Minneapolis: Fortress Press, 2000).

375

Cherry, Shai. *Torah through Time* (Philadelphia: Jewish Publication Society, 2007).

Eliade, Mircea. *The Sacred and the Profane: The Nature of Religion*, translated from French by W. R. Trask, 1957 (San Diego: Harcourt Brace Jovanovich, 1987).

Fishbane, Michael. *Biblical Interpretation in Ancient Israel* (New York: Oxford University Press, 1985).

———. *Sacred Attunement: A Jewish Theology* (Chicago: University of Chicago Press, 2008).

Fox, Everett., trans. *The Five Books of Moses : Genesis, Exodus, Leviticus, Numbers, Deuteronomy*; a new translation with introductions, commentary, and notes. *The Schocken Bible*, vol. I (New York: Schocken Books, 1995).

Fox, Matthew. *Original Blessing* (Santa Fe, N. Mex: Bear, 1983).

Friedman, Richard Elliott. *Who Wrote the Bible?* (New York: Simon & Schuster, 1987).

Gafni, Isaiah M. *Beginnings of Judaism* (Chantilly, Va.: The Teaching Company, 2008).

Ginzberg, Louis. *Legends of the Jews* (Philadelphia: Jewish Publication Society, 2003).

Gorion. *Mimekor Yisrael* (see entry under bin Gorion).

Halkin, Hillel. "Law in the Desert," *Jewish Review of Books*, Spring 2011.

Hauser, Alan J., and Duane F. Watson, eds. *A History of Biblical Interpretation: Volume 1, The Ancient Period* (Grand Rapids, Mich: Eerdmans, 2003).

Heschel, Abraham Joshua. *God in Search of Man* (Northvale, N.J.: Jason Aronson, 1987).

Josephus, Titus Flavius. *The Works of Josephus*, translated by William Whiston (Peabody, Mass.: Hendrickson, 1987).

Kamenetz, Rodger. *The Jew in the Lotus: a Poet's Rediscovery of Jewish Identity in Buddhist India* (San Francisco: Harper, 1994).

Kellner, Menachem. *Dogma in Medieval Jewish Thought* (Oxford: The Littman Library of Jewish Civilization, 1986).

————. *Must a Jew Believe Anything?* (Oxford: The Littman Library of Jewish Civilization, 1999; 2nd Ed. 2008).

Kugel, James L. *The Bible As It Was* (Cambridge, Mass.: Harvard University Press, 1997).

————. *Traditions of the Bible: A Guide to the Bible as it Was at the Start of the Common Era* (Cambridge, Mass.: Harvard University Press, 1998).

Lauterbach, Jacob Z., ed. *Mekilta de-Rabbi Ishmael* (Philadelphia: Jewish Publication Society, 1933).

Magid, Shaul. *American Post-Judaism: Identity and Renewal in a Postethnic Society* (Bloomington: Indiana University Press, 2013).

Mao Tse-tung. *Quotations from Chairman Mao Tse-tung* (Peking: Foreign Languages Press, 1966).

Menn, Esther. "Inner-Biblical Exegesis in the Tanak": Chapter 2 in Alan J. Hauser and Duane F. Watson, Eds., *A History of Biblical Interpretation, Volume 1.*

Neusner, Jacob. *The Oral Torah: The Sacred Books of Judaism: An Introduction* (San Francisco: Harper & Row, 1986).

————, ed. and trans. *The Babylonian Talmud, A Translation and Commentary*, 22 vols. (Peabody, Mass.: Hendrickson Publishers, 2005; revised edition, 2011).

————, ed. and trans. *The Jerusalem Talmud, A Translation and Commentary*, CD ROM, Hendrickson.

Otto, Rudolf. *Das Heilege* (Breslau, 1917). Translated into English as *The Idea of the Holy* (New York: Oxford University Press, 1923).

Philo Judaeus of Alexandria. *The Works of Philo*, translated by C. D. Yonge (Peabody, Mass.: Hendrickson, 1993).

Plaskow, Judith. *Standing Again at Sinai* (San Francisco, Harper & Row, 1990).

Rashi (Rabbi Shlomo Yitzhaki). See Section II, *Miqraot Gedolot* and מקרות גדולות, נביאים וכתובים

Russell, Peter. *The Global Brain* (Los Angeles: J. P. Tarcher, 1983).

Spinoza, Baruch. *Ethics* (Oxford: Oxford University Press, 2000).

Steinbeck, John. *East of Eden* (New York: Penguin, 1986).

Suzuki, Shunryu. *Zen Mind, Beginner's Mind* (New York: Weatherhill, 1970).

Teilhard de Chardin, Pierre. *The Phenomenon of Man* (New York: Harper & Row, 1961).

Tillich, Paul. *Systematic Theology*, 3 vols. (Chicago: University of Chicago Press, 1951–1963).

Tov, Emanuel. *Textual Criticism of the Hebrew Bible* (Minneapolis: Fortress Press, 1992; 2nd ed., 2001).

Twersky, Isadore. *A Maimonides Reader* (Springfield, N. J.: Behrman House, 1972).

Whorf, Benjamin Lee. *Language, Thought and Reality* (Cambridge, Mass: MIT Press, 1956).

Wilber, Ken. *The Atman Project* (Wheaton, Ill.: Theosophical Pub. House, 1980).

Wylen, Stephen M. *The Seventy Faces of Torah: The Jewish Way of Reading the Sacred Scriptures* (Mahwah, N. J.: Paulist Press, 2005).

Zaehner, Robert Charles, trans., ed. *The Bhagavad-Gita: With a Commentary Based on the Original Sources* (New York: Oxford University Press, 1969). Translation originally published 1966 by J. M. Dent & Sons Ltd. in *Hindu Scriptures*.

II. Works of Scripture and Traditional Commentaries

Bhagavad-Gita: With a Commentary Based on the Original Sources, trans. and ed. by Robert Charles Zaehner (New York: Oxford University Press, 1969). Translation originally published 1966 by J. M. Dent & Sons Ltd. in *Hindu Scriptures*.

Bible: *Biblia Hebraica Stuttgartensia,* ed. Karl Elliger and Wilhelm Rudolph (Stuttgart: Deutsche Bibelgesellschaft, 1987).

Bible: *The Five Books of Moses : Genesis, Exodus, Leviticus, Numbers, Deuteronomy*, trans. Everett Fox. *The Schocken Bible*, vol. I (New York: Schocken Books, 1995).

Bible: *The Five Books of Moses, trans. Robert Alter* (New York: W. W. Norton, 2004).

Bible: *The Holy Bible, King James Version*. Electronic edition of the 1769 edition of the 1611 Authorized Version (Bellingham, Wash.: Logos Research Systems, Inc., 1995).

Bible: *The JPS Hebrew-English Tanakh* (Philadelphia: Jewish Publication Society, 1999). The Hebrew text from the *Biblia Hebraica Stuttgartensia* and the English text from the *New JPS Tanakh* (1985).

Bible*: English Standard Version* (Oxford: Oxford University Press, 2009).

Bible: *The Soncino Books of the Bible*, ed. Dr. Rev. A. Cohen, 14 vols. (London: Soncino Press, 1983).

Bible: *Vetus Testamentum ex versione Septuaginta Interpretum* (Oxford: The Clarendon Press, 1875).

Lao-tzu. *Tao Te Ching* (Delhi: Motilal Banarsidass, Sacred Books of the East Vol. 39, 1891). J. Legge, Translator.

Mekilta de-Rabbi Ishmael, Lauterbach, Jacob Z., ed. (Philadelphia: Jewish Publication Society, 1933).

Midrash Rabbah, ed. Rabbi Dr. H. Freedman and Maurice Simon, 10 volumes (London: Soncino Press, 1939).

Miqraot Gedolot, ed. Rabbi A. J. Rosenberg (New York: The Judaica Press, 1993).

מקרות גדולות, נביאים וכתובים *Miqraot Gedolot Prophets and Writings* (Jerusalem: Machon HaMo'or, 2001). Volume 14, Rashi's commentary to Mishlei (Proverbs) and Volume 15, Rashi's commentary to Qohelet (Ecclesiastes). This edition entirely in Hebrew.

Ramban (Nachmanides). *The Torah: with Ramban's Commentary*, 7 volumes (Brooklyn: Mesorah Publications, 2004–2008).

Siddur: *The Complete ArtScroll Siddur* (Brooklyn: Mesorah Publications, 1984, 2001).

Talmud: *The Babylonian Talmud, A Translation and Commentary*, ed. and trans. Jacob Neusner, 22 vols. (Peabody, Mass.: Hendrickson Publishers, 2005; revised edition, 2011).

Talmud: *The Babylonian Talmud* (Hebrew/Aramaic). The Soncino Talmud DVD (Davka Corp.).

Talmud: *The Babylonian Talmud* (Hebrew/Aramaic and English with commentary). ArtScroll Mesorah Publications Digital Edition (iPad application), 2012.

Talmud: *The Jerusalem Talmud* (Hebrew). *Talmud Yerushalmi*. Bar Ilan Online Responsa Project, http://www.responsa.co.il

Talmud: *The Jerusalem Talmud*. (Brooklyn: Artscroll Mesorah Publications, Schottenstein *Talmud Yerushalmi* English Edition, Sanhedrin Vol 1, 2012).

Talmud: *The Jerusalem Talmud, A Translation and Commentary*, Jacob Neusner, translator, CD ROM, Hendrickson.

תורה הכתובה והמסורה. Ed., Rabbi Aaron Hyman (Tel-Aviv: Dvar Publishing Co., 1979).

III. Language Reference Works

Brown, Francis, Samuel R. Driver, and Charles A. Briggs, eds., *A Hebrew and English Lexicon of the Old Testament* (Oxford: Clarendon Press, 1906; Corrected edition, 1952). Cited as "BDB."

Frank, Yitzhak. *The Practical Talmud Dictionary* (Jerusalem: Ariel, 1994).

Harkavy, Alexander. *Yiddish-English-Hebrew Dictionary* (New Haven: Yale University Press, 1928).

Liddell, Henry George, and Robert Scott, *A Greek-English Lexicon* (Oxford: University Press, 1961).

Melamed, Ezra Tziyon. *Aramaic-Hebrew-English Dictionary of the Babylonian Talmud* (Jerusalem: The Samuel and Odette Levy Foundation, 2005).

Munīr Baʻlabakkī; Rūḥī Baʻlabakkī. *Al-Mawrid Al-Waseet. A Concise Arabic-English Dictionary* (Beirut: Dar El-ilm LilMalayin, 1997).

Monier-Williams, Monier. *A Sanskrit-English Dictionary* (Oxford: Oxford University Press, 1899).

Weinreich, Uriel. *Modern English-Yiddish / Yiddish-English Dictionary* (New York: YIVO Institute, 1968; Schocken Books, 1977).

Wigram, George V., ed., *The Englishman's Hebrew and Chaldee Concordance of the Old Testament* (London: Samuel Bagster and Sons, 1843). Many subsequent editions and reprints, most recently: *The New Englishman's Hebrew-Aramaic Concordance. Coded to the Strong's Concordance Numbering System* (Peabody, Mass.: Hendrickson, 1984).

IV. Works by Rabbi Zalman Schachter-Shalomi

1975. *Fragments of a Future Scroll: Hassidism for the Here and Now* (Mt. Airy, Pa.: B'nai Or Press).

1983. *The First Step: A Guide for the New Jewish Spirit* (Toronto: Bantam Books, 1983).

1988 *The Dream Assembly, Tales of Rabbi Zalman Schachter-Shalomi.* Collected and Retold by Howard Schwartz (Warwick, N. Y.: Amity House).

1993. *Paradigm Shift*, ed. Ellen Singer (Northvale, N. J.: Jason Aronson).

1995. *From Age-ing to Sage-ing: A Profound New Vision of Growing Older,* with Ronald S. Miller (New York: Warner Books).

1996. *Spiritual Intimacy: A Study of Counseling in Hasidism.* (Lanham, Md.: Rowman & Littlefield, 2005).

1997. *Words of Light: Shabbaton Writings.* Philadelphia: ALEPH Alliance For Jewish Renewal).

2000. *Gate to the Heart: An Evolving Process.* (Philadelphia: ALEPH Alliance For Jewish Renewal).

2000. *Tree of Life Sacred Time* (Philadelphia: ALEPH Alliance For Jewish Renewal).

2000. *Writings From the Heart of Jewish Renewal* (Philadelphia: ALEPH Alliance For Jewish Renewal).

2001. *A Guide For Starting Your New Incarnation: Teachings on the Modern Meaning of T'shuvah,* ed. Daniel Siegel (Philadelphia: ALEPH Alliance For Jewish Renewal).

2001. *Sparks of Light: Counseling in the Hasidic Tradition*, with Edward Hoffman (Boulder, Colo.: Shambala).

2002. *Spiritual Economics: You Can Get Anything You Want In A-don-I's Restaurant*, ed. Daniel Siegel (Philadelphia: ALEPH Alliance For Jewish Renewal).

2003. *First Steps to a New Jewish Spirit: Reb Zalman's Guide to Recapturing the Intimacy & Escstasy in Your Relationship with God*, with Donald Gropman (Woodstock, Vt.: Jewish Lights). New edition of *The First Step* (1983).

2003. *The Kabbalah of Tikkun Olam*, ed. Daniel Siegel (Philadelphia: ALEPH Alliance For Jewish Renewal).

2003. *Wrapped in a Holy Flame: Teachings and Tales of the Hasidic Masters*, ed. Nataniel Miles-Yepez (San Francisco: Jossey-Bass).

2005. *Credo of a Modern Kabbalist,* with Rabbi Daniel Siegel (Victoria, B.C., Canada: Trafford Publishing).

2005. *Jewish with Feeling: A Guide to Meaningful Jewish Practice,* with Joel Segel (New York: Riverhead Books).

2005. *Renewal Is Judaism NOW: To See the Power of Heart in Our Time,* ed. Daniel Siegel (Philadelphia: ALEPH Alliance For Jewish Renewal).

2007. *Integral Halachah: Transcending and Including*, with Daniel Siegel (Victoria, B.C., Canada: Trafford Publishing).

2009. *A Heart Afire: Stories and Teaching of the Early Hasidic Masters*, with Netanel Miles-Yepez (Philadelphia: Jewish Publication Society).

2010. *A Merciful God: Stories and Teachings of the Holy Rebbe, Levi Yitzhak of Berditchev.* with Netanel Miles-Yepez (Boulder, Colo.: Albion-Andalus).

2011. *A Hidden Light* (Santa Fe, N. Mex.: Gaon Books).

2011. *All Breathing Life* (Santa Fe, N. Mex.: Gaon Books).

2011. *The Gates of Prayer: Twelve Talks on Davvenology* (Boulder, Colorado: Albion-Andalus).

2012. *Davening: A Guide to Meaningful Jewish Prayer,* with Joel Segel (Woodstock, Vt.: Jewish Lights).

2012. *My Life in Jewish Renewal*, with Edward Hoffman (Lanham, Md.: Rowman & Littlefield)

2012. *The Geologist of the Soul: Talks on Rebbe-craft and Spiritual Leadership* (Boulder: Albion-Andalus).

Index

A

About Dana Densmore

Dana Densmore is a scholar with particular focus on the source texts in her fields of inquiry. Her gestation was passed with a mother who was working as a WWII Arlington Hall codebreaker and Densmore has carried on breaking codes ever since.

After earning her BA in 1965 studying the foundational texts of Western civilization at St. John's College in Annapolis, Densmore worked as a systems programmer at MIT for the Apollo Project and the Space Shuttle. One of her responsibilities there was integration of the real-time guidance, navigation, and control programs for the onboard guidance computer in the Apollo Lunar Lander.

She was a leading theorist for the emerging feminist movement and published the first journal of feminist theory beginning in August 1968 and running through 1974. She is a long-time board member of The Women's Institute for Freedom of the Press, and for two years was Senior Editor and Research Director for that organization.

In 1987, Densmore was appointed to the faculty of St. John's College, Santa Fe, where she led tutorials and discussions in the St. John's College great books curriculum. In 1993 she received an MA from St. John's for a thesis on the cause of gravity in Newton's *Principia*. While leading students through the *Principia*, she developed a series of notes and expansions which became the nucleus of her book, *Newton's Principia: The Central Argument*, published in 1995.

She has had a lifetime of involvement in theology and religious studies. She is an initiate of the Sufi Order brought to the West in

1927 by Inayat Khan, and is a Senior Teacher and Sheikha in that order and an ordained Cheraga of the Universal Worship. She has studied the texts of all the major religious and spiritual traditions, reading scriptures in the original languages of Greek, Sanskrit, Hebrew, Arabic, and the Aramaic of the Talmud.

Densmore is co-director and chief editor of Green Lion Press, a quality scholarly publisher of source texts and guided studies in history of science and history of mathematics.